# Insiders' Guide®

## to the

## Olympic Peninsula

# Help Us Keep This Guide Up to Date

Every effort has been made by the authors and editors to make this guide as accurate and useful as possible. However, many things can change after a guide is published—establishments close, phone numbers change, hiking trails are rerouted, facilities come under new management, etc.

We would love to hear from you concerning your experiences with this guide and how you feel it could be made better and be kept up to date. While we may not be able to respond to all comments and suggestions, we'll take them to heart and we'll also make certain to share them with the authors. Please send your comments and suggestions to the following address:

The Globe Pequot Press
Reader Response/Editorial Department
P.O. Box 480
Guilford, CT 06437

Or you may e-mail us at: editorial@globe-pequot.com

Thanks for your input, and happy travels!

*Insiders' Guide® Series*

# Insiders' Guide®
# to the
# Olympic Peninsula

By Rob McNair-Huff
and
Natalie McNair-Huff

Guilford, Connecticut
An imprint of The Globe Pequot Press

Cover photo: ©Mark Windom (IndexStock)
Back cover photos: Rob McNair-Huff, Natalie McNair-Huff
Map design: Trapper Badovinac

ISBN 1-57380-191-7

Manufactured in the United States of America
First Edition/First Printing

# Contents

# Directory of Maps

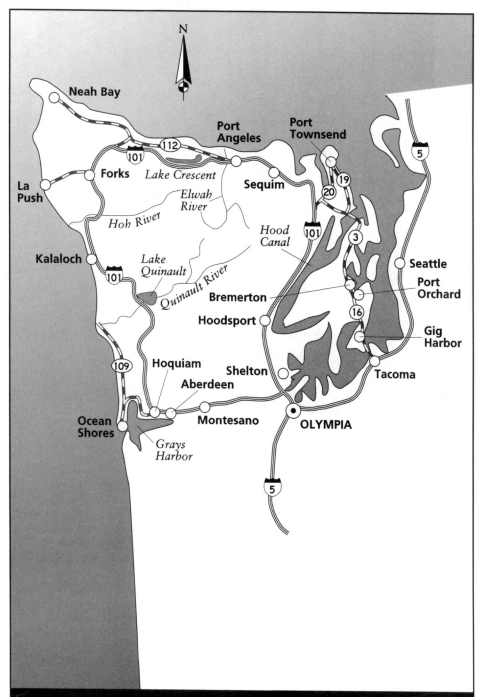

N

Neah Bay

Port
Angeles

Port
Townsend

5

112
101

Forks

*Lake Crescent*

Sequim

19

La
Push

*Elwah
River*

20

*Hoh River*

101

3

*Hood
Canal*

Kalaloch

*Lake
Quinault*

Seattle

101

Port
Orchard

*Quinault River*

Bremerton

16

Gig
Harbor

Hoodsport

109

Hoquiam

Shelton

Tacoma

Aberdeen

Montesano

OLYMPIA

Ocean
Shores

*Grays
Harbor*

5

# OLYMPIC PENINSULA

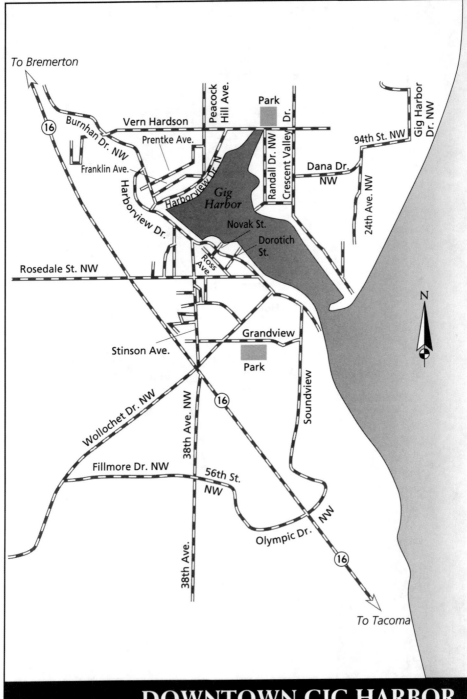

# DOWNTOWN GIG HARBOR

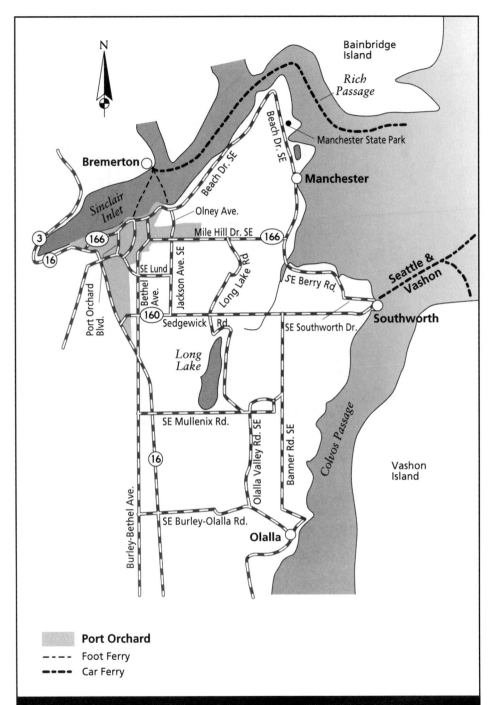

N

Bainbridge
Island

*Rich
Passage*

Manchester State Park

**Bremerton**

Beach Dr. SE

Beach Dr. SE

**Manchester**

*Sinclair
Inlet*

Olney Ave.

3

Mile Hill Dr. SE

166

166

16

SE Lund

Jackson Ave. SE

Long Lake Rd

SE Berry Rd.

Seattle &
Vashon

Bethel Ave.

160

SE Southworth Dr.

**Southworth**

Port Orchard Blvd.

Sedgewick   Rd.

*Long
Lake*

SE Mullenix Rd.

Olalla Valley Rd. SE

Banner Rd. SE

*Colvos Passage*

Vashon
Island

16

Burley-Bethel Ave.

SE Burley-Olalla Rd.

**Olalla**

**Port Orchard**

- - - - Foot Ferry
▬▬▬ Car Ferry

# PORT ORCHARD & VICINITY

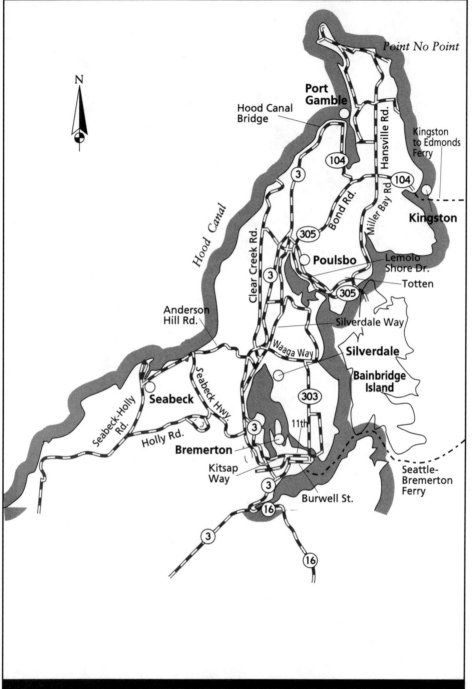

N

Point No Point

**Port Gamble**

Hood Canal Bridge

Hood Canal

104

3

Bond Rd.

Hansville Rd.

Miller Bay Rd

Kingston to Edmonds Ferry

104

**Kingston**

305

**Poulsbo**

Lemolo Shore Dr.

Totten

Clear Creek Rd.

3

305

Anderson Hill Rd.

Silverdale Way

Waaga Way

Silverdale Way

**Silverdale**

303

**Bainbridge Island**

Seabeck Hwy.

Seabeck-Holly Rd.

**Seabeck**

3

11th

Holly Rd.

**Bremerton**

Kitsap Way

3

Burwell St.

Seattle-Bremerton Ferry

16

3

16

# NORTH KITSAP PENINSULA

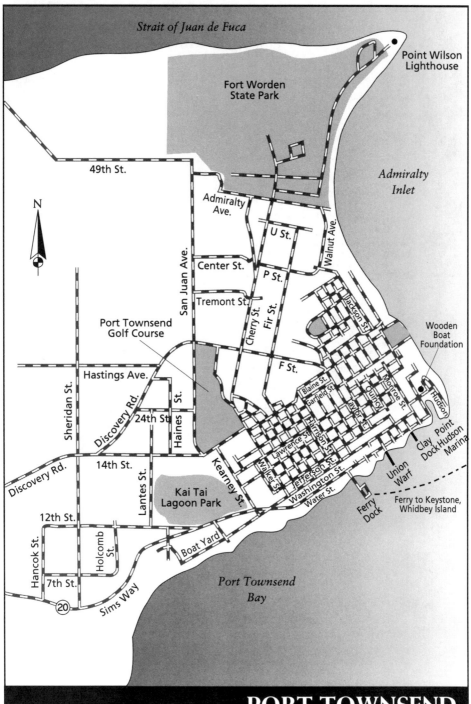

Strait of Juan de Fuca

Point Wilson
Lighthouse

Fort Worden
State Park

Admiralty
Inlet

49th St.

Admiralty
Ave.

U St.

Walnut Ave.

Center St.

San Juan Ave.

P St.

Tremont St.

Cherry St.

Fir St.

Port Townsend
Golf Course

Jackson St.

Wooden
Boat
Foundation

F St.

Hastings Ave.

Blaine St.

Garfield St.

Quincy

Monroe St.

Sheridan St.

Discovery Rd.

St.

24th St.

Haines

Harrison St.

Taylor

Hudson

Clay

Point Hudson
Dock Marina

Lawrence St.

Polk St.

14th St.

Lantes St.

Discovery Rd.

Kearney St.

Jefferson St.

Washington St.

Water St.

Union
Warf

Kai Tai
Lagoon Park

Ferry
Dock

Ferry to Keystone,
Whidbey Island

12th St.

Hancok St.

Holcomb
St.

Boat Yard

7th St.

20

Sims Way

Port Townsend
Bay

## PORT TOWNSEND

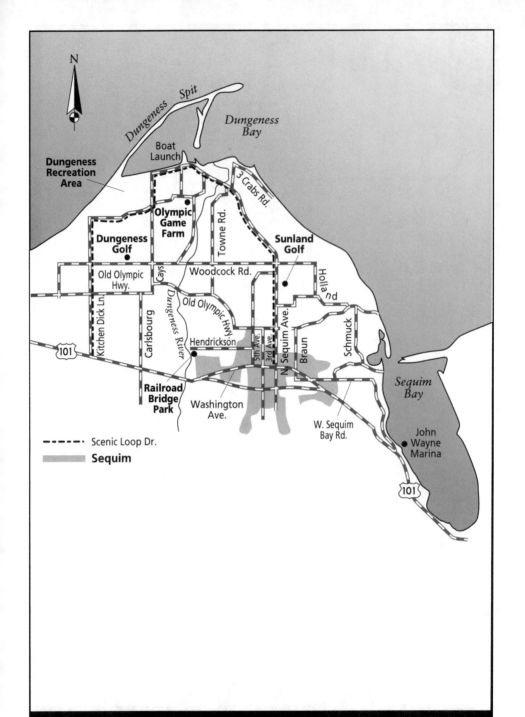

N

Dungeness Spit

Dungeness Bay

Dungeness Recreation Area

Boat Launch

3 Crabs Rd.

Olympic Game Farm

Towne Rd.

Dungeness Golf

Sunland Golf

Old Olympic Hwy.

Woodcock Rd.

Holland

Calys

Dungeness River

Old Olympic Hwy.

Kitchen Dick Ln.

Carlsbourg

Hendrickson

5th Ave.

3rd Ave.

N. Sequim Ave.

Braun

Schmuck

Sequim Bay

US 101

Railroad Bridge Park

Washington Ave.

W. Sequim Bay Rd.

John Wayne Marina

101

- - - - - Scenic Loop Dr.

Sequim

**SEQUIM–DUNGENESS VALLEY**

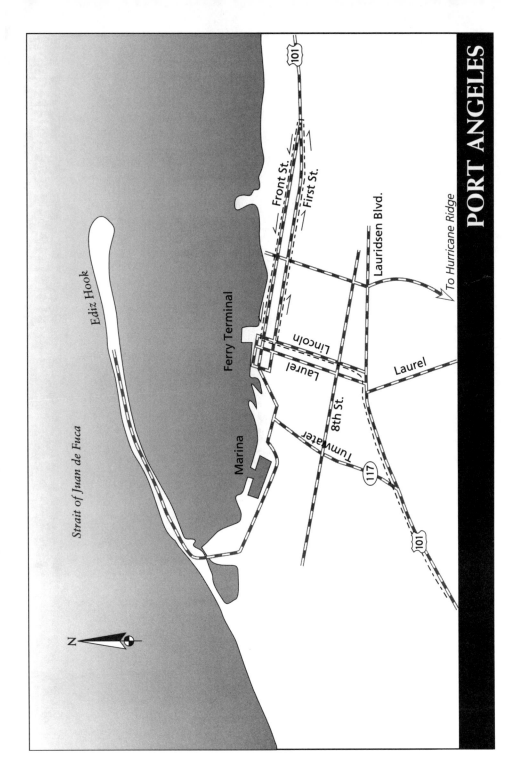

PORT ANGELES

Strait of Juan de Fuca

Ediz Hook

Marina

Ferry Terminal

Front St.

First St.

Lincoln

Laurel

Laurel

Lauridsen Blvd.

To Hurricane Ridge

8th St.

Tumwater

101

101

117

N

HOQUIAM & ABERDEEN

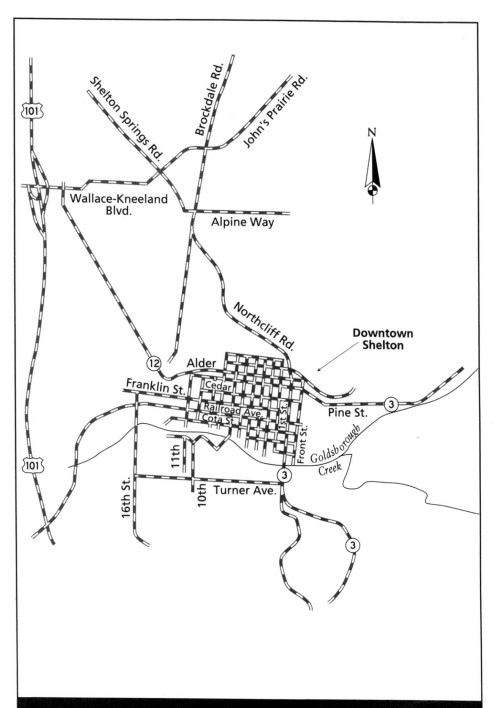

SHELTON

# Preface

It begins far beneath the Pacific Ocean in a molten line that pushes the continental plate eastward to form a sharp ridge of mountains. Whales and fish swim over the line in an instinctive eastward migration. The orcas and gray whales swim into the protected waters of Puget Sound chasing the salmon that swim to the streams and rivers where they spawn and lay their eggs. The land emerges from the water as a low fringe surrounding the Olympic Mountains. The mountains rise quickly, forcing the water-laden clouds blowing in from the Pacific to dump their loads in an almost constant drizzle. The rain and rich alluvial soil nourish the giants of the land—centuries-old fir, red cedar, spruce—all dripping with green moss to create a unique and delicate ecosystem where bald eagles, hawks, and owls flourish. The snow-capped peaks bite into the sky and throw a shadow on the fringe of land to the east. Here, on the east side of the mountains, the rain falls far less often creates an entirely different landscape before the waters of Puget Sound again swallow the land.

Many ages ago the first humans came. They clothed themselves with furs and woven cedar bark and paddled canoes made from giant red cedar trees. They called themselves Makah, Quileute, Quinault, Twana, S'Klallam. The land made them rich and fed them well on feasts of wild berries, tender greens, salmon, elk and deer, oysters, clams, mussels, crab, and whale. Then the white traders came in mysterious, white-sailed "canoes" for the otter pelts and cedar trees, the salmon, and the shellfish. They too decided to call this green, mountain-strewn paradise home. They built forts and ports and railroads. They explored the high mountain reaches and forever changed the face of the landscape with dams and roads and logging.

Many who have come here for short visits return to call it home, and many of us still think of it as Paradise. The craggy mountains entice climbers and hikers who escape to the backcountry for weeks at a time. The protected coves and bays of the Puget Sound beckon to kayakers and anglers and entertain others with tide pools and sea stacks set against beautiful sunsets. And the towns, filled with museums, four-star restaurants, art galleries, antiques and gift shops, and Victorian architecture beckon to tourists from around the world.

This is the Olympic Peninsula, and we are happy you have chosen us to be your guides. Let this book entice you and introduce you to the many pleasures that this corner of the nation has to offer. The Peninsula, as the locals call it, has something for nearly everyone, and we'll help you find just what you want.

# Acknowledgments

It takes more than two people to complete a book like this, and we owe thanks to a lot of people who have helped us, put up with us, and answered innumerable questions as we wrote and researched the Insiders' Guide to the Olympic Peninsula.

First we need to thank the hundreds of people we have interviewed and spoken to about the Olympic Peninsula while on our travels. Special thanks to the volunteers and staff at the chambers of commerce in each town, and to the shop owners, hotel and motel staff, and dozens of bed and breakfast inn owners. We thank some other notable individuals who have gone out of their way to help us, including Cheryl Sones for help in Neah Bay and Thatcher Bailey and the crew at Copper Canyon Press for the tour and explanation about how the press works.

Thanks to Marie Stewart for reading rough drafts, and a special thank you to Alexis Adams for prodding us to submit the book proposal. We also appreciate the staff of Olympic National Park, especially press contact Barb Maynes and Greg Marsh at the Olympic National Park Visitor Center in Port Angeles.

Many thanks go to our editors, Erin Turner and Erika Serviss, at Falcon Publishing. We both want our friends and family to know how appreciative we are that they stuck by us and for putting up with our absence while we have been on the road doing research or buried with writing at home.

Rob also wants to thank his parents for introducing him to the natural world and exposing him to the southern reaches of the Olympic Peninsula. Natalie thanks her parents for first introducing her to the Olympic Peninsula on one particularly rainy weekend about 20 years ago. The ant that crawled into her ear thinking it a dry refuge from the rain isn't her only memory of the trip. She also remembers camping in the rain, the view from Hurricane Ridge, the tunnel of trees near the Hoh, and a lot of fun. Thanks also for joining us on a couple of research trips, and, as always, supporting and encouraging us as we work our craft.

Thank you, everyone.

*Cities on the Olympic Peninsula go all-out in the summer to gussy up their storefronts with dramatic flower baskets.* PHOTO: ROB McNAIR-HUFF

# How to Use This Book

Welcome to the Olympic Peninsula, one of the most fascinating places on the planet! At least the authors and many of the Peninsula's residents think so. Why do we think this? Because it offers such richness and diversity for those who make their way to this corner of the United States.

Some folks come to the Peninsula to get away from it all. They may hike the backcountry trails and make do with a tent, sleeping bags, and the comforts of the outdoors. Others rent cabins on private coves where they spend their days writing, walking nearby trails, or fishing from porches. Some hearty souls strap the necessities on bikes or in kayaks to paddle around Puget Sound and take it all in at a slower pace.

For those who like to be pampered, the area offers all the comforts of home in lovely Victorian bed-and-breakfast inns and an eclectic assortment of hotels. Visitors can walk through local shops, art galleries, and antiques stores. Perhaps they'll end the day with a delicious dinner of salmon or crab at one of the excellent local restaurants. Of course, they may also opt to combine the pleasures of civilization with the excitement of the outdoors by walking along some of the rocky beaches or hopping on boats to go whale watching.

We have organized our book thematically and geographically so that it is easy for you to find the information you need. Each chapter is written so that it stands alone. You may elect to first read only those chapters that you need, but we hope you eventually read all of them as you'll learn more and more about the Peninsula with each one.

## Thematic Chapters

The first few chapters help you get a feel for the area. In fact, no matter what your plan, we suggest you first read Getting Here and Getting Around as well as Area Overview. Both provide essential information for navigating our winding roads and the ferry system as well as for learning more about what different regions offer for the adventurer.

We think that understanding the history, geology, and flora and fauna of an area gives people a greater appreciation of that region. We made a special effort to include chapters specifically addressing these topics. Learn about the roles played by Native Americans, timber, trains, and salmon when you read the History chapter. Then read The Natural World to find the names of all those trees, plants, and critters and to discover why the Peninsula is so unique geologically and meteorologically.

The next few chapters—Activities, Golf, Outdoor Recreation, The Arts, Antiques, Annual Events, and Kidstuff—will help you decide how to fill your days. If you're a golfer, the Golf chapter will show you the way to some fun and award-winning golf courses. Read the Outdoor Recreation chapter to get the scoop on camping, hiking, RVing, boating, fishing, and other outdoor activities. Check out the chapter on The Arts to find out where to listen to some great jazz music or see wonderful paintings and sculptures by Northwest artists. Antique hounds will want to read that chapter in order to find out where to go for the best deals on old books, Americana, and memorabilia.

To find fun things to do while you are visiting the area, thumb through the Attractions and Annual Events chapters. Both chapters are loaded with listings for museums, festivals, and cultural events. Keep the kids busy touring tide pools, playing miniature golf, or walking interpretive trails with the activities found in the A to Z list of the Kidstuff chapter.

Most of the information in each thematic chapter (except Kidstuff and Golf) is organized according to the same counterclockwise loop that we use in the geographic chapters. For example, following the introduction in the Antiques chapter, you will see a section for each city and within a city's section you will find an alphabetical listing of antique shops in that area.

## Geographic Chapters

The best way to see the entire peninsula is to drive a loop around the perimeter and take side trips into the interior. The geographic chapters begin with the Olympic National Park chapter since it covers so much of the Peninsula and can be easily reached from many areas on the perimeter of the Peninsula. Additionally, the park practically defines the Peninsula with its jagged peaks and boggy rain forests dripping with green moss and frequent rains. We start the loop in Gig Harbor, which is right across the bridge from our hometown, Tacoma. You may just as easily start the loop in Shelton, or in one of the towns accessible by ferry from Seattle or Vancouver Island, B.C.

Although we included a separate chapter for each of the larger towns, there are many smaller towns that dot the area. When we wanted to highlight something in one of those towns, we included it in the chapter for the nearest larger town. We also bundled all of the small cities on Hood Canal, a destination for scuba divers and shellfish harvesters, into one chapter. Each geographical chapter contains sections for hotels, bed-and-breakfast inns, restaurants, and shopping. Some include sections for nightlife and vacation rentals. If you are more interested in finding a spot to camp or park your RV, please refer to the Outdoor Recreation chapter.

Some folks who visit the area decide to return for good. For them we offer a few final thematic chapters. The Relocation Guide is filled with information on real estate, schools, health care, and religious organizations. The Media guide lists local papers and radio stations for visitors and new residents. And, although we think our guide is pretty thorough, we've included the For More Information chapter for those of you who want to learn even more about this beautiful part of the country.

Throughout the book you will see Insiders' Tips—little secrets, factoids, and fun things to do. Important information and contact lists are easily spotted in the gray boxes. We also provide some in-depth profiles of people, places, and events in our Close-Up sections scattered throughout the chapters.

As with all things, change is inevitable, and while we have taken strides to ensure that the information included in this book is accurate, we know that businesses move or close, trails change, and roads occasionally wash away. We encourage you to let us know if you find any changes or have recommendations for future editions.

# Area Overview

Following the route this book traces from the Narrows Bridge in Tacoma west to the Olympic Peninsula, and then traveling in a counterclockwise route, here is a glimpse of the communities and areas that make up the Olympic Peninsula.

## Olympic National Park

At the heart of the Olympic Peninsula is the Olympic National Park. One of the most popular parks in the nation with millions of visitors each year, the 922,651-acre park was designated on June 29, 1938.

Olympic National Park is often referred to as three parks in one because of the trio of distinct ecosystems within the park boundaries. It ranges from the alpine, high-mountain peaks that contain the widest range of glaciers for their elevation in the United States to the rain-soaked forest along the Pacific Ocean. And at its extreme western edge is a 60-mile-long stretch of largely undeveloped coastline.

The park also stands out for its biological diversity. Some of the largest trees, of various species, in the world are located within the park. And the park holds eight kinds of plants and five kinds of animals that are found nowhere else in the world.

## Gig Harbor

The small bayside community of Gig Harbor has a rich fishing heritage, and today the town of 6,400 people retains a heavy fishing influence. Located just off Washington Highway 16 across the Narrows Bridge from Tacoma, Gig Harbor serves as a bedroom community for commuters. But it also has a life of its own, with a thriving local art scene and well-known summer festivals.

Gig Harbor gets its name from the 1841 Wilkes Expedition when the bay was discovered by accident as the ship and its crew sought refuge in a storm. They named the harbor for the type of ship they were sailing, called a gig.

## Port Orchard

Once known as Sidney, the waterfront town of Port Orchard retains strong ties to the water and ferry services that put it on the map in 1890. Today's population of 7,255 people can still catch one of two boats remaining from the famous Mosquito Fleet—a once-huge network of walk-on passenger ferries—for a ride across Sinclair Inlet enroute to Bremerton.

Port Orchard serves as a bedroom community for workers in the nearby Bremerton Naval Shipyards as well as for workers who catch the Southworth ferry to head to Seattle. Notably, the Port Orchard waterfront offers the quintessential view of the Olympic Peninsula looking across Sinclair Inlet toward the Olympic Mountains in the distance. The view offers water, the city of Bremerton in the foreground, and the snow-capped mountains beyond.

## North Kitsap

The largest city in Kitsap County, Bremerton is best known as the northern home of the Pacific Fleet of the U.S. Navy. Founded in 1891 and named after its founder, German immigrant William Bremmer, the city's largest employer is the Puget Sound Naval Shipyard.

Naval history unfolds along the waterfront of Bremerton, with harbor tours of the mothballed ships floating offshore and the Bremerton Naval Museum downtown. The military influence doesn't end there, as a short drive down Washington Highway 3 past the town of Silverdale brings travelers to the Bangor Trident Nuclear Submarine base.

## Port Townsend

One of the oldest cities in Washington, Port Townsend—or Port Townshend as it was named in 1792 by Captain George Vancouver—is well known today for its Victorian architecture, abundant bed-and-breakfast inns, and thriving arts community. The official settlement of the city took place in 1851, nearly 40 years before Washington became a state.

> **Insiders' Tip**
>
> Watch the speed limit as you pass through the small towns on U.S. 101. Even though it's a highway, the speed limits in the towns drop drastically, which makes city limits a perfect place for a speed trap.

In its long history, Port Townsend has been a seaport, a logging and lumbering mill town, and most recently a tourist destination frequented by travelers from all corners of the world. It also offers one of the ferry routes to get onto the Olympic Peninsula, with a short ride from Whidbey Island.

## Sequim

Known as the "Banana Belt" of the Olympic Peninsula, the retirement community of Sequim (pronounced SKWIM) sits in the rain shadow of the Olympic Mountains. While the town of Forks on the west side of the mountains receives more than 160 inches of rain some years, Sequim averages just 16 inches of rain per year.

The other distinguishing feature of Sequim and the Dungeness River valley is the nearby Dungeness Spit—a five-mile-long natural sand spit that reaches into the Strait of Juan de Fuca and is one of the largest natural sand spits in the world.

## Port Angeles

The main city in Clallam County, Port Angeles is tied to the sea to the north and the Olympic National Park to the south. The city serves as a gateway to the park and to the popular viewing area at Hurricane Ridge, where visitors can see views of the city below as well as of Vancouver Island, B.C., across the Strait of Juan de Fuca.

Port Angeles is also an entry point to start exploration of the Olympic Peninsula, with ferry service running daily to and from Victoria, B.C. The city gets its name from Spanish explorers who entered the natural harbor formed by the 4.5-mile-long Ediz Hook sandbar in 1791 and named the city Puerto de Nuestra Senora de Los Angeles, "Port of Our Lady of Angels."

## Juan de Fuca Highway

The northwesternmost community in Washington, Neah Bay lies at the end of the road and the end of the continent on Washington Highway 112. Home of the Makah Indian Tribe, the town contains the Makah Cultural and Research Center, holders of the largest precontact Northwest Coastal Indian collection of artifacts in the country. As part of its heritage as an Indian village, Neah Bay plays host for the annual Makah Days festival in August.

Near Neah Bay is a one-mile trail to the northwesternmost point in the contiguous United States at Cape Flattery.

## Forks

After starting as an agriculture-based community in the1870s, Forks has grown to be synonymous with the logging industry and the spotted owl. Perched at the western edge of the Olympic National Park, Forks stands out as the westernmost town in the contiguous United States. It is also one of the wettest cities in the United States, with a record 162.14 inches of rain in 1997. As if those superlatives aren't enough, Forks contains the only stoplight in a 163-mile stretch of U.S. Highway 101.

Today Forks has grown into a tourist center based on outdoor recreation, including nearby fishing in the trio of rivers that form a fork that gave the town its name, and it is

*The Olympic Mountains rise dramatically over the northern Peninsula, where the elevation climbs from sea level to almost 8,000 feet in a span of 20 miles.* PHOTO: ROB McNAIR-HUFF

also known as home of the Forks Timber Museum, which pays homage to the city's lumbering heritage.

Just down the road from Forks is the world-famous Hoh Rain Forest. And a short distance out to the coast is the Indian village of La Push.

## Ocean Shores

Thousands of tourists rush to the vacation and retirement town of Ocean Shores every year, and the small town delivers with festivals, top-notch lodging, and the chance to catch howling winds and pounding surf with each winter storm. The city was built for tourism after a group of investors purchased a 6,000-acre cattle ranch that covered the entire peninsula that serves as the northern gateway into Grays Harbor.

## Hoquiam

What better name for a timber town than Hoquiam? The meaning of the Native American word is "hungry for wood," and throughout its history Hoquiam has lived up to its name more than most towns. At the height of lumbering in Grays Harbor County, Hoquiam joined with the nearby cities of Aberdeen and Cosmopolis to host some of the world's largest sawmills.

Current-day Hoquiam remains tied to its logging past with annual events like the Loggers Playday. Held early in September, the festival features national and international competitors battling in ax throwing, tree topping, log rolling, and other timber-related events.

## Aberdeen

Unlike its timber-dominated twincity of Hoquiam to the west, Aberdeen's roots are tied to both lumber and the fishing industry. Situated at the mouth of the Chehalis River, Aberdeen earned its name from an immigrant who founded a fish cannery that for years sent plentiful runs of sockeye, king, and silver salmon to cities across the United States.

Around 1900 Aberdeen's rough-and-tumble reputation had some people referring to it as the toughest town west of Chicago. The city has calmed considerably from its time as a mill town filled with saloons, gambling halls, and boardinghouses. Today Aberdeen is home to nearly 17,000 people and it is the largest city on Grays Harbor.

## Montesano

Founded in 1852 and incorporated as a city in 1883, Montesano is one of the oldest towns in Grays Harbor, and today it is the county seat. The town sits at the confluence of three rivers—the Chehalis River, the Satsop River, and the Wynoochee River—and throughout its history it has been notable for agriculture and, of course, logging.

Speaking of logging, one of the things that sets Montesano apart from the other timber-based towns of the Olympic Peninsula is the nearby 200,000-acre Clemmons Tree Farm, started in 1941 by a man named Weyerhaeuser. It is the nation's first commercial tree farm.

## Shelton

With city limits that only cover six square miles, Shelton is far from a sprawling city as it sits along the southern edge of Puget Sound. Founded in 1890, the city that is historically tied to logging has a population of 7,770 today.

*The sun sinks behind the Olympic Mountains.* PHOTO: NATALIE McNAIR-HUFF

Located along Washington Highway 3, Shelton is the turning point to head north along Hood Canal to explore the eastern portions of Olympic National Park and the northern portions of the Olympic Peninsula.

## Hood Canal

Despite its name, Hood Canal is not a canal at all. It is actually a narrow inlet of salt water that stretches from Port Townsend in the north southward to the town of Union, where it forms a huge bend before reaching the end of the inlet at the town of Belfair. Well known as a destination for scuba diving and shellfish gathering, a number of small towns and attractions dot the shores of Hood Canal. Among them are the towns of Hoodsport, Brinnon, and Quilcene.

# Getting Here, Getting Around

Water defines the boundaries of the Olympic Peninsula on three sides: the Pacific Ocean on the west, the Strait of Juan de Fuca on the north, and Puget Sound on the east. The steep, unsurpassable mountains at the center of the Peninsula make a southerly approach difficult. It is remote, wild, and a bit isolated, but those are the things that make it so special and unique. If you make the trek to the Peninsula, you will be rewarded amply with all it has to offer: mountain goats climbing the craggy cliffs of the Olympics, orcas—also known as killer whales—breaching in the sound, whitewater rafting, sea kayaking, great hiking, and more.

Getting here may be difficult, but it is far from impossible. Many roads eventually lead to the Peninsula as do many of the ferries that are part of Washington State's extensive ferry system. The number one Insiders' secret to enjoying the journey and the Peninsula? Take your time. Don't hurry. Winter storms have been known to wash roads into the sea. Deer and elk use the highways as salt licks and paths. Roads with switchbacks and more curves than a mountain goat's horn make for dangerous travel at high speeds with or without rain. And the traveler who is in a hurry is sure to miss some of the breathtaking sights around the next corner or up the last side road.

## Roads

### Getting to 101

Whether you are coming from the east, the south, or the north, you will travel Interstate 5 to Tacoma or Olympia before turning onto a state highway. The loop described throughout the book starts in Tacoma and travels counterclockwise around the Peninsula. From I-5, turn off at exit 132 onto Washington Highway 16, commonly referred to around here as Highway 16 or just 16. This highway leads you across the Tacoma Narrows Bridge and onto the Kitsap Peninsula. Sometimes locals refer to the Tacoma Narrows Bridge as the Narrows or as Galloping Gertie. On November 7, 1940, the Narrows was assaulted by a windstorm that blew the first bridge this way and that and created violent oscillations on the bridge deck. People abandoned their cars and ran to safety at either end of the bridge. Eventually the bridge disintegrated and fell into the Narrows below, taking with it a pet dog and several cars, but no people. So far we've seen no such problems with the new bridge, completed in 1950. Be prepared, however, for long lines and slow going if you try to cross near rush hour or on a Friday. Locals stream to the Peninsula for quick weekend getaways.

> **Insiders' Tip**
> If you drive, avoid the Seattle-Tacoma rush hour which starts around 3 P.M. each afternoon and around 6 A.M. each morning.

Gig Harbor sits right on the other side of the bridge. Farther along the highway you'll come to Port Orchard. Then, right before entering Bremerton, Washington Highway 16 becomes Washington Highway 3. Keep going on Washington Highway 3 until you reach a traffic light. Here you to turn left onto the very short Washington Highway 104 and the Hood Canal Bridge. Yes, Washington has a number of interesting bridges and bridge disasters. The Hood Canal Bridge is a floating bridge that crosses a two-mile span of the canal. On a winter day in 1979 when 100-mile-per-hour winds blew through the area, the water around the bridge was whipped into a froth and the bridge was jerked back and forth. The bridge, designed to rise and fall with the tide, was simply not able to survive the storm, and one of its pontoons filled with water. Piece by piece, the bridge sank. For the next three years, tourists and residents rode a ferry across the canal. Occasionally the bridge is still closed due to high winds.

Once across the bridge, you will be on the Olympic Peninsula. About seven miles after turning onto the bridge, Washington Highway 19 heads north to Port Townsend. We recommend this route into Port Townsend. When you leave Port Townsend to continue the tour around the Peninsula, take Washington Highway 20, which intersects with U.S. Highway 101.

## U.S. 101

U.S. 101 starts (or ends) in Olympia, Washington, our state capital, curls around the Olympic Peninsula, skirts Grays Harbor, and then keeps on going down the coast to end in the traffic jams of Los Angeles, California. We propose that the beginning of the highway is much more relaxing, peaceful, and beautiful than the other end.

Generally interstates and U.S. highways follow a strict numbering system in which all routes ending in an odd number are north-south routes. Normally if you start driving at the northern terminus of a highway, you begin by driving south. Even if you are driving east on one of these roads, the road signs will still say north or south depending on which end of the nation you'd end up on were you to keep driving. U.S. 101 is a renegade highway. The I-5/U.S. 101 junction at Olympia marks the northern terminus of U.S. 101. However, because of this quirk in planning and of the landscape, both ends of U.S. 101 are U.S. 101 North! Near the junction with Wash. 20, U.S. 101 becomes U.S. 101 West until the highway finally turns south about 25 miles beyond Port Angeles and becomes U.S. 101 South until the pavement ends at the southern terminus.

Sequim is the first significant city on U.S. 101 if you take the route we use in the book. The highway used to travel through downtown Sequim, but a recent change has rerouted it to skirt the southern edge of the city. The next significant town is Port Angeles where you can catch a ferry to Victoria, B.C., Canada. We suggest you check your gas gauge at Port Angeles. In fact, it's a good idea to check the gauge whenever you pass a gas station since the distances between them can be a tad too long for comfort.

After leaving Port Angeles the highway heads inland around the southern edge of Lake Crescent. At the small village of Sappho, the highway begins heading south to Forks. After Forks, the highway twists and turns its way through woods and along the coast for 105 miles before it comes to Hoquiam, Aberdeen, and the Grays Harbor area.

## Closing the Loop and Other Highways

Starting at Aberdeen, U.S. Highway 12 and Washington Highway 8 connect the two parallel sections of U.S. 101 to close the Peninsula loop. At Montesano, U.S. 12 and Wash. 8 merge for a few miles before U.S. 12 veers to the south at a small town called Elma. Continue on 8 until it ends near the terminus of U.S. 101. Sounds confusing, but from here U.S. 101 cuts through Shelton and heads north along the west side of Hood Canal until it intersects with Wash. 104 to end the Peninsula loop. If you elect to skip Hood Canal, you can either turn onto Wash. 3 at Shelton in order to head back to the Kitsap Peninsula, or you can head south on U.S. 101 and get on I-5 at Olympia.

All roads on the Peninsula seem to turn off of or lead to U.S. 101. One of these roads, Washington Highway 112, splits off of U.S. 101 shortly after Port Angeles. Wash. 112 is known also as the Strait of Juan de Fuca Highway, which is listed as a Scenic Byway. This road is a tortuous winding two-lane road that travels past prime fishing grounds. It ends at Neah Bay on the Makah Reservation. Washington Highway 113, a 10-mile stretch of road, connects Wash. 112 with US 101 so visitors don't have to backtrack all the way to Port Angeles in order to get back to the main highway. A few miles before Forks, Washington Highway 110 branches off U.S. 101 and heads west along the Sol Duc River to La Push, the Quileute Reservation, and the ocean. Then, at Hoquiam, Washington Highway 109 takes travelers west toward Ocean Shores and then north along the coast to Taholah on the Quinault Reservation.

## Ferries

Washington State maintains one of the most extensive ferry systems in the country. Every day, more than 70,000 people ride one of the 27 ferries serving 10 routes around the state. Many of these ferries serve destinations on the Olympic and Kitsap Peninsulas. Most people find riding a ferry relaxing and entertaining, not to mention the fact that doing so cuts down on the stress of driving. Occasionally ferry passengers enjoy the additional perk of glimpsing one of the area's resident pods of orcas (killer whales).

From Seattle, travelers may take one of two ferry routes to the Peninsula. The Seattle/Bremerton route is the most direct route to the Kitsap Peninsula. The crossing takes about an hour. Monday through Friday, a passenger-only ferry serves the Seattle/Bremerton route with a 30 minute crossing time. The Seattle/Bainbridge Island route is a more circuitous route to the Peninsula, but we certainly wouldn't stop someone from adding the beautiful island to the itinerary. A bridge links the island to the north end of the Kitsap Peninsula. The crossing takes about 35 minutes.

Another ferry terminal at Southworth serves as the terminus for the Fauntleroy/ Southworth ferry. This ferry crosses in about 35 minutes. Southworth is just a few miles north of Gig Harbor, and Fauntleroy is also known as the West Seattle ferry dock.

For a straight shot onto the Hood Canal Bridge, take the Edmonds/Kingston ferry. Edmonds is a suburb north of Seattle. The ferry, which crosses in about 30 minutes, joins two segments of Wash. 104, and the western segment starts at the northeastern edge of the Kitsap Peninsula.

If you wish to tour Whidbey Island as well as the Olympic Peninsula, then you may want to ride the

### Insiders' Tip

Ride the ferry from Seattle to the Peninsula to cut an hour or two off of your drive. It may not save you time, but the view of the Olympics from the water is breathtaking, and you may even see a few orcas.

*Cars load onto the Southworth ferry near Port Orchard, one of the gateways to the Olympic Peninsula for travelers from Seattle.* PHOTO: ROB McNAIR-HUFF

Keystone/Port Townsend ferry, which takes about 30 minutes crossing time.

When you get on a state ferry, be prepared to pay with cash, traveler's checks, or an in-state check. Credit cards and out-of-state checks are not accepted. Fares vary slightly according to route, but on average the peak season (mid-May to mid-October), one-way fare for an automobile and driver costs around $8.50 to $10.00. Each additional adult passenger costs $4.00. Fares for children five to eighteen are set at 70 percent of the standard fare, and children under five ride free. Senior citizen passenger fares cost half of the standard fare. Passengers may travel with a bike for an additional charge, around $1.00.

The last ferry route to or from the Peninsula takes visitors, mostly tourists, between Port Angeles and Victoria, B.C. This ferry, the M.V. Coho, is run by a private company, not the state. A one-way fare for automobile and driver costs around $30, each additional passenger older than twelve costs around $7.50, children five to eleven cost around $4.00, and children under five travel for free. For information on departure times and fares, call Black Ball Transport Inc. at (360) 457-4491.

For information on schedules, routes, and fares for the state ferry system, check the Web site www.wsdot.wa.gov/ferries/ or call (888) 808-7977. You can also pick up ferry schedules at any ferry dock, chamber of commerce, visitors center, or at many of the businesses in the area. For information on the Coho, call (360) 457-4491 or visit the Web site at www.northolympic.com/coho/.

# Renting a Car

If you are coming from far away and have decided not to drive cross-country or cross-state, you may want to look into renting a car once you've reached the state or the Peninsula. Several cities have rental agencies. Bremerton, since it serves a large military population and a major ferry line, may be the easiest place to rent a car. Five major car rental companies have offices in Bremerton: Alamo, Avis, Budget, Enterprise, and Hertz. In Port Angeles, you may pick up a car from Budget, (800) 345-8038, near the ferry terminal or airport. Budget also has offices in Port Townsend, (360) 385-7766, and Aberdeen, (360) 532-7579. You may also rent a car at the Sea-Tac Airport from one of many rental agencies there.

# By Bus

Surprisingly, for such a small and sprawling population base, the Olympic Peninsula has a great network of county bus lines. It won't be easy, and you may end up spending a lot of time waiting around, but it is possible to tour the Peninsula by a series of county buses. The fares on county buses range from 25 cents to $2. All county lines offer wheelchair access and most have bike racks on the buses. You can call or write to have schedules mailed to you, or you can pick them up at many local businesses and post offices.

# From Sea-Tac

**Bremerton-Kitsap Airporter**
**5748 Bethel Rd., Port Orchard**
**(360) 876-1737, (800) 562-7948 in-state only**
**www.kitsapairporter.com**

When you fly into Sea-Tac Airport, other than renting a car, this is your best bet for getting onto the Kitsap Peninsula. The shuttles leave the airport 20 times every day. In most cases you won't have to wait more than an hour. The driver will take you to your hotel or let you off at a central drop-off point in each of the cities served. Fares vary according to where you are going, but for an adult they range between $12 to Gig Harbor and $19 to Poulsbo. They accept cash and major credit cards but no checks.

**Olympic Bus Lines**
**(360) 417-0700, (800) 550-3858**
**www.olympicbuslines.com**

Olympic Bus Lines is the only Greyhound affiliate on the Peninsula. They make twice daily runs from downtown Port Angeles and Sequim to downtown Seattle and the Sea-Tac Airport. A one-way trip to downtown Seattle costs approximately $29, round-trip $49. A one-way trip to the airport costs approximately $43, round-trip $58.

# County Transit

**Clallam Transit**
**838 W. Lauridson Blvd., Port Angeles**
**(360) 452-4511, (800) 858-3747**
**www.clallamtransit.com**

The extremely friendly folks at Clallam Transit will help you plan a trip around the Peninsula if you visit their Web site and fill out the trip-planner form found on the "using the bus" page. This line runs from Diamond Point in Sequim where it connects with the Jefferson Transit line and as far west as LaPush and Forks, where it connects with the West Jefferson transit line.

**Grays Harbor Transportation Authority**
**705 30th Street, Hoquiam**
**(360) 532-2770, (800) 858-3747**
**www.ghcog.org/tranpage.htm**

This line serves most of the Grays Harbor area communities including Aberdeen, Hoquiam and Montesano, and Ocean Shores. It links into the West Jefferson line on the far side of Lake Quinault and also takes riders to Olympia for around $2 each way.

**Jefferson Transit**
**1615 W. Sims Way, Port Townsend**
**(360) 385-4777**
**www.jeffersontransit.com**

Jefferson Transit, centered in Port Townsend, also serves Port Hadlock, Port Ludlow, Irondale, and Chimacum. The line connects with Kitsap Transit at Poulsbo, with Clallam Transit at Sequim, and with the Mason County line at Brinnon, near Lake Quinault.

**Kitsap Transit**
**10 Washington Ave., Bremerton**
**(360) 377-2877, (800) 501-7433**
**www.kitsaptransit.org**

Pierce Transit serves the area around Gig Harbor, but Kitsap Transit serves the rest of the Kitsap Peninsula and Bainbridge Island. That means that each and every ferry to Bremerton, Southworth, and Kingston is met by a Kitsap Transit bus. This system connects to Mason County line at Bremerton and to Jefferson Transit at Poulsbo.

**Mason County Transportation Authority**
**(360) 426-9434, (800) 281-9434**
**www.olympicpeninsula.com/ travel/ gettingAbout/busMason.html**

If you want a ride in Mason County, you'll have to pick up the phone. All routes are "Dial-A-Ride," but they will also arrange for deviations from normal routes if you call ahead. This line serves Shelton and the Hood Canal area. It connects with Kitsap Transit at Bremerton, with Jefferson Transit at Brinnon, and at Olympia with Pierce Transit and Grays Harbor Transit.

## Charter Buses

If you prefer to leave all the driving to someone else without worrying about bus schedules and transfers, you might want to organize a tour with one of the charter bus services that serve the Peninsula.

**Gray Line of Seattle**
**4500 W Marginal Way SW, Seattle**
**(800) 544-0739, (206) 624-5077**
**www.graylineofseattle.com**

Gray Lines is the largest charter tour company in the Northwest. Most of its scheduled tours do not reach the Peninsula, but they will help you organize a tour of the area for groups sized 14 to 54. The company offers wheelchair accessibility and will arrange for tour narration and, in some cases, translation.

**Janssen's Charters & Tours**
**1623 Woods Rd. E, Port Orchard**
**(360) 871-2446, (800) 922-5044**

Normally Jannssen's organizes tours for locals to Leavenworth and Reno, but they have the most modern of buses to also help you see the Peninsula on a chartered tour.

**Majestic Charters & Tours, Bremerton**
**16952 Clearcreek Rd. NW, Poulsbo**
**(800) 696-6177**
**majesticcharterandtour.com**

In addition to organizing day and overnight trips to Seattle and other Washington hot spots, Majestic tours will arrange chartered tours for groups as small as two people or as large as 52. The buses are equipped with wheelchair lifts.

**Royal Victoria Tours**
**(888) 381-1800**
**www.royaltours.bc.ca**

During the summer months, Royal Victorian Tours takes tourists to the scenic Hurricane Ridge, one mile up the Olympic Mountains. From the ridge you can look out over the Strait of Juan de Fuca to Vancouver Island and down on Port Angeles. The company also offers tours of local golf courses, whale-watching excursions, and trips to Victoria, B.C.

## By Air

**Seattle-Tacoma International Airport**
**17801 Pacific Highway S., Seattle**
**(206) 433-5388**

Sea-Tac Airport is the nearest major airport to the Peninsula. You can rent a car at the airport and drive to Seattle to catch a ferry or drive down I-5 to Tacoma and take Wash. 16 to the Peninsula. Alternately you can catch a Horizon Air or Harbor Airline shuttle to the Port Angeles airport or hire a charter to one of the municipal airports on the Peninsula. Most major airlines fly to Sea-Tac. Contact your travel agent to book a flight.

**William F. Fairchild International Airport**
**1402 South Airport Rd., Port Angeles**
**(360) 457-1138**
**www.portofpa.com/airport.html**

The Port Angeles Airport, also known as the Fairchild International Airport, is the only airport on the Peninsula that is served by regular flights from Sea-Tac. Horizon Air (800-547-9308) has five daily round-trip flights. Harbor Airlines (800-359-3220) has four round-trip flights daily. Charter and sight-seeing flights may also be arranged here.

## Municipal Airports

Some of the Peninsula's municipal airports are little more than a paved runway. Others have control towers, on-site repair services, and family-style restaurants. Pilots who plan to fly to the area may want to consult the Washington State Department of Transportation's aviation Web site www.wsdot.wa.gov/Aviation/airports/airport-default.htm. Or, for even more information on airports here and around the nation, visit AirNav at www.airnav.com. AirNav provides navigational information as well as basic information about the services offered at each airport. Of course, we recommend you call the airport for the most accurate information.

| | |
|---|---|
| Tacoma Narrows Airport, Gig Harbor | (253) 853-5844 |
| Bremerton National Airport, Bremerton | (360) 674-2381 |
| Jefferson County Int'l Airport, Port Townsend | (360) 385-0656 |
| Sequim Valley Airport, Sequim | (360) 683-4444 |
| Fairchild Int'l Airport, Port Angeles | (360) 417-3433 |
| Bowerman Airfield, Hoquiam | (360) 533-9528 |

*Petroglyphs near Cape Alava.* PHOTO: NATIONAL PARK SERVICE

# History

The history of the Olympic Peninsula is closely tied to the land and the sea, and begins long before the white explorers arrived and written word was used here. To know that history we rely upon the oral traditions of the Native American tribes and upon the archeological artifacts found at different sites around the Peninsula. That history still impacts the region through the arts and cultural influences. To better understand the Peninsula, take time to learn about its history.

## Before *Discovery*

### First Peoples

We'll start our story nearly 12,000 years ago when bogs and open meadows covered the land that is now covered by giant trees. Small, nomadic groups of people wandered across the Peninsula in search of prey. Sometimes that prey was as large as the giant mastodon. How do we know this? In 1977 a farmer, Emanuel Manis, was digging around in a peat bog on his land when he happened upon the tusk of what turned out to be the complete skeleton of a mastodon. What is even more remarkable, is that the mastodon had what archeologists think might be a spear point imbedded in one of its ribs. There was also other evidence that people may have butchered part of the animal with chipped rock, bone, and antler tools, even if they didn't kill it.

People continued to populate the region through the end of the last Ice Age as the glacial ice retreated and the sea level rose. They, as well as the people who came after, are the ancestors of the current tribal groups that also lived in the area when the first European explorers sailed along the coast.

The coastal tribes had a unique way of life, and even though there were some differences between each tribe, they held much in common. Unlike inland tribes, the life of the coastal peoples was relatively easy, and water travel made trade efficient and easy. Food more or less came to them, and it was always available. They fished for salmon, cod, and other fish and cured them in the wind. The tribes on the west side of the Peninsula hunted for whales in dugout canoes carved from the largest cedar trees. They hunted deer, otter, and elk and dried the meat, and cured the skins, and used the bones for spear points and tools. Floats used in whaling were made from the skins of seals and sea lions. Shellfish were easily harvested by walking along the beach to pick up or dig for clams, oysters, mussels, shrimp, and crab. They also harvested berries, plant roots, and seaweed. They did not need to stray far from the shores, and myths tell of monsters and a mysterious and violent tribe of people who lived in the interior.

### Tribal Culture

Since they did not have to constantly move in search of food, and since the weather throughout the region is so moderate, the tribes were able to establish permanent villages with large, communal longhouses made of cedar slabs. Some, such as Old Man House of the Suquamish, grew to be 900 feet long and 60 feet wide. Family groups erected woven cedar screens for privacy. The soft, inner layer of cedar bark was also used to make baskets, hats, and clothing that was sometimes lined with the hair of white dogs that were specially bred for their soft, fluffy, woolly fur. In the warmer summer months, some tribe members traveled to summer camps in prime fishing areas where, for as long as the fish ran strong, they would camp, rising each morning to string nets across the rivers or to set out in canoes with fishing lines spun from nettle fiber. The fish were then cleaned and butterflied and either smoked or set on frames to bake in the sun and wind until they were dried and preserved. When the fall rains moved in, the summer encampment was disbanded, and the people returned to their winter villages.

It was through the long, dark, wet winter that the oral tradition was passed on to the next generation through stories, myths, and rituals. Artists carved and painted paddles, dishes, ceremonial masks, and clan totems, and others wove baskets and made new clothes. The Native Americans of the Pacific Northwest Coast developed a rich and varied culture due in part to the long winters when these common activities were refined into high art among the nobility of the tribes.

Among most area tribes a strict social hierarchy separated the people into three classes: nobility, commoners, and slaves. Chiefs, high and low, came from the nobility, and nobles married nobles, and only rarely did a commoner increase his or her rank by adoption by or marriage to a member of the nobility. Intermarriage among the tribes was common. The ruling class had more material goods, owned slaves, and held the allegiance of the commoners in a house and village. They had more leisure time to engage in artistic pursuits, although they were still expected to do their parts in feeding and especially protecting their village. The nobility also had certain rights such as the rights to the exclusive use of certain clan symbols and dances, the rights to fish on certain streams or in a particular bay, or the rights to certain names. In most areas there was little difference between commoners and slaves except that commoners were born into the tribe and were more independent in choosing their activities and mates.

The potlatch was one of the most important social and political occasions. To hold a potlatch, a chief or other high-ranking person would invite chiefs and other members of surrounding villages to the event. The entire village would prepare for the potlatch over months. Villagers would work weaving baskets, carving paddles, preserving and preparing food, and making gifts for guests to prepare for the potlatch. The greatest gifts were given to the highest ranking or most important guests. Sometimes, the people giving potlatches gave away nearly everything they owned. In turn, they would be invited to future potlatches given by others. It was in this way that people showed their status and preserved or increased their rank in the social order. The potlatches also gave tribes a chance to socialize, network, and set up new alliances. Sometimes guests helped to erect corner poles and longhouses. Potlatch gatherings could last for weeks as those invited traveled to the area and assembled before the feast. The feast was the crowning event with singing, ceremonial dancing, and of course, the distribution of gifts. The feast was when the guests witnessed the wealth and rank of their host. Potlatches could be described as a combination between a caucus and a festival.

## Slave Raids

When a chief needed more slaves, he launched a raid against surrounding tribes. Some slaves were the spoils of wars. In fact, the Quileute, who myths say descended from wolves, used James Island as a sort of defensive fortress. At one time, James Island was connected to the mainland by a tiny isthmus, much like the bridge across a mote. The Makahs, a tribe that lives by Cape Flattery in Neah Bay, would launch raids upon the Quileute. When the raiders were spotted, the entire village would move onto the island, where they would boil water in tightly woven baskets and then pour the water on the raiding warriors in their canoes at the base of the island. The island was also used as a burial ground for the chiefs, and the tribe grew nettles there as well.

North of James Island, and a few miles south of Cape Flattery, the Ozette established a village on Cape Alava. More than 800 years ago, that village was destroyed—smothered by a mudslide. The mud perfectly preserved the intact village until rain and time washed the silt away and revealed the site to a passing hiker. Archeologists excavated the village in the 1970s, and most of the artifacts are now housed in the Makah Cultural and Research Center. Those and other artifacts from sites around the two peninsulas tell us much about how the first peoples of this land lived.

Tribes on the Olympic Peninsula are often grouped with the Coastal Salish peoples. However, the Quileute seem to be unrelated, linguistically at least, to any other population in the world. The Quileute were linked through their unique language to the Hoh and the Chimakum, who, according to legend, were washed through the strait to the northeast corner of the Peninsula. Other tribes on the west side of the Peninsula include the Quinault with villages at Queets and Tahola as well as the Makah and Ozette. The Klallam territory extended from Port Townsend to Sekiu, and the tribe traded with the Indians on Vancouver Island as well as those on the Peninsula. The Twana, which included the Skokomish and Quilcene bands, occupied the shores of Hood Canal. The Suquamish lived on the east side of the Kitsap Peninsula, and the Chehalis lived around Grays Harbor.

These first peoples lived in harmony with the land for centuries, fishing, hunting whale, gathering wild fruits and vegetables, weaving, creating great works of art, and occasionally engaging in war and raiding for slaves.

# Exploration

## The Europeans

In 1592, approximately 100 years after the landslide at Ozette, Juan de Fuca, a Greek sailor sailing for Spain, claimed to have found the entrance to the mythical Northwest Passage. Although many doubt the veracity of that claim, the Strait of Juan de Fuca is nevertheless named after the explorer.

The first recorded contact between the European explorers and the people of the Peninsula came in 1775 when members of Juan Francisco de la Bodega y Quadra's crew—another Spanish exploration party—made landfall near the Hoh River. All six men in the landing party were killed on the beach by members of the Quinault tribe.

The first English explorer to visit the region was Captain James Cook, who explored the coast in search of the Northwest Passage. Cook charted and named Cape Flattery, and although he did not know it, his two ships, *Resolution* and *Discovery*, crossed briefly into the waters of the Strait of Juan de Fuca. George Vancouver, a man who later explored the area, was a member of Cook's crew. No other European explorers visited the area for seven years before the flurry of fur traders came to the area and traded trinkets for sea otter skins. One of these traders, Captain Charles William Barkley, recognized the strait for what it was and named it for Juan de Fuca when he charted it. John Meares, another English trader, accompanied by Captain William Douglas, named Mount Olympus and had a rather surly encounter with the Makah wherein four of his crew were wounded and one Makah was killed. Shortly afterwards, the Spanish established a short-lived fort at Neah Bay. After only five months of occupation, one Spaniard was dead, and since the Makah were on the verge of declaring war upon them, the Spanish abandoned the post.

The first American to explore the coast was yet another fur trader, Captain Robert Gray. He first came with John Kendrick in 1788. Gray sailed on the *Lady Washington* and Kendrick captained the *Columbia Rediviva*. On his first trip, Gray bought otter skins on the coast and then sailed around the world on his way back to Boston. Gray returned in 1792 aboard the *Columbia Rediviva* for more furs. On that trip Gray discovered two important bodies of water. To the south he discovered the Columbia River, which he named after his ship. He also sailed into a deepwater bay that measures 12 miles wide by 17 miles long and encompasses 200 square miles. He named the harbor after himself, Grays Harbor.

Before he charted both discoveries, Robert Gray met Captain George Vancouver, aboard a second ship named *Discovery*. It was Vancouver who named Puget Sound after one of his officers, Peter Puget, who was in charge of the team that explored the sound's southern reaches. Vancouver and his crew also charted much of the sound, including the Hood Canal.

## The *Press* Expedition

None of the Peninsula's interior was explored until after the arrival of American settlers. Even then, the early settlers only explored as far as they needed for establishing homesteads. Then in 1889, prompted by a comment made by the governor of the soon-to-be-state, the Seattle *Press* sponsored a team of would-be explorers who were charged with crossing the interior of the Olympic Mountains. A six-man team assembled by a foolhardy Scottish explorer named James Helbold Christie left Port Angeles in December of that year. Christie wanted to make a name for himself, and he knew if he waited to make the crossing until spring he would be competing against a bevy of similar teams. The men of the *Press* Expedition carried 1,500 pounds of provisions and were accompanied by four dogs. The first two mistakes came in quick succession. The team rented a wagon to carry lumber to the Elwha River. The wagon couldn't make it through the thick undergrowth to the river, and so the men bought two mules named Dolly and Jenny and cut a trail to the river. Cutting the trail took two weeks. Once there, they set about building a boat. That fiasco would lead one to believe that none of the men had ever built a boat—or perhaps it was that they drank the trip's allotment of whiskey. Once the boat was built and launched, it sank. The men dredged it out, dried it out, and spent two more weeks rebuilding it. When they launched it for the second time, it wouldn't go. Or rather, the only way they could get it to go was to pull it by man or mule power. By January 24, more than a month into the trip, they were only five miles up the river. They abandoned the boat.

The rest of the trip was plagued by even more problems, including a blizzard that hit just after they abandoned the boat. They hauled heavy packs through thick snow and their poor mules, which were ill-equipped for walking through snow, were cut and scraped by the sharp crust of ice. By early March, they were not even out of the Elwha watershed when Jenny the mule fell over a 400-foot ledge and had to be shot. They reapportioned her pack and set off again. A month and a half later, an injured Dolly laid down and would not get up. Christie unburdened her and set the starving mule free, never to be seen again. They forged onward, only to encounter more problems when, a week later, the dogs ate the last of their meat. Luckily for the men, their dogs turned out to be good at harassing bears. After they shot their first bear, the men were so hungry that they melted and drank its fat. By this time it was May, and 20 days into the month they finally attained their destination, the other side of the mountains. They caught a boat from the Quinault Indian Reservation to Grays Harbor, where they wired the *Press* to let them know they'd made it and to ask for money for haircuts and warm meals.

Although the journey sounds more like a dark comedy than a glorious adventure, the men did chart some significant landmarks and named quite a few of the peaks in the Olympic range.

# Settlement and Industry

You will have practically memorized the post-settlement history of the Olympic Peninsula if you remember these two things: timber and trains. Timber because it provided, and to a certain extent still does, the long-term economic base for the Peninsula, and trains because the railroad-that-never-was promised great riches and success.

## Timber, Mills, and the Customhouse

In April 1851, Alfred Augustus Plummer, a New England native enticed by tales of the region's opportunities, landed in Port Townsend after he and his friend Charles Bacheldor paddled up Puget Sound from Steilacoom. The two promptly built a cabin on the beach and planted a garden. Shortly afterwards, they were joined by Loren Hastings and Francis Pettygrove—Pettygrove was cofounder of Portland, Oregon. The four agreed that it would be a good idea to found a town, and so Port Townsend was born. It was the first city on the Peninsula, and although its first enterprise, a fishery, failed, the city prospered thanks to the customhouse and timber.

By this time, trees were already being harvested to serve as ship masts. The super tall and extremely straight Douglas fir trees took weeks to harvest, but the need was so great that the effort was still profitable. It was so profitable in fact, that in order to ensure that trees were not illegally harvested from U.S. territory, a U.S. Customs office was established in what was to become Olympia. In 1853, the second customs officer, Isaac Ebey, petitioned the government to move the Port of Entry to Port Townsend, which had a deep, accessible, and safe harbor.

The first ramshackle mills on the Peninsula were erected at Port Townsend and nearby Port Ludlow. Neither produced very much lumber, but the region's output of finished lumber rose sharply when the Pope and Talbot Company opened a steam mill on the northwest corner of the Kitsap Peninsula at Port Gamble. By the end of its first full year in operation, the mill had cut more than 3.5 million board feet. The company added more saws and production kept increasing. Under the leadership of Cyrus Walker, the company changed the way lumber and timber companies operated. The company built more mills, added more saws, bought land and held the living trees in reserve, stockpiled logs in log rafts for when times were tight, and bought a shipping company so it could transport its own lumber. By 1875 the company owned land throughout Puget Sound and was the largest landholder on the Peninsula and in the Washington Territory. While Pope and Talbot built mills on the Puget Sound, others built on-again off-again mills to the south around Shelton. It wasn't until the 1880s though that the mills there really took off, thanks in part to a railroad line that ran to Olympia.

Although timber and lumber made Port Townsend, it was not because it produced the goods. They made Port Townsend because of the customshouse. Any ship that left the region had to pass through customs at Port Townsend. The city turned into a boom-town as ship traffic increased. Merchants opened hotels, saloons, and stores to serve the sailors that passed through town. Some enterprising ladies even set up brothels. Shang-haiing—the practice of kidnapping men to fill a ship's crew—was common practice. Port Townsend was bigger than Seattle and had made the big time.

Then came Victor Smith who, as customs collector, did his best to cut Port Townsend down. Smith just didn't like Port Townsend and persuaded the Secretary of the Treasury, Salmon P. Chase, to convince President Abraham Lincoln to move the port of entry west to Port Angeles and create a military reserve. Of course, wouldn't you know it, Smith had previously invested in real estate in Port Angeles, some of the very land that Lincoln established as the reserve. So in 1862, Smith bucked accusations of embezzlement and the protestations of Port Townsend residents and forcibly moved the customshouse to Port Angeles. The disgruntled residents of Port Townsend sought revenge and justice and flooded President Lincoln with letters of complaint and affidavits of wrongdoing. Smith was fired, but appointed to the treasury department before he died a year later in a shipwreck. The next customs collector was a Port Townsend resident. He, of course, transferred the customshouse back to Port Townsend.

## Treaties

While the white people were battling over a customshouse, the first peoples were meet-ing with government agents to sign treaties. On January 26, 1855, the Klallam, Chi-makum, and Twana signed the Point No Point Treaty. A few days prior, the Suquamish signed the Point Elliott Treaty, which restricted them to the Port Madison Reservation. On January 31, the Makah and other tribes on the west end signed a treaty at Neah Bay. The treaties specified reservation boundaries and set down certain rules for the tribes, such as the prohibitions against drinking alcohol and owning slaves. The treaties also set the "purchase price" of the former tribal lands. In most cases the fee paid to the tribes averaged around $60,000 for all of their lands, and in exchange they were given a reser-vation on their own lands. Even after the treaties were signed, the Americans managed to take away more land through set-asides, which were later sold to whites. Such set-asides drastically changed the Port Madison Reservation when prime waterfront parcels were sold to white people for summer homes. Tribal identity was further fractured when Native children were removed from the reservations and placed in boarding schools where they were forbidden to speak their own languages or to practice their own reli-gions, rituals, and traditions.

James G. Swan assisted with treaty negotiations between the coast tribes and Isaac

Stevens, the territorial governor. Swan, who was originally from Boston, was a dabbler, and either a genius or a lunatic. He was a scientist, teacher, lawyer, author, artist, ethnographer, promoter, and historian. His diaries and books are still widely read. Swan happened to meet Chetzemoka, the Klallam chief from Port Townsend, in 1851 when the chief was visiting San Francisco while Swan was living there. The two became friends, and soon after the meeting Swan moved to the Willapa Bay area where he sold oysters by shipping them to California. While living on the coast he learned each tribe's language as well as the trading jargon called Chinook. Swan was the customs collector on the coast from 1854 to 1856, when he returned to the East Coast as Isaac Stevens' assistant. He was back in Washington inside of two years when he settled in Port Townsend long enough to reacquaint himself with Chetzemoka before heading to Neah Bay, where he tried and failed to run a trading post. Then he taught at Neah Bay for a few years before returning to Port Townsend in 1866, where he became one of the primary proponents for making Port Townsend the end of the railway line.

## The Railroad That Never Was

In 1869, the transcontinental railroad crossed the continent. Peninsula residents, especially those in Port Townsend, were ecstatic. They figured the city was the premiere candidate for the western terminus. After all, the customshouse was in Port Townsend. Speculators gambled on the location of the railroad up and down the Peninsula. Cities along Hood Canal such as Union, Brinnon, and Quilcene started spending money, cutting lumber, and building like crazy. Unfortunately for the Peninsula, the terminus was granted to Tacoma in 1873. Hopes were raised again when city boosters organized the Port Townsend Southern Railroad in 1887. They laid one mile of track before the company went bust. In 1889 the Oregon Improvement Company, which was held by Union Pacific, said that it was going to build a line from Portland to Port Townsend. The company acquired the Southern line and extended the line to Quilcene, but building stopped in 1893 when the company failed. In 1893, the people of Port Angeles held out hope for a line from Everett to Port Angeles. They even had fund-raising meetings, but the line never saw a single rail. Communities in the Grays Harbor area caught train fever when the Tacoma-Grays Harbor line was built. Several cities vied to be the western terminus, but Aberdeen won the bid when it built its own branch to meet the main line.

By 1900, all hopes for the train-to-greatness were dashed before being briefly revived during World War I. The planes that flew in the war were made of spruce, and spruce grew on the Peninsula. However, the spruce wasn't all that accessible and so a special military division was established, the Spruce Production Division. The division was charged with logging the spruce through the winter, and then in the spring it was to begin work on a mill at Port Angeles and on the spruce railroad from there to the Neah Bay area. Two short lines were also built for mills near Quilcene and Pysht. The division only took six months to build the mill and the railroad, but peace had just been declared by the time they finished. The mill at Port Angeles changed hands a number of times until a man named Rayonier bought it, and the railroad was eventually disassembled.

> **Insiders' Tip**
>
> The shortest railroad line in the state was laid by Norman Smith—son of customs collector Victor Smith—who bought a single rail, cut it in half, and laid it near Lake Crescent.

# Loggers, Trees, and the Environment

Throughout the war and after, timber was logged at a feverish pace. The budding conservation movement expressed concern that all of the trees would be logged in short order if nothing was done to slow down the process. Thanks to the efforts of conservationists and three U.S. presidents, Olympic National Park was created. The 922,653-acre park started much larger, as the 2,188,800-acre Olympic Forest Reserve, set aside by President Grover Cleveland. Later, after being pared down by timber interests, part of what would become the park was set aside by President Theodore Roosevelt in 1909 as the Mt. Olympus National Monument, a preserve for the elk in the heart of the Olympic Mountains and in their summer feeding areas. Hunters who collected their teeth for watch fobs decimated the elk. But the initial move to monument status still didn't protect the elk's winter habitat or many old growth timber stands that held some of the largest trees of their type in the world. President Franklin D. Roosevelt visited the monument in 1937 on a fact-finding mission and by the end of his visit he decided to add more property to the monument and make it Olympic National Park on June 29, 1938.

Although the timber barons were less than thrilled that so many trees had been made inaccessible to them, they did not let that stop them from logging. In fact, the pace of harvest accelerated as new equipment became available to the loggers, who started logging with axes and then saws. They first used bull teams and then steam donkeys to pull the logs out of the woods. By the time log trucks and chainsaws were heard throughout the woods, much of the forest had already been logged once, and the loggers were now cutting into second growth as the trees were put to new uses.

The logs were no longer just sold as raw lumber. Scientific and technological advances made it possible to use more trees in different ways. As Murray Morgan wrote in *The Last Wilderness*, "The research chemist was the fairy godfather who liberated the Cinderella tree [Western Hemlock] from the scullery. In 1909 the sulfate process was discovered for making newsprint out of wood. Hemlock wouldn't work at first, but scientists intensified their study of the structure of the tree. By the 1920s they had learned ways to take a hemlock apart and put some of it together as paper or cellulose for scores of purposes." A similar discovery made plywood more useable, waterproof, and durable. Soon pulp and paper as well as plywood mills were scattered throughout the Peninsula.

Logging peaked in the 1980s when timber companies raced to cut as many trees as possible before impending environmental legislation could take effect. New laws limiting where and what could be cut were enacted in order to preserve the few remaining stands of old-growth trees and the plant and animal diversity of the Peninsula, and to protect the habitat of the tiny and reclusive northern spotted owl. Timber companies still push to cut as much as possible, and the old-growth stands are still susceptible to the chainsaw, but tourist dollars have taken on a new importance to the region's economy, and communities that once relied upon timber have had to diversify in order to survive. Cities like Forks are trying to lure businesses by pushing the wired city concept with easy access to the Internet.

The communities of the Olympic Peninsula are defined by their relationship to the oceans and the trees. No matter what the future brings, the people who live here will always rely in some part upon the land for their livelihoods. Even the tourists who come to the Peninsula visit to see the giant old-growth trees dripping with moss and the broken peaks of the Olympic Mountains and the tumultuous waves on a stormy sea. When you visit the Peninsula, you cannot deny the land's impact on our lives, nor the impact of our lives upon the land. Such is the history of the Peninsula from the time before memory.

# Local Histories

## Gig Harbor

Discovered by the Wilkes Expedition while mapping lower Puget Sound in 1841, Gig Harbor was named for the fact that members of the expedition, some in a gig, used the harbor as shelter in a storm. Gig Harbor began like most Peninsula towns, as a logging area. It made the transition to a boating and shipbuilding capital in short order. Yugoslavian and Scandinavian immigrants moved into the area during its early years, and with the establishment of the Skansie Shipbuilding Company and the more than 180 purse seiners and cannery tenders built there, Gig Harbor was placed firmly on the map as a center for fishing and boating. Logging and sawmills added to the economic diversity of the area, and farmers grew berries and raised chickens and dairy cattle.

In 1897 a group of freethinkers established the Mutual Home Colony Association on a bay near Gig Harbor. They wanted to create a place where people could live with as few restrictions as possible. Once a person bought his or her membership and land allotment, the only rule was that of complete tolerance. Through word of mouth and a community newspaper that had subscribers throughout the nation, the community attracted freethinkers from everywhere. Anarchists, revolutionaries, libertarians, intellectuals, artists, even nudists called Home home. The community enjoyed a rich cultural and intellectual atmosphere fostered by the free exchange of ideas. Residents sponsored performances, lectures, and debates in Liberty Hall, and classes on art, yoga, Esperanto, and spiritualism. The famed anarchist Emma Goldman even gave a speech in Liberty Hall. In 1902, Home had attracted more than 100 inhabitants. People in neighboring communities, however, weren't quite as tolerant and found Home distasteful and controversial. Home was involved in a couple of national scandals, including the investigation of the 1901 assassination of President William McKinley. By 1913 the community was dying, and by 1917, with the outbreak of World War I, the community was all but dead.

In 1940, the first Narrows Bridge was built between Gig Harbor and Tacoma. Though it promised renewed growth for the city, the bridge fell into the Sound shortly after it opened on an extremely windy day. After the bridge was rebuilt, the community flourished, and today it attracts people who commute to Seattle and Tacoma for work. A strong arts community has also developed.

## Port Orchard

Port Orchard was the first incorporated city on the Kitsap Peninsula. It was originally named Sidney after Sidney M. Stevens, one of the founders. The name was changed in 1890 and named after H. M. Orchard, the member of Captain Vancouver's crew who discovered the bay. The first settlers grew fruit and berries, raised livestock, fished, and of course, logged and cut lumber. Some of the city's prominent business leaders also helped entice the Navy into establishing the shipyard just across the inlet in Bremerton.

Port Orchard residents rode steamboats known as the Mosquito Fleet to work at the shipyard. The Mosquito Fleet was a network of foot ferries that was the primary mode of transportation around Puget Sound. The Mosquito Fleet ran as far up the Sound as Everett and as far south as Olympia.

## North Kitsap

The three major towns in the North Kitsap area have histories tied to the sea. Bremerton, the largest community, has been a Navy town nearly from its beginnings. After exploration of the area in 1841 under Lt. Charles Wilkes, the Army Corps of Engineers visited in 1867 and proclaimed that the region had strategic significance. Groundbreaking took place in 1892 for the home of the Puget Sound Naval Shipyard along the Bremerton waterfront.

Development of the Bangor submarine base led to population explosions in Silverdale and Poulsbo. Poulsbo—known as Little Norway for its history of being settled in 1892 by Norwegian loggers—grew into a tourist and fishing town. Scandinavian farmers also settled Silverdale after loggers had cleared the land. The farmers actually rode one of the Mosquito Fleet boats to Seattle and sold their produce in Pike Place Market.

In 1971, the Navy established the Trident submarine base at Bangor, followed by the torpedo-testing base at Keyport. Both helped solidify the area's status as a naval peninsula.

North Kitsap also has a strong Native American heritage. The Suquamish tribe makes its home on the Port Madison Indian Reservation, and Chief Sealth is buried in the town of Suquamish. Several tribes, including the Klallam, Chimakum, and Twana, also signed treaties on the northern tip of the peninsula at Point No Point in 1855.

## Port Townsend

The Native American tribes used a lagoon and isthmus at Port Townsend as a portage point in order to avoid paddling through the treacherous currents off of Point Wilson. They called the place Kah Tai, which means "to carry." The Spanish explorer Manuel Quimper originally charted the small peninsula on which the city sits, but it was Vancouver who named the port in honor of the Marquis of Townshend.

Port Townsend had its own China-town by the 1880s. As the territory became more populated and there weren't quite enough jobs to go around, white people claimed that the Chinese laborers were to blame because they worked for less. In reality, the Chinese, who were hard workers hoping to make it rich so they could return home, were frequently paid more than their white, immigrant counterparts. That misinformed sentiment and unadulterated racism led to the federal Exclusion Act, and the accompanying race riots in nearby cities such as Seattle. Port Townsend avoided the riots, but the Chinese were still hassled and restricted, and a suspicious fire razed much of the Chinese section of town.

In the late 1890s, two forts were built near Port Townsend to create a harbor defense against any foreign threat. Fort Flagler was built on nearby Marrowstone Island, and Fort Worden was built on Point Wilson. Fort Worden was a welcome blessing when it was built because the decision to build it came just at the time that the city was in a tailspin due to the disappointments of failed railroads and a national depression. Gun batteries and rickety observation towers still remain at both forts.

The forts could do little to salvage Port Townsend's dashed hope of being the next New York City. In 1913, to add insult to injury, the hard-fought-for customshouse was moved to Seattle. The city revived briefly during WWI when the forts were in active use, but afterwards the city despaired again until the next war, when both forts were used as training centers and the city seemed to flourish again. But when the war ended, the people and the money left, and Port Townsend fell into a long local depression. The city began to revive itself in the 1970s as it reached out to tourists. Merchants opened bed and breakfast inns, restaurants, gift shops, and refurbished the long-vacant but beautiful-beneath-the-grime warehouses and sandstone block buildings that were built during the boom years. Dilapidated Victorian mansions were refurbished, remodeled, and painted, and soon the streets were bustling again with tourists and retirees with plenty of money to spend on curios, gourmet meals, and art.

## Sequim

Although Manuel Quimper was the first European explorer to chart and name the bay, it was the name given to it by George Vancouver that stuck. Vancouver recalled the coastline of Dungeness in the British Channel when he named Dungeness Bay. New Dungeness was the first white settlement in Clallam County. The Dungeness School House still marks the town site, but it is nearby Sequim that has stood the test of time. When the first settlers arrived, they looked at the wide-open plain and started planting crops. The crops foundered from lack of rain, and the homesteaders resorted to digging irrigation ditches from the Dungeness River to the fields. The settlers grew fruit and vegetables and raised dairy cattle, and that was the way life was in the valley until recently. You'll still find farmsteads, but today they are as likely to be growing lavender as they are to have crops of pumpkins, beans, and corn. Much of the former farmland however, has been supplanted by new subdivisions to accommodate the influx of retirees who flock to the area for the mild and sunny climate—a rarity on the Peninsula. The climate and beautiful surroundings attracted Sequim's most famous seasonal resident to the area. John Wayne vacationed here on land that now serves as the marina.

> **Insiders' Tip**
>
> Don't pass by another chance to learn. *Traveler's History of Washington: A Roadside Historical Guide* by Bill Gulick makes a great traveling companion and guide to historical attractions along the way.

## Port Angeles

In 1791, the Spaniard, Francisco Eliza, sailing with Manuel Quimper, explored the harbor at Port Angeles and named it Porto de Nuestra Señora de Los Angeles (Port of Our Lady of Angels). In 1857, Angus Johnson settled here, and five years later Victor Smith moved the customshouse to Port Angeles. It was a short-lived victory for the budding city. Although he tried every trick in his book, Smith could not convince more than 22 people to buy plots in the subdivided land extracted from the military reserve. Then, in 1863, a natural dam broke on a creek that ran through town. The deluge wiped the city out and carried the customshouse out to sea. Two customs agents died in the flood.

In 1887 Port Angeles was home to a utopian community. At this time the race riots against the Chinese were taking place in the Seattle area. Two men who helped organize the riots established the Puget Sound Cooperative Colony. The colony used local scrip in place of money, and all pay was based solely upon the amount of work performed, not upon the type of job. Of course, Chinese were not allowed to join the colony. The colony hoped to avoid the dreaded pitfalls of capitalism, but the social experiment lasted only seven years. The colony went bankrupt in 1894.

Many of the colony's 1,000 members stayed in the area even after the bankruptcy, and the fortunes of Port Angeles rose and flagged with the anticipation of the railroad. The mills and deep harbor anchorage kept the city going through the years, and in 1917, as part of the spruce railway project, the military paid for a new mill that was built in town. Rayonier eventually bought the mill, which is still in operation and now owned by a Japanese company.

# Juan de Fuca Highway

Some of the oldest history on the Olympic Peninsula is documented through places such as the ancient Native American fishing site at the Ozette dig near Cape Alava. The Makah Cultural and Research Center in Neah Bay unveils the history of the S'Klallam, Ozette, and Makah Tribes that have called the area home for thousands of years.

European influence on the Peninsula began in 1792, when Spain established a short-lived settlement in what would become Neah Bay. The area along Washington Highway 112, or the Juan de Fuca Highway, became part of the Oregon Territory in 1800 and it drew loggers and anglers to settle the area, with major settlements in Neah Bay, Clallam Bay, and Sekiu.

In 1999, the Makah Tribe in Neah Bay made news when it harvested a gray whale under the terms of its treaties with the United States. The status of the treaty and its legality were under international scrutiny at the time this book was written.

# Forks

Forks was originally called Indian Prairie because the Quileute hunted here. Forks was born in the 1870s as an agricultural town where farmers grew hops and peppermint and raised dairy cattle. But the rain-soaked area soon launched into the lumber business when the first sawmill was built in 1890. Logging has made the history of Forks a series of successes and failures. In 1951, a fire that started near Lake Crescent to the east swept past town along the banks of the Calawah River. According to witnesses, the intensity of the burn may have saved the town, along with the efforts of locals who fought the flames. The fire, which eventually consumed 30,000 acres of forest, burned so hot that it con-sumed most of the oxygen in the air, stifling the fire's spread.

Logging boomed well into the 1980s, before logging slowed to a crawl due to envi-ronmental regulations and a lack of trees outside the boundaries of the nearby national forest and park.

# Ocean Shores

Ocean Shores has a brief history, compared to the rest of the Peninsula. Once the site of a cattle ranch, land speculators purchased the sandy peninsula and developed it as a des-tination resort in the 1960s. The original development was never as popular as the investors imagined, but today the area draws more than three million visitors each year to the sandy seashores and canals along the inner sections of the city.

# Grays Harbor

Timber and fish dominate the history of the towns in Grays Harbor. The harbor, the largest and deepest natural harbor on the West Coast, was discovered and charted by Robert Gray in 1792. The deep harbor proved valuable for shipping timber logged from the hills surrounding the towns of Aberdeen, Cosmopolis, and Hoquiam, and eventually from areas such as McCleary and Elma. The first lumber mill in Grays Harbor went up in 1852, and by the early 1900s, Aberdeen had a reputation as the toughest town west of Chicago, with streets lined by bars, boardinghouses, and brothels that catered to loggers who ventured to town on the weekends. Fire destroyed much of downtown Aberdeen in 1903, but the town was rebuilt shortly thereafter with the plentiful local timber.

As the trees in the nearby forests dwindled, the town of Montesano became home to the first tree farm in the world, established by the Weyerhaeuser Company in 1941.

Today the region remains tied to timber, and while the number of mills and mill workers has dwindled, the area retains its logging heritage.

## Shelton

Thomas Webb and Franklin Purdy were the first white settlers in the area that would become Shelton when they arrived in 1851. But it was farmer David Shelton, who moved to the area in 1855, who is the namesake for the city. The town, which was originally called Sheltonville, grew to become one of the major timber towns on the Peninsula. The only incorporated city in Mason County, Shelton has lived and died by the cycles of logging and the employment offered by the Simpson Timber Company. During boom times, such as in 1887, three railroads operated in the area around Shelton.

In the 1940s, Shelton became the site of a major experiment in sustained forestry. In cooperation with the U.S. Forest Service and timber companies in Shelton and nearby McCleary, the Shelton Cooperative Sustained Yield Unit was established in 1946 to set up a logging cycle that would ensure that there will be as many board feet of timber standing on the 158,760 acres of timber company land and 111,466 acres of Forest Service land when the agreement ends in 2046 as there were when the agreement was signed. It remains to be seen how well the agreement will face the test of time.

## Hood Canal

Before white settlers moved to the region, Hood Canal was home to the Twana, who included the Skokomish and the Quilcene tribes. Captain Vancouver charted and named the fjord after a fellow Englishman, Lord Samuel Hood.

Most of the communities along the canal were founded in the 1860s by homesteaders such as Hampden Cottle, who founded Quilcene, and Elwell Brinnon. Others, such as Union, were developed in the 1880s as part of the speculating frenzy that was related to the railroad. The railroad from Port Townsend indeed made it to its first and last stop on Hood Canal at Quilcene. But when the railroads fell through, the canal turned into a string of ghost towns. It remains sparsely populated and the main industries of the 1880s are still the main industries: fishing, logging, and oysters. Coast Seafoods Company, the largest oyster hatchery in the world, is located on Hood Canal. When the Hood Canal Bridge was built in 1961, tourism was added to the list of primary industries, and fish hatcheries are another recent addition.

*Marymere Falls is surrounded by an old-growth forest in Olympic National Park.* PHOTO: NATALIE McNAIR-HUFF

# The Natural World

Geology

Climate

Habitat

An entire book could be written about the natural world of the Olympic Peninsula, and more than one book has been written about the topic. A combination of unique factors make the Peninsula, and the Olympic National Park that lies at its heart, a veritable island, surrounded on three sides by water—the Pacific Ocean to the west, the Strait of Juan de Fuca to the north, and Hood Canal and Puget Sound to the east. This geographical fact, along with the effects of past Ice Ages, sets the plants and animals of the Peninsula apart from the rest of Western Washington. To better understand the Peninsula, this chapter takes a look at the Peninsula's geological past and present, the climate, and the variety of plants and animals that populate the various habitats in the region.

## Geology

The origins of the Olympic Mountains baffled scientists for years, until geologists began to unravel the area's secrets in the 1960s when the theories of plate tectonics became widely accepted. One of the youngest mountain ranges in the United States, the Olympics rise abruptly from the Pacific Ocean to elevations around 8,000 feet and are part of what was once an ancient seafloor. Over millions of years the seabed was rammed and crumpled up against the North American continental plate. Most of the seafloor dives under the North American Plate to form what geologists call a subduction zone along the Washington coast, but for whatever reason, the portion of rock that formed the Olympic Mountains wasn't pushed under. Instead, it buckled and rose toward the sky.

The Olympic Mountains form a horseshoe shape, with the higher peaks mostly composed of basalt that was long ago erupted from volcanoes on the ocean floor. The basalt rammed against the coastline and thrust up into the air, stacked against the coast at an angle. Sedimentary rocks were added and overlay much of the basalt to form the rest of the mountains. Over millions of years, layer after layer of rock rafted in and stacked against the core rocks, creating the jumbled mountains that lie at the core of the Peninsula.

Mount Olympus, the highest peak in the Olympic Mountains, is nearly 8,000 feet tall. It and the other nearby peaks, many of which reach nearly as high, would undoubtedly be taller if not for the drastic glaciation that has carved the entire Olympic Peninsula and much of Western Washington over the ages. Despite their close proximity to the Pacific Ocean and the relative low elevation of the peaks, the Olympic Mountains sport 266 glaciers, the largest collection of glaciers at such a low elevation in the United States. The Olympics are more glaciated than the much taller Rocky Mountains largely due to weather patterns. Mount Olympus receives an average of 220 inches of precipitation each year, mostly in the form of snow. And as a result, the Blue Glacier that descends down its slopes—the largest glacier on the Olympic Peninsula—extends down to as low as 4,000 feet.

Almost as much as geology, ice has set the Olympic Peninsula apart as a special island along the Washington coast. Scientists believe that during each Ice Age, at least some portions of the Peninsula remained free of ice. Ice hundreds of feet thick filled the valley east of the mountains. When it retreated, the fjord formed by the glacier's work filled with water to form Hood Canal. To the north, the same thing happened to create the Strait of Juan de Fuca. The southern and western sections of the Olympic Peninsula largely escaped the ice, other than in places such as the Hoh River valley or the Quinault River valley, where glaciers likely ground down the valley toward the coast.

# Climate

The departure of the last Ice Age didn't signal an end to the effects of weather on the Olympic Peninsula. The cycle of precipitation and runoff back to the sea is pronounced on the Peninsula, as witnessed by the Hoh Rain Forest and the Quinault Rain Forest with their 140-plus inches of rain each year. Storms blowing in from the Pacific Ocean dump their loads of rain and snow as they rise and cool before passing over the Olympic Mountains, and this precipitation spawns 11 major rivers that send the runoff back to Hood Canal, the Strait of Juan de Fuca, and the Pacific Ocean. Once the water is rung out of the clouds along the upslopes of the mountains, the clouds skim westward without their cargo of rain, casting a huge rain shadow across portions of the Peninsula and sections of Western Washington. While Mount Olympus averages more than 220 inches of rain and snow each year, a few miles to the northeast the town of Sequim receives an average of just 17 inches of rain each year.

In the rainiest sections of the Peninsula, near Forks in the northwest and near Shelton in the south, most of the rain falls in the spring, fall, and winter. The Hoh Rain Forest receives an average of 12.5 inches of rain each month in the spring, 13.1 inches each month in fall, and 15.75 inches each month in the winter. Across Olympic National Park, three-quarters of the annual rainfall falls between October 1 and March 31.

One thing you can count on with weather conditions on the Olympic Peninsula is that they are extremely unpredictable. If it is raining and windy on the Hood Canal, it is very likely to be sunny in Sequim or Port Townsend. Traveling just a few miles in one direction or another can make all the difference. During the spring and fall months, what might be a soft drizzle near sea level in Port Angeles could be a blinding blizzard with whiteout conditions on Hurricane Ridge. While rain is less likely during the summer months, occasional thunderstorms strike the higher elevations and fog can occur along the ocean beaches.

## Insiders' Tip

If you want to view wildlife on the Peninsula, the best bet is to check one of the wildlife refuges or to wander a favorite spot in Olympic National Park. The best viewing times are usually around dawn and dusk.

# Habitat

The unique climate conditions and the fact that the core of the Olympic Peninsula has been isolated from surrounding areas during long periods of time has led to the evolution of many plants and animals that are found nowhere else in the world. Olympic National Park contains a number of endemic plants and animals—eight plants, five mammals, one amphibian, three fish, five insects, and two mollusks. These plants and animals are distributed throughout the Peninsula in six separate life zones: intertidal, rain forest, lowland forest, montane, subalpine, and alpine.

The best way to get to know the flora and fauna of the Peninsula is to start at the lowest point along the coast and work your way inland.

The intertidal zone hugs the shoreline, and its plant life is composed mostly of wind-battered Sitka spruce trees and sea vegetation such as feather boa kelp, sea moss, and eelgrass. When the tides shift and fall, the animals that live in the sea-spray habitat—starfish, white cap limpets, and green-, red-, and orange-colored sea anemones—are unveiled for tidepoolers. The falling tide also reveals a variety of shoreline surfaces, from sandy beaches to the south near Ocean Shores to cobble and stone beaches near Rialto Beach and Hole in the Wall all the way north to the sea stacks strewn offshore and rock outcroppings near Cape Flattery. The rock outcroppings make the best places for investigating the intertidal zone. The crevices and holes in the rocks fill with water allowing the sometimes colorful and camouflaged sea life to retreat there during low tide. A walk along the outcrops will reveal rocks slimy with kelp and seaweed; sand shrimp, hermit crab, and crab; the occasional sea cucumber; and starfish, limpets, and delicate anemones.

The intertidal zone is also home to sea mammals. Sea otter and California and Stellar sea lions haul out of the water and intermittently bask along the shore. And if the season is right, during March and April visitors might spy migrating California gray whales off the shore near Cape Alava, Cape Flattery, or Kalaloch.

On the inland side of the Peninsula, the intertidal zone includes the shores of Hood Canal, with its odd geoduck, razor clam, butter clam, and oysters. Hood Canal is a popular stop for Scuba divers who spend days exploring the underwater wonderland crawling with crab, shrimp, cod, and giant octopus. Visitors to the inland tidal areas may also spy foraging great blue heron and kingfishers.

The extra rich waters of the canal feed an immensely diverse world, and one of its unique inhabitants is the huge bi-valve known as the geoduck (pronounced gooeyduck). The geoduck grows up to 16 pounds, has a soft, fleshy neck that extends up to 18 inches beyond the shell, and can live to be more than 100 years old. It's not a delicate looking creature, and it is best hunted in small groups of strong diggers since the clam burrows three or four feet into the sand.

Many birds also make their home in the intertidal zone. Thousands of migrating birds pass through notable estuaries such as the Grays Harbor National Wildlife Refuge

# Endemic plants

Olympic Mountain milkvetch
Piper's bellflower
Flett's fleabane
Thompson's wandering fleabane
Henderson's rock spirea
Olympic Mountain Groundsel
Olympic Mountain synthyris
Flett's violet

# Endemic animals

### Mammals
Olympic marmot
Olympic yellow-pine chipmunk
Olympic snow mole
Olympic Mazama pocket gopher
Olympic ermine

### Amphibians
Olympic torrent salamander

### Fish
Olympic mudminnow
Beardslee rainbow trout
Crescenti cutthroat trout

### Insects
Hulbirt's skipper
Olympic grasshopper
Mann's gazelle beetle
Quileute gazelle beetle
Tiger beetle

### Mollusks
Arionid slug
Arionid jumping slug

in Bowerman Basin. Oystercatchers, sandpipers, and semipalmated plovers flock to the shores, and other migrating birds such as raptors—bald eagles, osprey, and thousands of hawks—fly overhead on their invisible route to Vancouver Island and beyond. No matter what time of year you explore the intertidal zone, you are sure to see a variety of gulls and cormorants.

Farther inland, along the west side of the Peninsula, the rain forest zones on the Hoh River, the Queets River, and the Quinault River valleys are draped with vegetation more dense than any other forest region in the world. The forest floor near the Hall of Mosses Nature Trail in the Hoh Rainforest is carpeted with a verdant covering of oxalis, thick mosses, and ferns, and curtains of moss hanging from stands of Douglas fir, Sitka spruce, and western hemlock hosts even more plant life. Mushrooms sprout from the sides of trees, and nurse trees—blown-down trees or fallen trees and stumps—host new seedlings that grow up and feed on the decaying wood.

Many of the biggest trees on the Olympic Peninsula are contained in this rain forest. The Quinault Loop Trail on Southshore Road near Lake Quinault offers a glimpse of large western red cedar, Sitka spruce, and western hemlock, and the adjoining Rainforest Nature Trail is a 0.5-mile loop that wanders through huge stands of Douglas fir. Record-setting trees also grow within this zone, such as the Queets Fir, a 14-foot-diameter and 212-foot-tall fir located about two and a half miles up the Queets River Trail, and a record-sized Sitka spruce that is just under 200-feet tall can be seen alongside Southshore Road near Lake Quinault. A record western red cedar, 20 feet in diameter and about 159 feet tall, grows on the north shore of Lake Quinault. Many more record-setting or near-record trees grow deeper in Olympic National Park.

Animals that roam the rain forest zone include the Roosevelt elk, which can often be seen wandering the valleys along the Hoh, Quinault, and Queets Rivers, as well as the much smaller salamanders, the tiny Pacific tree frog, and water-loving insects, such as the Almond-scented millipede. All feel at home in a place where rain and mist are constant companions. Birds such as the controversial Northern spotted owl—a predator that requires large tracts of old-growth forest to live and reproduce—and the Chestnut-backed chickadee also find a hideaway in the thick forest canopy.

Most of the Peninsula lies within the lowland forest category. Douglas fir, western hemlock, and western red cedar forests predominate, with plants such as Oregon grape, salmonberry, and wild rose creating a lush and fertile undergrowth. Many of the old-growth forests fall within this zone as well. Old-growth forests are defined by the combination of mature trees, dead and standing trees, fallen and rotting trees, and multi layered upper canopy. Underneath, oxalis and other shade-tolerant plants dominate in the darker areas. The best examples of old growth on the Peninsula can be found within Olympic National Park. The Ancient Groves Nature Trail, just off the Sol Duc River Road in the north end of the park, meanders for a half mile through ancient hemlock and fir. Other good places to see old growth include the trail to Marymere Falls near Lake Crescent, on trails in the Elwha River Valley, and in the southeastern corner of the park near Lake Cushman and Staircase.

> **Insiders' Tip**
>
> Bird-watchers may want to plan their trips to coincide with the raptor migrations that take place in April or October. Bald eagles, hawks, falcons, and other raptors cross the Peninsula and seek refuge as they fly to and from winter feeding grounds.

*Bird-watchers can feast their eyes on the millions of migrating birds seen in the region.* PHOTO: ROB McNAIR-HUFF

The American dipper, gray jays, and chestnut-backed chickadees, as well as the aforementioned Northern spotted owl, nest in the lowland forest. Black bear, cougar, raccoon, and more Roosevelt elk make their homes in the lowland forests. The national forest and Olympic National Park that occupy the center of the Peninsula exist in large part due to the elk. The park was originally set aside as a preserve for the elk herds, which were being decimated by hunters who sought their teeth to use as fobs on watches. Elk are so significant to the installation of the park that it was nearly named Elk National Park.

Above the 2,000-foot mark and heading toward the heart of the Olympic Mountains, the montane zone is marked mostly by the predominance of Pacific silver fir trees. The montane stretches from around 2,000 to 3,600 feet in elevation. The roads to Hurricane Ridge and Deer Park are some of the best places to see this zone. Besides the silver fir, the forests here include mountain hemlock and Pacific yew. Huckleberry, with its small, bright-red berries and little leaves, and false lily of the valley, trillium, and deerfern make up the understory.

Many of the same animals that are at home in the lowlands also cross into the montane. Roosevelt elk work their way through this zone en route to summer feeding grounds, as do Columbia black-tailed deer. Predators such as cougar, bobcat, and black bear also wander the montane.

Moving even higher into the hills, the subalpine zone is epitomized by what visitors can see on the trails and in the meadows around Hurricane Ridge. The subalpine zone is home to the subalphine fir, silver fir, and mountain hemlock. The lower reaches of the zone often include continuous forest, but as you move up the mountains, the trees thin out and grow in bunches, interspersed with low-growing meadow plants such as Sitka columbine, pink mountain heather, avalanche lily, lupine, and magenta paintbrush.

The variety of animals in the subalpine diminishes along with the tree cover. Roosevelt elk and deer still make their way up to these higher meadows for summer feeding, but the subalpine is also the first place where visitors can see the Olympic marmot and the nonnative mountain goats. The marmot can often be seen and heard in the spring near the Hurricane Ridge Visitor Center. Take a walk along the Hurricane Hill Trail or the trail through the Big Meadow and look for the hairy creatures that are one of the endemic species within Olympic National Park. If you have problems finding the marmot, just listen for the tell tale whistle. Mountain goats, which are not native to the Olympic Peninsula but were introduced by residents in the 1920s, also can often be seen in the subalpine zone.

The most severe climatic conditions on Olympic Peninsula dictate life in the alpine zone, and due to the short seasons, heavy snowfall, and blistering winds that whip over the mountaintops, few plants and animals make their home in this zone. But, many of

# Close-up

## Birding the Peninsula

Millions of birds migrate through and over the Olympic Peninsula each year, and their passage is so important to locals and bird-watchers from across the region that they celebrate the occasion each year at the end of April at the Grays Harbor Shorebird Festival. The festival marks the peak of the spring migration of thousands of Western sandpipers, and dunlins descend on the Grays Harbor National Wildlife Refuge in Bowerman Basin. They are closely followed by peregrine falcons and merlins.

Bowerman Basin is one of the largest wild shorebird estuaries on the West Coast, and it is considered one of four major staging areas for migrating shorebirds in the United States. The national wildlife refuge formed in response to a plan by businesses to fill in the basin for industrial use in the 1970s. Local conservationists and members of groups like the Audubon Society fought to have the 1,800-acre basin, which includes tidal flats, salt marshes, freshwater ponds, and deciduous woodlands, set aside as a refuge for the millions of birds that pass through the area each year. Although much of the land within the basin is still owned by the Port of Grays Harbor, the refuge includes a boardwalk at the tip of Bowerman Peninsula, the Sandpiper Trail, and a number of great places for viewing and photographing birds.

Although it is the largest bird refuge on the Peninsula, Bowerman Basin is far from the only place to view resident or migrating birds. Bird refuges dot the entire region. The Dungeness National Wildlife Refuge includes 631 acres of the Dungeness Spit near Sequim, and is a key wintering area for brant, a duck-like bird, and other waterfowl. The Dungeness Bay, which is formed by one of the world's longest natural sand spits, is also home for harbor seals, and orca whales can occasionally be seen by visitors who walk the spit.

The nearby Protection Island National Wildlife Refuge at the mouth of Discover Bay in the Strait of Juan de Fuca is closed to the public to protect nesting seabirds and harbor seals, but the 364-acre island is home to 72 percent of the nesting seabirds in Puget Sound. More than 17,000 pairs of rhinoceros auklets are estimated to nest on the island, which can be viewed from passing boat tours and private boats. Even bird-watchers on boats are required to stay at least 200 yards offshore to avoid scaring the nesting birds.

Another less accessible bird refuge is the Washington Maritime National Wildlife Refuge Complex, which includes the Dungeness and Protection Island areas as well as refuges just off the Washington coast at Copalis, Flattery Rocks, the Quillayute Needles, and in the San Juan Islands. The section of the maritime refuge along the coast covers more than 100 miles from Flattery Rocks near Cape Flattery in the north to Copalis Beach in the south, and the rocks in the region are nesting grounds for more than 100,000 pelagic birds such as black oysterhatch, common mure, and glaucous-winged gulls. The 870 coastal rocks and reefs within the refuge are also a wintering home to bald eagles and peregrine falcons.

Fans of raptors such as bald eagles, hawks, and falcons will want to head toward Neah Bay and Cape Flattery in the spring to witness the gathering of raptors riding the thermals at the south side of the Strait of Juan de Fuca as they gather before making the crossing to Vancouver Island and beyond.

Even common river valleys such as the Elwha River valley in the northern end of Olympic National Park are good places for birding, with colorful birds such as Harlequin ducks bobbing in the river waters. The park itself is home to more than 200 species of resident and migrating birds.

*Deer are some of the many animals that inhabit the Olympic Peninsula.* PHOTO: NATALIE McNAIR-HUFF

the Peninsula's endemic plants are found in this extreme area, such as the Olympic Mountain milkvetch, Piper's bellflower, Olympic groundsel, and Flett's violet. These plants emerge from winter snows in the late summer months and bloom in bunches. In order to survive the conditions, many plants in this zone grow in bunches or mats. Trees are not a major feature of this zone, since they struggle to deal with the weather conditions. One-hundred-year-old trees in the alpine zone may be no larger that two or three feet tall.

Despite the conditions, a few animals do make appearances in the alpine zone, such as the Olympic marmot, mountain goats, cougar, black bear, and the dark-eyed junco. But few of these animals actually live full-time in the alpine. Rather, they wander through the zone when conditions are at their peak during the late summer months.

The isolation of the Olympic Peninsula has also resulted in a number of animals that are missing from the native species on the Peninsula, although some have been introduced either inadvertently or otherwise by settlers over the years. Although animals such as grizzly bears, wolverine, red fox, and coyotes are native to other parts of Western Washington, they are not native to the Peninsula. Also missing are lynx, water voles, Golden-manteled ground squirrels, porcupines, and mountain goats. The non native mountain goats have become a destructive force within the park, and park managers are working on strategies to deal with the exploding population of mountain goats.

If you venture out into the woods looking for the plants and animals of the Peninsula, be sure to pack some patience. Try taking a short hike on one of the many nature trails scattered around the Olympic National Park and its periphery. You are likely to find something new in this environment, which stands out so much that the park has been named as a biosphere reserve and a World Heritage Site, recognizing the scientific value of the park as well as its scenic beauty

# Attractions

What do you want to do today? The Peninsula offers plenty to keep you busy and entertained. If you hear, "I'm bored. Are we there yet?" coming from the backseat, just flip through this chapter. No matter where you're headed, you'll find something to do or see just down the road.

The natural world has its own attractions that you'll see when you go hiking, camping, backpacking, shellfishing, sight-seeing, boating, or kayaking. But there are even more attractions, including history and art museums, forts, walking tours, wineries, casinos, marine science centers, and more. If you missed an attraction, just drive on a few more miles to find another.

In addition to the attractions listed here, you'll find more listed in the Olympic National Park and Outdoor Recreation chapters. During the off-season, many of the attractions open later, close earlier, and may open only on the weekends; and, while we have done our best to ensure that the information listed for each attraction is accurate, details do change. We recommend you call ahead to verify prices and hours, especially if you visit between October 1 and May 1.

## Gig Harbor

**Gig Harbor Peninsula Historical Museum**
**4218 Harborview Dr, Gig Harbor**
**(253) 858-6722**
**www.gigharbormuseum.org**

Fishing, logging, and agriculture all played an important part in establishing Gig Harbor. Through pictures, dioramas, and videos, the museum highlights those industries and the people who worked to settle this part of the Kitsap Peninsula. Of course, Galloping Gertie makes a prominent appearance as well. Admission costs nothing, but donations are welcomed.

The museum is open Tuesday through Saturday.

**History Walk**
**Gig Harbor**

Grab the self-guided tour map from the chamber of commerce and then hit the streets. As you walk, stop at the spots indicated on the map to learn about the history of this quaint fishing village. The tour loops through downtown and will take you by historical landmarks, including the marina.

## Port Orchard

**Sidney Museum & Log Cabin Museum**
**202 Sidney Ave. & 416 Sidney Ave.,**
**Port Orchard**
**(360) 876-3693**
**www.portorchard.com/museums**

Port Orchard was originally called Sidney in honor of one of the original pioneers. The simple Sidney Museum retains the name and pays homage to the city's history. The museum is housed on the second floor of the Sidney Art Gallery in the town's original Masonic Lodge. The velvet Masonic benches still line the walls of the museum that is filled with historical scenes, including a schoolroom, a ferry dock, and a dry goods store. Downstairs the Sidney Art Gallery displays and sells works by contemporary artists. All you have to do to get into the museum is ask at the galley. The museum is open Monday through Saturday.

If you continue walking up Sidney Avenue from the museum, you will come to one of the original town-site cabins, which was built in 1914 by a Civil War Veteran, Allen Bartow. The two-floor cabin has been restored and now serves to remind visitors about the city's origins. The cabin is open on Saturdays from May through December or by prior arrangement. Admission costs nothing although donations are encouraged.

**Navy Ship Harbor Tours**
**110 Harrison Ave., Port Orchard**
**(360) 377-8924**

Take a 45-minute tour of Sinclair Inlet, the Naval Shipyard, and the Mothball Fleet. Naval vessels awaiting repair, as well as those that have been retired from service are anchored in Sinclair Inlet between Port Orchard and Bremerton. When you take one of these tours you'll get a close look at aircraft carriers, warships, cruisers, and nuclear submarines. From June through the end of August, the tours leave hourly every day. In May and September the tours leave hourly but only on the weekends. Purchase tickets at the Ship's Store in Port Orchard, 110 Harrison Avenue. Adult fares cost around $8.50, and fares for children between 5 and 12 cost around $5.50. Children under 5 ride free, and a senior discount is available.

**Horluck Foot Ferries**
**Port Orchard waterfront**
**www.portorchard.com/chamber/visitor/ferries.htm**

Take a ride on the *Carlisle II*, one of the ferries that was part of the Mosquito Fleet, which was a fleet of foot ferries that carried people to all points around Puget Sound. The *Carlisle* still serves as a foot ferry between Port Orchard and Bremerton with trips leaving every 30 minutes. The ride only costs around $1.25 for a ten-minute cruise across the harbor. The ferry runs every day of the week except for Sunday. Kids ride free, and everyone rides free on Saturdays in the summer.

## North Kitsap Peninsula

**Elandan Gardens**
**3050 W. State Hwy. 16, Bremerton**
**(360) 373-8260**
**elandangardens.8m.com**

Elandan Gardens looks unassuming if you drive by it on the highway. Locals have made that mistake for years, but make sure you don't do the same thing. The site that was once a landfill has been transformed into a unique attraction. Walk through the gallery gift shop and out the back door to see an amazing collection of bonsai plants set amidst an intriguing, natural sculpture garden. Large stone structures set in a reflecting pond could very well overpower the delicate and ancient bonsai, but bonsai artist Dan Robinson and his wife Diane have achieved an almost perfect balance in the 2.5-acre garden. Some of the bonsai are more than 1,000 years old, and they seem to perfectly complement their natural surroundings on the shores of Sinclair Inlet. When you've finished your leisurely stroll through the garden, don't forget to visit the gallery filled with antique dolls and textiles from Asia, jewelry, specialty clothing, and other treasures. The adjoining nursery carries hard-to-find plants, including everything you'll need to start your own bonsai garden. Perusing the gallery and nursery costs nothing, but admission to the garden costs around $5 for adults and $1 for children under 12. Elandan Gardens is closed Mondays and for the month of January.

**Bremerton Naval Museum**
**130 Washington Ave., Bremerton**
**(360) 479-7447**

Learn about the history of the Puget Sound Naval Shipyard and the Mosquito Fleet when you take a tour of the Bremerton Naval Museum. History buffs and

*The USS* Turner Joy. PHOTO: NATALIE McNAIR-HUFF

Navy fans will especially appreciate all that the museum has to offer. The museum is open seven days a week during the summer. Admission costs nothing although donations are suggested.

### Kitsap County Historical Society Museum
### 280 4th St., Bremerton
### (360) 479-6226
### www.waynes.net/kchsm

Trace the Kitsap Timeline at the Kitsap County Historical Society Museum. The timeline will take you on an imaginary journey that starts at the last Ice Age and ends with World War II. On your journey you will see dioramas of a Suquamish settlement, a floating log camp, the Mosquito Fleet, and more. Other exhibits include models of various businesses and an impressive collection of old photographs, including some taken by the famous photographers Asahel and Edward Curtis. The admission price is a suggested donation of $2 per adult. The museum is closed on Sundays and Mondays, but it is open until 8 P.M. on the first Friday of each month so that it may take part in the "First Friday" art walks.

### USS *Turner Joy*
### Bremerton Boardwalk
### (360) 792-2457

In 1964, the destroyer USS *Turner Joy* was involved in an incident in the Gulf of Tonkin that instigated the Vietnam War. The ship was also one of the last to leave at the end of that war. Today it serves as a permanent exhibit for the Bremerton Historic Ships Association, which maintains the ship in its original condition and offers year-round tours. The tour includes the All-Veteran's Memorial, which honors the POWs of the Vietnam War. During the summer, tours are offered daily; the ship is closed on Tuesdays and Wednesdays from late fall to early spring. Admission costs around $7 for adults, $6 for seniors, and $4 for children under 12. Tickets can be purchased at the ship's gift shop on the Bremerton Boardwalk.

### Naval Undersea Museum
### Naval Undersea Warfare Center, Keyport
### (360) 396-4148
### num.kpt.nuwc.navy.mil

You will definitely remember a visit to the Naval Undersea Museum. As you wander through the museum you will learn about military history, marine biology, and the technological advances that have created today's naval equipment. Among other exciting displays, you will see a Japanese mini suicide submarine, a replica of a keg mine, and the *Trieste II*—a deep-sea sub that descended to 20,000 feet. Many more displays and artifacts will give visitors a greater understanding of a part of the depths of the sea. The museum is open seven days a week in the summer, and admission costs nothing. Take Wash. 3 to Wash. 308 and follow the signs to the museum.

**Poulsbo Marine Science Center**
**18743 Front St. NE, Poulsbo**
**(360) 779-5549**
**poulsboMSC.org**

Most of the time when children go to museums all they see are signs saying, "Do NOT touch." At the Poulsbo Marine Science Center the motto is please do touch, and to facilitate the touching, the center has several touch tanks set right at kid height. Children of all ages—even those who call themselves adults—can let starfish

> ## Insiders' Tip
> Nature is the biggest attraction around here. Enjoy one of nature's greatest attractions when the whales make an appearance. Orca whales can be seen in Puget Sound nearly any time of the year. Gray whales can be seen during their annual migrations.

tickle their hands, caress the tentacles of anemones, and pick up slimy sea cucumbers. If that's not enough, the helpful staff will be happy to answer any of your questions. The museum is open seven days a week except for major holidays. Admission costs around $4 for adults and $2 for children between the ages of 2 and 12. Seniors, students, and active military with ID receive a $1 discount.

**Suquamish Museum**
**15838 Sandy Hook Rd., Suquamish**
**(360) 598-3311**
**www.telebyte.com/suquamish/museum**

Experience the history of the Chief Sealth's Suquamish Tribe. The story of the tribe is shown through historical photographs, interviews, and authentic tribal artifacts such as baskets, carved bowls, and story poles. The museum is open seven days a week during the summer, and admission costs around $4 for adults and $2 for children 12 and under. Guided tours are also available for a fee if arranged in advance.

**Port Gamble Historic Museum**
**1 Rainier Ave., Port Gamble**
**(360) 297-8074**

The entire village of Port Gamble is registered as a National Historic Site, and a trip through town will feel as if you are living in the late nineteenth century. To learn more about the company town and the history of the Pope & Talbot Company, visit the Port Gamble Historic Museum, which occupies the lower level of the Port Gamble General Store. The museum has reproduced significant scenes from Port Gamble's history, including the captain's berth from the *Oriental*, the ship that carried William Talbot and Cyrus Walker to Port Gamble's deep harbor. Other scenes depict the master bedroom from Walker's Admiralty Hall, the sitting room of the Puget Hotel, and logging and mill equipment. Admission costs approximately $2 for adults, $1 for students and seniors, and children under 6 are admitted free.

# Port Townsend

### Fort Worden
### Port Townsend
### www.olympus.net/gov/ftworden/
### index.htm

If you visit Port Townsend and don't make it to Fort Worden, you'll miss one of the city's major attractions. Fort Worden has so many things to do that doing it all would take far more than a single day. Walk through the Chinese and rhododendron gardens, take a walk on the beach, or tour the officers' quarters and the Coast Artillery Museum. You could spend a day playing hide-and-seek at the gun batteries and then buy a book of poetry at Copper Canyon Press before heading to the Marine Science Center to hold a starfish. Then you could finish the day by watching the sunset over the Strait of Juan de Fuca or by attending a concert at the McCurdy Pavilion. Fort Worden offers more for the adventurous, but we'll leave it to you to discover all that the park has to offer.

### Fort Flagler
### Marrowstone Island
### www.parks.wa.gov/ftflaglr.htm

Pack a picnic lunch, take a light jacket along, and make sure you are wearing sturdy walking shoes before you head to Fort Flagler. In addition to campgrounds, a public fishing pier, and over 19,000 feet of saltwater shoreline, the 783-acre park features some of the best bird-watching opportunities in the area. If sitting around looking for birds is too sedate an activity for you, then walk along the beach collecting shells and rocks or explore the gun emplacements. Fort Flagler was established in order to protect Puget Sound from any possible foreign invasion. Although it was never called into active duty, the Fort did play an important role in West Coast military history.

### Historic & Scenic Tours
### Port Townsend

You can take tours of Port Townsend by foot or car. The visitor information center at 2437 E. Sims Way will provide you with a map of the scenic tour route. The downtown portion of the tour is best accomplished on foot. You will see most of the city's landmarks, such as the Haller Fountain, the Old City Hall (now the site of the history museum), the Union Wharf, and some of the city's original commercial buildings. The driving segment of the tour takes you to Kah Tai Lagoon, Fort Worden, the courthouse, the customshouse, and by many of the historic and beautiful Victorian homes. You can also make reservations for an hour-long walking tour. Three different tours are offered: waterfront, homes, and saloons. Call Guided Historical Sidewalk Tours at (360) 385-1967 to reserve space on a tour. Tours cost approximately $10 per person.

### Jefferson County Historical Society
###   Museum
### 210 Madison St., Port Townsend
### (360) 385-1003
### www.jchsmuseum.org

Wander through four floors of historical exhibits housed in the original City Hall and town jail. An extensive collection of photographs, documents, and artifacts presents visitors with a rich lesson on the history of this Victorian Port. Permanent exhibits explore the cultures of the Native peoples, including the Hoh, S'Klallam and Chimacum; others are dedicated to mariners, local industries, the military, and the original settlers. The museum also sponsors several special exhibits that change throughout the year, so even if you've visited once, a second trip will be well worth your time. The museum is open seven days a week except major holidays, and a donation gets you in the door.

### Kah Tai Lagoon
### Port Townsend

The Kah Tai Lagoon was once a large bog that was a thorn in the side of the early city leaders because visitors heading into town over land got stuck in the mud. Before the white settlers came, the lagoon served as the portage point for the Native tribes. They would paddle into the lagoon and then carry their canoes across a small strip of land to the Strait of Juan de Fuca. By doing so, they avoided the treacherous waters around Point Wilson. Over the years the lagoon has been filled in, but what remains is still a favorite spot for migratory birds. The 80-acre park serves as a nesting and feeding site on the Pacific Flyway. The U.S. Fish and Wildlife Department declared the lagoon to be one of the state's most important wildlife habitats. It is a perfect place to eat a picnic lunch, walk groomed trails, and go bird-watching. The lagoon is just behind Haines Place park-and-ride.

## Sequim

**7 Cedars Casino**
**270756 Hwy. 101, Sequim**
**(360) 683-7777, (800) 4-LUCKY-7**
**www.7cedarscasino.com**

Feeling lucky? Then head to the 7 Cedars Casino to play the slots or bingo or hit the tables for some blackjack, craps, or roulette. If luck isn't on your side, you may want to skip the gambling and go for the entertainment ranging from comedy to jazz to country and rock and roll. The casino is worth stopping at if only to see the totem poles guarding the front of the building. You'll find more poles and sculptures inside as well as an art gallery and a restaurant. The casino is open seven days a week.

**Dungeness Spit**
**Sequim**
**www.visitsun.com/dungeness.html**

Lighthouse fans, bird-watchers, and hikers flock to the Dungeness National Wildlife Refuge and the Dungeness Spit. The six-mile long sand spit is yet another example of the many natural wonders on the Olympic Peninsula. To fully experience the spit, take the 4.5-mile walk to the lighthouse, where volunteers will give you a tour. On your way back, scramble over driftwood or take a break to build a sandcastle or eat a picnic lunch. Some areas are closed to foot traffic, but much of the spit is open for saltwater fishing and shellfishing during legal seasons. The Dungeness Wildlife Recreation area sits atop the bluff overlooking the spit and offers picnic tables, RV sites, and campsites. Admission to the spit costs $3 per family. To get to the spit from U.S. 101, turn north onto Kitchen-Dick Road and follow it to the Dungeness Recreation Area. Drive through the recreation area to the parking lot overlooking the spit.

*Dungeness Spit reaches into the Strait of Juan de Fuca for nearly 5 miles.* PHOTO: ROB McNAIR-HUFF

**Olympic Game Farm**
**1423 Ward Rd., Sequim**
**(360) 683-4295, (800) 778-4295**
**www.olygamefarm.com**

His animals may be more famous than he is, but without Lloyd Beebe, some of Disney's most popular animal films would never have been made. Lloyd trained animals that were used in more than 50 Disney movies, including some used in the original version of *The Incredible Journey*. This farm is where Lloyd trained his animals; it also served as a studio for many of the films that he directed. In 1972, Lloyd and his wife and partner, Catherine, opened the Olympic Game Farm to the public. Today the family still runs the farm, which is home to more than 200 animals, many of which are rare and endangered, including elk, zebras, timber wolves, lions, and bear. Visitors can see the animals up close with a walking tour and a driving tour. The farm is open seven days a week except for major holidays. Admission starts at $8.

**Railroad Bridge Park**
**Hendrickson Road, Sequim**
**(360) 582-9345**
**www.dungenessrivercenter.org**

Stand on an old railroad bridge trestle and watch the scenic Dungeness River speed beneath you on its way to the sea. The bridge has been transformed into a walking and biking trail. The park also serves as home to the Dungeness River Center and the Riverstage Amphitheater, where educational and conservation programs are held, and where visitors can see interpretive displays.

**Sequim-Dungeness Valley Museum**
**& Arts Center**
**175 W. Cedar St., Sequim**
**(360) 683-8110**
**www.sequimmuseum.org**

In 1975 a local farmer found the nearly complete skeleton of a 12,000-year-old mastodon. One of the mastodon's bones was found with a spear point imbedded in it. The find proved that people lived and hunted on the Peninsula far earlier than previously thought. Bone and tusk from that mastodon are now housed in this museum. Other exhibits explore the history and heritage of the Dungeness valley. Local artists also use the museum to display recent works. The museum is open daily through the summer, and admission costs nothing, although donations are always accepted.

## Port Angeles

**Arthur D. Feiro Marine Life Center**
**City Pier, Port Angeles**
**(360) 417-6254**
**www.olypen.com/feirolab**

Have you ever picked up a sea cucumber? Visit the Arthur D. Feiro Marine Life Center at Port Angeles' City Pier to find out what happens when you pick up this intriguing invertebrate. Touch tanks, aquariums filled with native oceanic fauna, and permanent exhibits educate visitors about the interaction of life and the sea. The center is closed Mondays during the summer months, and in the winter the center is only open on Saturdays and Sundays. Admission costs around $2.50 for adults and $1 for children between 5 and 12 and seniors. Children under 5 are admitted free.

**Olympic National Park Visitor Center**
**3002 Mount Angeles Rd., Port Angeles**
**(360) 452-0330**
**www.nps.gov/olym**

Before heading deeper into the park, stop at the visitor center. Exhibits will explain the plants and animals in the park, and park rangers will answer any questions you might have about the weather, the animals, the trails, and the campgrounds. You'll also find a comprehensive collection of maps and books about the park. It's a good idea to stop here in winter to check on road and trail conditions: The

*The Olympic National Park Visitor Center.* PHOTO: ROB McNAIR-HUFF

buy lunch at the lodge, and if you're lucky, you may see deer, elk, goats, or a marmot or two while you eat.

### Clallam County Museum
### 223 E. 4th St., Port Angeles
### (360) 452-2262

After you visit this museum, you may leave and look at Port Angeles and say, "But it looks so normal." A walk through the museum will shed light on the city's tumultuous past from the flash flood that destroyed half the town to the utopian community of the 1880s. Of course, no local history would be complete without the stories of the trees and the sea, and those stories are told here as well. The museum is open Monday through Friday. Donations are accepted for admission.

Hurricane Ridge road sometimes closes as early as late October due to white-out conditions. The center is open seven days a week.

### Hurricane Ridge
### Olympic National Park

Hurricane Ridge is the park's busiest spot. More visitors go to Hurricane Ridge every year than to any other single point in the park. You'll understand why after you take the 17-mile drive from Port Angeles to the mile-high ridge. Incredible views surround the ridge. To the north you will see Port Angeles, the Strait of Juan de Fuca, and Vancouver. To the south, the toothed peaks of the Olympics stretch as far as you can see. Easy-to-hike and wheelchair-accessible trails may be explored alone or with a ranger. You can

### Port Angeles Fine Arts Center
### 1203 E Lauridsen Blvd., Port Angeles
### (360) 457-3532 www.olympus.net/community/pafac

Set on a wooded lot with views of the Olympic Mountains and the Strait of Juan de Fuca, the Port Angeles Fine Arts Center features art outdoors in the sculpture garden as well as changing exhibits in the gallery. Past exhibits have included shows by local painters, sculptors, and a digital art exhibit. Admission costs nothing, but donations are welcomed. The gallery is closed on Sundays, but the art outside is on display daily from dawn to dusk.

## Juan de Fuca Highway

### Salt Creek Recreation Area

During low tides, the Salt Creek Recreation area offers easily accessible tide pools on a basalt formation called Tongue Point. Check your tide table and make sure you have sturdy shoes on before heading out to poke around nature's touch tanks. The rocks drip with

seaweed, barnacles, limpets, and urchins. Crab scurry in cracks, and if the tide is low enough, you may even glimpse an octopus hiding in a crevice. While waiting for the tide to change you can also walk the trails around the gun emplacements once used by the Army or sit at one of the many picnic sites.

# Close-up

## Olympic Peninsula Wineries

The Hoodsport Winery, which opened in 1979, was the first winery to open on the Olympic Peninsula. Since then, a number of wineries have cropped up around the Peninsula. They all feature traditional wines, and some specialize in fruit wines. The wineries we have included here offer public tours and tastings.

**FairWinds Winery**
**1984 Hastings Ave. W., Port Townsend**
**(360) 385-6899**
**www.fairwindswinery.com**

A small winery housed in a former horse stable, FairWinds features a moderately dry Gewürztraminer and a rare Aligoté among its offerings.

**Lost Mountain Winery**
**3174 Lost Mountain Rd., Sequim**
**(360) 683-5229**
**www.lostmountain.com**

Lost Mountain winery produces small batches of sulfite-free wines. The winery has been making robust red varietals and blends for more than 20 years.

**Olympic Cellars**
**255410 Hwy. 101 E., Port Angeles**
**(360) 452-0160**
**www.olympiccellars.com**

An old barn that sits along U.S. 101 between Sequim and Port Angeles houses Olympic Cellars winery, which has been producing wines for more than 20 years. The winery makes several varietals and a few blends as well as a popular honey wine.

**Black Diamond Winery**
**2976 Black Diamond Rd., Port Angeles**
**(360) 457-0748**
**pages.prodigy.net/sharonlance**

Black Diamond Winery is a newly opened winery that specializes in fruit wines using such fruits as plum, apricot, rhubarb, and berries.

**Hoodsport Winery**
**23501 Hwy. 101, Hoodsport**
**www.hoodsport.com**

Hoodsport wines can be bought in supermarkets and wine shops throughout the Northwest. The winery makes traditional as well as fruit wines. Some of its more limited productions are available only at the winery.

*The Makah Cultural Research Center.* PHOTO: NATALIE McNAIR-HUFF

**Makah Cultural Research Center
(360) 645 2711
www.makah.com/museum.htm**

Nearly 500 years ago a mudslide covered a Makah village at Ozette. While disastrous for the people of the village, the thick mud perfectly preserved thousands of artifacts over the centuries until rain and erosion revealed the village site. The Makah Cultural Research Center is the only place in the nation where you can see the recovered artifacts. Nearly every person who visits the museum leaves impressed and simply can't stop talking about all they saw and learned; many make the trip to Neah Bay just to see the museum. In addition to the artifacts, you'll see a replica of a full-sized longhouse, dug-out canoes, and many of the day-to-day implements used by the tribe. The museum is open seven days a week through the summer months. Admission costs $4 for adults and $3 for students and seniors.

**Cape Flattery Trail
www.northolympic.com/capeflatterytrail**

If you've driven all this way, you might as well go to the land's end: Cape Flattery. Just follow the signs in Neah Bay to the Cape Flattery Trail. Park at the trailhead and walk the three-quarter-mile trail to the northwestern most point of the contiguous United States. There you will see one of the most beautiful scenes anywhere on earth. The seals and sea lions on Tatoosh Island will bark as the surf pounds into the steep bluffs pitted with caves. These are the rocks that spelled doom for so many ships and mark the opening of the Strait of Juan de Fuca. Wear hiking boots or sturdy walking shoes. Although much of the trail has been boardwalked by the Makah Tribe, it is still steep and very slippery.

*The Cape Flattery Trail leads visitors to spectacular scenery.* PHOTO: ROB MCNAIR-HUFF

# Forks

### Forks Timber Museum
### 1421 S. Forks Ave. (U.S. 101), Forks
### (360) 374-9663

Discover the tools and techniques that loggers used to cut down the gigantic trees that once grew around here. Exhibits at the museum include a steam donkey and steam tractor, one of the first chainsaws, a fire lookout tower, and samples of the types of trees that grow here. The nearby Logger Memorial is dedicated to the loggers who lost their lives while working in the forest. The Forks Timber Museum also sponsors tours of logging and mill sites, and it is one of the most popular attractions on this part of the Peninsula. It is open every day during the summer months. Guided tours may be arranged in advance. Admission costs around $2.

### Hole-in-the-Wall
### Rialto Beach

You simply have to take at least one walk on the beach when you make the trip to this side of the Peninsula. The walk to Hole-in-the-Wall is an easy and pleasurable 1.5 miles along the cobbled beach starting at Rialto Beach in front of James Island. By the time you reach the sea stacks, the cobbles will have given way to rocks and tide pools. When the tide is low you can explore the tide pools and even walk through the hole in the giant sea stack. Don't forget your camera because this is one of the best vantages for picture taking on the coast.

### Hoh Rainforest & Hall of Mosses
### (360) 374-6925

This is what most people think of when they think of rain forests: trees decorated with cascades of verdant, thick mosses, and frothy white lichens. The Hoh Rainforest and its Hall of Mosses will intrigue and amaze you with their wonderland setting. The relatively flat and easy 0.75-mile Hall of Mosses begins next to the Hoh Rainforest Visitor Center. A longer, 1.25-mile Spruce Nature Trail, and a shorter wheelchair-accessible trail are also nearby. All three trails and a walk through the visitor center can be accomplished in an afternoon. In the summer stay into the evening for interpretive programs presented by the park rangers.

# Ocean Shores

### Damon Point State Park

Each year thousands of birds descend on the Grays Harbor Estuary. Damon Point, a 300-acre preserve, offers a unique ecosystem where many of these birds land for a rest during their long journeys. In fact, it is the only place in the world where the rare snowy plover and the semi-palmated plover breed in the same area. The park's location, a hook of land stretching nearly two miles into Grays Harbor, makes it a perfect spot for watching ships and harbor seals.

### Ocean Shores Interpretive Center
### 1013 Catala Ave. S.E., Ocean Shores
### (360) 289-4617

Located next to the Ocean Shores marina, this interpretive center is dedicated to educating visitors about the human and natural history of the region. History exhibits explain the relationship between the Native tribes and the early fur traders, and later the lumber barons. Other exhibits highlight the distinct ecosystems of field, marsh, and ocean. The center is only open during the summer months or by special arrangement.

### Pacific Paradise
### 767 Minard Ave., Ocean Shores
### (360) 289-9537

Ocean Shores can be the ultimate family getaway, and a trip to Pacific Paradise adds a large dose of fun to any trip. An elaborate, 36-hole miniature golf course with water traps and many decorative obstacles will challenge the best putt-putt golfers. The course is lit for nighttime play. After a round of putting, cool off with a spin in the bumper boats or head inside for a game of air hockey or a go at one of the many video and arcade games.

**Quinault Beach Resort**
**78 S.R. 115, Ocean Shores**
**(360) 289-9466**
**www.quinaultbeachresort.com**

Head to the Quinault Beach Resort for an evening of gambling or live music. The resort's casino features slot machines, electronic games, and card and roulette tables. The cabaret features live music: jazz, blues, country, and rock. While their parents play, children can also have fun at the youth activity center

---

## Insiders' Tip

The sea is both beautiful and dangerous. Keep an eye on the weather and the water when you are exploring the beaches and tide pools. Sneaker waves and logs carried on the tide can kill, and people have been trapped by quickly turning tides.

---

# Grays Harbor

**Hoquiam Castle**
**515 Chenault Ave., Hoquiam**
**(360) 533-2005**
**secure.insideoutweb.com/hoquiamscastle**

It took Robert Lytle, a local lumber baron, three years to build this mansion. He completed it in 1900, and its turrets and 10,000 square feet impress visitors today as much as they did upon its completion. David and Linda Carpenter, the current owners, have turned the house into a bed and breakfast, but they still offer daily tours to the public between 11 A.M. and 3 P.M. The tour cost approximately $4 for adults and $2.50 for seniors and children between 5 and 11.

**Lady Washington**
**712 Hagara Street, Aberdeen**
**(800) 200-5239**
**www.ladywashington.org**

Captain Robert Gray sailed the original *Lady Washington* from Boston to the Northwest Coast, and on his voyage he discovered the body of water that now bears his name: Grays Harbor. Today, a replica of his ship sails the same waters.

The ship is a popular attraction for tourists and locals, who can take a tour or a cruise on the ship. The *Lady Washington* is a working ship, and as a result, it is not always in port. Call ahead to inquire about the ship's schedule and make reservations.

**Polson Museum**
**1611 Riverside Ave., Hoquiam**
**(360) 533-5862**
**www.polsonmuseum.org**

Housed in a 6,500-square-foot, 26-room mansion, the Polson Museum features 17 rooms of historical exhibits. The rooms are filled with thousands of pictures, antiques, historical documents, dolls, and other artifacts. The museum also sponsors several events throughout the year, including the annual Loggers' Play Day Parade. The museum is open Wednesday through Sunday during the summer, and on the weekends during the off-season. Admission costs $2 for everyone over 12, 50 cents for children under 12, or $5 for families.

# Shelton

**The Kimberly T. Gallery and
The Bronze Works**
**W. 50 Fredson Rd., Shelton**
**(360) 427-3857**
**www.olywa.net/bronzeworks**

The Bronze Works is a working foundry where fine art sculptures are poured. Sculptures in glass, metal, and stone are displayed along with drawings and paint-ings in the accompanying gallery. To see the foundry in action, visit on Tuesdays and Thursdays when the molten bronze is poured around 1:30 P.M. Visitors can watch the pour through a glass screen, and a video explains the process. The Bronze Works is open Monday through Friday.

# Hood Canal

**Hood Canal/Theler Wetlands**
**NE 22871 SR 3, Belfair**
**(360) 275-4898**

Freshwater and saltwater marshes meet in the Theler Wetlands to create one of the Peninsula's unique ecosystems. A wheelchair-accessible trail leads visitors on a 3.8-mile tour of the 135-acre preserve. Visitors will have a chance to see a wide variety of wildlife, including otter, salmon, more than 150 species of birds and insects, and more than 200 types of plants. The wetlands are open every day of the year until 10 P.M. Admission to the wetlands costs nothing, but donations are requested.

**Whitney Gardens**
**306264 Hwy. 101, Brinnon**
**(360) 796-4411**

Late each spring, the rhododendrons and azaleas around the Peninsula put on a dis-

*Whitney Gardens offers gardeners a chance to view and take rare plants home.* PHOTO: ROB McNAIR-HUFF

# Chamber of Commerce Information

Gig Harbor Chamber of Commerce
3302 Harborview Dr., Ste. 2, Gig Harbor
(253) 851-6865
www.gigharborchamber.com

Port Orchard/South Kitsap Chamber of
Commerce
1014 Bay Street, Ste. 8, Port Orchard
(360) 876-3505
www.portorchard.com/chamber

Kitsap Peninsula Visitor & Convention
Bureau
2 Rainier, Port Gamble
(360) 297-8200, (800) 416-5615
www.visitkitsap.com

Bremerton Chamber of Commerce
301 Pacific Ave., Bremerton
(360) 479-3579
www.bremertonchamber.org

Silverdale Chamber of Commerce
3100 Bucklin Hill Rd., Ste. 108, Silverdale
(360) 692-6800
www.silverdalechamber.com

Poulsbo Chamber of Commerce
19168-C Jensen Wy., Poulsbo
(360) 779-3115
www.poulsbo.net

Port Townsend Visitor Center
2437 E. Sims Wy., Port Townsend
(360) 385-2722
www.ptguide.com

Sequim-Dungeness Chamber of
Commerce
1192 E. Washington St., Sequim
(360) 683-6197
www.visitsun.com

Port Angeles Visitor Information Center
121 Railroad, Port Angeles
(360) 452-2363
www.portangeles.org

Clallam Bay–Sekiu Chamber of Commerce
P.O. Box 335, Clallam Bay
(360) 963-2339
www.clallambay.com

Forks Visitor Information Center
1411 S. Forks Ave. (U.S. 101), Forks
(360) 374-2531, (800) 44-FORKS
www.forkswa.com

Grays Harbor Chamber of Commerce
506 Duffy St., Aberdeen
(360) 532-1924
www.graysharbor.org

Ocean Shores Chamber of Commerce
120 W. Chance-A-La-Mer
(360) 389-2451, (800) 76-BEACH
www.oceanshores.org

Shelton-Mason Chamber of Commerce
230 W. Railroad, Shelton
(360) 426-2021, (800) 576-2021
www.sheltonchamber.org

Greater Quilcene/Brinnon Chamber of
Commerce
P.O. Box 774, Quilcene
(360) 765-4999
www.northolympic.com/qb

play that entices hummingbirds from their nests, bees from their hives, and people out of their homes. One of the best places to see this show, and to see other plants in bloom through the summer, is at the 6.8-acre display garden at Whitney Gardens. The garden draws so many people that you'll often find tour buses sharing space with cars in the parking lot. The garden takes between one and two hours to tour, and the trails are wheelchair accessible. The garden is open daily until dusk from February through November. If you see plants in the display garden that you'd like to see in your garden, visit the adjoining nursery to buy one of the many rare plants it carries. Expect to pay a small admission fee to tour the garden.

**Mount Walker**

The time it takes to drive to the top of Mount Walker will be well rewarded, especially on clear days. The summit offers some of the best views on the Peninsula. On one side you will see the crisp, broken peaks of the Olympic Mountains. On the other side you will look down on the deep blue waters of Hood Canal. In the late spring, the mountain will be dotted with color from the blossoms of thousands of azaleas and rhododendrons. The summit offers a pleasant break even on cloudy days. Sometimes the sun peaks through at the summit while a lake of clouds sits in the valleys below you. If you prefer, you can also hike the challenging four-mile trail to the summit. Take plenty of water and wear hiking boots and sunscreen for the hike.

# The Arts

Art Museums

Galleries

Music

Theater

Literary Arts

Art and Music Festivals

Arts Organizations

Here, where rain and gray clouds dominate the sky for nine months of the year, residents turn to the arts for color, pizzazz, and entertainment. The arts have always played an integral role in the cultures of the Pacific Northwest. The First Peoples were well known for their totems and intricate carvings on even the most mundane items. Today, the Native arts still play an important role on the Peninsula with Native art galleries scattered throughout. The intricately carved masks, bentwood boxes, and cedar baskets are practically synonymous with the area tribes. That tradition has carried on and is amplified by the role the arts play on the Peninsula today. Public art appears as murals, permanent and temporary installations, sculptures placed here and there, and the occasional chalk drawing on the city sidewalks.

Around the Peninsula you will find enclaves of artists. Areas like Gig Harbor and Port Townsend seem to attract visual artists and sculptors by droves. Nearly every town has at least one art gallery while many boast half a dozen or more.

But the Peninsula's art scene isn't limited to visual arts. Classical music aficionados will want to check out the Olympic Music Festival for some of the finest offerings anywhere. And don't forget to check out the locally produced plays. Although most community theater has a spotty reputation, we think you'll be pleasantly surprised with the local offerings. If you are an artist, you may be interested in joining one of the organizations listed at the end of this chapter.

Since the Peninsula teems with art galleries, we have listed them alphabetically by city. The festivals are listed by time of year, and the other entries are listed in alphabetical order. We suggest you call ahead to check on performance schedules and ticketing information. While we have highlighted some of the more popular and accessible places and events, new galleries open, and more events are added every year. Use this chapter as a starting point, but make sure you ask around to see what else is happening when you are in town. You may be pleasantly surprised, as we were one weekend in Port Townsend. We were sitting eating lunch when a troupe of English country dancers invaded the restaurant to give an impromptu performance. Art is alive and well on the Olympic Peninsula—we think it must be all that clean air.

## Art Museums

**Port Angeles Fine Arts Center**
**1203 E. Lauridsen Blvd., Port Angeles**
**(360) 457-3532**
**www.olympus.net/community/pafac**

A long time Port Angeles resident, artist, and art lover, Esther Barrow Webster established the Port Angeles Fine Arts Center and bequeathed her home to the organization upon her death in 1985. Today the center is the "west-most museum of contemporary art in the contiguous United States." The center is tucked into a wooded lot with an incredible view of the Strait of Juan de Fuca. The setting makes a perfect backdrop for the modern paintings, sculptures, and drawings that are displayed here throughout the year. One recent exhibition centered on digital art. Visitors can also stroll the grounds to see the sculptures displayed in the "Art Outside" exhibit. Admission is free, but the museum is closed on Mondays.

# Galleries

## Gig Harbor

**Ebb Tide Gallery of Gifts**
**8825 N. Harborview Dr., Gig Harbor**
**(253) 851-5293**

The rear windows of the Ebb Tide Gallery perfectly frame the inner harbor, and they could very well be mistaken for art. The windows are surrounded by real works of art all painted, drawn, sculpted, or photographed by local artists. You'll find art in all sorts of flavors here from the bright and quizzical soft sculptures to traditional and calming paintings of nature scenes.

**Gallery Row**
**8825 N. Harborview Dr. #1, Gig Harbor**
**(253) 851-6020**

Eight local artists display their wares in an ever-changing display. The artists span the disciplines from raku pottery and sculpture to watercolor paintings to photography. The studio offers classes and workshops throughout the year to aspiring artists, and it sits right next door to the Ebb Tide Gallery of Gifts.

**Harbor Gallery**
**3177 Harborview Dr., Gig Harbor**
**(253) 851-8626**

Suitably housed in the Anchorage Building in downtown Gig Harbor, Harbor Gallery boasts what may well be the most extensive collection of maritime art on the West Coast. In addition to a unique collection of indoor fountains, the gallery displays paintings, prints, sculptures, and glass art created by well-known artists from the Pacific Northwest and the world.

**The Preuit Collection and Framery**
**3115 Harborview Dr., Gig Harbor**
**(253) 851-3792**

The Preuit Collection and Framery specializes in works by local artists. In fact, 85 percent of the artists represented here live within 25 miles of Gig Harbor. You'll see catching sculptures made from string and driftwood sitting next to more classically constructed bronze pieces next to photographs and paintings and imported crystal. The gallery also frames pieces you bring in.

> ## Insiders' Tip
> If you want tickets for an event in Gig Harbor, visit the Arts & Entertainment kiosk at 6950 Kimball Drive.

## Port Orchard

**Sidney Gallery**
**202 Sidney Ave., Port Orchard**
**(360) 876-3693**
**www.portorchard.com/sidneygallery**

Sidney Gallery, taking the original name of this small city as its own, has taken over the old Masonic Hall. Fine art prints, paintings, ceramics, and sculptures by some of the Northwest's most well-known artists decorate the rustic walls. New shows premier monthly, but you'll always find a great assortment of artistic gifts as well. You'll find something in nearly every price range. Send the kids upstairs to look through the museum while you stay downstairs to check out the art.

*The Olympic Peninsula brims with unique art and crafts.* PHOTO: NATALIE McNAIR-HUFF

## North Kitsap

### Amy Burnett Fine Art Gallery
**402 Pacific Ave., Bremerton**
**(360) 373-3187**

Amy Burnett is a nationally known artist; her paintings hang on walls and in galleries across the nation. Amy also owns the largest art gallery on the Kitsap Peninsula. You'll see her paintings hanging next to the works of other nationally recognized and regional artists. The works displayed range from oversized woodcarvings to delicate glass art to traditional and contemporary paintings. The gallery also hosts musical groups on occasion. It is closed on Mondays.

### Artists' Edge
**2009 Harkins St., Bremerton**
**(360) 377-2930**

Cross the bridge to the Manette neighborhood to see the Artists' Edge—it's worth the trip. Each month the Artists' Edge hosts a new show featuring the works of a single artist from the Pacific Northwest. Shows range from controversial installations to collections of smaller paintings, photographs, and sculptures. Artists' Edge's main service is framing, but the art shows are a definite bonus that keep visitors coming back. You'll also find Artists' Edge stores in Silverdale and Poulsbo.

### Collective Visions
**331 Pacific Ave., Bremerton**
**(360) 377-8327**

Visual artists from the Bremerton area have banded together to create Collective Visions. When you wander in, you'll see a constantly rotating display of paintings, collages, and pottery. Since the artists staff the gallery, you may be lucky enough to talk with them about their works. The gallery also sponsors musical concerts one Friday each month. Collective Visions is closed on Sundays and Mondays.

**Metropolis The Gallery**
**247 4th St., Bremerton**
**(360) 373-4709**

Metropolis is Bremerton's second cooperative art gallery. The small space is filled with an eclectic collection of mostly ultramodern art. If you're looking for something unusual and thought provoking, you'll find it here. Some visitors may find some of the pieces to be quite shocking, such as a female torso carved out of blood-red wood, while other pieces feel whimsical and fun.

**Olympic Inn Artworks**
**18830 Front St., Poulsbo**
**(360) 697-5677**
**www.olyinnartworks.com**

Think flowers and fairies, dolls and delicate glass, lace and porcelain, and you'll have a good idea about what you'll find at Olympic Inn Artworks. The small shop is jam-packed with light and airy, original works that would look at home in an English cottage, a Victorian sitting room, or a contemporary dining room. There's so much to look at here that it may seem overwhelming, but the patient shopper will be amply rewarded when she spies that perfect painting to go over the mantel.

**Potlatch Gallery**
**18830-B Front St., Poulsbo**
**(360) 779-3377**

Potlatch Gallery is small, but it is packed with beautiful pieces that are filled with the flavor of the Northwest. You'll find ceramic tiles with northwest scenes printed on them as well as fine woodcarvings, stone sculptures, and jewelry all made by regional artists. The gallery is closed on Sundays and Mondays.

**Raven Blues**
**18827 Front St. N.E., Poulsbo**
**(360) 779-4662**

One side of Raven Blues is filled with contemporary women's clothing. The other side of the store is filled with contemporary artworks imbued with that special Northwest flavor. We especially liked the glass-topped tables held up by stone and stick pedestals. The tables hold a plethora of smaller pieces from boxes to vases to bowls. The walls are hung with paintings and sculptures. Although the space is limited, the displays are pleasing and far from overwhelming. One caution when you visit Raven Blues—the resident cat may entice you into petting it so much that you forget to look around.

**Verksted Gallery**
**18937 Front St., Poulsbo**
**(360) 697-4470**
**www.verkstedgallery.com**

Local artists sell their artwork in Poulsbo's cooperative Verksted Gallery. Fiber artists create intricate and detailed European costumes for dolls, wall hangings, and baskets. Painters hang works in watercolor, oils, and mixed media. Sculptors work with glass, wood, stone, and cloth. The displays at the gallery change frequently so you're sure to see something new every time you visit.

# Port Townsend

**Ancestral Spirits Gallery**
**701 Water St., Port Townsend**
**(360) 385-0078**
**www.Ancestralspirits.com**

Be careful when you go into Ancestral Spirits Gallery. You may very well lose an hour or two to the spirits of the gallery. Ancestral Spirits boasts Port Townsend's and the Peninsula's largest collection of Native American art work. Most of the pieces have been created by artists from the Northwest Coast First Peoples such as Haida, Inuit, Kwakwaka'wakw, and the Coast Salish. You'll also find the collection dotted with dolls, prints, paintings, and carvings by artists from other tribes across the nation. We love to drop by each time we're in town so we can drool over the collection of masks and traditional carvings hanging on the old brick walls.

### Artisans on Taylor
**236 Taylor St., Port Townsend**
**(360) 379-8098**
**www.andreaguarino.com/Studio.html**

Bright, colorful, fun, unique, and innovative. All work perfectly to describe the art you will see in this small gallery. Most of the pieces reflect the eclectic nature of the Peninsula from fish sculptures created with recycled wire to collages created with found objects. The gallery specializes in glass beads, many made by owner Andrea Guarino, and handblown art glass. Handmade baskets and dolls, stone and wood sculptures, and ceramic and turned bowls complete the collection.

### EarthenWorks Gallery
**713 Water St., Port Townsend**
**(360) 385-0328**

EarthenWorks Gallery is one of the larger galleries in Port Townsend, and more than 300 artists are represented here. You'll find pieces for every space from office to garden to living room. Tom Torrens' metal sculptures and bells are specifically created for the garden while glass sculptures are well suited for the dining-room table. One-of-a-kind necklaces, earrings, and bracelets sit next to carved decoys and exquisitely assembled hardwood boxes. Any art collector will find something to whet his appetite at EarthenWorks.

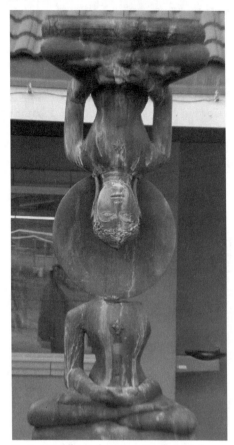

*Bronze Buddha at the Bronze Works in Shelton.*
PHOTO: ROB McNAIR-HUFF

### Forest Gems
**807 Washington St., Port Townsend**
**(360) 379-1713**
**www.forestgemsgallery.com**

When you buy something from Forest Gems, you'll be taking a piece of the Northwest home with you. Susan and Harvey Windle love wood in all its forms, and they think it makes a perfect "canvas" for creative expression. Woods from up and down the coast have been carved and sanded and polished into small and large works: coffee tables made of redwood burls, turned vases made from myrtlewood, and whale sculptures carved from alder.

### North by Northwest Indian Art Gallery
**918 Water St., Port Townsend**
**(360) 385-0955**

Enter into a spacious gallery in a building from another era, and you'll feel as if you are taking a peek at a different world. The walls of the gallery are hung with masks representing the mythical creatures of the Northwest Native oral tradition: Eagle, Raven, Whale, Frog. Display cases hold antique cedar bark baskets and other artifacts. Liz Smith, the owner of Port Townsend's first Native American art gallery, has assembled a unique collection that must be seen by any collector of tribal arts.

**Old World Glass Studio**
**1005 Water St., Port Townsend**
**(360) 379-9568**
**www.oldworldglass.net**

Anneliese and Gordon Redmond combine Italian and Pilchuck glassblowing techniques to create the works displayed here. Gordon honed his craft at the Pilchuck school, which was founded by world-renowned glass artist Dale Chihuly. Now Gordon sells his pieces at the couple's studio in downtown Port Townsend. Tour the shop to see his vases, bowls, and paperweights. If you have something special in mind, talk to the artists—custom work is one of their specialties.

**Pacific Traditions**
**637 Water St., Port Townsend**
**(360) 385-4770**

Pacific Traditions occupies the lobby of the Water Street Hotel. It's a tiny gallery, and it is easy to miss, but the smart collector will make sure to drop by. The gallery was once run by the Jamestown S'Klallam Tribe and was recently sold to a local owner who has made a point of maintaining the excellent collection of Northwest Native artworks. You'll find limited edition prints, a small but exquisite collection of masks, and an assort-

## Insiders' Tip
If you want an art-filled weekend, head to Port Townsend. You'll find a concert, a play, or an art exhibit in town nearly every week.

ment of bentwood and carved cedar boxes and bowls, baskets, and drums. Jewelry, cards, and a collection of reference and art books round out the collection.

**Stepping Stones Gallery**
**1011 Water St., Port Townsend**
**(360) 379-6910**

A small group of prolific artists, mostly painters, have banded together to create the Stepping Stones Gallery. Almost every painting and sculpture in the gallery reflects the flavor of the Pacific Northwest. Some incorporate the symbols of the Native American groups while others reflect the natural world in all its manifestations from the stormy sea to the calm and tranquil mountain lakes. Most days, visitors can talk with gallery artists hard at work painting and drawing.

# Sequim

**Blue Whole Gallery**
**129 W. Washington St., Sequim**
**(360) 681-6033**
**bluewholegallery.tenforward.com**

From eclectic and unique to traditional and familiar, you'll find it all at Blue Whole Gallery. More than 40 artists display their works at this cooperative gallery where ultra-modern, sleek steel sculptures sit next to traditional watercolor paintings of flowers. Funky and whimsical ceramics share space with woodcarvings based on the designs of the Native tribes. The gallery hosts free demonstrations where visitors can see artists at work each Thursday afternoon. Different artists are featured each month.

**Northwest Native Expressions**
**1033 Old Blyn Hwy., Sequim**
**(360) 681-7828**

Located in the Jamestown S'Klallam Tribal Center, Northwest Native Expressions serves as the one of two galleries operated by the tribe. The second is just down the road in the lobby of the 7 Cedars Casino. Contemporary works based on traditional techniques share space with more standard works. The pieces range from masks and carvings to basketry, jewelry, and prints. A small collection of books and cards complement the art.

# Port Angeles

**Bergsma Showroom**
**139 W. First St., Port Angeles**
**(360) 452-5080, (800) 923-5080**

Eileen Knight is a big fan of Jody Bergsma. While many gallery owners claim to have helped a budding artist, few can claim the role that Eileen played in Jody's life. Eileen is Jody's aunt, and when Jody was a teenager, Eileen encouraged her to enter her paintings in a Port Angeles art show. Today, Eileen continues to support Jody at this gallery. In addition to the Jody Bergsma prints, the gallery carries prints by Rie Muñoz and many other artists as well as smaller home decor items.

**The Clallam Art Gallery**
**The Landing Mall, 115 Railroad Ave.,**
**Ste. 206, Port Angeles**
**(360) 452-8165**

Port Angeles and Peninsula artists have taken over this large space in The Landing Mall. They have decked the walls with paintings of the Dungeness River and the bay and ferries. They have filled display cases with hand-etched gourds and hand-crafted silk dolls and jewelry. They have filled the shelves with pottery and sculptures. In short, they have created a cooperative gallery where they can share their life's works with you.

**Olympic Stained Glass**
**112 N. Laurel St., Port Angeles**
**(360) 457-1090**

If you have an idea for the perfect stained-glass window, take it to Olympic Stained Glass, where they will take your vision and make it reality. You can also pick out one of the many premade pieces or browse the gift collection that includes glass pieces from Seattle's famous Glass Eye studio as well as gemstone and amber jewelry.

**Reigning Visions Artwork**
**The Landing Mall, 115 E. Railroad Ave.,**
**Ste. 208, Port Angeles**
**(360) 452-8743**

When you're in The Landing Mall, make a point of walking upstairs to see Reigning Visions Artwork. Bill Lohnes' detailed woodcarvings alone are worth the trip, but you'll find much more here. Wood bowls, turned vases, intricate inlaid boxes, soft sculptures, and ceramic tiles augment a collection of more traditional ceramics, paintings, and art glass. The collection is eclectic and exciting and retains that special Northwest feeling that is indicative of so many of the region's galleries.

# Forks

**West Wind Gallery**
**120 Sol Duc Wy., Forks**
**(360) 374-7795**

Forks is better known for logging and clear-cuts than it is for art, but several area artists are working hard to change that perception. West Wind Gallery serves as the cooperative gallery for artists on the west side of the Peninsula. More than 50 artists display their wares in a constantly changing collection that includes fiber arts such as weaving and sweaters knitted from hand-spun wool, woodcrafts made with local wood, whimsical multimedia pieces, and finely detailed jewelry. Many of the paintings and photographs reflect the familiar seascapes and mountain scenes of the Peninsula. The gallery also offers on-site framing. It is closed on Sundays.

## Insiders' Tip

For a current list of upcoming shows for the galleries and art museums on the Peninsula, visit www.artguidenw.com.

### Gallery Marjuli
**865 Point Brown Ave., Ocean Shores**
**(360) 289-2858**

In a town where kitsch and clutter are as commonplace as beach blankets and swimsuits, the Gallery Marjuli is a refreshing change of pace. Local artists working in clay, wood, glass, and paint are well represented and augmented by an assortment of unique gifts such as pendulums, art supplies, and home decorating items. Owners Julie Bitar and Marj McBride have also assembled a unique collection of Asian artworks that meshes seamlessly with the Northwest flavor of the other paintings and sculptures on display here.

# Shelton

### Kimberly T. Gallery & Sculpture Garden
**50 W. Fredson Rd., Shelton**
**(360) 427-3857, (888) 821-0372**

A visit to the Kimberly T. Gallery & Sculpture Garden is a real treat, especially if you visit on a Tuesday or Thursday around 1 P.M. That is when the Bronze Works pours the super-heated, molten bronze into ceramic molds as part of the centuries-old process of creating bronze sculptures. It is an impressive sight, and one not often seen by the public. After the pour, take a walk around the sculpture garden to look at the larger-than-life sized sculptures that have been created at the Bronze Works. Smaller pieces are displayed in the gallery. Even if you miss the pour, a walk through the sculpture garden is worth pulling off of U.S. Highway 101.

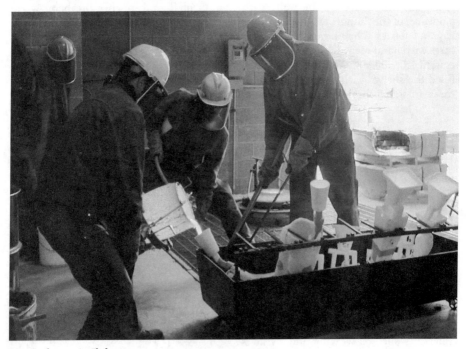

*Pouring bronze in Shelton.* PHOTO: NATALIE McNAIR-HUFF

# Music

## Admiral Theatre
**515 Pacific Ave., Bremerton**
**(360) 373-6810**

The Admiral Theatre opened as a movie theater in the 1940s. In 1997, the community refurbished the 1,000-seat venue with money donated by residents and other notable contributors such as Microsoft founders Bill Gates and Paul Allen. The theater's ground floor is set up like a dinner theater with chairs and tables, and catered dinners precede some performances. The balcony offers more traditional row seating. Although other arts organizations and civic groups also rent the theater, the Admiral Theatre Foundation presents a varied season of entertaining acts. Past musical acts have included Dr. John playing his New Orleans inspired music, a group of Taiko drummers, and the Seattle Symphony. The theater also presents plays such as *James and the Giant Peach*, ballets, comedy troupes, and quirky variety shows. The Admiral Theatre also houses the Evergreen Children's Theatre.

## Bremerton Community Concerts
**P.O. Box 2404, Bremerton**
**(360) 373-4850**

For more than 60 years, Bremerton Community Concerts has brought the performing arts to the Kitsap Peninsula. Each year a new slate of performers includes such diverse acts as the Black Mountain Male Chorus of Wales to a celebration of jazz and blues music. Subscriptions for individuals and families are quite reasonably priced, but tickets to individual performances are not available.

## Bremerton Symphony
**535-B 6th St., P.O. Box 996, Bremerton**
**(360) 373-1722**
**www.symphonic.org**

The Bremerton Symphony brings classical music to the North Kitsap Peninsula. The 65-member orchestra presents up to nine concerts each year. Although they perform popular classical favorites such as Mozart and Tchaikovsky, their repertoire also includes less well-known pieces such as Franck's Symphony in D-minor. On occasion the orchestra is joined by a 70-voice choir and guest artists. Most concerts are held in the Bremerton High School performing arts center with some performances taking place in local churches or the Admiral Theatre. Tickets may be bought for the season or for individual performances.

## Community Chorus of Port Townsend
**1320 Jefferson St., Port Townsend**
**(360) 385-2233**

If you can sing, you can join the Community Chorus of Port Townsend. The all-volunteer chorus gives two concerts each year in the spring and fall, as well as a Christmas concert. Performances take place in local churches and at the high school auditorium. The repertoire consists mostly of classical choral works such as pieces by Vivaldi and Copland. Call or write for a current performance schedule.

## Grays Harbor Symphony
**1620 Edward P. Smith Dr., Aberdeen**
**(360) 538-4066**

The Grays Harbor Symphony performs two annual concerts featuring popular classical favorites. Approximately 40 community

> ## Insiders' Tip
> If you're in the mood for some hot jazz, cool blues, or down-home country, check out some of the local bars. Many host excellent local and traveling musicians and admission is the price of a beer or two.

members volunteer to be in the symphony. Performances take place at Grays Harbor College's Bishop Center. Call or write for a current performance schedule.

### Juan de Fuca Festival of the Arts
### P.O. Box 796, Port Angeles
### (360) 457-5411
### juandefucafestival.com

In addition to sponsoring the annual Memorial Day arts festival, the Juan de Fuca Festival of the Arts (JFFA) features a season of live acts. Members of JFFA receive advance notice of events, and a chance to buy discounted tickets. Past performers have ranged from the fiddle group Barrage to Kartik Seshadri on the Sitar.

### Kitsap Peninsula Opera
### P.O. Box 1071, Bremerton
### (360) 377-8119

Most people are surprised to find that the Kitsap Peninsula has its own opera company, but that just proves how important people think the arts are on the Peninsula. Members of the Bremerton Symphony join the full opera company. Professional singers, most in transition from college to major opera companies, perform classic and traditional operas in their original languages. English supertitles allow the audience to follow the story as it is sung. In the past, the company has performed *La Boheme, Faust*, and the *Magic Flute*. Call for current production schedules and tickets.

### Mason County Community Concert Association
### 481 S.E. Channel Pt. Rd., Shelton
### (360) 426-5982

As part of a national network, the Mason County Community Concert Association brings up-and-coming performers to the residents of Shelton. To see the concerts you must be a member of the association or one of the sister associations located in small communities nationwide. The Mason County branch of the association was established over 50 years ago when the loggers and millwrights in the area expressed an interest in bringing the performing arts to town. Programs include dance groups, soloists, and small musical ensembles.

### Port Angeles Symphony
### 216 C N. Laurel, Port Angeles
### (360) 457-5579
### www.olypen.com/pasymphony

This 80-member, volunteer symphony has two separate performance seasons. The full orchestra, led by music director and conductor Nico Snel, performs classical favorites such as Verdi's "Overture" and occasionally a Pops concert during the first season. Following the symphony season, a smaller chamber orchestra presents six more performances: three in Port Angeles and three in Sequim. Snel and other symphony members also work with the North Olympic Youth Symphony. The full symphony concerts take place at the Port Angeles High School auditorium. If you want your music at a discount, or you want to take children, check out the open dress rehearsals that take place before each performance. The chamber music concerts take place in local churches. Tickets may be bought for a season or single performance. Call, write, or visit the Web Site for a current schedule and ticketing information.

### Port Townsend Community Orchestra
### 3115 Regent St., Port Angeles
### (360) 457-4250

Under the leadership of conductor Dewey Ehling, who is from neighboring Port Angeles, the 50-member Port Townsend Community Orchestra plays four concerts each year. It is occasionally joined by a special guest musician to play classical favorites as well as the occasional pops concert. Concerts take place in the Chimacum High School auditorium.

### Turtle Bluff Orchestra
### 5162 Flagler Rd., Chimacum
### (360) 385-3626

Each year the Turtle Bluff Orchestra—a small orchestra composed of professional musicians—gives three classical concerts in October, January, and May. The concerts take place in the Chimacum High

School auditorium. Part of the goal of the orchestra is to pair younger musicians with more experienced musical veterans. From what we have heard, the concerts are quite a treat.

**Victorian Chamber Singers**
**30 Patison St., Port Hadlock**
**(360) 379-0223**

The Victorian Singers entertain Port Townsend-area residents with Victorian choral works and programs featuring the operas and songs of Gilbert and Sullivan. Recent performances included the *Mikado* and *Pirates of Penzance*. The community group performs a Christmas concert and also has concerts in March and June. Call or write for a performance schedule and more information.

# Theater

**7th Street Theatre**
**311 7th St., Hoquiam**
**(360) 532-0302**

Will Rogers, Paul Robeson, and Lilly Pons have graced the stage of the 7th Street Theatre, an 1,100-seat theater built in 1928. Then, as it does today, the theater provided a forum for the performing arts. Although the theatre does not have its own company, community groups use it as a venue for musical acts, plays, and lectures. The theater is undergoing a progressive restoration in order to return it to its former glory and to reveal its fine details and unique accents. Call for a current schedule of upcoming events.

**Bishop Center for Performing Arts**
**1620 Edward P. Smith Dr., Aberdeen**
**(360) 538-4066**

Although other organizations such as the Grays Harbor Symphony use and rent the Bishop Center for Performing Arts, the center also puts on its own season's worth of entertainment. The acts vary widely from operas, musical groups, and plays. Tickets may be bought for individual events or for the season.

**Driftwood Theater**
**120 3rd St., Aberdeen**
**(360) 538-1213**

The Driftwood Players, a community group, has been entertaining Grays Harbor residents since the late 1950s. In 1981 the players bought and remodeled a former Christian Science building, which became the group's permanent home. The company produces five plays per year, and each play runs for four weekends. Past plays have included *I Hate Hamlet*, and *Daddy's Dying, Who's Got the Will?*

**Key City Players**
**419 Washington St., Port Townsend**
**(360) 385-7396**
**www.olympus.net/community/kcplay**

The Key City Players number between 55 and 60, and they produce five plays each year in the group's playhouse in downtown Port Townsend. The volunteer actors, directors, costume designers, and stagehands have produced such plays as *The Dresser* and *One Flew Over the Cuckoo's Nest*, as well as musicals like *Little Shop of Horrors*. Each play enjoys a run of ten performances. Call, write, or visit the Web site for information on the current season and for tickets.

**Paradise Theatre**
**9916 Peacock Ave., Gig Harbor**
**(253) 851-7529**
**www.paradisetheatre.org**

Not long ago, all the performances put on by the Paradise Theatre Company took place on the Meadows on Peacock Hill. But the company recently acquired a Victorian house that has been transformed into a playhouse so performances extend throughout the year. During the summer months, performances still take place on the meadow, and the company also sponsors a children's acting camp. During

# Close-up

## A Passion for Poetry

Writers and poetry lovers owe a debt of gratitude to Copper Canyon Press, which makes its home in a small building on the Centrum campus at Port Townsend's Fort Worden. The independent, non-profit press started humbly in the winter of 1972 when poet Sam Hamill lugged an old galley press up three flights of stairs to his Denver, Colorado, apartment. He bought the galley press, and two cases of type using the $500 award he received for excellence in literary publishing for his work on *Spectrum*, the literary magazine at the University of California, Santa Barbara. He had enough type to print two pages of poetry at a time—slow going for a literary press. In 1974 Centrum offered to house Copper Canyon at Fort Worden.

Hamill and original partner in poetry, Tree Swenson, moved the press to the Northwest. Swenson kept the galley press connected and running while Hamill made ends meet by working odd jobs, teaching workshops, and working with prison inmates. Miraculously, he still made time to write poetry and work at the press. Through their incredible devotion, Hamill and Swenson carved a niche in the publishing world for their little press. The two published limited-edition books of poetry, all hand printed and hand sewn. Copper Canyon also helped several other small, independent presses get their starts by teaching the art of bookbinding and printing to the founders.

Over the years, Copper Canyon's reputation and resources grew through the assistance of Centrum and the National Endowment for the Arts as well as private contributions and a lot of hard work. Along the way, Hamill and his helpers realized that the press would need to turn to digital printing to make it in the competitive world of publishing. Nevertheless, they continued to focus on the look and craftsmanship of the book as well as the work enclosed between the covers. The move made Copper Canyon an important literary institution as has been proven by ever increasing sales as well as grants from the Andrew W. Mellon Foundation and the Lila Wallace–Reader's Digest Fund.

The growth did not diminish Copper Canyon's dedication to poetry in all its forms. Collections range from the melodious lines of Olga Broumas to the questioning couplets of Pablo Neruda to the porcine tales of David Lee. The press produces books by some of the world's most well-known poets, including Hayden Carruth, Lucille Clifton, W.S. Merwin, Octavio Paz, Denise Levertov, and Carolyn Kizer. Hamill—Zen Buddhist, devotee of Asian literature, and translator of the Japanese poet Basho—has ensured that Copper Canyon main-

the cooler, wetter months, the shows move inside as part of a dinner theater. The company is a professional theater that specializes in popular and cabaret-style plays, including such shows as *You're a Good Man Charlie Brown, West Side Story, The Mystery of Irma Vep,* and *I Do, I Do.* The theater also sponsors late-night improv groups on Friday nights. Tickets for individual performances cost around $30; season tickets may also be purchased.

**The Performing Arts Guild of South Kitsap**
**820 Bay St., Port Orchard**
**(360) 876-6610**
**www.pagsk.org**

The Performing Arts Guild of South Kitsap has made it its goal to bring live theater to the small community of Port Orchard. Each year, the guild produces six plays, including dramas, comedies, mysteries, and a musical. Volunteers from all

tains a commitment to publishing Asian poetry. That dedication has led to the recent creation of the Kage—an imprint for translated poetry. And since listening to poetry is such an important part of enjoying it, Copper Canyon also produces CDs of select poets reading their poems.

Just in the last decade, the press has grown from publishing 10 books a year to now publishing between 18 and 20 books each year. Each of the books it publishes is as important to Copper Canyon as the first book. It's as if each poem becomes a gift in the hands of the publisher. As a result, when you buy a book from Copper Canyon Press, you buy a work of art in all senses of the word, from poetry to type to paper to book design. Beautiful, limited-edition broadsides are still printed on the manual press—Copper Canyon has not abandoned the time-honored art that launched it on its way to brilliance.

You can visit Copper Canyon Press Monday through Friday. After you enter the main gates to Fort Worden, follow the signs to the press by going straight on the entrance road rather than turning right toward the beach. You can buy the books published by the press and take a quick look around. If you are lucky, you may even get to see the old galley press in operation. If you can't make it to the press, you can still buy its books at The Imprint Bookstore (820 Water St.). To receive a free catalog, write to Copper Canyon Press, P.O. Box 271, Port Townsend, Washington 98368; call (360) 385-2925; or visit the Web site at www.coppercanyonpress.org.

*Copper Canyon Press.* PHOTO: ROB McNAIR-HUFF

over the Kitsap Peninsula join the productions as actors, directors, costume and stage designers, and members of the support crew. Past seasons have seen such plays as *The Odd Couple, One Flew Over the Cuckoo's Nest, Oliver,* and *A Midsummer Night's Dream.* The plays are performed in the Bay Street Playhouse in downtown Port Orchard. Tickets cost around $8 for students and seniors and $10 for general admission: musicals cost slightly more.

Call or visit the Web site for a current schedule.

### Port Angeles Community Players
### 1235 E. Lauridsen, Port Angeles
### (360) 452-3350

The actors and members of the volunteer-based Port Angeles Community Players perform five plays from September to July. Each season includes dramas, comedies, and at least one mystery. The Players, who have been performing for Port Angeles residents for more than 48 years, hold the plays in their own playhouse, which was originally built as a theater. Past performances have included *Under the Sycamore Tree*, *Real Inspector Hound*, and *The Octet Bridge Club*.

# Literary Arts

### Olympic Poets and Writers Workshop
### Shelton
### (360) 426-2268

Each week at Shelton's St. David's Hall (218 N. 3rd), local writers gather to critique each other's work and support each other. Visiting writers give readings once a month, and the group also takes part in the annual Write in the Woods writer's conference at Olympic College.

### Port Townsend Writer's Conference
### Centrum, P.O. Box 1158, Port Townsend
### (360) 385-3102
### www.centrum.org/Writers.html

Writers of poetry, fiction, and non fiction gather for 10 days each July at Port Townsend's Fort Worden for Centrum's writer's conference. Critiqued and non-critiqued workshops are led by nationally recognized writers such as Terry Tempest Williams and Dorothy Allison and poets Carolyn Kizer and David Lee. Readings, lectures, and open-mike readings complete the offerings. The spaces for this conference fill quickly, so get your application in early. Call or visit the Web site for more information and an application form.

### Port Townsend Shorts
### Pope Marine Park Building, Port
### Townsend

During the First Saturday art walks in Port Townsend, area actors read short stories from 5 to 8 P.M. in the Pope Marine Park Building next to the City Dock. The readings are quite creative and lively. If you're in town during the art walks, make sure you swing by to listen for a while.

# Art and Music Festivals

## Winter

### Chamber Music Port Townsend
### Port Townsend
### (360) 385-5320, (800) 733-3608
### www.centrum.org/Chamber.html

Relax to the melodious sounds of chamber music during the first weekend in February. Centrum sponsors this weekend-long concert series that features a different string quartet or chamber music group each year. Tickets for a single concert cost approximately $16 to $20; tickets for the series can also be bought at a slight discount.

## Spring

### Jazz in the Olympics
### Port Angeles

Jazz bands and ensemble groups gather in Port Angeles to play the weekend away. Performances take place in venues throughout the city, and admission varies according to performance. So if you hanker for some springtime jive, join the party during the third weekend in April.

### Juan de Fuca Festival of the Arts
### Port Angeles
### (360) 457-5411
### juandefucafestival.com

Five stages throughout the city host musicians, jugglers, acrobats, actors, and dancers during this Memorial Day weekend festival. Arts and crafts and food vendors will be happy to sell you a few gifts or nibbles. Kids will have fun at the "action stations," where they can play games or make some crafts. More than 60 performers present more than 120 performances from Friday night to Monday evening.

## Summer

### Arts by the Bay
**Poulsbo**
**(360) 697-1397**

Join the residents of Poulsbo for a summer arts fair for music, dancing, and, of course, booth upon booth of art. Artists from near and far sell their works, which range from sweaters made with handspun wool, carved whales and dolphins, vibrant weavings, and pastoral paintings or local scenes. If all that looking makes you hungry, head to the food vendors for some crisp and crunchy funnel cakes or a piece of lefse sprinkled with cinnamon and sugar. The festival takes place on the third Saturday and Sunday in August.

### Country Blues Festival
**Fort Worden, Port Townsend**
**(360) 385-5320, (800) 733-3608**
**www.centrum.org/Bluesfest.html**

This festival marks the end of Centrum's weeklong Country Blues Workshop. Centrum draws some of the best blues performers from around the nation, and at the end of the workshop performers and workshop participants adjourn to McCurdy Pavilion to give three rousing concerts. The workshop and festival take place during the last week of June. Call Centrum for more information on the workshops. Concert tickets cost around $14 to $16.

### Festival of American Fiddle Tunes
**Fort Worden, Port Townsend**
**(360) 385-5320, (800) 733-3608**
**www.centrum.org/Fiddle.html**

Hordes of fiddlers descend on Port Townsend's Fort Worden each year during the first week in July. The fiddlers come to take part in Centrum's Fiddle Tunes workshop. You'll hear fiddle tunes all over the city throughout the week, but for the most impressive taste of old-time fiddle music, buy tickets to the evening concerts. Concert tickets cost around $14 for adults and $3 for children. Call Centrum for more information on the workshops and concert schedule.

### Gig Harbor Summer Art Festival
**Judson St., Gig Harbor**
**(253) 858-8920**

Gig Harbor has a rich community of artists working in every media imaginable. This Art Festival, sponsored by the Peninsula Art League, celebrates the artists, their works, and the community with an arts and craft fair. You'll find raku pottery, watercolors, oil paintings, sculptures, food vendors, and more. Join the weekend-long celebration in the middle of July.

### Jazz Port Townsend Festival
**Port Townsend**
**(360) 385-5320, (800) 733-3608**
**www.centrum.org/Jazz.html**

Centrum's series of summer music festivals and workshops continues with the Jazz Port Townsend Festival during the last week of July. Workshop attendees experience classes presented by internationally known jazz artists such as Bud Shank, Bill Ramsay, and Don Lanphere. Port Townsend residents and visitors reap the benefits of having so many jazz musicians in town when the artists jam and perform in local bars and restaurants. Three extended concerts are also presented on Thursday, Friday, and Saturday evenings at Fort Worden's McCurdy Pavilion. Concert tickets range from around $15 to $24.

**Olympic Music Festival**
**Quilcene**
**(206) 527-8839**
**www.musicfest.net**

From the middle of June to the beginning of September, classical-music lovers from across the nation drive to an old barn in Quilcene on Saturdays and Sundays. There they listen to some of the best music in the nation. The Philadelphia String Quartet and special guests play from a broad repertoire. A recent festival included the New Zealand String Quartet playing Shostakovich and Beethoven. Other programs feature pieces by Prokofiev, Fauré, Mozart, and other classical masters. The music festival is family friendly with an on-site farm animal petting zoo, and boxed lunches are available.

Tickets for barn seating cost around $24 for adults and $15 for children ages 6 to 17. Lawn seating costs around $14. Children under 6 are admitted free to the lawn, but they are not allowed to sit in the barn. A discount is offered for advance purchase tickets.

**Summer Bluegrass Festival**
**Olalla**
**(253) 857-5604**

Located between Gig Harbor and Port Orchard, Olalla is the place where bluegrass fans gather to dance to the music. The festival takes place near the end of August. Children's activities and a kids' parade keep the little ones entertained. Adults will have fun with the arts-and craft-booths and all the live music.

## Autumn

**Forest Storytelling Festival**
**Port Angeles**
**(800) 457-0030, (360) 457-3169**

Professional and amateur storytellers visit Port Angeles each year during the third weekend in September. Some storytellers use puppets and props, while others simply use their colorful personalities to charm the audience into a world of myth and wonder. The festival participants also give workshops and presentations. Other activities include a raffle, dinner, and a children's bookstore.

**Open Studio Tour**
**3412 Lewis St., Gig Harbor**
**(253) 858-8920**

Most people like to look at art, but we don't often get to see it as it's being made.

Each Labor Day weekend Gig Harbor area artists open their studios to the public so that visitors can see what happens in a working studio. The artist line-up changes each year, but every year more than 10 studios are included in the self-guided tour. Each artist who participates works in a different medium: pottery, fabric, lithography, metal sculpture, or painting. On Friday evening the Cultural Arts Commission holds a Gala Auction to kick off the tour. Tickets for the auction cost around $35. Call or write for more information and a tour map.

# Arts Organizations

**Centrum**
**Fort Worden, P.O. Box 1158,**
**Port Townsend**
**(360) 385-3102, (800) 733-3608**
**www.centrum.org**

Centrum has been organizing workshops and bringing the arts to the Peninsula for

close to 30 years. Artists come from every corner of the nation to take part in the annual workshops sponsored by Centrum. Many of the artists stay in Fort Worden's old officers' quarters while they perfect their work in dance, music, visual arts, acting, and writing. Well-known performers

*Stunning handcrafts, such as this Chris Mathey vase, are sold throughout the Peninsula.* PHOTO: NATALIE McNAIR-HUFF

such as dancer and choreographer Bill Evans and saxophonist Bud Shank teach at the workshops. The community benefits from the workshops as well, since most conclude with a music or arts festival of some sort. Most of the associated festivals are listed above. Centrum also sponsors artist residencies throughout the year so that artists working in any discipline have the space, time, and resources needed to work on their creations.

### Cultural Arts Foundation Northwest
**P.O. Box 291, Poulsbo**
**(360) 697-1397**

Poulsbo's Cultural Arts Foundation Northwest supports artists practicing in all disciplines. The foundation organizes arts summits and quarterly arts walks and publishes a quarterly newsletter. The foundation also sponsors Arts by the Bay, an annual arts festival that takes place on the third weekend in August in downtown Poulsbo.

### Gig Harbor/Key Peninsula Cultural Arts Commission
**12109 102nd Ave. Ct. N.W., Gig Harbor**
**(253) 851-9462**
**www.ghkp-culturalArts.org**

The Gig Harbor/Key Peninsula Cultural Arts Commission aims to bring arts to the area regardless of the income level of the people involved. To that end, the commission acts as a sort of information distribution center for artists. The commission sends artists and arts organizations information about grants, contests, and exhibits, and helps them find the resources that they need. Then the commission takes information such as performance and exhibit schedules from the artists and publishes it in a newsletter, a quarterly newspaper insert, and a community flyer. It also sends the information to local media outlets. The commission also sponsors public art programs, including public bronze sculptures selected by the community and a planned student art gallery and retail space. Commission members are also provided with free Web space, and with an invaluable resource in attaining grants and the support that is so often lacking for individual artists in small communities.

### Peninsula Art Association
**P.O. Box 11, Shelton**
**(360) 877-5435**

Visual artists in the Shelton area band together as the Peninsula Art Association. The association sponsors juried art shows and public exhibitions. Members also teach workshops in disciplines ranging from carving to screen printing to watercolor painting. Members receive a newsletter to keep them up-to-date on programs and events, and they meet on the second Tuesday of each month to network and plan upcoming workshops and shows. Membership costs around $15.

### Peninsula Art League
**P.O. Box 1422, Gig Harbor**
**(360) 858-7612**

The Peninsula Art League promotes the visual arts in the Gig Harbor/Key Peninsula area. The league organizes the Gig Harbor Summer Art Festival and sponsors workshops and gallery shows throughout the year. A monthly newsletter keeps league members up-to-date with league events and also publishes requests for submissions and information about workshops and classes.

## Insiders' Tip

Once a month, many local galleries stay open late for gallery walks. Participating galleries will be able to fill you in on the specifics. Some galleries also provide hot coffee, tea, cider, and snacks, as well as live music.

**Port Townsend Arts Commission**
**540 Water St., Port Townsend**
**(360) 379-8642**
**www.olympus.net/community/ptarts**

The Port Townsend Arts Commission is funded by the city to "promote and encourage the arts of Port Townsend." The nine-person commission includes actors, writers, visual artists, and musicians. The commission sponsors arts events for every discipline, including juried art shows, writing workshops, an annual one-act play competition, and the Port Townsend Shorts—short story readings by local artists during the monthly art walks. Local artists can also register with the commission's artists registry.

**Port Townsend Arts Guild**
**P.O. Box 246, Port Townsend**
**(360) 379-3813**

By organizing arts-and-craft shows, the Port Townsend Arts Guild supports arts in the community that may not otherwise receive financial support. The guild also supports the local food bank, and donated money to the Haller Fountain restoration. The guild's six arts-and-crafts shows are featured prominently during many of Port Townsend's annual events, including the Rhody Festival in May and the Wooden Boat Festival in September. Artists from across the state take part in the shows, and art fans can buy dried flower wreaths, handmade stamps, and ceramic bowls, as well as paintings, sculptures, and works of wood.

*An antique gas tank greets shoppers at Cottage by the Sea in Ocean Shores.* PHOTO: ROB McNAIR-HUFF

# Antiques

The Olympic Peninsula may not be known as an antiques hunter's paradise, but the area is dotted with antiques shops. Towns like Port Townsend and Port Orchard have an abundance of shops. Some sell mostly furniture, but most sell an assortment of antiques and collectibles, and since the lumber, logging, and fishing heritage of the area is still strong, you will find an abundance of the tools of those trades. Nearly every antiques shop you visit will have at least one corner full of tools.

If you want an intensive weekend worth of antiques shopping, you'll find the highest concentration of shops on the Kitsap Peninsula. Port Townsend, Sequim, and Port Angeles also feature a number of well-established shops where you can find nearly everything ever made. Everyone has a different definition of what "antique" means, and while you will find a few places with nineteenth-century offerings, you'll find most shops around here filled with classic American and vintage antiques.

More antiques stores dot the area than we could cover in this section, but we have highlighted a few in each region. We recommend that you use these shops as a start to your antiques hunting, but don't forget to stop by the others you see on your trip. You're sure to find something special in each one. Most antiques stores on the Peninsula are open year-round, but a few do close during the winter. Nevertheless, you may want to call ahead to double-check hours and that the store you want to visit will be open.

Happy hunting!

## Gig Harbor

**Vintage America Antiques**
**3102 Harborview Dr., Gig Harbor**
**(253) 857-7374**

Going into Vintage America Antiques is like opening a treasure box full of goodies from the last two centuries. Old books and vintage quilts look like they just emerged from Grandma's attic, and plumb bobs, oil cans, and architectural accessories could have come from Grandpa's tool shed. We were especially impressed with an eighteenth-century panetierre that looked as if it should still be filled with loaves of freshly baked bread. This shop also boasts an extensive collection of letters and type from printers and advertisers. Proprietors Roberta and David Keyes include information about some of the items on handwritten cards so you'll even know what you're buying.

**Yvonne Leone Antiques & Interior Design**
**3226 Harborview Dr. #2, Gig Harbor**
**(253) 853-6191**

Yvonne Leone is an interior designer, and she visits Europe twice each year to hand select the antiques that she carries in her store and uses in her designs. You'll find wonderfully preserved furniture from Italianate tables to French sofas and more. Smaller accessories complement the furniture. Yvonne is also happy to talk with you about how to best fit a piece into your existing spaces.

# Port Orchard

**Antiques by the Bay**
**802 Bay St., Port Orchard**
**(360) 876-4397**

The mission-style and Craftsman furniture displayed in the front of the store and in the windows will draw you in. Once inside you will find more items that will be sure to capture your attention, including a fun collection of antique dolls, jewelry, plenty of china, and glass. More modern collectibles are also represented here, including Pez dispensers and action figures. Antiques by the Bay is open seven days a week.

**Olde Central Antique Mall**
**801 Bay St., Port Orchard**
**(360) 895-1902**

More than 50 dealers have set up shop at this Antique Mall in downtown Port Orchard. You'll find a little bit of everything here, from Depression glass to furniture to porcelain figurines. It will take you close to an hour to sort through everything downstairs, but don't think you're done there. Head upstairs for even more browsing, and before you leave buy a tune on the unique Empress Queen Player Piano by the front door. The mall is open seven days a week.

**PV Teeks**
**113 Sidney, Port Orchard**
**(360) 895-2786**

Just a little way up the Sidney hill, you'll find a small shop filled with "newer" antiques. Most of the items date post 1940s and include advertising art, kitchenware, glassware, postcards, marbles, and other collectibles.

**Sidedoor Antiques**
**701 Bay St., Port Orchard**
**(360) 876-8631**

Michael O'Brien and Nancy Minor have amassed a large collection from the barely vintage to classic American antiques. As you walk in the front door, you will see a collection of refurbished and operable vintage radios, large and small. The radios share space with bed frames, sofas, tables, chairs, armoires, and a few long display cases filled with dolls, jewelry, and smaller items. Walk farther into the building and you'll find a conglomeration of more furniture and other odds and ends. Among them you'll find a few hidden treasures such as a large bank of post office boxes or a few steamer trunks. Sidedoor Antiques is closed Monday through Wednesday.

## North Kitsap Peninsula

**Antique Junction**
**18980A Jensen Wy. N.E., Poulsbo**
**(360) 779-1890**

Antique Junction is exactly that, a junction between classic American antiques, vintage wares, and primitive pieces ranging from artworks to hand made furnishings. You won't grow tired of looking at a monotonous and cluttered collection here because what you'll find is a varied and well-displayed assortment of antiques in a wide range of styles and price ranges.

**The Cats Meow**
**18940 Front St., Poulsbo**
**(360) 697-1902**

The Cats Meow displays the merchandise of several vendors. You'll find a bit of this and a dash of that here. The collected pieces cover everything from American furniture to Depression glass to dolls. To the rear of the store you will also find a display case filled with antique and vintage guns, swords, and other weapons.

**Granny & Papa's Antique Mall**
**Poulsbo Village, 19669 7th Ave., Poulsbo**
**(360) 697-2221**

Located in a strip mall just beyond downtown Poulsbo, Granny & Papa's Antique Mall features all kinds of antiques. Several merchants keep displays here, and Judy Haag (a.k.a. Granny) makes sure that the

*Many antiques stores include one-of-a-kind gems, such as these postal boxes for sale at a shop in Port Orchard.* PHOTO: ROB McNAIR-HUFF

displays are attractively presented. As a result, this mall has avoided the cluttered and overwhelming feeling to which many antiques malls succumb. You'll discover some unusual finds here, such as Civil War artifacts and stunning examples of folk art as well as plenty of furniture, toys, china, crystal, and collectibles for all tastes and pocketbooks. Papa (Al Haag) also repairs crystal, china, porcelain, and glass.

### The Hiding Place
### 18850 Front St., Poulsbo
### (360) 779-7811

The Hiding Place has a bit of a split personality, but that's what makes it fun. One half of the store is dedicated to Christmas decorations. The other half contains antiques. A few select pieces of furniture hold accessories, curios, jewelry, and other samples of vintage Americana.

### Poulsbo Antique Mall
### 18955 Anderson Parkway, Poulsbo
### (360) 779-4858

The Poulsbo Antique Mall is stuffed full of nearly everything ever made. The mall specializes in furniture and collectibles. The front of the shop is strewn with dining sets, chests, and armoires. Chairs hang from the rafters, and the display cases filled with knickknacks and smaller items stretch throughout the large warehouse. Coin collectors and sports-card collectors may also find a few treasures in a couple of display cases. You might have to look hard

here, but the patient browser will be sure to find something to take home.

### Silverdale Antiques
### 9536 Silverdale Wy. N.W., Silverdale
### (360) 692-2462

If you are looking for furniture, especially an armoire for your linens or television, visit the spacious warehouse of Silverdale Antiques. Owners Denis and Deborah Housen also offer smaller items such as an extensive collection of glass and china. And for the truly eclectic collector, check out the complete set of chain mail. Silverdale Antiques is closed on Mondays.

### Victoria's
### 18967 Anderson Pkwy., Poulsbo
### (360) 779-8456

Victoria Robinson loves antiques, and it shows in her eclectic and varied collection. The furniture she sells, although not plentiful, runs the gamut from American primitive to ornate German bureaus. The walls are hung with art and Native American baskets, and display cases are filled with attractively arranged tools, jewelry and buttons, collectible toys, kitchenware, and more. Bakelite collectors will spy a few precious pieces for their collections. Victoria likes to keep her shop organized and comfortable so that people in wheelchairs can wander. A sign on her door also advertises that she welcomes children, dogs, and food.

## Port Townsend

### The Antique Company
### 10894 Rhody Dr., Port Hadlock
### (360) 385-9522

This 5,000-foot showroom is not to be missed if you are looking for furniture, as it is filled with furniture in nearly every style and from every age imaginable. Each piece is ready to use. You won't find peeling veneer and water rings here. Instead you'll find oak mission-style tables and desks, walnut bed frames, mahogany armoires, and a lot more. You'll also be

## Insiders' Tip

If you don't see what you want, ask someone who works in the shop. There may very well be a treasure or two hidden in a box somewhere.

pleased at the prices. You'll find a well-balanced assortment of American and European pieces since the owners regularly travel to Europe to hand select more merchandise. The store, which has been open for more than 10 years, is located on Washington Highway 19, also known as Rhody Drive through Port Hadlock.

### Finders Keepers
### 909 Water St., Port Townsend
### (360) 379-4662

You'll swear you walked into a kitchen gadget shop from the 1930s when you pop into Finders Keepers. The shop is small, but it is jam-packed with American vintage from eggbeaters to wall hangings to porcelain figurines. You'll also find plenty of glassware and vintage prints. Finders Keepers is just a fun place for a quick stop.

### Insatiables
### 821 Washington St., Port Townsend
### (360) 385-9262

Karen Graham, the owner of Insatiables, used to maintain a booth full of books just across the street in the Antique Mall. Her collection far outgrew the space, so she jumped at the chance to expand when this space opened. She finagled her family

into building sturdy bookshelves, and then filled them with an impressive collection of "old, rare and curious books." She specializes in technical books, and since Port Townsend is a maritime city, she also has a hefty selection of nautical books. Kids will have fun looking through the assortment of old children's books. Insatiables stands out in this six-bookstore town.

### Port Townsend Antique Mall
### 802 Washington St., Port Townsend
### (360) 385-2590

The Port Townsend Antique Mall has been open for more than 20 years. Two floors worth of antiques and collectibles entice browsers to spend whole afternoons perusing the booths. It's all here. You'll find fine furniture in nearly every style and from every age, plus jewelry, figurines, and art. Some of the merchants specialize in Native American artifacts, and a few specialize in Asian art and decor. Don't forget to check the downstairs display that tells the saga of the Chinese community in Port Townsend around 1900. If you want to see everything in the mall, plan on spending at least an hour.

# Sequim

### Lighthouse Antiques and Collectibles
### 261321 U.S. Hwy. 101, Sequim
### (360) 681-7346

When Roger and Nancy Neidinger opened their store in 1994, most of the antiques stores in the area sold the typical assortment of porcelain figurines, china, and glass, but the Neidingers decided to buck the trend and sell antique and vintage tools alongside all the "pretty things." You'll find plenty of pretty things here too, but the collections of tools, advertising art, and handmade furniture and toys is even more impressive. You will definitely find the odd and unusual here, such as seed display boxes, marble ramps, and the occasional coal bucket. Grease

monkeys can spend their time sorting through the wrenches, adzes, plumb bobs, and hand drills. Lighthouse Antiques is located on U.S. 101 at the western edge of Sequim, and it is easy to miss it when you are speeding by, but turn around and go back. You won't be sorry.

### Sunnyside Antiques
### 132 E. Washington St., Sequim
### (360) 582-9258

You might not think that there is much to Sunnyside Antiques when you first walk inside, but keep walking past the check-out counter, and you'll find two more rooms. Chairs and cameras and clam baskets and dolls hang from the ceiling. Wooden and vintage toys line the top shelves, and every nook and cranny is filled with more. The owners arrange estate sales so they have been able to selectively assemble a collection of unusual and sometimes hard-to-find pieces. If you don't see what you are looking for, ask—they may have it hidden away somewhere. Sunnyside Antiques is closed on Sunday.

## Port Angeles

### The Corps Shop
**129B W. 1st St., Port Angeles**
**(360) 457-7041, (800) 457-7041**

Although technically it may not be an antiques store, The Corps Shop is definitely worth checking out. Here you'll find military memorabilia, and plenty of it. Proprietor Robert W. Mingram, a former Marine, has gathered an incredible collection. He displays the fatigues and dress blues on mannequins, each named after the service man or woman who once owned the clothes. The mannequins are housed in display cabinets and surrounded by more military paraphernalia, including canteens, jackets, posters, pictures, and more. Even if military collectibles are not your thing, check the shop out just for the historical value; a trip through The Corps Shop is definitely a history lesson. The Corps Shop is closed Sunday.

### Marion's Port Angeles Antiques
**123 W. 1st St. Ste. B, Port Angeles**
**(260) 452-5411**

Marion Magiera has been selling antiques in Port Angeles for more than 18 years, although she recently moved her shop to a new downtown location where she can better display the collection. She specializes in American antiques, including furniture, china, and glass. When we visited we drooled over a couple of curved-glass and maple hutches and a colonial secretary. The shop is spacious and well organized so you won't feel cramped or overwhelmed, and there is plenty of room to move around and look at everything.

### Retroville
**133 E. 1st St., Port Angeles**
**(360) 452-1429, (877) 399-1429**
**www.retroville.com**

Retroville is a fun place to shop. Take the kids and show them what life was like from the 1930s to the 1950s. You'll find plenty of vintage everything here. Need a tacky ashtray for your lounge? You'll find it here. How about a Bauer flowerpot or a flamingo shaped vase or a metal display cabinet? Yep, they're here too. Wander to the back of the store to thumb through racks of vintage loungewear, Hawaiian print shirts, and letter jackets. Keep going to the next room to browse kitschy wall art and folk paintings. A walk through Retroville is practically a journey back through the mid-1900s.

### Small Treasures Antiques
**129A W. 1st St., Port Angeles**
**(360) 452-3350**

Some antiques stores are cluttered and can feel overwhelming. Some antiques stores look junky and spare. Small Treasures Antiques looks intriguing and inviting. Although the shop is housed with several other stores all separated by partial walls, Small Treasures has created a space all its own with vignettes that are reminiscent of those in history museums. The bedroom contains a bed, of course, plus a vanity and all the accoutrements while a magazine shop vignette displays books, magazines, and advertising art. We especially liked the soda fountain and general store vignette filled with everything you might find at either location. Small Treasures has quite a bit to see, but it's easy on the eyes.

# Forks

**Tinker's Tales & Antiques**
**71 N. Forks Ave., Forks**
**(360) 374-9433**
**www.tinkers-tales.com**

Tinker's Tales & Antiques has new things, old things, and in-between things. You just have to stop by to see all that they have, and while you visit you can sip an espresso. The shop is a hybrid between a bookstore with old and new books, an antiques shop with American collectibles, and an art store. Antiques range from Native American artifacts to porcelain figurines to china, all of which will fit just right in that empty corner of your suitcase.

# Ocean Shores

**Cottage by the Sea**
**810 Point Brown Ave., Ocean Shores**
**(360) 289-9046**

The friendly folks at Cottage by the Sea will be more than happy to share stories about their antiques. Make sure you ask about the Poly gas tank, an impressive and colorful fixture that is sure to catch your eye. Walk behind the gas tank to find cast iron and tin toys as well as advertising art for oil and soda pop companies. You'll also find American furniture dating mostly from the 1930s, including armoires, desks, and some nice chairs. The store also displays a collection of historical pictures of the region, and display cases are filled with jewelry, china, silver, and plenty of knickknacks.

**Ocean Shores Antiques**
**817 Point Brown Ave. N.W., Ocean Shores**
**(360) 289-9840**

Ocean Shores Antiques is a potpourri of the barely old to the truly antique. Display cases near the cash register hold rare china and flow ware and other small, rare pieces. But that is only the beginning. This old house is positively overflowing with antiques and collectibles. It's a bit difficult to maneuver, but if you are patient and take your time, you'll find something priceless to you. You'll also find newer collectibles like a whole room worth of Star Wars memorabilia and another full of comic books and old magazines. Doll lovers will find silk, porcelain, and hard plastic dolls in nearly every room.

# Grays Harbor

**Keepsake Cottage**
**519 N. Maple, Aberdeen**
**(360) 532-1863**

A mother-daughter team, Christy and Rovena Brooks, maintains this collection dedicated primarily to "women's things." You'll find more vintage kitchen tools than you could fit in a kitchen, from eggbeaters to potato mashers to cast-iron pans. Hand embroidered flour sack towels and other kitchen towels are folded in neat piles, and porcelain figurines and other collectibles fill the spaces in between. Keepsake Cottage is small, but charming, and makes a nice diversion on a long drive.

> **Insiders' Tip**
> Many antiques shops provide free maps that show where other shops are located. If you're a serious hunter, pick one up and keep it in your glove compartment.

a display space for the "antiques and desirables" that she sells at Many Moons. She specializes in old books and Asian antiques. Most of the antiques here will fit on a shelf, but she does have some furniture as well. We spent a few minutes contemplating a rare, triangular, blue-glass poison bottle and a porcelain Betty Boop doll. When asked how she selects her wares, Donna replied that she just buys what she likes. As a result, you'll find a lot of unique pieces from architectural details to bamboo baskets to trade beads. You can't miss her shop if you look for the green Statue of Liberty light outside the house.

*Bullwinkle the Moose overlooks the wares at Frontier Antiques in Shelton.* PHOTO: ROB MCNAIR-HUFF

**Many Moons**
**2701 Simpson Ave., Hoquiam**
**(360) 538-1809**

Donna Shine is an interesting character. Not only will you see her art on sale at a co-op in Forks, but she has also turned two rooms of her home in Hoquiam into

**Peoples Emporium Antiques**
**2200 Simpson Ave., Hoquiam**
**(360) 532-9129**

Peoples Emporium has been plying antiques to tourists and residents in Hoquiam since 1992. Inside this radio station turned antiques store you'll find an ample collection of American antiques, all collected from local residents. One corner is hung with fish creels for the angler in your life. Furniture ranges from stick chairs to primitive hutches to fashionable furniture dating from the 1920s and 1930s. You'll find plenty of old glass and curios as well as a small collection of comics and sports memorabilia. Peoples Emporium Antiques is closed on Monday and Tuesday.

## Shelton

**Frontier Antiques**
**317 1st St., Shelton**
**(360) 426-7795**

Bullwinkle, the giant moose head, greets you as you walk through the door of Frontier Antiques. From there you can browse display case upon display case filled with every sort of antique imagina-

ble: jewelry, pens, toys, tools. Every few feet another example of taxidermy hangs from the walls or is piled on a table. This store is large and as you wander deeper inside you'll find dolls, china, silver, and plenty of lighting fixtures. In fact, owners Joseph and Annette Kiser say they try to specialize in lighting fixtures. Most of the furniture is American made, but you'll find a few pieces of European furniture as well. During our visit we saw an amazingly ornate rolltop desk and an imposing chest of drawers dating from the late 1800s.

# Hood Canal

**The Daisy Pot**
**6960 WA Hwy. 106, Union**
**(360) 898-2424**

The Daisy Pot is small, but the linens, household goods, and oddities you'll find here are well worth a quick trip through it. Even though it is tiny, you won't feel cramped because it is bright and well lit. Vintage linens and antique quilts make it hard to leave empty-handed. Architectural accessories, rugs, dishes, and French country items complete the collection.

**Walker Mountain Trading Post**
**300103 U.S. Hwy. 101, Brinnon**
**(360) 796-3200**

The building that houses Walker Mountain Trading Post started its life in 1929 as a restaurant and tavern. It was heated by a woodstove then just as it is today, and you'll find antiques from that era displayed on the shelves surrounding the stove. A former storage space is filled with old glass jars and bottles, including a castor oil bottle that still contains castor oil. A small room holds tools once used by the loggers and lumber workers of the region. Yet another room is filled with linens and kitchenwares. The walls are hung with pictures, wall hangings, and some truly antique tapestries and samplers. Walker Mountain Trading Post has been a family-run business for more than 20 years. Hazel Munday, the proprietor, took over the business from her aunt, who sold antiques here for 15 years. The rustic atmosphere makes a perfect backdrop for the rustic antiques in the collection.

## Insiders' Tip

Most of the antiques stores listed here buy antiques and will offer free appraisals.

*The marina at Port Townsend makes a great place to test the sea-worthiness of a model boat.* PHOTO: NATALIE McNAIR-HUFF

# Kidstuff

Kids will find plenty to do on the Olympic Peninsula. You can rent kayaks, boats, and mountain bikes to explore the mountains and the bays. If you're adventurous you can dig around in the tide pools—maybe you'll discover a new type of limpet—or hike in the Olympic National Park with llamas.

In town you can sleep in a castle, eat gigantic apple pancakes, or order a custom-made ice-cream sundae. You can try to run your friends off the track with bumper boats or beat them at miniature golf. For some high-flying fun you can send a kite to the skies. You'll also find quite a few history museums, including The Makah Cultural and Research Center in Neah Bay, which contains one of the world's most unique collections of Native American artifacts. You can walk to the edge of the continent at Cape Flattery, or see ancient petroglyphs by walking around the Ozette Loop.

This chapter covers the Peninsula from A to Z with a list of kid-friendly activities. These are just a sampling of the area's opportunities for family fun. Read the Annual Events, Activities, and Outdoor Recreation chapters for more ideas.

## A is for Apple Pancake

Kids (and adults) can eat breakfast all day at the Oak Table (292 W. Bell St.) in Sequim. The giant Apple Pancake—a baked pancake filled with apples and glazed with brown sugar and cinnamon—is gargantuan. Few adults and fewer children could eat the whole thing. Other breakfast favorites are featured as well. More great, kid-friendly breakfast spots include Port Townsend's Salal Cafe (634 Water St.), The Home Port Restaurant in Ocean Shores (857 Point Brown Ave. N.W.), and Chestnut Cottage Restaurant in Port Angeles (929 E. Front St.).

## B is for Bumper Boats

Head to Ocean Shores for a weekend's worth of family activities including miniature golf, bumper cars, bumper boats, bumper golf, go-carts, and arcade games. BJ's Family Fun Center (752 Point Brown Ave.) offers go-carts, bumper cars, bumper boats, and water wars. Pacific Paradise (767 Minard Ave.) has an elaborate 36-hole miniature golf course and a video arcade and amusement center.

## C is for Castles

Did you know you could sleep in a castle? The Olympic Peninsula features several castles, and at least one is rumored to be haunted. In Port Townsend, the Manresa Castle (7th & Sheridan Sts., Port Townsend) serves as a hotel and restaurant. The castle was built by a local business owner, Charles Eisenbeis, as a wedding present for his wife.

**Washington State Trivia:**

The state tree is the western hemlock.

The state bird is the goldfinch.

The state's nickname is "The Evergreen State."

The state flower is the coast rhododendron.

A ghost is said to inhabit one of the gabled rooms on the third floor. Visit for dinner or Sunday brunch and take a tour to look at the collection of historical pictures and the fine woodwork. Also in Port Townsend, Fort Worden's Alexander Castle (220 Battery Way) was built in 1888 as another wedding gift. Hoquiam sports another castle: the Hoquiam Castle (515 Chenault Ave.). At one point, the town's children claimed the then-vacant house was also haunted. Today it is a bed and breakfast inn, and the owners offer daily public tours between 11 A.M. and 3 P.M. The tour costs approximately $4 for adults and $2.50 for seniors and children ages 5 through 11.

## D is for Dungeness

You can eat Dungeness crab for dinner. You can walk to the Dungeness Spit to take a tour of the lighthouse. And, you can fish along the Dungeness River or eat a picnic lunch at Railroad Bridge Park on the shores of the river.

## E is for Eagles

Bald eagles love the Peninsula so much that they never leave. You'll see them along rivers and on the coast, where the hunting is easy and nesting spots are plentiful. The Peninsula is on the Pacific Flyway so you'll have ample opportunity to see plenty of other birds as well. A few prime bird-viewing locations include Cape Flattery near Neah Bay, Fort Flagler, the Dungeness Spit, and Grays Harbor National Wildlife Refuge. It's fun to try to see how many different bird species you can count in one place.

## F is for Flying Kites

Go fly a kite. You'll find plenty of parks and beaches just right for kite flying. Some of our favorite spots include the beaches at Fort Worden, Ocean Shores, and Kalaloch, and the playfield at Salt Creek. Don't worry if you didn't bring a kite along, nearly every city has at least one store that sells kites.

## G is for Giant Trees

Giant trees, some as wide as 12 feet and nearly 300-feet high, used to cover the lower reaches of the Peninsula. These trees clothed and housed the people of the Native tribes, and later they attracted loggers and lumber barons to the area. The hunger for wood fueled a logging frenzy that resulted in a drastic reduction in the number or old-growth trees left standing, but a few record trees still stand on the Peninsula. To learn more about the trees, visit the Olympic Park Field Guide online (www.northolympic.com/onp/recordtrees.html) or talk to a park ranger. A visit to the Forks Timber Museum (1421 S. Forks Ave. (U.S. Hwy. 101) will let you see how the trees were logged.

## H is for Hoh Rainforest

Ancient, old-growth trees dripping with green moss and an understory, thick with more moss and millions of ferns, is what most people think of when they imagine a rain forest. To see such a setting, travel up the Hoh River to the Hoh Rainforest in the Olympic National Park. Several easy-to-hike interpretive trails will let you see one of the world's unique forests. During the summer, park rangers lead educational activities. One of the most impressive sites in the forest is the Hall of Mosses, which you can see on an easy walk of less than a mile.

# I is for Ice Cream

Elevated Ice Cream in Port Townsend (631 Water St.) is a popular stop for kids, small and big, no matter what the weather. The shop makes its own ice cream, Italian ices, and candies. You can even get a real, old-fashioned ice-cream soda because they make their own soda syrups, too. No trip to Port Townsend is complete without a trip to this busy shop, especially on a hot summer evening.

**Insiders' Tip**

Drink your water! It's especially important that children drink plenty of water while hiking or playing on the beach in the sun. Keep that water bottle full.

# J is for Journey Through Time

Learn more about the history of the Peninsula and the people who live here when you visit the many history museums. Nearly every city on the Peninsula has at least one history museum. We especially like the Polson Museum in Hoquiam (1611 Riverside Ave.) for its impressive collection of artifacts, pictures, and documents that take up 17 rooms in a 26-room mansion.

# K is for Kayak

Spend an hour or a day on the water in a kayak. Kayaking is one of the best ways to explore the shores of the Peninsula. Several companies provide guided tours along with a kayak, life jacket, and sometimes lunch or a snack. Tours can last anywhere from an hour to a day. Children can ride and paddle in a two-person kayak with a parent. In Gig Harbor call the Gig Harbor Kayak Center, (253) 851-7987 Two companies in Port Townsend offer guided tours: Kayak Port Townsend, (360) 385-6240 and PT Outdoors, (888) 754-8598. In Port Angeles call Olympic Raft & Kayak, (360) 452-1443.

# L is for Llamas

Trek into the Olympics with a pack of llamas. Strap your gear onto a llama, and you will be free to trek into the hills unencumbered. The llama pack trips make great family outings since the llamas do all the heavy work and a guide travels with you. To arrange a tour or for more information call Kit's Llamas at (253) 857-5274 or Wooley Packer Llama Company at (360) 374-2243.

# M is for Makah

The Makah Tribe is only one of the tribes on the Peninsula. Others include the S'Klallam, Suquamish, Skokomish, Quillayute, Quinault, and Hoh. The Makah Reservation is located at the end of WA Hwy. 112 encompassing Neah Bay and Cape Flattery. Each August the tribe celebrates the Makah Days with dancing, singing, canoe races, and feasting. The Makah also run an incredible museum that is the only place where you will be able to see artifacts recovered from a tribal village that was buried by deep mud more than 500 years ago. You'll see canoes, baskets, fishing gear, and a replica of a longhouse at the museum.

# N is for Navy

Aircraft carriers, cruisers, destroyers, and other naval ships are anchored in Sinclair Inlet next to the naval shipyard in Bremerton. You can get a close look at the ships by taking

# Close-up

## Raven Steals the Light

The Northwest Native tribes passed their culture and history to the next generation through stories and art. Most of the stories center on animals, spirits, and magical creatures. Raven played an important role in the stories of nearly every coastal tribe. This is a retelling of one of Raven's many adventures.

Many ages ago, long before humans walked the Earth, the world was as dark as night. Darker than night because there was no light—No sun. No moon. No stars. Not knowing any differently, nobody was concerned about the darkness until the day that Raven sat upon a rock, bored with his trickery and looking for a new adventure.

It so happened that the rock he perched upon sat by a river near the house of a chief of the gods. He heard shuffling in the house, and suddenly the house glowed eerily in the darkness. Raven thought this very strange and watched closely, but the glow disappeared. He turned his ears to the longhouse and listened as the chief bragged about his great treasure. The chief sang the story of his secret, which he guarded jealously.

Raven, much more curious than a cat or a two-year-old child, began to nose around the longhouse, and a great house it was, too. He found the house quite well made, but curiously so, as he could find no way in. While he looked around, he heard the chief's daughter leave the house—although he had no idea how she did so. As she walked to the stream to fetch water, Raven thought up a crafty plan. He hopped over to the stream and turned himself into a spruce needle. The needle floated down the stream and into the basket that the chief's daughter used to scoop the water. The sound of the cool water running down the stream made her thirsty. She took a drink from the basket and swallowed the spruce needle along with the water. Raven sat inside her while he thought about his plan, and when he was ready he transformed himself again. Soon the daughter gave birth to a black-haired boy with a sharply pointed nose and covered with feathers.

Raven's cry was raucous and loud, but the chief loved the baby more than anything and would run to play with him whenever he began to cry. As the boy grew, the grandfather would make toys for Raven and play games with him. But Raven grew bored quickly and would cry even more loudly. Still, the grandfather loved his grandson and would do anything to make him happy and stop the crying. The only thing that the chief would not do for Raven was allow him to play with the giant bentwood cedar box in the middle of the room.

Every day Raven would beg to see inside the box, and every day the chief would say no. Every day Raven would cry louder and louder and throw a fit, and every day the grandfather would create a new toy or a new game. Then one day the chief ran out of things to make and games to play. Raven begged to see inside the box. The grandfather once again said no. Raven began to cry louder than he ever had before. Raven cried so loudly that the chief thought his head would explode from the noise, and so he relented. He told Raven that he would allow him to see inside the box, but that Raven must never ever speak about its contents.

The chief took off the lid of the box. Inside was another box just like the first but smaller. And inside that was another box just like the first but even smaller. And so it went until the chief came to a tiny box. When he took off the lid, the room lit up. For the first time the chief saw how ugly his grandson was—he could never tell before since there was no light by which to see.

Raven instantly transformed himself again and plucked the smallest box from the hands of the startled chief and flew around the house. The chief was so angry that he had been tricked that he started bellowing like an elk. Raven flew out the smoke hole in the long-house, but the loud yell from the chief startled him, and he began to lose his grip on the box. As he flew, bits of light dribbled from the box and became the stars. Raven flew higher hoping to find a cedar limb where he would be safe from the chief. He found a high limb and thought he was safe, but then he heard the chief below him. He jumped and flew away, and a chunk of light fell from the box and became the moon. Raven flew higher and higher and found the highest limb he could. When he landed he looked inside the box and saw the remaining light. Raven was so happy that he sang a crowing song and danced around in triumph. But Raven was careless and forgot that the box of light did not have a lid. The light slipped from the box and fell into the sky where it became the sun. Ever since, Raven has cried over his lost light. And that is how Raven stole—and lost—the light.

There are many tales about Raven and the light, and this is mine. Others will tell you different stories, and theirs are just as true.

a harbor tour; call the Ship's Store in Port Orchard at (360) 377-8924. You can also take a tour of the USS *Turner Joy*, which is anchored off of the Bremerton boardwalk. And for more naval history, visit the Bremerton Naval Museum (130 Washington Ave.) and the Naval Undersea Museum at the Naval Undersea Warfare Center in Keyport.

# O is for Olympic National Park

Olympic National Park has three faces: the face of the mountains, the face of the rainforest, and the face of the ocean. You can camp, hike, backpack, ski, ride horses, and see wildlife in all three regions. Drive to the top of Hurricane Ridge to view the mountaintops and read about the park at the visitors center, or head to the area around Forks for a drive inland along the Hoh River to the world-famous Hoh Rainforest. To play around on the sand, drive farther south to Kalaloch and watch the waves pound the shore.

# P is for Parks

Spend a day at the park. If you go to Fort Worden you can tour museums, pet starfish, play a game of soccer, camp, hike, kayak, listen to a concert, and even spend the night. You'll find city, county, and state parks practically around every corner. Some parks, such as Salt Creek, are dedicated to marine life, while others feature slides, swings, and open fields.

# Q is for Quilcene Oysters

Kids may not like to eat oysters. After all they are kind of gooey and slimy and squishy, but they sure can be fun to harvest. You can also go clam digging for the giant geoduck (say it like gooey-duck) or the smaller razor clam. Then, of course, you may want to drop a pot for crab or simply drop a line for a couple of fish during fishing season. Children under 14 may fish without a license when accompanied by a licensed adult.

# R is for Riding Horses

Imagine galloping along the seashore on a big, chestnut-colored quarter horse with the wind in your face and the waves crashing near by. Sound like fun? You'll get your chance

*Roadside farms such as this pick-your-own pumpkin patch can be great places to stop with kids.* PHOTO: NATALIE McNAIR-HUFF

when you hit the beach at Ocean Shores. You can either walk to where the horses are tethered on the beach, or you can call Chenois Creek Horse Rentals at (360) 533-5591, Nan-Sea Stable at (360) 289-0194, or Rising Star Ranch at (360) 581-3141.

## S is for Swimming & Sandcastles

What else can you do with so much sand other than build a sandcastle, sand igloo, or maybe a sand witch. Although much of the Washington coast is rocky or cobbled, you'll still find plenty of sandy beaches. As for swimming, we generally recommend that you stick to your hotel's pool. The ocean water around here is very cold, and there are other hidden dangers as well: Riptides, sneaker waves, and undertows can pull you out to sea quickly. Even if you go wading in the ocean (brrrrr!), make sure you keep an eye on the rising tide and watch out for big waves.

## T is for Tide Pools

Splashing around in tide pools can be tons of fun, and if you're not careful, you might learn something by accident. Tide pools are nature's version of touch tanks. As the tide goes out, holes and crevices in the rocks fill with water to create magical pools where you can see shrimp, anemones, urchins, starfish, and several different seaweeds. You'll also see crab and hermit crabs, limpets, and barnacles, and if the tide is low enough you can see octopus and sea cucumbers. Most bookstores on the Peninsula can sell you a guide to tide pools. If you touch and pick up the animals, make sure you put them back in the same place and don't throw them around. That way you'll do your part to keep the sea alive, and while you're at it, you may want to take a bag along so you can pick up any litter that you see. Some of the best tide-pooling areas we've found include the Salt Creek Recreation Area off of WA 112 and Hole-in-the-Wall north of Rialto Beach near Forks. Make sure you keep an eye on the tide so that you don't get trapped on a promontory. The tide can rise quickly and cut off beach access. You can buy tide tables at most local convenience stores.

## U is for Under the Sea

When you can't make it to the tide pools, head indoors to one of the marine science centers. Each center has touch tanks, aquariums, and permanent interpretive displays. The nice thing about the marine science centers is that the trained docents will answer any questions you have about the animals and plants that you see. They can tell you exactly why that sea cucumber looks so weird when you pick it up or how an octopus changes its dots. The centers also offer interpretive walks, classes, and fun activities throughout the year. The Poulsbo Marine Science Center (18743 Front St. NE) is open seven days a week and has the complete skeleton of a young gray whale named Slick. On the pier at Fort Worden you'll find another center that has an underwater camera. The third center, the Arthur D. Feiro Marine Life Center, is on the city pier in Port Angeles and is open Tuesday through Sunday during the summer months and Saturday and Sunday during the winter. Entrance fees vary at each center but all fees are less than $5 for an adult and between $1 and $3 for children.

## V is for Violin

Eat a picnic lunch, pet some sheep, and sit on the lawn in front of an old barn while you listen to a string quartet play beautiful music. There aren't too many places in the world where you can do that! The Olympic Music Festival features classical music played by chamber orchestras and string quartets. Every summer from the middle of June to September you can attend Saturday and Sunday concerts at the barn near Quilcene on Hood Canal. Call (206) 527-8839 or visit the web site (www.musicfest.net) for a schedule and to buy tickets. In Port Townsend, Centrum also sponsors several music festivals all year long, including the Chamber Music Port Townsend concert series in February and the Festival of American Fiddle Tunes in July. Call Centrum at (800) 733-3608 or visit its Web site, www.centrum.org, for more information and to buy tickets.

## W is for Whales

Several whale species swim in the waters off of the Washington coast. Orca whales are year-round residents and can often be seen in Puget Sound or swimming in the Strait of Juan de Fuca. Gray, blue, and Minke whales as well as dolphins and porpoise migrate seasonally to their northern feeding grounds and southern breeding grounds.

> **Insiders' Tip**
> Park rangers will happily answer kids' questions about the plants and animals in the park. The park's visitors centers all have interpretive displays and sometimes feature guided tours.

If you're patient and in the right place at the right time, you may see one from the shore. But you'll have better luck if you hop on a charter boat and take a whale-watching cruise. Then, even if you don't see a whale you'll still have a fun time on the boat. Whale-watching cruises leave from Port Townsend, Port Angeles, Clallam Bay, and Neah Bay. Check the visitor information center or chamber of commerce in each town for more information.

## Insiders' Tip

How long can you hold still? Wild animals are easily startled, so if you want to see one, pick a spot and sit as still as you can for as long as possible.

## X is for X-Country Skiing

Kids love snow, and cross-country skiing is a great way to enjoy it. The easily accessible park trails and closed roads at Hurricane Ridge draw skiers from all over the Peninsula. On the weekends, rope tows and a Poma lift serve downhill skiers, and in the afternoons, free, guided snowshoe hikes depart from the visitors center. Hurricane Ridge is equally fun in the summer, when park rangers lead guided interpretive tours, and all the trails are open to hikers.

## Y is for Yawl and Yardarm

You'll see plenty of yawls and yardarms at the Wooden Boat Festival in Port Townsend in September. You can also make your own model boat and take it for a float at the festival. Wooden boats are what the explorers used when they first came to this region and wooden boats are still used by sailors and anglers. One of the largest and most important wooden boats in the area is the *Lady Washington*. Capt. Robert Gray sailed on the *Lady Washington* in 1788 when he became the first American explorer to make landfall in the region. A replica of the famous ship now calls Aberdeen home. When it's in port you can take tours, and sometimes cruises are offered as well. Call (800) 200-5239 for the schedule.

## Z is for Zebras

Children can feed the zebras and other animals at the Olympic Game Farm. More than 200 animals live at the farm, including Siberian tigers, lions, wolves, and cougar. Many of the animals have starred on the silver screen in some of Disney's most popular animal films. The game farm is open daily, and admission costs $8 and up. The game farm is located at 1423 Ward Rd., Sequim; (360) 683-4259 or (800) 778-4295. Visit the Web site at www.olygamefarm.com.

# Annual Events and Festivals

January
February
March
April
May
June
July
August
September
October
November
December

Around here we like to party, and we don't need much of an excuse. You'll find a festival or special event nearly every weekend of the year. Some are one-time events, while others have been held annually for more than 50 years. If you want to experience the friendly atmosphere of the Northwest, attend any of the annual events and festivals highlighted in this chapter. Many are free in whole or in part.

Some festivals such as Sequim's Irrigation Festival and Poulsbo's Viking Fest celebrate local heritage and history. Makah Days, Quileute Days, and Chief Seattle Days are tribal celebrations where local tribes gather to honor their cultures. These festivals are fun as well as educational. Other events celebrate the natural world. Bird lovers will especially appreciate the Grays Harbor Shorebird Festival. Gardeners and flower fanatics will want to attend Port Townsend's Rhododendron Festival or the Lavender Festival in Sequim.

Of course, coastal areas are famous for wind and sand, and both of these natural elements are celebrated with kite festivals and sand sculpture contests. For the ultimate in zaniness, make sure you check out the Kinetic Skulpture Race in Port Townsend or the Seagull Calling Festival in Port Orchard. You'll find great food offered at most of these events, and some feature the freshest seafood you'll ever find unless you catch it yourself.

We have tried to list these events within each month according to when in the month they take place. Take note however, that sometimes these events are rescheduled, canceled, or otherwise modified. We recommend that you call before attending to check on where and when these events take place. If a number is not provided for a specific event, call the city's chamber of commerce. Music, art, and literary events are listed in the Arts chapter, and we definitely recommend that you put some of them on your itinerary.

## January

**Sun Lover's Indoor Beach Bash**
**Ocean Shores**

We don't often see the sun around here during the winter months, but the residents of Ocean Shores don't let that stop them from having fun in the sun in January. Join them for a beach party at the convention center, where you can eat snow cones and hot dogs as well as other summertime foods. Family activities and kite flying add to the festivities.

### Insiders' Tip

Events and festivals are added every year. Call the chambers of commerce for up-to-date schedules. See the Attractions chapter for a list of chambers of commerce and visitor information center phone numbers.

# February

**Native New Year Celebration**
**Suquamish**
**(360) 394-5266**

The Suquamish Tribe makes its home on the northeastern tip of the Kitsap Peninsula. Join tribal members near the beginning of February as they celebrate the new year. The celebration includes a salmon dinner, a Native dance presentation, and storytelling.

## Insiders' Tip

Carry plenty of cash if you plan on eating at one of these events. Although some arts-and-crafts vendors will take checks, the admission gates and food vendors won't.

# March

**Victorian Festival**
**Port Townsend**
**(888) 698-1116**
**www.VictorianFestival.org**

Port Townsend is well known for its Victorian architecture, but during the third week of March, the whole town dresses up in Victoriana. During the festival, many city residents wear period costumes and many Victorian inns and homes are opened for tours and teas. A Victorian costume ball is preceded by antiques shows, art shows, plays, lectures, and odd contests such as the mustache and beard contest. Workshops on home restoration and Victorian crafts and hobbies such as soap and candle making, woodworking, and gardening are also held. Admission fees and venues vary. Some events are free. If you plan on staying in Port Townsend during the festival, we suggest you make your reservations early.

# April

**RainFest**
**Forks**
**www.forks-web.com/rainfest**

Around here, the rain is as good an excuse for a party as anything else, especially in Forks—the city often receives more than 140 inches of rain each year. By the time spring rolls around, the city residents are ready for some fun. Local artists give demonstrations in basket making, spinning, weaving, chainsaw carving, and other art forms. Children can make a splash by making their own crafty creations, or they can attend a Kiddy Carnival at Tillicum Park. Musical and dance presentations round out the festival events.

# May

**Farmers' Markets**
**Most Peninsula cities**

Weekend Farmers' Markets are held in most of the Peninsula cities from May through October. You'll find locally grown produce, arts and crafts, and baked goods all sold by friendly vendors. Call the chambers of commerce for more information.

**Festival of Colors**
**Ocean Shores**

Three days of beachcombing, live entertainment, and family fun mark this springtime celebration during the first weekend in May. Head to the convention center for an arts and crafts fair, or stick to the beach for kite flying and other recreational activities.

### Sea Gull Calling Festival
### Port Orchard

This festival gives people permission to act like a cuckoo, and maybe a little crazy. The point of this festival is to celebrate the ubiquitous seagull. Of course, it also celebrates community and the arrival of warmer, drier weather. The festival takes place on the first weekend in May, and individuals and families gather on the shore and compete to see who can "call" the most seagulls. All techniques are fair game from unique "seagull dances" to secret calls to baiting with bread and sardines. The festival champ is the seagull caller who is able to attract the most seagulls to her spot on the beach.

### Grays Harbor Shorebird Festival
### Hoquiam
### (360) 495-3289, (800) 321-1924
### www.audubon.org/chapter/wa/ghas/
### bowerm.html

Every year the songbirds and birds of prey migrate from South America to the Northern Hemisphere. During the long journey, the birds make pit stops along the coast. One of the best places to see them is at Bowerman Basin and other spots around the Grays Harbor estuary. Join other bird lovers, the Audubon Society, and U.S. Fish and Wildlife rangers for lectures and special presentations, and field trips. Bring good walking shoes, your binoculars, a bird guide, and your birding-life list. You're sure to see something special during this festival, which takes place in early May.

### Irrigation Festival
### Sequim
### (360) 683-5774, (800) 500-8401
### www.visitsun.com/waterfest

When white settlers first moved into the Sequim-Dungeness valley, it was so dry that crops would not grow with the small amount of rain afforded in the rain shadow. The settlers dug irrigation ditches running from the Dungeness River to the growing fields. The residents of Sequim celebrate that accomplishment with this festival, which takes place during the first full week in May. Arts-and-crafts and garden shows; luncheons; logger competitions; plays; carnivals; and fun, kid-friendly activities mark the week long festival.

### Rhododendron Festival
### Port Townsend
### www.ptguide.com/rhodyfest

The beautiful, colorful, and varied rhododendron is Washington's much-loved state flower, and it grows all over the place on the Olympic Peninsula. Port Townsend's homage to the blossom, also affectionately known as the rhody, takes the form of this fun-filled, week long festival during the third week in May. Port Townsend residents have been celebrating the flower for more than 65 years. The newly-crowned Rhododendron Queen presides over the festivities, which include an arts-and-craft fair, several parades and kooky races such as the bed race, a golf tournament, and a road race. Of course, the rhody flower show is included as well. Events take place at several locations throughout the city.

### Chainsaw Carving Contest
### Ocean Shores

Most people think chainsaws are only used for cutting down trees, but these artists know how to use a chainsaw like a painter uses a paintbrush. The carvings created during this three-day contest blow the ubiquitous little bear carvings out of the water. You'll see impressive whale and dolphin sculptures, delicate mermaids, and more, all made from a few huge chunks of wood, chainsaws and other power tools, and a bit of varnish.

### Armed Forces Festival
### Bremerton
### www.bremertonchamber.org/
### AFFcalendar.htm

The Bremerton Chamber of Commerce claims that the Armed Forces Parade, which is part of this festival, is the largest in the country. Kitsap County is home to five Naval facilities, and the people who work at them come out in droves at this festival, which was first celebrated in 1948. Visit the Naval Station open house or tour the Naval Museum, history museum, and the USS *Turner Joy*. See Navy equipment displays, a vintage car show, or local bands performing on the boardwalk. The festival takes place over the third weekend in May. Events take place on the boardwalk and other venues in downtown Bremerton. Many activities are free to the public, but some venues charge admission.

**Viking Fest**
**Poulsbo**
**(360) 779-3378**

Celebrate Poulsbo's Norwegian heritage at the Viking Fest. Tour the medieval Viking village, ride carnival rides, listen to live music, and shop at the arts-and-crafts booths. Of course, no festival is complete without food, and here you can try authentic Norwegian delicacies such as pickled herring, lutefisk, lefse, and sugared rosettes. A parade, complete with villagers in authentic costumes, trails through town on Saturday. The festival takes place over three days during the third weekend in May.

# June

**Maritime Gig Festival**
**Gig Harbor**

Join the residents of Gig Harbor for this family-oriented festival that takes place the first full weekend in June. The festival celebrates the fishing heritage of this maritime village. In addition to arts-and-crafts vendors, a parade, and children's activities, the bay fills with boats for the blessing of the fleet.

**International Kite Challenge**
**Ocean Shores**

During this three-day festival, the sky will be dotted with bright, colorful banners, samurai heads, elaborate birds, and darting arrows. The gently sloped and sandy beach at Ocean Shores is the perfect spot for kite flying, and this is one of the state's largest kite festivals. Bring or buy your own kite or just enjoy the pros as they make their kites dive, circle, and dip during the stunt kite competition. If your kite simply refuses to take flight, you can even get free kite flying lessons.

**Fathoms O' Fun Festival**
**Port Orchard**

Join the residents of Port Orchard for this family-friendly celebration of summer. On the third weekend in June, Port Orchard takes on a carnival atmosphere complete with old-fashioned frog-jump contests for the kids, a baseball tournament, a parade, and food and crafts vendors.

**Forest Festival**
**Shelton**

Timber made Shelton what it is. This festival celebrates loggers and logging culture with a parade and a street fair where food and arts-and-crafts vendors will tempt you with their goods. The centerpiece of the festival features a logging show where the skills of old are displayed by the pros. You'll see ax throwing, tree climbing, and more.

**Skandia Midsommerfest**
**Raab Park, Poulsbo**

The Skandia Folkdance Society of Seattle sponsors this mid summer festival, which takes place near the weekend after the summer solstice. An afternoon parade, with participants dressed in authentic Scandinavian costumes, precedes a Midsommer Pole raising. Scandinavian dancing and music are featured at several performances on different stages. Visitors are invited to join in the dancing, of course. Admission for adults costs $5, and children under 18 get in free.

### Sand Sculpture Festival
### Ocean Shores

Be prepared to be impressed during this three-day festival that takes place at the end of June. These sand sculptures are much more elaborate and artistic than the average sand castle. Master sand sculptors build their masterpieces next to amateurs and families. Sculptures range from detailed, fairy-tale castles to frightening alligators and dragons to the occasional hog on a Harley. Look quick because with the high tide these creations will be history.

> ## Insiders' Tip
> Our weather is rather mercurial, so no matter which of these festivals you attend, you should plan on bringing an umbrella as well as the sunblock.

# July

### 4th of July
### Various cities

Nearly every city and village on the Peninsula has a 4th of July celebration with a street fair, live music, and fireworks. Just head to the waterfront or the main street of whichever town you are in to celebrate independence and the pioneering spirit.

### Lavender Festival
### Sequim
### www.lavenderfestival.com

Crush a lavender bud between your fingers and you'll be transported to olfactory heaven. For more than five years, people in Sequim have been celebrating this fragrant and versatile Mediterranean herb during the third weekend in July. Walk or drive through the valley to tour the lavender farms where you can buy gifts made with lavender and other herbs. You can even take a few plants home to your garden. Attendees can also attend demonstrations on growing and using lavender. A street fair rounds out the festivities with an open-air market and family-friendly activities.

### Quileute Days
### La Push

The Quileute Tribe holds an annual heritage festival each year on the third weekend in July. Traditional crafts, foods, singing, and dancing take center stage. Sports tournaments and arts-and-crafts vendors add to the festive atmosphere.

### River Festival
### Hoquiam

During the third weekend in July, the residents of Hoquiam hold a street fair to honor the Hoquiam River and the people who live and work along it. Food and craft vendors set up booths while musicians keep the crowd dancing. The Coast Guard even joins the fun by staging a river rescue.

### Whaling Days
### Silverdale
### (360) 692-1107

Head to the east shore of the Kitsap Peninsula to join Silverdale as it celebrates summer fun. Limited hydroplane races, a duck race, a road race, and a destruction derby are included in the highlights. A street fair provides more sedate entertainment with musicians, dancers, and arts-and-crafts booths. Food aplenty can also be found among the vendor booths. The celebration takes place during the last weekend in July, so good weather is practically guaranteed.

### Feast of Forks & Forks Fly-In
### Forks

No, this isn't a challenge to eat forks. Instead it's a celebration of community in

Forks. Vendors and food booths take over downtown. Live music and dancing keeps everyone moving. Kids' activities such as a carnival and a petting zoo keep children entertained. A free bus shuttle takes visitors to the airport to see the planes that have arrived as part of the Fly-In. A salmon dinner served by the Lions Club highlights Saturday afternoon as the center mark of this three-day, end-of-July festival.

# August

### County Fair Season
### Various cities

Yep, it's time for an old-fashioned county fair complete with giant pumpkin contests, bake-offs, canning and gardening demonstrations, quilting contests, and all that good stuff. Kids will have fun at the petting zoos or riding carnival rides, and you can even lose good money at the carney game booths. The Mason County Fair in Shelton is held the last week in July. The Jefferson County Fair takes place during the second weekend in August. The Clallam County Fair in Port Angeles and the Kitsap County Fair in Bremerton take place during the third week in August.

### Pioneer Days
### Key Peninsula Civic Center
### 17010 Vaughn Rd., Vaughn
### (360) 884-3456

Family fun is promised during the Key Peninsula Pioneer Days, which take place on the first full weekend in August. Before the festival the fish pond is stocked with fish just ripe for the catching from poles held in little hands. Ven-

*From May through October many towns on the Olympic Peninsula host farmers' markets, such as this one offering lavender in Sequim.* PHOTO ROB McNAIR-HUFF

dors sell crafts, plants, and snacks. Bands entertain the festival goers while they sit in the beer garden or line up for the parade.

### Gig Harbor Renaissance Fair
### 10215 SR 302, Gig Harbor
### (800) 359-5948

Grab your lances and your swords, cinch your corsets, don your caps, and head to the Renaissance Fair to peruse the period wares made by master crafters. You'll find wall hangings, textiles, medieval garb, beeswax and hand-dipped candles, and many delectable edibles. After you've wandered the market, take a break and watch while some of the 300 performers entertain you. You'll see medieval jousting and sword fights, minstrels, jugglers, storytellers, and maybe even a joker or two. The fair takes place on Saturday and Sunday during the first two weekends in August.

### "The Cruz" Custom Car Show
### Port Orchard

If you're feeling nostalgic for the cars of yesteryear, then look no more. Each August, Port Orchard turns into one giant vintage car lot. More than 700 hot rods and custom cars are on display, and a street fair takes over the main street.

### Joe Kuhn Clambake & Uptown Fair
### Uptown Port Orchard
### www.ptguide.com/mainstreet/clambake

Joe Kuhn, a one-time mayor of Port Townsend, started the tradition of an annual clambake. Today, the community gathers on the lawn of the community center during the Uptown Fair. Clams by the bucketful are baked, steamed, and slurped by the hungry hordes on a mid-August Saturday. Tickets for the clambake cost approximately $8.50 for adults and $5 for children 12 and under. After you've had your fill of clams, adjourn to the beer garden, browse the arts-and-crafts booths and sidewalk art, or take a hay ride. In the evening, join movie fans at Memorial Stadium for an outdoor movie.

### Chief Seattle Days
### Suquamish
### (360) 394-5241

Chief Sealth—the chief for whom Seattle was named—was a member of the Suquamish Tribe, and he is buried at Suquamish, where the tribe holds this yearly festival to honor him. A powwow, war canoe races, and authentic salmon bake mark the day. Visitors will also be treated to a Native arts-and-crafts fair as well as singing and traditional dancing. Admission is free.

### Makah Days
### Neah Bay
### www.makah.com/days.htm

Experience a bit of the Northwest Native lifestyle at Makah Days. Visitors will be treated to traditional dancing and singing performed by the villagers. Dug-out canoe races display the skills needed on the high seas during the whale hunt. You'll find cedar-bark baskets, hats, weavings, beadwork, and other crafts from the vendors. When you're hungry you can eat salmon staked and cooked next to a traditional, open-pit cedar fire. The two-day festival, which takes place on the last full weekend in August, promises to be a fun cultural experience. If you want to learn more about the tribe's history, make sure you visit the Makah Cultural Center, and later hike the trail to Cape Flattery.

### Insiders' Tip

The festivals in Port Townsend, especially the Wooden Boat Festival, attract thousands of visitors. Make your reservations well in advance if you want to stay in town.

*Most annual events include entertainment such as this marimba band playing in Port Townsend.* PHOTO: NATALIE McNAIR-HUFF

# September

### Blackberry Festival
### Bremerton
### (360) 377-3041
### www.blackberryfestival.org

Blackberries grow prolifically around here, and this end-of-summer festival celebrates the sweet, juicy, and popular fruit with a vendor fair, outdoor cinema, and a carnival. Sample blackberries in the form of wine, beer, jelly, jam, cobbler, cider, pie—whatever you can imagine. Work all those berries off in the fun run, or for a more leisurely interlude, listen to local bands playing on various stages. The Blackberry Festival takes place on the Saturday and Sunday of Labor Day weekend and coincides with the Bremerton Fly-In and the Tour de Kitsap bike ride. Most events take place at the park next to the ferry terminal.

### Arts & Crafts Show
### Ocean Shores

The Ocean Shores Convention Center will be stuffed to brimming with arts-and-crafts booths during this three-day show, which is billed as the largest in Southwest Washington. Admission to the show is free, but with so many vendors and artists, you likely won't make it out of the building without buying something.

### Logger's Play Day
### Hoquiam

Hoquiam is a timber town. In fact, the city's name means "hungry for wood." This festival, held the first Saturday after Labor Day, celebrates the logger heritage of the city. A large parade of floats and logging trucks winds through town to cheers and waves. In the afternoon loggers compete in log rolling contests and other events such as ax throwing, tree climbing, speed sawing, and chopping.

### Mosquito Fleet Maritime Festival
### Port Orchard

No, this festival isn't in honor of the blood-sucking insect. It's in honor of the fleet of ferries that used to connect all the towns of Puget Sound. Learn about the history of the fleet through museum displays, cruises, and harbor tours. Steam donkeys and tractors share the stage with touch tanks for the kids.

### Wooden Boat Festival
### Port Townsend
### (360) 385-3628
### www.woodenboat.org/festival

Hundreds of wooden boats, old and new, and thousands of boating enthusiasts converge on Port Townsend for three days during the second weekend in September. The foundation presents special programs and lectures on such topics as navigation, carving, rigging, maintenance, and more. Vendors ply marine equipment, wooden canoes, kayaks, and all things nautical. Several cruises are offered, and regattas and boat parades draw all eyes to the bay. Live music and an arts-and-crafts fair entice the crowds from the festival grounds to downtown. Tickets for the festival cost around $10 for a one-day pass and around $20 for a three-day pass. Children and seniors receive a discount. We suggest you park at the park-and-ride near Safeway and ride the free shuttle to the Point Hudson Marina rather than struggling with the traffic and crowds.

### Sea Kayak Festival
### Fort Worden, Port Townsend
### (262) 242-5228
### www.gopaddle.org

This is the festival for you if you're into kayaking, whether you're a beginning kayaker, or an experienced veteran who long ago mastered the Eskimo roll, or if you're in the market for a new kayak.

Sponsored by the Trade Association of Paddlesports and billed as the largest sea kayak symposium in the world, the festival draws people from all over the world. More than 80 classes cover such topics as self-rescues, stroke technique, and expedition planning. Outfitters and manufacturers sell everything from single and two-person kayaks and canoes to outerwear to survival gear.

### Historic Homes Tour
### Port Townsend
### (360) 385-2722
### www.ptguide.com/homestour

If you want to see inside some of Port Townsend's majestic Victorian homes, this is your chance. The Jefferson General Hospital Auxiliary sponsors the tour, which is held during a mid-September weekend. The tour is self-guided via a tour map and may be completed in one day, although touring over two days allows for

*Wooden boats of the Wooden Boat Festival in Port Townsend.* PHOTO: NATALIE-McNAIR-HUFF

*Kayakers from across the United States and around the world visit Port Townsend each September for the annual West Coast Sea Kayak Symposium.* PHOTO: ROB McNAIR-HUFF

a more leisurely pace. Private homes are included on the tour, and some homeowners will provide booties for you to place over your shoes to protect the floors and carpets. Tickets for the tours cost around $15 for adults and $7 for children if bought on the day of the event; a discount is offered for advanced purchase.

### Septemberfest
### Poulsbo
### (360) 779-3378

Join the community of Poulsbo for this celebration. Septemberfest takes place on the third weekend in September, and starts off with Prom Night (adults only) on Friday night. Kayak races, a children's talent show, live entertainment, and a beer and wine garden complete the activities. Of course, vendors fill many booths with arts, crafts, and edible goodies.

### The Big Hurt
### Port Angeles
### (800) 942-4042

It's not called the Big Hurt because it's easy. The Big Hurt is a grueling race that starts with 17 miles of mountain biking, followed by a 5 mile kayak course, 40 miles of road biking, and it ends with a 10K run. Are you tough enough? If so, join the challenge. Participants are treated to a high-carb spaghetti dinner the night before the race.

### Port Townsend Film Festival
### Port Townsend
### (800) 359-4202
### www.ptfilmfest.com

International independent films are the focus for this festival. Three days of screenings, day and night on several screens, may wear out even the most diehard movie fan, but we doubt it. If you're not sitting in a theater, you might be sitting in a lecture hall or eating and dancing at one of the evening events offered so that attendees may meet some of the actors and directors. The first festival featured actor Tony Curtis and the host of Turner Classic Movies, Robert Osbourne. Call or visit the Web site to buy a festival pass. Single-event tickets will also be available during the festival.

**Dungeness River Festival**
**Sequim**
**www.dungenessrivercenter.org**
Head to Railroad Bridge Park on the Dungeness River for a weekend filled with folk music, dancing, stories, native plant walks, and educational programs. The family-friendly festival teaches visitors about the watershed ecology and natural treasures of the region.

# October

**Hickory Shirt & Heritage Days**
**Forks**
**www.forks-web.com/heritagedays.htm**
This week long festival recalls the pioneer days around Forks when the trees were so thick that the sun barely peeked through. Each night of the week, stories of the pioneering days are shared at dinners and lectures so that the rich oral history of the region will be passed to the next generation. Don't be surprised to hear a tall tale or two. The week ends with the Fish and Brew Tasting Contest and the Shipwreck Symposium.

**Oysterfest**
**Shelton**
Head to the Mason County Fairgrounds during the first weekend in October to get your fill of oysters and seafood. The West Coast Oyster Shucking Competition also takes place during the festival. The winner of the competition will compete at the national contest in Maryland. The festival also includes a seafood cook-off and an art contest. A beer garden, wine tasting, and live music will entertain you as you eat and browse the booths.

**Kinetic Skulpture Race**
**Port Townsend**
**www.kineticrace.org**
This may very well be the strangest and wackiest event in the nation. It's a race to be mediocre, since the winner is the person who ends the race in the middle of the pack; cheating is de rigueur. Each entrant or team must contrive a vehicle that will travel on ground, water, and deep mud. The vehicle must be human-powered. A zany costume helps, although we're not quite sure how. Friday and Saturday nights are celebrated with more inanity at the Rose Hip Queen competition and coronation, where bribing the judges is perfectly acceptable and expected. Beware the Kinetic Kops who are wont to hand out tickets when the rules are broken by race participants and spectators—and believe us, the rules are easily broken by the breathing. As one resident said of the race weekend, "It's as if somebody dropped a circus in town."

**Pumpkin Festival**
**Port Orchard**
Getting ready for Halloween is even more fun when you attend the Pumpkin Festival in Port Orchard. Carving benches with free pumpkins are set out for the kids, and a pumpkin carving contest gives the adults something to do, too. A free, indoor carnival for children under 12 is held at the community center.

# November

**Dixieland Jazz Festival**
**Ocean Shores**
Five venues around the city play host to Dixieland bands from around the nation. Admission to the concerts is charged, but a free shuttle bus transports attendees between the venues and the hotels. The festival takes place during the first weekend in November.

# December

### Yule Fest
### 18891 Front St. NE, Poulsbo

The Sons of Norway sponsor this traditional celebration over the first weekend in December. The festival opens with a Christmas bazaar complete with a Norwegian Smorgasbord that includes authentic ethnic dishes such as lefse, krumkake, cheese boards, and herring. Vikings escort the Lucia Bride, the bringer of light, into the hall before the lighting of the Yule log closes the evening.

### Gig Harbor Lights Festival
### Gig Harbor

Are you ready for the holidays? This is how Gig Harbor gets ready with a tree lighting, a lighted boat parade, and a holiday lights display contest. Of course, the white-bearded old man makes an appearance as well.

### Santa Boat Parade
### Port Orchard

Santa comes by boat around here, and if Mom and Dad call ahead, Santa will even stop his boat on the parade route to call the children out by name for a special "Ho-ho-ho." The Port Orchard Yacht Club sponsors the parade, which starts near Southworth and travels the shoreline to the Port Orchard marina. At the marina, the Sinclair Inlet Yacht Club creates a Nautical Christmas Lane with all the boats tied up and decorated in lights.

# Outdoor Recreation

Outdoor activities dominate the fair-weather season on the Olympic Peninsula. Thousands of campsites call out to campers, miles of shoreline and open water invite boaters, and countless miles of trails draw hikers out into the heart of the forest.

In this chapter we present an overview of the outdoor amenities and attractions on the Peninsula. Keep in mind that many of these campgrounds, parks, and trails get very busy on sunny weekends, and in the heart of the summer it is wise to plan ahead and make reservations for as many of your planned activities as possible. To avoid the crowds, consider visiting the Peninsula outdoors in the late fall or early spring. Many times the weather will cooperate and offer a great, less-crowded experience. The other option is to head into the outdoors during the weekdays rather than on weekends.

## State Parks

Washington State Parks has a number of campsites and picnic areas on the Olympic Peninsula. Here we take a look at the state park offerings in each area covered by this book. To reserve a campsite, be sure to plan ahead and make a reservation using the Reservations Northwest telephone system by calling (800) 452-5687. You can also check the Washington State Parks information number at (800) 233-0321, or check the Web site at www.parks.wa.gov.

## Parks

### Gig Harbor

**Kopachuck State Park**
**www.parks.wa.gov/kopachck.htm**

This 109-acre park offers 41 standard campsites, 79 picnic sites, 5 kitchen shelters, and 1,500 feet of unguarded beach on Henderson Bay. Trailers no larger than 35 feet can use the park, which also offers trailer dump facilities. The park has trails with views of Henderson Bay and the Olympic Mountains, in addition to an underwater marine park for divers.

### Port Orchard

**Manchester State Park**
**www.parks.wa.gov/manchstr.htm**

Formerly a U.S. Coast Artillery Harbor Defense installation, this 111-acre park offers a 53-unit campground with two comfort stations, two small picnic shelters, and a group day-use area that can be reserved for up to 150 people. Of special interest in this park is the turn-of-the-century Torpedo Warehouse, a large brick building with arched doorways and windows. The park also holds a primitive campsite that is part of the Cascadia Marine Trail.

## North Kitsap

### Illahee State Park
www.parks.wa.gov/illahee.htm

Do some saltwater fishing off the dock or use one of the 88 picnic areas in this park near Bremerton. The 74-acre park also offers 25 camping sites, a dock with 4 floats, 5 mooring buoys, and parking for 155 cars. Illahee State Park is popular with boaters, hikers, and those interested in oyster harvesting and clamming.

### Kitsap Memorial State Park
www.parks.wa.gov/kitsapm.htm

Just three miles south of the Hood Canal Bridge, Kitsap Memorial State Park is a 57-acre property offering saltwater frontage, 25 standard campsites, 18 campsites with electrical and water hookups, and 3 primitive sites for hikers or cyclists. The park also has 51 picnic sites, one mooring buoy, and more than a mile of trails.

### Scenic Beach State Park
www.parks.wa.gov/scenicb.htm

Located just a mile south of Seabeck on Hood Canal, this 88-acre park features a natural forested area with views of the Olympic Mountains along with a camping area for 52 tents or trailers, 75 picnic sites, and parking space for 75 cars. Besides the scenery that gives the park its name, Scenic Beach State Park is also known as a popular spot for fishing and oyster gathering.

## Port Townsend

### Anderson Lake State Park
www.parks.wa.gov/anderson.htm

Eight miles south of Port Townsend off WA Highway 113, this 410-acre park offers more than 8,000 feet of shoreline on Anderson Lake along with a boat launch, toilet, and one picnic site. The park also holds 4.4 miles of trails.

### Fort Flagler State Park
10541 Flagler Rd., Nordland
(360) 385-3701, (360) 902-8600
www.parks.wa.gov/ftflaglr.htm

Once part of the triad of forts that protected the shipping channels into Puget Sound, Fort Flagler State Park is a 783-acre park at the north end of Marrowstone Island, across the bay from Port Townsend. It offers 102 campsites, 14 utility sites, and 2 group sites, in addition to 4 primitive sites for cyclists. Fort Flagler also has 59 picnic sites, 256 feet of moorage space at moorage floats, and 7 moorage buoys. The major draw at this former military installation is four miles of hiking trails that lead to five gun emplacements that are open to the public. An American Youth Hostel is also located within the park.

Fort Flagler also holds the Fort Flagler State Park Environmental Learning Center and a series of vacation houses.

### Fort Worden State Park
www.parks.wa.gov/ftworden.htm

Another of the former military bases that once held guns and lookouts whose mission it was to keep enemy ships from the main shipping channel into Puget Sound, Fort Worden State Park is bordered on two sides by the waters of Admiralty Inlet to the east and the Strait of Juan de Fuca to the north. Fort Worden encompasses 433 acres, including 80 trailer camping sites, 3 primitive campsites, and 60 picnic sites. But camping is just part of the offerings at Fort Worden. It is also home to three dormitories, a youth hostel, a dock, two mooring floats, nine mooring bouys, and a marine interpretive center. Another 25 vacation homes that were originally built as officers' quarters are also available for rent.

Like Fort Flagler to the southeast, Fort Worden holds remnants of its military past, including 12 gun emplacements ready for exploration and the remains of lookout towers in some of the trees. Even the restored Balloon Hangar is put to use, holding concerts in a 1,400-seat audito-

*Hikers set out on one of the many trails through Olympic National Park.* PHOTO: NATIONAL PARK SERVICE

rium at events such as Jazz Port Townsend.

### Mystery Bay State Park
**www.parks.wa.gov/mystery.htm**

This small 10-acre park on the west side of Marrowstone Island offers four picnic sites, a dock, seven moorage buoys, and a boat launch ramp. The park is situated on a bay that gets its name from the Prohibition era, when smugglers would hide from the Coast Guard along the wooded shorelines to avoid detection. Moorage and launch fees are collected at the park year round.

### Old Fort Townsend State Park
**www.parks.wa.gov/oldftwns.htm**

Open from 6:30 A.M. to dusk each day from the second weekend of April until the third weekend in September, this former U.S. Army fort has 40 campsites, each with a table and fireplace. Several hiking trails run through the park, which is also home to an interpretive-history walk that begins at a large display board near the front of the park. Larger groups can also reserve a large kitchen shelter, or a large camping area for overnight use.

### Rothschild House State Park
**www.parks.wa.gov/rothschd.htm**

Built in 1868, this Victorian-style house is a 0.54-acre park in downtown Port Townsend. It is open on a seasonal basis for interpretive tours. For more information, contact the Port Townsend Chamber of Commerce. It is on both the State and National Registers of Historic Places.

## Sequim
### Sequim Bay State Park
**www.parks.wa.gov/sequim.htm**

A 91-acre park at the end of Sequim Bay, this site features 60 standard campsites, 26 utility campsites, and 3 primitive sites. Groups can reserve a group camp area, or spend the day at one of the 53 picnic areas. The park is also a mecca for boaters, with 424 feet of saltwater moorage space, a boat launch ramp, and six mooring buoys. Hikers can also check out the 2.5 miles of trails.

## Forks

**Bogachiel State Park**
www.parks.wa.gov/bogachl.htm

Just six miles south of Forks, this 123-acre park offers 36 standard campsites, 6 sites with hookups for RVs, 2 primitive sites, and a 35-foot limit for trailers. The park includes frontage along the Bogachiel River and has trailer dump facilities, kitchen shelters, and a day-use area with six picnic sites.

## Ocean Shores

**Pacific Beach State Park**
www.parks.wa.gov/pacbeach.htm

Pacific Beach State Park packs a lot of punch in just 10 acres of land. Located in the North Beach section of the coast north of Ocean Shores, it features 31 campsites with electrical hookups, 33 standard campsites, a trailer dump station, and six day-use picnic areas. The park is a popular destination during the clam-digging season, but it is also popular for fresh and saltwater fishing, beachcombing, and kite flying.

**Griffiths-Priday Ocean State Park**
www.parks.wa.gov/griffith.htm

A popular day-use area with more than 8,000 feet of Pacific frontage, Griffiths-Priday Ocean State Park encompasses 364 acres near the town of Copalis. Besides bordering the ocean, the park also borders the mouth of the Copalis River. It offers 10 picnic sites, 3 pedestal grills, and a kitchen shelter with 4 picnic tables. The entire park can be reserved for up to 200 people. Activities to do at this park include canoeing, fishing, and beachcombing.

**Ocean City State Park**
www.parks.wa.gov/oceancty.htm

Set on 169 acres with nearly 3,000 feet of Pacific Ocean shoreline, Ocean City State Park is located just 1.5 miles north of Ocean Shores along WA Highway 115. It features 149 standard campsites, 29 util-ity campsites, and 3 primitive campsites. A popular destination during razor clam season, the park also has 4 restrooms, 10 picnic tables, and a group camp with a log shelter that can accommodate up to 40 people camping in tents. The park is also a great place for beachcombing, bird-watching, and both saltwater and surf fishing.

## Grays Harbor

**Lake Sylvia State Park**
www.parks.wa.gov/lksylvia.htm

The site of a former mill pond, Lake Sylvia State Park is a 233-acre park just north of Montesano. The park has 35 standard campsites, 2 primitive sites, and a group camp that can hold up to 120 people. One hundred eighteen picnic sites and a beach-side kitchen are also offered along with 270 feet of developed swimming beach. Besides a children's play area, the park also holds more than five miles of hiking trails.

**Schafer State Park**
www.parks.wa.gov/schafer.htm

This 119-acre park with shoreline along the Satsop River offers 47 tent camping sites, 6 trailer sites, and 2 primitive sites along with 75 picnic sites and 2 kitchen sites. The park is a popular destination for river activities such as fishing and rafting, and it also offers hiking and a children's play area with swings.

## Shelton

**Jarrell Cove State Park**
www.parks.wa.gov/jarrell.htm

A 42-acre park at the northwest end of Harstine Island, Jarrell Cove State Park has 20 tent sites, 17 picnic sites, 2 picnic shelters, and a group camp. In addition, the park has 2 docks with moorage piers and 14 mooring bouys, with a marine pump-out. Besides camping and boating, the park draws hikers and clam diggers.

## Hood Canal

### Belfair State Park
410 N.E. Breck Rd., Belfair
(360) 275-0668
www.parks.wa.gov/belfair.htm

Located on the far end of Hood Canal, Belfair State Park packs 184 campsites, 47 of which include trailer hookups within its 62 acres. The park sits on a site believed to have been a meeting place for generations of Native Americans. It includes an unguarded swimming area.

### Dosewallips State Park
www.parks.wa.gov/dosewall.htm

Just one mile south of Brinnon, Dosewallips State Park covers 424 acres along Hood Canal and the Dosewallips River. The winter home to an elk herd numbering about 75 animals, the park is popular in summer months for picnicking, camping, and fishing. When the water conditions permit, it offers oyster picking and clamming as well. The park includes 88 standard campsites, 40 trailer sites, 2 primitive sites, and a group camp. Thirty-five picnic sites dot the grounds, and hikers can explore more than four miles of trails with five footbridges.

### Harvey Rendsland State Park
www.parks.wa.gov/harvey.htm

This eight-acre park alongside Jiggs Lake on North Shore Road has no facilities. It is open for fishing and hiking.

### Hoodsport Trail State Park
www.parks.wa.gov/hoodsprt.htm

Two miles west of Hoodsport on Lake Cushman Road, this 80-acre park surrounds a creek. It offers three picnic tables, one toilet, and two miles of trails with a pair of footbridges over Dow Creek.

### Lake Cushman State Park
N. 7211 Lake Cushman Rd., Hoodsport
(360) 877-5491
www.parks.wa.gov/lkcushmn.htm

Set at one end of the 4,000-acre Lake Cushman reservoir, which is formed by a dam used to generate power for the city of

> ## Insiders' Tip
>
> Even if you think you are taking a short day hike, be prepared with the essentials: map, compass, water and a way to purify it, extra food, rain gear and extra clothing, fire starter and matches, first-aid kit, army knife, flashlight and extra bulbs, sunscreen, and sunglasses.

Tacoma, this 602-acre park holds 50 tent camping sites, 30 full hookup sites, and 2 primitive walk-in campsites. The park also has a camp area with a cooking shelter that can be reserved by groups. The kitchen shelter may be necessary since this area receives an average of 98 inches of rain each year. Lake Cushman also has 40 picnic sites, rest rooms, and hot showers in the camping areas. Boaters will also want to note that there is a ramp to launch small, motorized boats into the lake.

### Pleasant Harbor State Park
www.parks.wa.gov/pleasant.htm

Located 2 miles south of Brinnon along U.S. Highway 101, this moorage facility is adjacent to Dosewallips State Park. It offers beachcombing, fishing, and scuba diving.

### Potlatch State Park
www.parks.wa.gov/potlatch.htm

Potlatch State Park sits 12 miles north of Shelton on U.S. Highway 101. The park site was once a Native American gathering place used by the Skokomish and Twana Tribes, who held potlatches here. The park offers 81 picnic sites, 85 parking spaces, 17 tent camping sites, 18 trailer sites, and 2 primitive campsites. Five moorage bouys are just offshore in Hood Canal, and the site also offers a kitchen shelter and rest room. The park is popular for clamming, fishing, and scuba diving.

### Shine Tidelands State Park
www.parks.wa.gov/shinetl.htm

Mostly composed of wetlands just north of the Hood Canal Bridge off Highway 104, this 13-acre park includes 18 primitive campsites, and portable toilets are provided between April 1 and October 31 each year. The park is popular for clamming and crabbing during low tides, and it also draws divers and wind surfers.

### Triton Cove State Park
www.parks.wa.gov/triton.htm

A 28-acre park five miles north of the town of Eldon on Hood Canal, this park features a boat launch and six picnic sites. The facilities also include an outhouse and a small moorage dock.

### Twanoh State Park
12190 WA Hwy. 106, Union
www.parks.wa.gov/twanoh.htm

About eight miles west of Belfair along WA Highway 106, Twanoh State Park features a boat dock, seven mooring buoys, two boat launch ramps, and a boat pump-out facility along the south side of lower Hood Canal. The park covers 182 acres, with 9 trailer campsites, 38 tent campsites, a group camp, and 15 walk-in camps. It also holds 111 picnic sites and 5 day-use kitchens.

# Olympic National Forest

In addition to the camping offered in state parks and in Olympic National Park at the core of the Olympic Peninsula, the Olympic National Forest offers a number of campgrounds in the woods that surround the national park. The forest accounts for 632,000 acres of prime timberland, managed for multiple uses, including recreation, wildlife habitat, timber, watershed, and wilderness. Campgrounds within the national forest are available on a first-come, first-served basis, and forest officials ask that campers take their litter and garbage home from the campsites so that limited maintenance funds can be spent on activities rather than on garbage dump fees.

Here is a basic listing of the campgrounds available in Olympic National Forest:

### Big Creek

Northwest of Hoodsport on WA Highway 119, this campground offers 25 tent/trailer sites ($10 per night), along with a nature trail and picnic sites.

### Brown Creek

Twenty-two miles northwest of Shelton, Brown Creek has 12 tent/trailer campsites ($10 per night) and 8 tent-only sites, in addition to rest rooms and picnic areas.

### Campbell Tree Grove

This campground on the West Fork Humptulips River offers five tent/trailer campsites, six tent-only sites, and toilets, along with a picnic area and on-site water.

### Chetwoot

Hike in or boat in to this rustic campground 39 miles north of Montesano with 8 tent campsites.

### Coho

Thirty-eight miles north of Montesano and above the Wynoochee Dam, this large site offers 46 tent/trailer campsites ($12 per night) and 12 tent sites ($10 per night for walk-in sites), along with a fishing boat ramp and rest rooms. Some of the sites are wheelchair accessible.

### Collins

Ten tent/trailer campsites ($10 per night) and six tent-only sites are among the amenities here, north of Hoodsport along the Duckabush River.

### Dungeness Forks

Near U.S. Highway 101 on the Dungeness

*Campers are welcome at private campgrounds, many state parks, and within Olympic National Park.*

PHOTO: NATALIE McNAIR-HUFF

River, this site offers 10 tent campsites ($10 per night), along with picnic areas and toilets.

### East Crossing

South of Sequim along U.S. Highway 101, the East Crossing campground features 10 tent/trailer campsites ($10 per night), along with rest rooms and a picnic area. The site is popular for fishing.

### Elkhorn

Northwest of Brinnon and along the Dosewallips River, the Elkhorn campground offers 16 tent-only sites and 4 tent/trailer sites ($10 per night), along with access to fishing and rest rooms.

### Falls Creek

Along South Shore Road on Lake Quinault, Falls Creek features a boat ramp to launch onto the lake, a nearby nature trail, 16 tent/trailer campsites ($11 and $14 per night), and 15 tent-only sites. The camp also has a cooking shelter, and it is a popular swimming spot in warm summer months.

### Falls View

Located along the Quilcene River Trail near U.S. Highway 101, Falls View has 30 tent/trailer campsites ($10 per night), along with a picnic area and toilets.

### Gatton Creek

Ten tent camping sites ($11 per night) and five walk-in campsites are among the amenities at Gatton Creek, located along South Shore Road near Lake Quinault. The camp also has rest rooms and picnic sites.

### Hamma Hamma

One mile north of Eldon and close to U.S. Highway 101 on the Hood Canal, the Hamma Hamma campground features 16 tent/trailer campsites ($10 per night), along with toilets and access to fishing. Visitors can also rent a cabin near the campground . For more information, call (360) 877-5254.

### Interrorem

Four miles west of U.S. Highway 101 near the Duckabush River, Interrorem offers

night), and a picnic area are highlights of this campground about eight miles west of U.S. Highway 101 near the town of Eldon.

### Mt. Walker Viewpoint

A popular byway along U.S. Highway 101 south of Quilcene, the Mt. Walker Viewpoint sits at an elevation of 2,800 feet, and offers two viewing areas with toilets and picnic areas. The views overlook the Puget Sound basin and across the forest to the eastern peaks of the Olympic Mountains.

### Rainbow

A group camp available by reservation only, Rainbow is five miles southwest of Quilcene along U.S. Highway 101. It offers nine camp sites and vault toilets. For reservations, contact the ranger station at (360) 765-2200.

three picnic sites, a nature trail, a historical site, and a rental cabin. For information about cabin availability, call (360) 877-5254.

### Klahowya

Near U.S. Highway 101 on the Soleduck River, not far from the town of Sappho, you'll find the Klahowya campground, which offers 20 tent/trailer campsites ($10 and $12 per night) and 30 tent-only campsites in addition to bathrooms and trails leading to fishing on the river.

### Lebar House

A horse-only campground 22 miles northwest of Shelton, Lebar House features 13 campsites ($5 per night), along with a vault toilet.

### Lena Creek

Fourteen tent/trailer campsites ($10 per

### Seal Rock

Thirty-seven tent/trailer campsites ($10 and $12 per night) are joined by 5 tent-only sites and a group camp area that can be rented separately for $25 and can hold up to 15 people at this scenic camp along Hood Canal. The site also has wheelchair-accessible rest rooms and access for fishing and swimming.

### Willaby

Set in the forest along South Shore Road near Lake Quinault, Willaby features 27 tent/trailer campsites ($14 per night) as well as 7 tent-only sites, a boat ramp, trails, and picnic areas within two miles of U.S. Highway 101.

# Ranger Stations

**Hoh Ranger Station**
Hoh River Rd., Forks
(360) 374-6925

**Hood Canal Ranger District**
295142 U.S. Hwy. 101, Quilcene
(360) 765-2200

**Hoodsport Ranger Station**
150 N. Lake Cushman Rd., Hoodsport
(360) 877-5254

**Kalaloch Ranger Station**
U.S. Hwy. 101, Forks
(360) 962-2283

**Lake Crescent Ranger Station**
U.S. Hwy. 101, Port Angeles
(360) 928-3380

**Mora Ranger Station**
Mora Rd., Forks
(360) 374-5460

Olympic National Forest Headquarters
1835 Black Lake Blvd. S.W., Olympia
(360) 956-2300

Olympic National Park
Park Superintendent
600 E. Park Ave., Port Angeles
(360) 452-4501

Pacific Ranger Station
437 Tillicum Ln., Forks
(360) 374-6522

Pioneer Memorial Museum
3002 Mt. Angeles Rd., Port Angeles
(360) 452-5401, ext. 230

Quinault Ranger Station
353 S. Shore, Quinault
(360) 288-2525

U.S. Fish and Wildlife Service
Dungeness National Wildlife Refuge,
2109 Old Olympic Hwy., Sequim
(360) 683-7040

# County Campgrounds

### Dungeness Recreation Area

Located above the Dungeness Spit near Sequim, this recreation area holds 65 campsites in addition to rest rooms, showers, a dump station, and access to fishing and a boat launch. Located four miles north of U.S. Highway 101 along Kitchen Dick Road, the camping area is also adjacent to the Dungeness National Wildlife Refuge. For more information about camping and facilities, call (360) 683-5847.

### Haven Lake County Park

Four campground sites and access to fishing are the highlights of this park that is 15 miles southwest of Bremerton along WA Highway 300. The park does not contain trailer sites..

### Lake Leland County Park

Just north of Quilcene along U.S. Highway 101, this park offers primitive campsites, fishing, and a boat launch.

### Pillar Point County Park

Thirty-five campsites, a cooking shelter, and rest rooms are among the amenities at this county park west of Port Angeles

along WA Highway 112. The park also has picnic facilities, a boat launch, and access to fishing and crabbing. For more information, call (360) 928-3201.

### Pleasant Harbor

Primitive camping facilities and access to fishing are the highlights of the Pleasant Harbor park just south of Brinnon on the Hood Canal. The park also has toilets.

### Quilcene Jefferson County Park

Located in Quilcene, this park offers a small campground, picnic tables, rest rooms, and a cooking shelter.

### Salt Creek Recreation Area

One of the more popular camping destinations west of Port Angeles, the Salt Creek Recreation Area holds 87 campsites. The park also has picnic tables, hiking trails, and access to great tide-pooling at low tides. The area, just 3 miles north of WA Highway 112 on Camp Hayden Road, also offers rest rooms and access to fishing and swimming. For more information, call (360) 928-3441.

# Recreation Areas

### Green Mountain State Forest
### (360) 825-1631, (800) 527-3305

Just a few miles west of Bremerton, the 6,000-acre Green Mountain State Forest is a mecca for hikers, mountain bikers,

motorcyclists, and ATV users. The forest also draws horseback riders. Green Mountain Campground offers limited amenities.

### Tahuya State Forest
**(360) 825-1631, (800) 527-3305**

Located west of Belfair on the Kitsap Peninsula, this 23,100-acre forest is laced with trails for mountain bikers, motorcycle riders, horseback riders, and hikers. The forest also contains primitive campsites open on a first-come, first-served basis. The forest is managed by the Washington State Department of Natural Resources.

# Boating and Marinas

Whether you ply the waters of Hood Canal, Puget Sound, or the Strait of Juan de Fuca with a motorboat or sailboat, the Olympic Peninsula is a mecca for boating. Nearly every town along the counterclockwise route around the Peninsula has at least one marina. And numerous small, private docks and marinas cater to boaters as well.

Reservations are advised to ensure you will find moorage at many marinas, particularly during the busy summer months. In this section we note some of the major marinas.

## Gig Harbor

**Arabella Landing**
**3323 Harborview Dr., Gig Harbor**
**(253) 851-1793**
**www.vici.com/arabella/marina.htm**

Permanent, short-term, and overnight mooring is available at Arabella Landing. The marina offers a pump-out station, power, and water.

## Port Orchard

**Illahee Marine State Park**

Located on Port Orchard Narrows, the dock here offers 350 feet of side-tie dock space and 5 mooring bouys. The park has 3 kitchen shelters, picnic tables, a horseshoe pit, ball fields, and hiking trails. Rest rooms and porta-potty dumps are also nearby.

**Port Orchard Marina**
**8850 S.W. WA Hwy. 3, Port Orchard**
**(360) 876-5535, (800) 462-3793**

Boats up to 44-feet long can use one of the 40 slips offered year-round at the Port Orchard Marina. Open daily except for Christmas and Thanksgiving, the marina also features side-tie dock space, and gas and diesel fuel are available on site. The marina is located just a block from downtown.

## North Kitsap

**Keyport Marina**
**Washington St., Keyport**
**(360) 779-4360**

Adjacent to the Naval Undersea Warfare Center at Keyport, this marina offers a handful of guest moorage spots on a first-come, first-served basis.

**Port of Bremerton Marina**
**Bremerton Waterfront, Bremerton**
**(360) 373-1035**

Located along the boardwalk on the Bremerton waterfront, this marina offers a number of slips for guest moorage, along with power, rest rooms, showers, laundry facilities, and pump-outs.

**Port of Brownsville**
**9790 Ogle Rd. N.E., Brownsville**
**(360) 692-5498**
**www.portofbrownsville.org**

Open every day of the year, this marina, north of Bremerton and south of Keyport, offers full amenities and a fuel dock for guests.

**Port of Manchester**
**P.O. Box 304, Manchester**

The bare essentials are offered at this year-round marina with 200 feet of guest moorage. Boaters are warned to study tide charts before entering the area.

**Port of Poulsbo**
**Liberty Bay, Poulsbo**
**(360) 779-3505**

One of the busiest marinas on the Olympic Peninsula, this popular spot offers 130 guest moorages along with full-service fueling, rest rooms, showers, and laundry facilities. Administered by the Port of Poulsbo, the marina fills quickly on summer weekends.

**Port of Silverdale**
**P.O. Box 310, Silverdale**
**(360) 698-4918**

One of the larger marinas in the area, the Port of Silverdale offers 1,300 feet of guest moorage with a minimum depth of 10 feet at low tide. Amenities at the marina include access to the Silverdale waterfront parks and rest rooms. Due to its large size, this marina often has moorage available on busy summer weekends.

**Port Washington Marina**
**1805 Thompson Dr., Bremerton**
**(360) 479-3037**

Beware of the six-foot minimum depth areas at this Bremerton area marina. Open year-round, it offers 100 feet of tie-up space with amenities, including 30/50 amp power, bathrooms, showers, laundry facilities, and pump-out facilities.

**Seabeck Marina**
**15376 Seabeck Hwy., Seabeck**
**(360) 830-5179**

Less than a mile from Scenic Beach State Park, the Seabeck Marina is open year-round with rest room facilities and marine fuel available on the dock.

# Port Townsend

**Port Hadlock Bay Marina**
**310 Alcohol Loop Rd., Port Hadlock**
**(360) 385-6368**

Port Hadlock Bay Marina offers 160 slips year-round, and reservations are advised. Facilities at the marina include rest rooms, showers, and a pump-out. A restaurant and lodging are featured.

**Point Hudson Marina**
**103 Hudson St., Port Townsend**
**(360) 385-5160, (877) 385-4500**

Recreational and limited commercial moorage are offered at the Point Hudson Marina. The marina, at the north end of Port Townsend, accepts reservations on 45 slips for boats up to 40 feet, but no reservations are accepted on the 800 feet of linear dock set aside for vessels up to 65 feet. Besides moorage, the marina offers a public boat ramp, rest rooms, showers, laundry, and a pump-out. The marina is open year-round.

## Insiders' Tip

Make sure you leave your itinerary with someone just in case something happens and you get hurt or lost. If at least one person knows what your plans are, it's that much easier for search and rescue to know where to look.

*Boating on the Penisula covers a wide range of activities.* PHOTO: NATALIE McNAIR-HUFF

**Port of Port Townsend Boat Haven**
**2601 Washington St., Port Townsend**
**(360) 385-2355**

Port Townsend Boat Haven offers 425 slips for recreational and commercial moorage. Facilities include fuel, rest rooms, showers, laundry, pump-out, and a public boat launch. The marina also offers access to boat repairs and construction.

## Sequim

**John Wayne Marina**
**2577 Sequim Bay Rd., Sequim**
**(360) 417-3440**

One of the largest marinas on the Peninsula, the John Wayne Marina is so named because the land on which it sits was once

**Port Ludlow Marina**
**1 Gull Dr., Port Ludlow**
**(360) 437-0513**

Open year round, the Port Ludlow Marina offers 300 slips, including 49 for guests. Management requires that boaters make reservations. Facilities include fuel, rest rooms, showers, laundry, and pump-out. Guests can also purchase fishing licenses or browse the gift shop.

owned by the famous actor. The marina offers 300 slips, but most are reserved for area residents. Approximately 20 slips are available for nightly moorage, and no reservations are accepted.

## Port Angeles

**Port Angeles Boat Haven**
**832 Boat Haven Dr., Port Angeles**
**(360) 457-4505**

More than 700 feet of dock space is avail-

able for guest moorage at the Port Angeles Boat Haven, which does not accept reservations.

# Juan de Fuca Highway

**Makah Marina**
**1321 Bayview Ave. S., Neah Bay**
**(360) 645-3015**

This basic marina in Neah Bay offers approximately 200 slips, along with fuel, power, and water.

**Olson's Resort and Marina**
**Sekiu**
**(360) 963-2311**

Olson's Resort and Marina offers transient moorage with no covered slips. No reservations are accepted for the 200 slips

available. Amenities include a motel, a store, and RV parking.

**Van Riper's Resort and Charter**
**280 Front St., Sekiu**
**(360) 963-2334**

Two hundred fifty slips, including transient moorage are offered at Van Riper's Resort. No reservations are accepted, but guests who stay in the RV campground or in the motel are guaranteed moorage. Facilities include fuel, power, and water.

## Forks

**Quilleute Marina**
**71 Main St., La Push**
**(360) 374-5392**

The Quilleute Marina has 70 slips avail-

able on a per-night basis, with amenities including fuel, sewer pump-out, and lighted docks.

## Hood Canal

**Pleasant Harbor Marina**
**308913 U.S. Hwy. 101, Brinnon**
**(800) 547-3479**
**www.pleasantharbormarina.com**

Open year-round, the Pleasant Harbor Marina features 312 slips, but reservations are advised for anyone counting on tying up here. The marina has permanent and transient moorage, with laundry and shower facilities, pump-out, fuel, and power. The connected resort also has a grocery, a gift shop, and a swimming pool.

**Summertide Resort & Marina**
**15781 N.E. Northshore Rd., Tahuya**
**(360) 275-9313, (253) 925-9277**
**www.SummertideResort.com**

This Hood Canal resort offers nightly

moorage and a boat launch, in addition to cottages and RV camping sites near the town of Belfair.

**Quilcene Boat Haven**
**1731 Linger Longer Rd., Quilcene**
**(360) 765-3717**

Open throughout the summer and in winter when needed, the Quilcene Boat Haven offers 48 slips on a first-come, first-served basis. Facilities include rest rooms, showers, pump-out, and a public boat ramp.

# Scuba Diving

Hood Canal and the Strait of Juan de Fuca are widely known as popular diving destinations. Divers are drawn to the area's number of accessible deep-shore dives, wreck dives, and the abundant sea life on the floor and along the shores of the dive sites. Among the sea life, divers commonly see giant lingcod, urchins, abalone, starfish, wolfeels, crab, and a wide variety of other invertebrates.

The following is a list of shops along the Olympic Peninsula that offer scuba diving instruction, gear, and repair. These shops are the best source for local expertise about where to go to make the most of your dive on the Peninsula.

### Curley's Resort and Dive Center
**291 Front St., Sekiu**
**(360) 963-2281, (800) 542-9680**
**www.curleysresort.com**

Located along the Strait of Juan de Fuca, Curley's diving supplies include full service air, rentals, and sales of top diving gear. The resort caters to diving groups and it is near many popular diving sites. Check the shop's Web site for details about local dive destinations.

### Hood Sport 'n Dive
**27001 U.S. Hwy. 101, Hoodsport**
**(360) 877-6818**
**hood.hctc.com/~hsd/**

Three miles north of Hoodsport, in the Rest-a-While Marina, Hood Sport 'n Dive is a full-service shop on Hood Canal. The shop features gear for rent and for sale, as well as service, repairs, and technical diving gear. Since the shop is right on the water, divers are allowed to dive with their new gear before buying it. The shop also offers exclusive, no-bank beach access to the Sund Rock Marine Preserve.

### Mike's Beach Resort
**38470 U.S. Hwy. 101, Lilliwaup**
**(800) 231-5324**
**www.mikesbeachresort.com**

Besides offering affordable lodging alongside Hood Canal, Mike's Beach Resort is known as a great destination to area scuba divers. Along the back side of the resort, artificial and natural structures support sea life in a diving park that is rated as suitable for classes and novice divers. People can also do night diving. Nearby, the canal floor drops off to a depth of more than 100 feet.

### Mike's Diving Center
**22270 U.S. Hwy. 101, Shelton**
**(360) 877-9568**

Located north of Shelton in the Native American village of Potlatch, Mike's Diving Center offers scuba gear rentals and supplies for divers venturing into the southern end of the Hood Canal.

### Port Townsend Dive Shop
**2200 Washington St., Port Townsend**
**(360) 379-3635**
**www.ptdive.com**

With a staff with more than 25 years of diving experience, the Port Townsend Dive Shop offers the latest dive suits and accessories along with information about local dive sites and seasonal charters. Check the shop's Web site for maps with info about area diving destinations.

### Sound Dive Center
**4954 Wheaton Way, Bremerton**
**(360) 373-6141**
**www.sounddive.com**

Billed as the only Kitsap County dive shop open on Sundays, the Sound Dive Center in Bremerton offers classes and a full selection of scuba dive gear. Check out the schedule and information about upcoming guided trips, or fill up your tanks.

### Sound Dive Center
**625 E. Front St., Port Angeles**
**(360) 457-3749**

Clallam County's only dive shop, this sister store to the Bremerton shop of the same name is open seven days a week. It features scuba gear in addition to classes and information about all of the great diving spots in the Port Angeles and Strait of Juan de Fuca area. The Port Angeles shop also offers nitrox.

*Fishing is a popular past time on the Peninsula.*  PHOTO: ROB McNAIR-HUFF

# Fishing

More than a dozen rivers, creeks, and lakes draw fishing fans to the Olympic Peninsula. Add the saltwater fishing in Hood Canal, the Strait of Juan de Fuca, and along the shores of the Pacific Ocean, and this region is a fishing destination.

Within Olympic National Park, all waters are closed to the removal of any fish, shellfish, aquatic plants, or wildlife, with some exceptions. The park offers a detailed yearly breakdown of what kinds of fishing are allowed and where. Stop by a ranger station or the Olympic National Park Visitor Center in Port Angeles to get the information before heading out to a stream, river, or lake. Anglers within the park are not required to have a Washington State Personal Use Food Fish License except when fishing in the Pacific Ocean from shore. A Washington State catch record card is required to fish for salmon or steelhead, and a Washington State Shellfish/Seaweed license is required for harvest of shellfish along the Pacific Coast section of the park.

Outside the park, anglers need to obtain a fishing license for most waters. And they are advised to pick up a current fishing pamphlet at local outdoors shops.

### Bogachiel River

Just south of Forks, the Boggie, as it is known to local anglers, is well known for its salmon and steelhead runs. You will find easy access at Bogachiel State Park and at other points along the river.

### Chehalis River

A popular river for spring and fall chi-nook salmon, as well as coho and chum salmon, the Chehalis flows from the Willapa Hills in the south to mark the southern end of the Olympic Peninsula as it empties into Grays Harbor and the Pacific Ocean. The river is also known for its steelhead, sturgeon, and sea-run cut-throat that have been planted into the lower inter tidal area of the river. For more information about the Chehalis River, call the Grays Harbor Trout Unlimited chapter at (360) 533-4648.

### Elwha River

The section of the Elwha between Lake Mills and Lake Aldwell offers native rainbow trout. Anglers need to check current regulations pamphlets for seasons and restrictions on fishing this river, and keep in mind that sections of the river that fall within the boundaries of Olympic National Park are regulated by park fishing rules.

### Hoh River

Upper sections of the Hoh River within Olympic National Park are regulated by the park. Lower sections of the river, which can be accessed along public access sites as well as by boat, fall under state rules. Depending on the season and river conditions, the Hoh can be an excellent salmon and steelhead stream.

### Hoquiam River

Bring a canoe for access to the most difficult sections of the Hoquiam River, which is known for its winter steelhead, chinook, chum, and coho salmon runs.

### Queets River

The entire length of the Queets River falls either within Olympic National Park or the Quinault Indian Reservation. Like the other west-end rivers, the Queets is known for its salmon and steelhead runs. Be sure to check the Olympic National Park regulations for seasons and daily limits.

### Quillayute River

Several boat and bank access areas offer a starting point for anglers on the Quillayute River. By the time this river reaches the sea near La Push and Rialto Beach, it includes the waters of the Dickey, Sol Duc, Bogachiel, and Calawah Rivers. All the rivers in this system offer excellent salmon, steelhead, and cutthroat fishing. And many of the rivers are popular with fly fishers.

### Satsop River

The Satsop River is most known for its winter steelhead and chinook, coho, and chum salmon. It also holds resident and sea-run cutthroat. All wild cutthroat and steelhead have to be released, and there are a number of public access points and boat launches along the shore.

### Wishkah River

An easy river to fish by canoe, the Wishkah holds winter steelhead, coho salmon, and sea-run cutthroat. All wild steelhead and wild cutthroat have to be released. The river pours into Grays Harbor near Aberdeen.

### Wynoochee River

Starting at the Wynoochee Reservoir and dam, this river is known for its chinook, chum, and coho salmon runs as well as winter steelhead. Resident and sea-run cutthroat trout round out the highlights for anglers.

### Lake Crescent

Encompassed within Olympic National Park, the rules for the park govern fishing in this lake alongside U.S. Highway 101 west of Port Angeles. This lake, which was formed by glaciers, holds two of the endemic fish species in the park, a type of rainbow called the Beardslee trout, and a type of cutthroat called the crescenti trout. For more information about fishing on Lake Crescent, call the National Park Service at (360) 452-4501.

### Lake Cushman

At nearly 4,000 acres, Lake Cushman is one of the largest lakes on the Olympic Peninsula. Its waters gather up behind a hydroelectric dam run by Tacoma Public Utilities. Just four miles northwest of Hoodsport, the lake holds such fish as kokanee, which are the prize catch in the summer months, and late-season cutthroat trout. The lake is closed to taking Dolly Varden or bull trout, but it is open year-round for other species.

### Lake Quinault

You'll find this lake in the Quinault Rain Forest, within U.S. Forest Service lands. Lake access is offered at a number of state and National Forest Service parks, and fishing in the lake is dictated by tribal rules of the Quinault Tribe.

### Ozette Lake

The largest natural freshwater lake in the state, Ozette Lake sits within the boundaries of Olympic National Park. Fish found in this lake include cutthroat trout, yellow perch, largemouth bass, and northern pikeminnow. For more information about other Olympic National Park waters regulations, call (360) 452-4501.

# Hiking

Besides the trails offered within Olympic National Park, a number of popular hiking destinations can be found in the Olympic National Forest. Here is a brief listing of the more popular hiking spots.

### Lena Lake Trail

This popular day hike departs from Forest Service Road 25, about eight miles west of U.S. Highway 101 near Hoodsport, and winds three miles up to the Lena Lake Campground.

### Mt. Ellinor Trail

A challenging day hike with great views, this hike climbs 2.5 miles before reaching an alpine meadow. In the summer, wildflowers cover the ground in this meadow, which is the turn around point for day hikes. More experienced climbers can finish the scramble to the summit. To reach the trailhead, take WA Highway 119 nine miles from Hoodsport, then turn onto Forest Service Road 24 and go 1.6 miles to FS Road 2419. Go 4.9 miles on road 2419 to reach the lower trailhead, or 7.5 miles to reach the upper trailhead.

### Mt. Walker Trail

Just south of Quilcene along U.S. Highway 101, the Mt. Walker Trail climbs two miles through a forest dotted with wild rhododendrons. The reward at the top of the mountain is a pair of panoramic viewpoints offering views to the east toward Hood Canal and Mt. Rainier, and to the west toward the eastern crags of the Olympic Mountains.

# Kayaking and Rafting

Surrounded by water, the Olympic Peninsula is one of the world's most popular areas for kayaking. Each year hundreds of kayaking fans and top kayak makers from around the world converge on Port Townsend for the West Coast Sea Kayak Symposium in September. As a result of this exposure to the sport, it is not uncommon at all to see kayaks atop cars and trucks on the major highways around the Peninsula.

In this section we offer a glimpse of some of the shops, 129, and guides that offer kayak rentals, sales, tours, and instruction. In addition, we highlight one whitewater rafting guide and a company that outfits river floats.

> ## Insiders' Tip
> The Olympic Peninsula is a big draw for hikers. Hundreds of miles of trails crisscross Olympic National Park and Olympic National Forest.

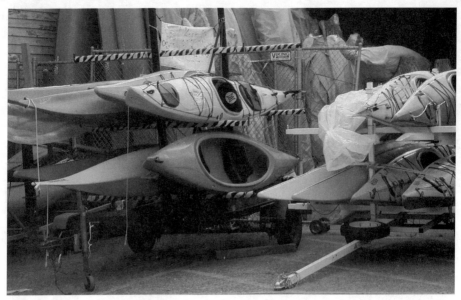

*Outdoors shops, such as the Olympic Outdoor Center in Poulsbo cater to a wide range of sporting enthusiasts, including kayakers.* PHOTO: ROB McNAIR-HUFF

### Extreme Adventures
**P.O. Box 1991, Forks**
**(877) 374-8747**

Extreme Adventures offers float trips that range from two hours to overnight on a river near Forks. The longest trip begins within Olympic National Park and floats about 32 miles of the Hoh River.

### Kayak Port Townsend
**435 Water St., Port Townsend**
**(360) 385-6240, (800) 853-2252**
**www.kayakpt.com**

Offering tours and rentals seven days a week, Kayak Port Townsend is a great place for beginning paddlers to learn about the sport of sea kayaking. The shop offers basic instructions for anyone on a tour. Tours range from two hours to deluxe overnight trips to such destinations as the Strait of Juan de Fuca and Protection Island, to Discovery Bay, or a four-day and three-night tour of the San Juan Islands. Custom tours can also be arranged. Rentals of either single, double, open double, or WindRider sea kayaks are also available.

### Olympic Adventures
**1001 Water St., Port Townsend**
**(360) 379-7611**

Set out on a kayak tour in a wooden sea kayak from Olympic Adventures. The tours include waterfront trips as well as longer, wildlife-viewing excursions.

### Olympic Outdoor
**773 Pt. Brown Ave. N.W., Ocean Shores**
**(360) 289-3736**

Rent a single or double kayak by the hour, half a day, or full day at Olympic Outdoor. The shop also rents mountain bikes and offers bike repair, as well as clam digging and crabbing gear.

### Olympic Outdoor Center
**18971 Front St., Poulsbo**
**(360) 697-6095**
**www.kayakproshop.com**

Check out the latest kayaks, rent a kayak for a water tour of Poulsbo, or sign up for a kayaking class at the Olympic Outdoor Center. The shop's courses include introductory techniques for kids and adults. Ask about group paddles to off-site places such as Hood Canal, the north Olympic Peninsula coast, or Blake Island.

**Olympic Raft & Kayak**
**123 Lake Aldwell Rd., Port Angeles**
**(888) 452-1443**
**www.northolympic.com/olympicraft**

River rafting trips and kayaking trips within and around Olympic National Park are the specialty of Olympic Raft & Kayak. Whitewater trips take place on the Elwha River, while float trips in rafts or kayaks are held on the Hoh River.

**PT Outdoors**
**1017B Water St., Port Townsend**
**(360) 379-3608, (888) 754-8598**
**www.ptoutdoors.com**

PT Outdoors offers daily classes and rents kayaks. The shop, located in the heart of downtown Port Townsend, also has daily

sea kayaking tours ranging from two-hour trips to a sunset paddle to all-day paddles. Andy Gale, a certified Coastal Kayak Instructor, also teaches classes along the waterfront for beginners and experts.

**Sound Bikes & Kayaks**
**120 E. Front St., Port Angeles**
**(360) 457-1240**

Rentals and sales of kayaks, as well as kayaking accessories and books, are highlights of Sound Bikes & Kayaks. Kayaks can be rented by the hour or by the day. The shop sells touring and whitewater boats, as well as a selection of specialty kayaks.

# Outfitters and Guides

A number of fishing and hunting guide services offer tips for making the most of your outdoor experience on the Olympic Peninsula. Listed below are some of the companies that offer such unique outdoor opportunities as llama packing, mountain climbing, or fly fishing on the Bogachiel or Sol Duc Rivers.

**Brown's Outdoor**
**112 W. Front St., Port Angeles**
**(360) 457-4150**

Browse the large inventory of quality outdoor gear at Brown's Outdoor. The shop offers a wide variety of products at many price ranges, including tents, backpacks, climbing gear, accessories, and dehydrated food items.

**Captain Jack's Sea Charters**
**Port Townsend**
**(360) 379-4033, (877) 278-5225**
**www.Cpt-Jack.com**

Captain Jack's offers whale-watching tours departing from the Port Townsend Boat Haven. Tours follow orca, Minke, and gray whales as they move through the waters around the Victorian town.

**Diamond Back Guide Service**
**140 Dolan Ave., Port Angeles**
**(360) 452-9966**
**www.northolympic.com/diamondback**

With guided fishing trips on the Hoh,

Bogachiel, Calawah, Sol Duc, and Quillayute Rivers, the Diamond Back Guide Service offers chances to catch trophy-sized steelhead and salmon. The service also offers scenic float trips

**Elk Horn Ranch 129**
**716 South Shore Rd., Quinault**
**(360) 288-2750**

Offering guided horseback trips into the Upper Quinault Valley, the Elk Horn Ranch 129 is a Forest Service concessionaire for the South Shore area. In addition to the horseback trips, the company offers three lakeside campgrounds along Lake Quinault, bicycle rentals, and a limited number of openings for deer and elk hunting trips.

**Jim Leons Outdoor Adventures**
**Forks**
**(360) 374-3157**
**www.fishingnorthwest.com/jimleons**

Hunting and fishing trips along the western edges of the Olympic Peninsula are

*Sport fishing for salmon near Hoodsport on the Hood Canal.* PHOTO: ROB McNAIR-HUFF

the specialty of Jim Leons from Forks. He guides clients in search of summer and winter steelhead, salmon, and sea-run cutthroat trout.

**John Monk's Guide Service**
**P.O. Box 1012, Forks**
**(360) 374-5817, (360) 458-3593**
**valleyint.com/guide-steelhead-salmon**

A guide with more than 30 years of experience on the Bogachiel, Sol Duc, Hoh, and Calawah Rivers near Forks, John Monk specializes in helping clients in the search for trophy steelhead and salmon.

**Kit's Llamas**
**P.O. Box 116, Olalla**
**(253) 857-5274**
**www.northolympic.com/llamas**

Kit's Llamas specializes in llama trekking in the Olympic Mountains. Trips offered range from day hikes with llamas packing gear to extended overnight trips into the heart of Olympic National Park. Kit's also offers educational trips with the llamas, as well as services packing gear in to selected drop sites for solo hikers.

**Mike Schmitz Olympic Peninsula Fishing Guides**
**P.O. Box 2688, Forks**
**(360) 364-2602, (888) 577-4656**
**www.forks-web.com/mschmitz**

Mike Schmitz offers guide services on rivers in the Forks area, including the Bogachiel, Sol Duc, Hoh, and the Clear-

water. Mike's son, Mike Schmitz Jr., also works for the guide service.

**North Coast Guide Service**
**3055 E. Hoquiam Rd., Hoquiam**
**(360) 533-9896**
**www.northcoastguide.com**

Trips to fish for winter and summer steelhead, sturgeon, and salmon along the Olympic rain forest rivers are the specialty of the North Coast Guide Service. The service is run by Michael Dennis, a long-time resident and expert on Olympic Peninsula streams.

**Olympic Mountaineering**
**140 W. Front St., Port Angeles**
**(360) 452-0240**
**www.olymtn.com**

Olympic Mountaineering offers all levels of guided hikes and climbs in Olympic National Park and the Olympic National Forest. So whether you want to climb to the summit of Mt. Olympus with a guide, or you just want to go for an interpretive walk along the Elwha River or on Hurricane Hill, this company can help. The company also has an indoor climbing gym, and it hosts clinics and classes on climbing and outdoor topics.

**Olympic Mountain Outdoors**
**P.O. Box 1468, Port Townsend**
**(360) 379-5336**
**www.olympicguides.com**

From guided day hikes to custom

overnight trips into the heart of the Olympic Mountains, Olympic Mountain Outdoors works to serve its mission—to make it easier for those who want to travel and explore the Olympic Peninsula. In addition to hikes, OMO offers camping trips, snowshoeing excursions, backcountry skiing, and naturalist trips.

**P.S. Express**
**431 Water St., Port Townsend**
**(360) 385-5288**
**www.pugetsoundexpress.com**

Daily cruises between Port Townsend and the San Juan Islands, with whale watching along the way, are part of the services offered by P.S. Express.

**Puffin Adventures**
**P.O. Box 157, Sekiu**
**(360) 963-2744, (888) 305-2437**
**www.olypen.com/puffinadventures**

Ride a charter boat to scuba diving destinations or kayaking sites, on a fishing trip, or to tour a wildlife area with Puffin Adventures. Fishing trips include charters to try to catch halibut, bottomfish, or salmon.

**Quillayute River Guide Service**
**P.O. Box 71, La Push**
**(360) 374-2660**
**forks-web.com/jim**

Specializing in salmon and steelhead fishing on the Quillayute River system and its tributaries, Jim Richeson offers expertise to help anglers better their chances of catching fish in the Forks and La Push areas. Richeson also offers guide services on the Hoh River.

**Sport Townsend**
**1044 Water St., Port Townsend**
**(360) 379-9711**

Backpacking gear, hiking boots, food supplies, and climbing gear join kayaks, canoes, and a wide range of outdoor books on the shelves at Sport Townsend. The shop also serves as a central place in Port Townsend to sign up for guided trips into the woods or into the local waters for a kayaking excursion.

# RV Parks

Recreational vehicle campgrounds and parks dot the perimeter of the Olympic Peninsula. The following is a listing of some of the facilities available to travelers.

## Gig Harbor

**Gig Harbor RV Resort**
**9515 Burnham Dr. N.W., Gig Harbor**
**(253) 858-8138, (800) 526-8311**

This resort offers 100 wooded sites with full hookups, tent sites, cable TV, showers, rest rooms, laundry, ice, propane, RV supplies, and ice. Guests also enjoy a heated pool, playground, and game room.

## Port Townsend

**Port Ludlow RV Park**
**1 Gull Dr., Port Ludlow**
**(360) 437-0513**

This park offers 33 full hookups and 3 partial hookups with daily, weekly, and monthly rates. All sites can double as tent sites. Register at the marina store.

**Smitty's Island Retreat RV Park**
**9142 Flagler Rd., Nordland**
**(360) 385-2165**

Right next to Fort Flagler State Park, this park offers 40 sites with full hookups, including water, power, and sewage available for daily, weekly, and monthly rates.

# Sequim

**Olympic Paradise RV Park and Woodcarving Shop**
**137 Pierson Rd., Sequim**
**(360) 683-1264**
**www.olympicparadise.com**

Select from 10 full hookup sites and 8 tent sites at the Olympic Paradise RV Park. While you stay, take a tour of the gift shop, walk the nature trail, or watch owner and chainsaw carver Don Dykema in the carving shop. Additional amenities include a 24-hour laundry, rest rooms, and showers.

**Rainbow's End RV Park**
**261831 Hwy. 101, Sequim**
**(360) 683-3863**

In addition to 39 full hookups, a laundry, showers, and 30 tent sites, guests at Rainbow's End RV Park also enjoy a trout pond and a creek.

**Sunshine RV Park**
**259790 U.S. Hwy. 101, Sequim**
**(360) 683-4769**

Sunshine RV Park, conveniently located off of U.S. Highway 101, offers 50 full hookups with cable TV, showers, pull-thru sites, 15 tent sites, laundry facilities, and a recreation room.

# Port Angeles

**Al's RV Park**
**521 N. Lee's Creek Rd., Port Angeles**
**(360) 457-9844, (800) 357-1553**

With nightly, weekly, and monthly rates, Al's RV Park offers 31 full hookups, cable TV, phone connections, rest rooms, showers, laundry, 10 tent sites, and a clubhouse.

**Arney's Dam RV Park**
**47 Lower Dam Rd., Port Angeles**
**(360) 452-7054**
**www.northolympic.com/arneys**

Arney's Dam and RV Park has 36 full hookups, two acres for tent sites, RV and boat storage, rest rooms, showers, laundry, propane, public phone, and an on-site store.

**Conestoga Quarters RV Park**
**40 Sieberts Creek Rd., Port Angeles**
**(800) 808-4637**

With 34 full hookups, 8 tent sites, rest rooms, showers, a pavilion with lighting, a BBQ pit, and water, Conestoga Quarters suggests reservations.

**Shadow Mountain Campground**
**232951 U.S. Hwy. 101, Port Angeles**
**(360) 928-3043**

Fire pits and an on-site store and deli top off the offerings at Shadow Mountain Campground, which has 40 full hookups, 11 tent spaces, laundry, showers, and gas, propane, and diesel.

**Welcome Inn RV Park**
**1215 U.S. Hwy. 101, Port Angeles**
**(360) 457-1553**

In addition to 80 full hookups, Welcome Inn RV Park also offers permanent spaces with storage, cable TV, phone connections, rest rooms, showers, laundry, propane, clubhouse, and a van for rent on site.

# Juan de Fuca Highway

**Crescent Beach RV Park**
**2860 Crescent Beach Rd., Port Angeles**
**(360) 928-3344**
**www.olypen.com/crescent**

Located on the site of the logging community of Port Crescent, this park offers 40 full hookup sites along with 24 tent sites, rest rooms, showers, and laundry facilities.

**Silver Salmon Motel and RV Park**
**P.O. Box 156, Neah Bay**
**(360) 645-2388**

In addition to 12 full hookups (some with picnic tables), this park also has an on-site gift shop, which sells souvenirs as well as local art. Monthly rates are available.

**Snow Creek Resort**
**P.O. Box 248, Neah Bay**
**(360) 645-2284**

Snow Creek Resort offers 17 full hookups and 25 with only power and water, 30 tent sites, showers, a boat launch, a dock and moorage, and an on-site store.

**Shipwreck Point Campground**
**6850 WA Hwy. 112, Sekiu**
**(360) 963-2688**
**www.olypen.com/tretsrvp**

Located along the Strait of Juan de Fuca, this park offers 25 full hookup sites and 25 tent sites. Guests also enjoy hot showers and laundry facilities, and the park also rents kayaks so guests can tour the 1,000 feet of protected waterfront. Pets are allowed on leash only.

## Forks

**Bear Creek Motel & RV Park**
**P.O. Box 236, Beaver**
**(360) 327-3660**
**www.northolympic.com/bearcreek**

The RV Park at Bear Creek Motel offers 14 full hookups and 4 sites with just electricity, as well as the amenities at the motel and attached restaurant.

**Forks 101 RV Park**
**P.O. Box 1041, Forks**
**(360) 374-5073, (800) 962-9964**

Forks 101 RV Park includes cable TV and optional Internet connections along with the traditional amenities offered with its 35 full hookups that features large pull-thru sites. If you don't want to cook dinner, just walk across the street to eat at an area restaurant.

**Lonesome Creek RV Park**
**590 Ocean Dr., La Push**
**(360) 374-4338**

The Lonesome Creek RV Park offers 44 full hookups, including 22 on the ocean, as well as showers, an on-site grocery store, and a clubhouse. The park also has 12 campsites and 7 tepees.

## Ocean Shores

**Blue Pacific Motel and RV Park**
**2707 WA Hwy. 109, Ocean City**
**(360) 289-2262**

With easy access to the beach, this park offers 13 full hookups with cable TV, and 6 with only water and power. Additional amenities include rest rooms, showers, laundry facilities, and a large play area. Rates are available in daily, weekly, and monthly allotments.

**Driftwood Acres Ocean Campground**
**Copalis Beach**
**(360) 289-3484**

Close to the beach and the Copalis River, this campground offers 21 RV sites, most offering full hookups, 21 tent sites, free firewood, and showers. Guests can also stay in one of the eight new cabins.

### Insiders' Tip

If you go into the backcountry, take a compass or handheld GPS locator and know how to use them.

**Echoes of the Sea Motel & Campground**
3208 WA Hwy. 109, Copalis Beach
(360) 289-3358, (800) 578-3246

This location permits pets and offers 20 full hookups, rest rooms, showers, a recreation room, and 7 tent sites. Two of the tent sites are large enough to accommodate groups.

## Grays Harbor

**Elma RV Park**
P.O. Box 1135, Elma
(360) 482-4053

## Shelton

**Lake Nahwatzel**
W. 12900 Shelton Matlock Rd., Shelton
(360) 426-8323

Call ahead for reservations at Lake Nah-

## Hood Canal

**Cove RV Park**
303075 U.S. Hwy. 101, Brinnon
(360) 976-3452

Along with a mini grocery, Cove RV Park has 34 full hookups, cable TV, showers, laundry, propane, and phones.

**Ocean Shores Marina RV Park**
1070 Discovery Ave. S.E., Ocean Shores
(360) 289-0414

This park offers 96 full hookups (some with cable TV) and 10 camping sites. Guests also enjoy on-site showers, laundry facilities, and access to a boat launch.

Open year-round, this park welcomes pets and offers 50 pull-thru sites cable TV, and laundry facilities.

watzel, which offers 11 full hookups and 2 sites with just electricity along with a restaurant, cocktail lounge, recreation hall, antiques shop and cabins.

**Glen-Ayr Canal Resort**
25381 U.S. Hwy. 101, Hoodsport
(360) 877-9522, (800) 367-9522

With 45 full hookups as part of the resort, Glen-Ayr Canal Resort also offers cable TV, marina, clubhouse, spa, laundry, and propane.

**Minerva Beach RV Resort**
21110 U.S. Hwy. 101, Shelton
(360) 877-5145

With some secluded sites in the woods, Minerva Beach RV Resort offers 28 full hookup pull-thru sites, as well as 25 tent sites, an on-site store, propane, laundry, rest rooms, and showers.

**Summertide Resort & Marina**
15781 N.E. Northshore Rd., Tahuya
(360) 275-9313, (253) 925-9277
www.SummertideResort.com

Sumertide Resort and Marina offers moorage as well as 25 full hookups with nightly, monthly, and yearly rates.

## Insiders' Tip

Heading into the backcountry? Remember to follow zero impact principles for the backwoods. Plan ahead, camp and travel on durable surfaces, dispose of waste properly, leave what you find, minimize campfires, respect wildlife, and respect other visitors to the backcountry.

# Golf

Water and trees form the backdrop for more than a dozen public and semi-private golf courses that form a ring around the Olympic Peninsula. So links lovers have no need to go without their putting, chipping, and driving fix during a visit to the region. All 18 courses included in this chapter offer their own unique spin on local golfing, with a few award-winning course designs and many laid-back, high-quality courses set out by golf enthusiasts over the last 80 years. All of the courses are open year-round, but it is wise to call ahead for a tee time in most cases, just to be sure that a tournament or other activity isn't tying up the particular course you want to play.

All of the courses listed accept Visa and MasterCard, and they all take advance tee times. Many also have Web sites, and some allow online tee time reservations and offer detailed course information. The majority of these courses also offer pro shops with a full range of services, from club rentals to lessons.

The survey of Olympic Peninsula courses is listed alphabetically, and it includes links all along the course covered in this book, from Tacoma in the east and heading west to Bremerton, then around the Olympic Peninsula in a counter clockwise trail along the major highways that ring the peninsula.

## Bayshore Golf Club
**E. 3800 Hwy. 3, Shelton**
**(360) 426-1271**

Bayshore Golf Club stands out among courses along the Hood Canal as one of the older sets of links around. The nine-hole, par 36 course takes advantage of its water theme on its signature hole number four, a par four that offers a view of the bay. The relatively flat course that plays at 3,058 yards from the white tees features three holes that are lined by a creek, and there are bunkers near just about every green. The course was designed by a group of local golfers.

Bayshore is classified as a semi-private course, limiting the public from the course only on Tuesdays and Wednesdays and at times when tournaments are on the links. But for a semi-private course, Bayshore is pretty laid-back. There is no tight dress code, just so long as people wear clothes, according to golf pro Brian Davis. Golfers are also able to choose metal spikes if they prefer them, although soft spikes are preferred.

The course also offers a full-service pro shop with a snack bar, and golf pros are on hand to offer lessons. Fees for nine holes during weekdays are $11 and $13 on weekends, and golfers are encouraged to line up tee times up to two weeks in advance. Walk-on golfers may be able to get on the course in afternoons and in the slow winter season, but Davis says it is a good idea to call ahead since a lot of tournaments are held on the course.

**Directions:** From Shelton, head north on Wash. 3. The course is just a few miles north of town, right off the highway.

## Chevy Chase Golf Club
**7401 Cape George Rd., Port Townsend**
**(800) 385-8722**
**www.chevychasegolf.com/**

From Sequim and Port Angeles, take U.S. 101 to Discovery Bay and turn left onto Wash. 20. After about six miles watch for the sign for the Chevy Chase Golf Course. Turn left at the Four Corners Store onto Discovery Bay Road. Travel straight ahead for a mile and watch for the Chevy Chase Inn on the left. Turn onto Cape George Road and the clubhouse is on the right.

One of the oldest golf courses in the area, the front nine of the 18-hole Chevy Chase Golf Club near Port Townsend first opened to the public in 1925. Seventy-two years later, in 1997, was the opening of the back nine designed by Mike Asmundson. The year-round, par 72 course plays at 6,177 yards from the standard white tees. The course takes advantage of its setting along the west side of Discovery Bay with views on the back nine holes that overlook the water, and most golfers consider hole 11 to be the most scenic, with a great view of Mt. Baker off to the north.

The tree-lined course presents a number of challenges, with water coming into play on holes four and five, as well as sand traps on nearly every hole. The greens are small with undulating greens on the front nine holes. Otherwise, most of the greens are flat and play a little slow.

Golf pro Shawn Yim watches over the daily activities in the full-service pro shop that offers lessons, a driving range, and a putting green, in addition to merchandise for sale. The pro shop also has a snack bar, and a lounge is nearby. Golfers who purchase drinks in the lounge can take them onto the course.

The course is rated as definitely walkable, but many players choose to rent golf carts for as little as $20 for a power cart on 18 holes, or $14 for nine holes. Pull carts are also available. Fees for 18 holes range from $22 on weekdays to $25 on weekends. Senior and Junior rates are also available.

Tee-time reservations are available via phone or by checking the course's Web site. Golfers are advised to set a tee time seven days in advance.

**Directions:** From Seattle and points south, cross the Hood Canal Bridge on Wash. 104 and continue west up the hill to the turnoff for Port Townsend on Wash. 19. Follow Wash. 19 north through Chimacum and approximately two miles past the light to the intersection with Four Corners Road. Turn left and travel one mile to the intersection with Cape George Road. Take a left just past the tennis courts and the clubhouse is on the right.

> ## Insiders' Tip
> Bring your camera to the golf course to take pictures of the unobstructed views of the Olympic Mountains, Puget Sound, and other sights from the wide-open expanses of area courses.

### Dungeness Golf & Country Club
1965 Woodcock Rd., Sequim
(800) 447-6826 or (360) 683-6344

A tough third hole and views that include the Olympic Mountains behind the course and peek-a-boo glimpses of the Strait of Juan de Fuca are among the unique features of the Dungeness Golf Course. The 18-hole, par 72 course opened in 1970, initially with just nine holes. Today is it open year-round and located in one of the drier areas on the Peninsula, making it a good bet for rain-free golfing.

The par five third hole, known as Old Crabby, features a sand trap shaped like a crab's claws that can snag golf balls as they approach the green. The sand trap on the third hole is one of 52 sand traps along the course, and golfers also have to play precisely on three holes that have water to contend with.

Aside from the standard course, Dungeness also offers a full-service pro shop with a snack bar, a full restaurant, and lessons taught by teaching pro John Lucas. The course also has a driving range, putting green, and chipping green.

Although the course is generally considered walkable, the back nine does have a few minor hills that can make renting a golf cart a wise idea. Dungeness charges $26.50 to play 18 holes on weekdays and $29.50 on Fridays through Sundays. Cart rentals are extra and twilight rates are also

*The threat of rain doesn't deter golfers along the Olympic Peninsula, especially in the north where the mountains leave many courses in a relatively dry rain shadow.* PHOTO: NATALIE McNAIR-HUFF

available. It is a good idea to line up a tee time in advance, and the course offers reservations up to 60 days in advance. But walk-on play is definitely a possibility on weekday afternoons.

**Directions:** From all points to the west, take U.S.101 to the Carlsborg Road exit and turn north at the end of the off-ramp. Then turn right onto Old Olympic Highway and proceed about a half-mile before turning left onto Cays Road. Turn left onto Woodcock Road and follow signs to the course.

**Gold Mountain Golf Course**
**7263 W. Belfair Valley Rd., Gorst**
**(360) 415-5432, (800) 249-2363**
**www.goldmt.com**

With two courses and annual ratings as one of the top golf destinations in the state, the Gold Mountain Golf Course is a premier place for golfers on the Peninsula. The par 72, 6,034-yard Olympic course designed by John Harbottle opened in 1996. And the older par 71, 6,059-yard Cascade course that opened in

1970 still draws hordes of golfers.

The new Olympic course is highlighted by the signature par five 18th hole, a downhill finishing shot with water on the right and sandtraps near the green. Olympic has more water come into play than the other course—including a pond stocked with fish on one hole—and it also offers sand traps around the greens on every hole.

Cascade, on the other hand, is highlighted by the par 3 eighth hole that plays across a valley, with the tee and green at about the same elevation. The Cascade course has water on one hole and it also has fewer sand traps than the newer course.

Aside from two courses, Gold Mountain also offers a full restaurant in addition to a full pro shop with a full range of gear, along with lessons and a nearby driving range, putting green, and chipping green. To guarantee a tee time on either of the courses at Gold Mountain, plan to call ahead for a reservation up to 30 days in advance. Walk-on golfing is possible, but mostly on weekdays and afternoons.

To play the Cascade course, golfers will pay $22 during the weekdays, $16 for weekday twilight rates, and $28 for weekends. The Olympic course costs $32 on weekdays, $18 for weekday twilight rates, and $39 on weekends.

**Directions:** From Tacoma, take Wash. 16 west across the Narrows Bridge and continue on Wash. 16 until it intersects with Wash. 3 in Gorst. Turn left and head south on Wash. 3 toward Belfair. Merge onto Sam Christopher Road West, then turn left onto West Belfair Valley Road.

### Highland Golf Course
**300 Yard Dr., Cosmopolis**
**(360) 533-2455**

The Highland Golf Course in Cosmopolis opened in 1929 with nine holes, but in 1994 it grew into a full-fledged par 70, 18-hole course that plays at 5,830 yards from the standard men's tees. With eight holes that have water in play and scenic views from the back nine holes, Highland is a popular destination near Grays Harbor.

A par five, 490-yard 17th hole serves as the signature hole for the course. It offers hazards on both sides of the fairway, with water on one side and trees on the other, and a downhill section adds another dimension to the challenge of the hole.

In addition to a standard driving range and putting green, the course offers a full pro shop, on-site lessons, and a snack bar. It is recommended that golfers line up tee times in advance. Greens fees are $15 during weekdays for 18 holes and $17 during weekends. Cart rentals are an additional $20 for a power cart or $10 for a handcart.

**Directions:** Taking U.S. 101 south from Aberdeen, take the First Street exit and look for the entrance to the course on the right.

### Horseshoe Lake Golf Course
**15932 Sidney Rd. SW, Port Orchard**
**(800) 843-1564**
**www.hlgolf.com**

Many golfers may look at the yardage total for the Horseshoe Lake Golf Course

and think they are in for an easy day, but even at 5,600 yards the par 71 course offers its share of tree-lined challenges. The fairways are narrow with a few sand traps and water comes into play on a number of holes. Add the hilly back nine to the mix and the course offers enough challenging terrain that golf carts are highly recommended.

Horseshoe Lake opened in 1992 after being designed by local golfer Jim Richardson. Placed as it is on a peninsula between Puget Sound to the east and Hood Canal to the west, the course offers stunning views of the Olympic Mountains, especially along the back nine that borders Minter Creek. The course record to date is 67.

The course is open year-round and services on-site include a full restaurant, a pro shop that offers merchandise, and lessons taught under the leadership of PGA pro Chris Morris. Golfers can stop by to use the driving range or putting green, and there is no need to worry too much about the dress code since all the proprietors require is common golf attire.

Reservations for tee times are accepted up to two weeks in advance for foursomes and a week in advance for individuals, and the best way to get a reservation is to stop by the course's Web site. Costs range from $29 for 18 holes on weekdays to $34 for 18 holes on the weekends. The course also offers winter rates.

**Directions:** From the Tacoma area, head west on Wash. 16 to the Purdy/Key Center exit about seven miles from the Narrows Bridge. Follow the exit to the first light and turn left onto Wash. 302. Go approximately two miles to 94th Avenue and turn right, then follow it about one mile to the golf course on the left side of the road.

### Lake Cushman Golf Course
### North 210 W. Fairway Dr., Hoodsport
### (360) 877-5505

Since opening in 1972, the nine-hole Lake Cushman Golf Course has been a popular destination for players along the Hood Canal. The par 70 (for 18 holes, playing from separate tees) course plays at 5,871 yards out and back. Like most courses along the Olympic Peninsula, Lake Cushman is open year-round, but if heavy rains pound the area day after day, it is wise to call ahead for an update on course conditions.

The toughest hole on the course at Lake Cushman is the seventh, with a slight dog-leg to the right and a lake and stream around the hole as obstacles. The course has five holes with water—either streams or small ponds. Sand traps are not prevalent.

Lake Cushman also offers a full pro shop with some merchandise and gear for sale, lessons taught by a PGA golf pro, and a nearby driving range and putting green. Golfers will also find a snack bar serving common refreshments and beer.

It costs $10 to play nine holes on weekdays during the peak season and $12 for nine on weekends. Golfers are advised to call ahead for tee times, which can be reserved up to two weeks in advance.

**Directions:** From Olympia, take U.S. 101 north for about 40 miles to the town of Hoodsport. In Hoodsport, turn left at the signs for the golf course and head up the hill for three miles. The course is on the left side of the road.

### Lakeland Village Golf & Country Club
### E. 200 Old Ranch Rd., Allyn
### (360) 275-6100

The Lakeland Village Golf & Country Club course looks easy to play on paper, but with narrow fairways and small greens, the par 36, nine-hole course is a challenge for many golfers. It plays at 2,900 yards.

Lakeland Village's sixth hole is the trickiest on the course because of a water hazard along the way to the green, and the eighth is the most scenic with a view of the lake down the hill. Despite the mention of hills though, the course is rated as very walkable. Golfers will find a full-service pro shop that offers lessons and club rentals, a nearby putting green, and a full restaurant serving beer and wine at Lakeland Village. Drinks are allowed on the course, as long as they are purchased on-site.

Lakeland Village, as a semi-private course that allows public play, is becoming popular through word-of-mouth promotion, so golfers are advised to line up a tee time up to a week in advance. It costs $11 to play nine holes and $16 to play 18 holes on weekdays. Weekends run $15 for nine holes and $20 for 18 holes.

**Directions:** From I-5 north or south, take the Wash. 16 exit westbound and go across the Narrows Bridge toward Bremerton. When Wash. 16 intersects with Wash. 3 southbound, take the exit and head south through the town of Belfair to the town of Allyn. The course is situated just west of Wash. 3 on East Old Ranch Road.

## Insiders' Tip
Leave your clubs at home and lighten your load. Pro shops will rent a set to you by the round.

**Lake Limerick Country Club**
**E. 790 St. Andrews Dr., Shelton**
**(360) 426-6290**

Another of the Olympic Peninsula golf courses that opened in the 1960s is the Lake Limerick Country Club near Shelton. The nine-hole, par 36 public golf course that debuted in 1967 plays at 2,900 yards.

The long eighth hole is the most scenic on the links with a view of a lake. Other than this view hole, two others have water in play—holes six and seven. And bunkers abound on the tree-lined and narrow course.

Lake Limerick allows metal spikes on the course, although soft spikes are preferred. When golfers arrive they find a full-service pro shop with on-site lessons. A snack bar is also offered with breakfast and lunch food, as well as a full grill.

The cost to play nine holes during weekdays runs $11, or $16 for eighteen holes. Weekends are $16 for nine holes and $21 for eighteen. Golfers can also rent carts, although the course is walkable with only a few rolling hills.

**Directions:** From downtown Shelton, follow Wash. 3 northbound out of town to turn left on E. Lincoln Place. Go straight onto E. Mason Lake Road and follow it around a curve to E. St. Andrews Drive.

**Madrona Links Golf Club**
**3604 22nd Ave. NW, Gig Harbor**
**(253) 851-5193**

Just across the Narrows Bridge in Gig Harbor, Madrona Links offers 18 holes of quality golfing on a par 71, 5,193-yard course that is open year-round. Fittingly for the course's name, it is well-known for the number of trees on the course, and golfers have to beware along the narrow fairways to avoid tree trouble.

Mardrona Links debuted in 1978. It features a difficult 13th hole where the fairway slants right to left. The course that was designed by Ken Tyson also has four holes with water hazards.

When golfers arrive at the links they will find a full-service pro shop offering apparel and other gear, along with a full restaurant with a banquet room and lounge. The course also offers a small 150-yard driving range along with putting and chipping greens.

Playing 18 holes on weekdays costs $21, and it's $23 on weekends. The price for nine holes is $15 on weekdays and $17 on weekends. Golfers are encouraged to get advance tee times, and reservations are accepted up to seven days ahead of time.

**Directions:** From I-5 north or south, take the Wash. 16 exit westbound and cross the Narrows Bridge. Proceed west to the Wollochet/Pt. Fosdick exit to Gig Harbor. Merge onto Stone Drive NW, then turn right onto Jahn Avenue NW. Jahn Avenue NW becomes 32nd Street NW. Follow this to turn right onto 22nd Avenue NW.

**McCormick Woods**
**5155 McCormick Woods Dr. S.W.,**
**Port Orchard**
**(360) 895-0130, (800) 323-0130**
**www.mccormickwoods.com**

Consistently ranked as one of the top courses in the state, McCormick Woods has just about everything a golfer could want in an Olympic Peninsula course. It offers 18 holes that play at 6,658 yards from the standard men's tees. Recently the course was chosen by Golf Digest as one of the top 201 best places to play golf in the United States.

*Native plants and course-side wetlands help make McCormick Woods one of the most environmentally friendly golf courses in the state.* PHOTO: ROB McNAIR-HUFF

McCormick Woods opened as a 9-hole course in 1986, and it expanded shortly thereafter to a full 18-hole course. A couple of holes serve as signature holes for the course—the par four 12th hole that offers a great view of Mount Rainier in the distance and the par five 18th hole coming back to the clubhouse. Overall, the course is extremely wooded, but it isn't real narrow along the fairways. It is well known for its rolling fairways and undulating greens.

Aside from the award-winning course, McCormick Woods also sports a full- service pro shop and a stellar restaurant called Marymac's. Golfers interested in playing McCormick Woods should line up a tee time in advance, and reservations are accepted up to seven days in advance.

McCormick Woods costs $43 on weekdays during the summer and $57 on weekends. Off-season rates are $22 on weekdays and $30 on weekends. Golf cart rentals cost an additional $13 per person, and carts are not required.

**Directions:** From Wash. 16, take the Tremont Street exit, then go south. In about a mile, turn left onto McCormick Woods Drive S.W. and follow the signs to the clubhouse.

### Oaksridge Golf Club
**1052 Monte-Elma Rd., Elma**
**(360) 482-3511**

A popular golf course for seniors because of its relative flatness, Oaksridge began its life as a nine-hole course in 1921 before expanding years later to become the par 72, 18-hole course that it is today. The 5,423-yard course is highlighted by the 486-yard 10th hole, that serves as the signature hole with a huge oak tree along the fairway.

Aside from its namesake trees, Oaksridge has three holes on the back nine with water in play, and the course has nine major sand traps in all.

Outside of the course itself, Oaksridge also has a full pro shop with clothing and merchandise for sale, as well as some food items. Cost for playing 18 holes during the week is $16, and 9 holes costs $9. Senior rates are $7 for 9 holes and $13 for 18 holes. And cart rentals are extra—$10 for 9 holes and $17 for 18 holes. Tee-time reservations are not terribly critical, except for on weekends, when golfers are advised to call a day or two in advance.

**Directions:** From Olympia, take Wash. 12 going west, then turn right on Shouweiler Road. Make a left onto Monte Elma Road then go a half-mile to the course, look for the entrance on the left.

### Ocean Shores Golf Course
### 500 Canal Drive, Ocean Shores
### (360) 289-3357

Ocean breezes and playing across a canal are two of the features that make the Ocean Shores Golf Course stand out. The 18-hole course that opened in 1961 offers a mostly flat surface on an out-and-back design. It is a par 71 course that plays at 5,983 yards from the standard men's golf tees.

The signature hole at Ocean Shores is a par 3 ninth hole that has golfers play across a canal on the way back toward the clubhouse. The course has more of a links-style design on the front nine and a more northwest-style design on the back nine.

Ocean Shores also has a full pro shop with on-site lessons taught by a pair of PGA pros. There is also a nearby chipping green and putting green, as well as a snack bar on the course with simple foods like hot dogs and sandwiches.

Playing at Ocean Shores during the summer season from April through October costs $25 for 18 holes. And it costs $17 for 18 holes between October and March.

**Directions:** From Wash. 109 going north, make a left onto Hogans Corner (Wash. 115) and go straight to Point Brown Avenue, then make another left onto J K Louis Drive. Turn left again, then make a right on Canal Drive. Look for the clubhouse on the left side of the road.

### Port Ludlow Golf Course
### 751 Highland Dr., Port Ludlow
### (360) 437-0272, (800) 455-0272
### www.portludlowgolf.com

The award-winning Port Ludlow Golf Course bills itself as a semi-private resort, and it does sell memberships, but it is also a favorite of golfers from the general public who hunger for the views, playing among second-growth trees, and the course designed by Robert Muir Graves. Port Ludlow offers 27 holes, with the first 18 holes designed in 1975 and the last nine holes added in 1992. Golfers can play different courses at different times of the day, but all of the course options add up to being par 72 links that play at around 6,900 yards.

Ponds and creeks play a part in making Port Ludlow a challenging golf course, but scenery and views of Puget Sound, Ludlow Bay, Whidbey Island, and Mount Baker in the distance combined with the fact that no two holes are next to each other makes it a favorite of area golfers. Golfers also enjoy the amenities, such as a full-service pro shop with just about everything you would expect in a pro shop. The course also has an on-site deli and food and beverage service.

Golfers making the trip to Port Ludlow need to line up tee times in advance. Reservations are accepted from non-members up to five days in advance. Greens fees run to $59 for 18 holes from June through September, and to $29 for 18 holes during the off-season.

**Directions:** From the Hood Canal Bridge heading west, take the exit onto Paradise Bay Road immediately after the bridge. Go 3.5 miles to Teal Lake Road, then turn left and go one block before taking a right onto Highland Drive. Go to the top of the hill and look for the clubhouse.

### Port Townsend Municipal Golf Club
### 1948 Blaine St., Port Townsend
### (360) 385-4547

The nine-hole Port Townsend Municipal Golf Club offers options for visitors to the Victorian-themed town. They can choose to either play the par 35, 2,755-yard, nine-hole course, or use the separate tees to transform the course into a par 70, 2,904-yard 18-hole course. Either way, golfers will get scenic views of the Olympic Mountains in the background and they will be challenged by playing around a large pond that comes into play on three different holes.

Port Townsend's course, which opened in 1925 is rated as very walkable, although the course does sit on a hillside. Golf carts are available for rent. The club also offers a full pro shop with a selection of golf clothing, gear, shoes, and clubs. PGA pro Mike Early teaches lessons on-site.

Costs for playing 9 holes are $12 plus tax during the summer season from April 15 through September 15, and $18 plus tax for 18 holes. Golfers are advised to line up tee times at least a day in advance, although walk-ons are possible in the early afternoons.

**Directions:** Entering town northbound on Wash. 20, turn left onto Kearney Street, then go straight to Blaine Street.

### Rolling Hills Golf Course
**2485 NE McWilliams Rd., Bremerton**
**(360) 479-1212**

The 18-hole Rolling Hills Golf Course designed by Don Hogan opened in 1972, and since its opening the par 70, 5,936-yard course has drawn area golfers with its challenging small greens. A couple of holes stand out as most memorable for players— a par three, 175-yard 16th hole that challenges golfers by hitting over a pond and the par five 10th hole that is billed as one of the hardest par 5 holes in the county.

Rolling Hills gets its name because much of the course is located on top of a hill, but the course is still quite walkable and golfers are not required to use carts. The course features two ponds and a couple of creeks in addition to sand traps that serve as obstacles on most holes.

The pro shop at Rolling Hills offers merchandise and some food items, and players can also opt to eat at the full- service restaurant on the course. Golfers can also sign up for lessons or stop by to use the driving range or putting and chipping greens. Rates for playing at Rolling Hills are $23 for 18 holes on weekdays and $25 for 18 holes on weekends. And tee-time reservations are accepted up to seven days in advance.

**Directions:** From Wash. 16, take Wash. 303 north. Continue north on Wash. 303 until reaching N.E. McWilliams Road, then turn right. In a short distance, turn right again to reach the clubhouse.

### Trophy Lake Golf & Casting
**3900 SW Lake Flora Rd., Port Orchard**
**(360) 874-8337**
**www.trophylakegolf.com**

One of the newest golf courses in the state, Trophy Lake Golf and Casting features a unique combination of 18 holes of golfing along a lake-speckled course that also offers fly fishing in five lakes. It is safe to say it is one of the few golf courses in Washington where the pro shop offers golf gear right alongside fly-fishing gear.

The par 72 course designed by award-winning John Fought plays at 6,162 yards from the standard men's tees. The combination of lakes and streams make the signature 18th hole, a par 5, 465-yard hole with a pond on the right and a creek on the left, stick in the memory of golfers as they finish their rounds.

Although the course is quite walkable, Trophy Lake includes cart rental as part of its standard playing fees. It costs $39 during the week to play during the winter months and $59 during the week in summer. Weekend rates are higher. To line up a tee time, call ahead. Tee times are accepted up to a month in advance. Golfers are required to use spikeless shoes at Trophy Lake.

**Directions:** From Wash. 16, take the Sedgewick Road exit and turn south. Continue down Sedgewick Road until it turns into Glenwood Road S.W. Continue down Glenwood Road S.W. until it turns into S.W. Lake Flora Road. The course is down the road on the left.

### Village Greens Golf Course
**5180 Country Club Way SE, Port Orchard**
**(360) 871-2236**

The tree-lined Clover Valley Country Club course offers 18 holes with plenty of water in play. The par 69 course opened in 1963, and today it features year-round

*Rolling hills and on-course amenities such as this gazebo are some of the features of Peninsula golf courses.*

PHOTO: ROB McNAIR-HUFF

play over its 5,350 yards with a full range of services, from lessons taught by a teaching pro on staff to a full pro shop with rental clubs and a snack bar. Rated as walkable, Clover Valley also offers motorized golf carts in addition to standard pull carts. Gas-powered carts are $18 for 18 holes or $10 for 9, and pull carts are $3. Fees for weekday play during the summer season is $12.50 for 18 holes and $9 for 9. Weekend fees are $16 for 18 holes and $9 for 9. The course also offers twilight rates and senior discounts.

Golfers are advised to line up tee times in advance, and times can be arranged up to a year in advance by calling the pro shop.

**Directions:** From Tacoma, take Wash. 16 across the Narrows Bridge to the Sedgwick Road exit and take a right. Drive about 2.5 miles to Country Club Way and turn south; then go a short distance down the road to the course.

# Olympic National Park

Visitor Centers

Entrances

Lodging and Dining

Camping

Day Hikes

The crown jewel of the Olympic Peninsula, and one of the most popular national parks in the United States, Olympic National Park draws more than 4 million visitors each year to its rugged mountains, rain forests, and coastal wilderness. Looking at this 922,653-acre park today, it is hard to imagine the Herculean efforts and battles that took place between conservationists, nature lovers, local residents, and large timber companies leading up to the park's designation on June 29, 1938.

The area started on the road to becoming a national park in 1897, when President Grover Cleveland established the 2,188,800-acre Olympic Forest Reserve. Not all of this huge reserve would become the national park. Before a survey of the forest reserve could even be completed three years later, timber interests and land speculators convinced government officials to open up more than 75 percent of the richest forest lands to settlers and to logging.

In the early 1900s, efforts to protect the elk herds on the Olympic Peninsula moved the area closer to national park status. On March 3, 1909, as one of the last acts of his time in office, President Theodore Roosevelt designated a 600,000-acre area as the Mt. Olympus National Monument, largely to help protect the elk that would later carry his name, Roosevelt elk. The elk, which are a subspecies found on the Peninsula, were being killed extensively by hunters who would harvest their teeth for watch fobs. Designation of the national monument protected the elk's summer feeding grounds and much of the inner core of the Olympic Mountains, but it failed to protect winter feeding areas. Repeated efforts to create a larger and more permanent reserve for the elk failed over the following years, until President Franklin D. Roosevelt was inaugurated in 1933.

President Franklin D. Roosevelt visited the Peninsula in 1937 on a fact-finding mission to determine once and for all if the area should be set aside as a national park. During his visit, Roosevelt stayed at Lake Crescent Lodge, stopped in Forks, and visited Lake Quinault Lodge. Early in the visit he made it clear that he not only wanted to proclaim the area a national park, but that he was going to include valuable timberlands within the park boundaries to preserve some of the gigantic trees and rain-forest lands that were coveted by the National Forest Service and logging interests.

Olympic National Park became official on June 29, 1938, when President Roosevelt signed a bill setting aside 638,280 acres as park land. He also included a provision to add more lands at a later time, and over the ensuing years, more lands have been added to bring the park to its present 922,653 acres, including the 60-mile-long section of wilderness coastline that is the longest section of coastal wilderness in the lower 48 states.

Visitors flock to Olympic National Park because of the unique natural world unveiled along its hiking trails and at its visitor centers and beaches. Nowhere else in the world can someone ski at a place like Hurricane Ridge in the morning, and then travel a few dozen miles to walk ocean beaches or rain-forest lowlands in the afternoon—all within the boundaries of the same national park. Its designation as a park has preserved a large ecosystem valued by leading scientists to the extent that in 1976 it was designated by UNESCO as an International Biosphere Reserve. Five years later, in 1981, it was named as a World Heritage Site for its outstanding natural and cultural values.

# Park Statistics

**Land area:** 922,653 acres

**Visitors:** More than 4 million a year

**Established:** 1938

**Hiking:** 600 miles of trails

**Coastal area:** 62 miles

**Campsites:** 955

**Plants:** More than 1,200 species, 8 found nowhere else in the world

**Animals:** More than 200 birds and 70 types of mammals, 18 animals found nowhere else in the world

In 1988, nearly 95 percent of the park was designated as wilderness, a designation that prohibits road building, mining, timber cutting, hunting, and the use of motorized vehicles within the wilderness boundary.

# Visitor Centers

Three major visitor centers offer in-depth information and on-duty park staff throughout much of the year. The park also has a number of information centers that open in the summer only, such as the Storm King center at Lake Crescent (360-928-3380) and the station at Kalaloch. Information about the east side of the park is offered at the Hood Canal Ranger Station in Hoodsport (360-877-5254).

**Olympic National Park Visitor Center**
**3002 Mt. Angeles Rd., Port Angeles**
**(360) 452-0330**
**www.nps.gov/olym**

Open year-round, the main park visitor center is located on the road to Hurricane Ridge. It offers a small theater and exhibits on the plants and animals found within the park, all open from 9 A.M. to 4 P.M., with extended hours in the summer. Stop by to let the kids play in the children's activity room or to walk one of the short nature trails adjacent to the center. This is also the place to stop and ask park staff about road conditions heading toward Hurricane Ridge, especially in the winter months, or to pick up brochures or buy books about the park in the bookstore.

**Hurricane Ridge Visitor Center**
**(360) 928-3211**

This visitor center at the top of Hurricane Ridge serves sandwiches and drinks along with offering gifts and park information. The center is open daily from the end of April through late September, and open on weekends and holidays, weather and road conditions permitting, during the winter months. It is also open when the area is open to skiing. Park rangers also lead guided snowshoe hikes in the winter, and interpretive walks in the summer along the wheelchair-accessible trails.

**Hoh Rainforest Visitor Center**
**(360) 374-6925**
Exhibits about the rain forest and three short nature trails are the highlights of the Hoh Rainforest Visitor Center. The Hoh center is open daily from 9 A.M. to 4 P.M., but it isn't staffed in the winter months. During the summer, rangers lead guided activities and give lectures at the center and in the nearby campground.

# Entrances

Entrance to the park costs $10 per car, or $5 per person for those walking, cycling, or riding a bus into the park at entrances that include fee collection booths—Elwha, Hurricane Ridge, Hoh, Sol Duc, and Staircase. Passes are good for one week from the day of purchase. As an alternative, an Olympic Park pass is $20 and it offers unlimited park access for a full calendar year. Other alternatives include the 12-month Golden Eagle Passport, good for access to all federal recreation areas and national parks, for $50.

Senior citizens who are U.S. residents or citizens over the age of 62 can also get into the park at reduced rates by buying the $10 Golden Age Passport. Meanwhile, the Golden Access Passport is free to U.S. citizens or residents with lifetime disabilities.

Here we take a look at the amenities offered at the major entrances to Olympic National Park.

## Deer Park

Located in the northeast corner of the park, the high-elevation camping at Deer Park draws visitors looking for a less-developed outdoor experience. Deer Park includes a summer-only ranger station and a primitive campground that can only be reached by turning south off U.S. Highway 101 on Deer Park Road and driving toward the road's conclusion at 6,007-foot Blue Mountain. Deer Park offers a great glimpse of the backcountry and a location from which to explore hikes along the Gray Wolf River or farther along the ridge line into the heart of the Olympic Mountains.

## Heart O' the Hills

As its name implies, the Heart O' the Hills entrance to the park leads deep into the heart of the mountains. The most popular park entrance, Mt. Angeles Road, leads into the park, passing by the Olympic National Park Visitor Center en route to the Heart O' the Hills campground and Hurricane Ridge some 17 miles south of the city of Port Angeles. At nearly a mile high, Hurricane Ridge opens access to the core of the Olympic Mountains. From here, trails branch out along Klahhane Ridge, Hurricane Hill, and down into the Elwha River valley far below.

## Elwha

Just a few miles west of Port Angeles and a few miles south of U.S. Highway 101, the Elwha entrance to the park follows the river into the folds between the mountains. This entrance offers hikes along the river that was once a prodigious salmon fishing destination, before dams blocked the water's flow in the 1920s. It also offers a pair of popular campgrounds, access to Lake Mills for boating and fishing above the dam, and for hikers, access via the road to Whiskey Bend to hiking along the main north-south route through the park to Elkhorn, Hayes River, Low Divide, and finally North Fork on the Quinault River.

Movie buffs will like this park entrance as well, since a short hike in to Humes Ranch will reveal the setting for the 1950s Disney movie *Olympic Elk*.

## Insiders' Tip

Want to learn more about Olympic National Park? Be sure to check the park's official Web site at www.nps.org/olym.

## Sol Duc

Continuing west, and after skirting the southern end of Lake Crescent, the Sol Duc entrance leads south along the Sol Duc River into the forest. Besides the Sol Duc Hot Springs Resort, this entrance offers access to many hiking trails and pictur-esque Sol Duc Falls. The Eagle campground is an alternative for staying overnight along the Sol Duc River, and hikers looking for scenic conditions in the high country can venture into Seven Lakes Basin or try one of the hikes linking with either the Elwha River trails, trails down the Bogachiel River, or even the Olympus Ranger Station and trails leading down to the Hoh Rainforest entrance.

## Ozette

Way off in the northwesternmost corner of the lands that make up Olympic National Park is the Ozette Lake entrance. This lake, located at the end of Hoko-Ozette Road, is the largest natural freshwater lake in Washington. It is open to non-motorized boat use. A nearby pair of popular hiking trails lead to the coastal portion of the park. The northern trail goes to Cape Alava, while the southern trail leads to Sand Point. There are also camping facilities along Ozette Lake, picnic areas, and a ranger station.

This entrance is a must-see for those interested in the Native American tribes that have made their homes along the coast for thousands of years. Just south of Cape Alava and along the beach, petroglyphs can be found on the rocks. The area also holds the Ozette Village archeological dig, which is not open to the public. Artifacts from the village can be viewed at the Makah Cultural Heritage Center in Neah Bay.

## Mora

Just west of the rain capitol of Forks sits Mora campground and entryway to the park along the coast at Rialto Beach. Just north of the Quillayute River and the Native American village of LaPush, Rialto Beach offers a cobbled surface with views of the ocean and James Island, and a short hike north from the parking lot brings visitors to the popular Hole-in-the-Wall area, with its sea-carved rock gateway and tidepools that offer hours of exploration during low tides.

## Hoh Rainforest

South of Forks and turning inland from U.S. Highway 101 on Hoh River Road, the famous Hoh Rainforest entrance to the park is one of the most popular destinations on the Olympic Peninsula. Besides the Hoh Rainforest Visitor Center, the entrance offers access to camping, picnic facilities, interpretive trails, and hiking trails that wind into the core of the Olympic Mountains all the way to the base of Mount Olympus and the Blue Glacier, the biggest mountain and biggest glacier in the Olympics.

## Queets

One of the least-developed entrances into the heart of the park, the Queets River area offers trailheads for hikers as well as access to campgrounds along with the Queets Ranger Station. Nestled in the rain forest, one highlight of the Queets area is the park's largest Douglas fir tree, just a little more than a mile down the main trail along the Queets River.

## Quinault Rain Forest

Between the park offerings on the north side of Lake Quinault and the historic Lake Quinault Lodge on the south side of the lake, the entryway into the Quinault Rain Forest has a lot to offer visitors. Among the features of the park's southwesternmost entrance are the Quinault Rain Forest, North Fork, and Graves Creek Ranger Stations, camping at Graves Creek, North Fork, and July Creek, and access to major trailheads to the Enchanted Valley area and Low Divide. In addition to these trails that lead into the temperate rain forest, the south side of Lake Quinault on U.S. Forest Service lands offers camping at Willaby and Falls Creek, as well as the Quinault U.S. Forest Service station.

## Staircase

Just past Lake Cushman and into the southeastern corner of Olympic National Park is the Staircase Ranger Station, camping area, and picnic facilities. Hike along the North Fork of the Skokomish River and to areas such as Flapjack Lakes.

## Dosewallips

The main eastern entrance into the park, Dosewallips offers camping and a ranger station in addition to trails that lead along the Dosewallips River and to popular destinations such as Lake Constance, Constance Pass, Hatana Falls, and the Anderson Glacier. Trails link into the heart of the park from here, including routes that can cross the park to the Quinault area, Staircase, and Deer Park.

# Lodging and Dining

Formal lodging and dining facilities are limited within Olympic National Park. Here we mention the major options for luxury lodging and dining within the park boundaries.

**Lake Crescent Lodge**
**416 Lake Crescent Rd., Port Angeles**
**(360) 928-3211**
**www.olypen.com/lakecrescentlodge**
Nestled among hemlock and fir trees on the edge of Lake Crescent, this lodge, built in 1916, has hosted President Franklin D. Roosevelt within its five-room confines. Open from late April through October, the lodge also offers 30 rooms outside the main building and 17 rustic cottages, four of which include fireplaces. In addition to lodging, visitors can also dine on fine food, including dishes such as salmon and oysters. The lodge offers a full menu of breakfasts, lunches, and dinners. No reservations are required for dining.

**Lake Quinault Lodge**
**Southshore Rd., Quinault**
**(360) 288-2900, (800) 562-6672**
**www.visitlakequinault.com**
Although not technically located within the park, the venerable Lake Quinault Lodge played a significant role in the formation of Olympic National Park.

**Insiders' Tip**

Twice a year more than 20,000 gray whales migrate past the coastal portion of Olympic National Park. Many pass within two miles of the coast, so those looking out for the whales can spy them during their passage in March and October.

Franklin D. Roosevelt visited the lodge in 1937 while on a fact-finding trip that eventually led to the park's designation. Open year-round, the lodge has 31 rooms in the main lodge, 36 lakeside rooms, 16 rooms with fireplaces, and 9 annex rooms. The lodge is rustic, with period wicker furniture and open beam ceilings, and the rooms don't include TVs, making this a great place to get away from the world. In addition to lodging, visitors can rent boats or wander one of the nature trails near the lodge.

Diners can stop by the Lake Quinault Lodge for cuisine that features fresh fish, seafood, chicken, steak, and pasta. Breakfast, lunch, and dinner are served at the lodge, and reservations are recommended.

**Lake Quinault Resort**
**314 North Shore Road, Amanda Park**
**(360) 288-2362, (800) 650-2362**
**www.lakequinault.com**
Located on the road to the Quinault Ranger Station, this 50-plus-year-old resort with a stellar view along the north shores of Lake Quinault offers townhouse suites, one-bedroom kitchenettes, and two-bedroom kitchenettes. Altogether, the resort offers nine year-round rooms with TVs, coffeemakers, hair dry-

ers, and daily housekeeping. The resort also features summertime lakeside campfires each night, along with a gas BBQ and a covered gazebo. The resort does not allow pets, but quiet, well-supervised children are welcome.

**Kalaloch Lodge**
**157151 U.S. Hwy. 101, Forks**
**(360) 962-2271**
**www.visitkalaloch.com**
A popular destination for storm watchers, the Kalaloch Lodge sits on a bluff overlooking the Pacific Ocean, just 30 miles south of Forks. The main lodge, built in 1953, includes 10 rooms. Another 10 rooms are offered in the nearby Sea Crest House. For those who want a private cabin, the lodge includes 44 rustic cabins, many of which have views of the Pacific and nearby Kalaloch Creek. Kalaloch is open year-round, and since the rooms don't offer TVs or telephones, it is a good place to escape. In addition to the lodging, Kalaloch offers a gas station, a small grocery store, a gift shop, and a cocktail lounge.

Dining at Kalaloch is popular as well. Reservations are recommended for travelers who want to partake of the menu, which includes fresh seafood, chicken, and steak. The lodge serves breakfast, lunch, and dinner. For fast-food fare, stop by the lodge coffee shop for espresso, hamburgers, chicken, and ice cream.

**Log Cabin Resort**
**3183 E. Beach Rd., Port Angeles**
**(360) 928-3325**
**www.logcabinresort.net**
Located on the sunny northeast side of Lake Crescent, the Log Cabin Resort offers lakeside chalets, lodge rooms, rustic cabins, camping cabins, and full RV hookups. Built in a setting that held a log cabin in the mid 1880s, the lodge and its surrounding buildings have been built gradually since the 1920s. All rooms have private baths, with the exception of four cabins that share a bathhouse. Open February through October, the lodge also has

*Elk played an integral role in the formation of the park, since the land was orginally set aside as a reserve for elk herds.* PHOTO: NATIONAL PARK SERVICE

a gift shop and small grocery store, and boats are available for rent as well.

Diners can sit back under the log-beamed ceilings and take in a lake view along with local seafood on the breakfast and dinner menus.

**Sol Duc Hot Springs Resort**
**(360) 327-3583**
**www.northolympic.com/solduc**
Set 12 miles deep into Olympic National Park, the Sol Duc Hot Springs Resort features three mineral pools alongside a

lodge built in the late 1960s. There has been a resort in this location since 1914. Today's incarnation includes 32 cabins, all with private baths, and some with full kitchens. The resort is open from May through September, and the hot springs and nearby hikes to waterfalls make it a popular destination.

Dining at the resort includes a pool-side deli serving sandwiches, burgers, and ice cream, in addition to the full breakfast and dinner menus in the restaurant.

# Camping

The park has 17 major camping areas offering 955 campsites. The list below includes the campground name, how many sites are available, whether the site offers facilities for recreational vehicles, and the cost per night to stay in the campground.

Campsites are offered on a first-come, first-served basis, so be sure to show up early to land a spot on a weekend. Most campgrounds offer fresh water, flush or pit toilets, a table, and a fireplace or fire pit.

In addition to these sites, backcountry camping sites are available to hikers making treks farther into the park. Check with ranger stations and at the trailheads to investigate backcountry campsite status, or call the Wilderness Information Center at (360) 452-0300.

**Altaire**—30 sites, RVs OK, $10 per night

**Deer Park**—14 sites, $8 per night

**Dosewallips**—30 sites, $10 per night

**Elwha**—41 sites, RVs OK, $10 per night

**Fairholm**—88 sites, RVs OK, $10 per night

**Graves Creek**—30 sites, RVs OK, $10 per night

**Heart O' the Hills**—105 sites, RVs OK, $10 per night

**Hoh**—88 sites, RVs OK, $10 per night

**July Creek**—29 sites, $10 per night

**Kalaloch**—175 sites, RVs OK, $12 per night

**Mora**—94 sites, RVs OK, $10 per night

**North Fork**—7 sites, Free

**Ozette**—13 sites, RVs OK, $10 per night

**Queets**—20 sites, $8 per night

**Sol Duc**—82 sites, RVs OK, $12 per night

**South Beach**—50 sites, RVs OK, $8 per night

**Staircase**—59 sites, RVs OK, $10 per night

# Day Hikes

To really get to know the plants and animals of Olympic National Park, you should consider taking a day hike during your visit. Here are some suggestions for trails that are easy to get to, relatively quick to complete, and that offer a great glimpse of the park.

## Hiking Rules

1. Pets are not allowed on park trails and beaches except at Rialto Beach north from the parking lot to Ellen Creek and all beach access from the Hoh Indian Reservation south to the Quinault Indian Reservation, where they are allowed on a leash. Pets are allowed on a leash in campgrounds and parking areas.

2. Pack out all garbage.

3. Use the privies or pit toilets where they are available. Otherwise, make your own toilet in a shallow trench away from campfires and trails, and at least 100 feet from any water source. Be sure to cover the trench when you finish.

*The lodge at Hurricane Ridge sits more than a mile above sea level.* PHOTO: NATALIE McNAIR-HUFF

## Heart O' the Hills and Hurricane Ridge

Heart of the Forest Trail—This trail through lowland forest is 2 miles one-way, starting at Loop E in the Heart of the Hills campground.

Hurricane Hill Trail—A wheelchair-accessible, paved trail, the 1.5-mile Hurricane Hill loop starts at the end of Hurricane Ridge Road and heads to the top of the hill, offering views of Port Angeles, the Strait of Juan de Fuca, and in early summer, wildflowers are present along the route. Wheelchairs can maneuver the first half-mile of the trail, but passage beyond that point requires assistance.

Meadow Loop Trails—Some of the most popular and accessible trails in the park, the Meadow Loop Trails start near the Hurricane Ridge Visitor Center and wind through the subalpine environment along the ridge. Be sure to stay on the trail, much of which is paved and wheelchair accessible. These trails often offer glimpses of Columbia black-tailed deer, and if you listen carefully you may hear the whistle of an Olympic marmot. But remember not to feed any wildlife along the trail. For a longer walk, venture onto the primitive adjoining Klahhane Ridge Trail.

## Elwha

West Lake Mills Trail—Check out this out-and-back trail that begins at the Lake Mills boat launch and meanders along the lakeside for two miles.

Griff Creek Trail—From its starting point behind the Elwha Ranger Station, this steep, 2.8-mile, one-way switchback trail climbs to an overlook at the 1.8-mile mark, and then continues up along the creek bed before reaching its conclusion.

Krause Bottom Trail—If you want to take a little more aggressive hike, drive to the end of Whiskey Bend Road and set off on this 4-mile round-trip hike above the Elwha

River. The trail sets out along a wooded ridge above the river for about 1.5 miles, then veers to the right down a steep descent to the riverside in an area called Krause Bottom. When you reach the bottom, be sure to wander to the right to a ledge that offers a view of a rocky gorge called Goblin Gates. To finish the hike, either return the way you came in, or continue along the river and up a hill to Humes Ranch in another half mile. Then rejoin the main trail back to the parking lot.

## Lake Crescent

Moments in Time Nature Trail—Wander this easy, half-mile loop trail to view Lake Crescent and old-growth forest in an area that once held homesteads between the site of the present Olympic Park Institute and Lake Crescent Lodge.

Marymere Falls—View a 90-foot-tall waterfall at the end of this one-mile trail that leaves the side of Lake Crescent and winds through old-growth forest after departing from the Storm King Ranger Station. The first three-quarters of a mile of the trail is wheelchair accessible.

Mount Storm King Trail—Climb a steep trail for another 1.7 miles from Marymere Falls for good views of Lake Crescent.

Pyramid Peak Trail—Starting on the north side of the lake, this trail climbs 2,600 feet in just 3.5 miles before reaching the summit, which offers views of Lake Crescent and the Strait of Juan de Fuca. Be sure to explore the World War II aircraft spotter station at the summit.

Spruce Railroad Trail—Connecting the North Shore and Lyre River Trailheads, this four-mile trail is popular with hikers and mountain bikers for its flat grade and views of Lake Crescent. The trail follows the route of the World War I Spruce Railway.

## Sol Duc

Sol Duc Falls—Drive to the end of Sol Duc River Road and walk less than a mile one-way to view the much photographed Sol Duc Falls. For a longer hike, try the six-mile Sol Duc Falls/Lover's Lane Loop. Sections of the loop are rough and rocky.

Mink Lake Trail—Bring a fishing pole on this rigorous, 2.5-mile, one-way hike from the Sol Duc Hot Springs Resort to a mountain lake. The trail climbs 1,400 feet to the lakeside.

Ancient Groves Nature Trail—This half-mile trail winds through old-growth forest from one road turnout to another along the Sol Duc River Road.

## Insiders' Tip

Learn more about the plants, wildlife, and history of Olympic National Park by checking out the programs offered by the Olympic Park Institute. The institute offers classes and seminars every year between spring and fall on topics including geology, intertidal life, marine mammals, and Native American art. For more information about the institute, check its Web site at www.yni.org/opi/ or call (360) 928-3720.

*A hiker rests and takes in the view of the Blue Glacier in the heart of the Olympic Mountains.* PHOTO: NATIONAL PARK SERIVCE

## Lake Ozette

Cape Alava Trail—Hikers have their choice of two trails to the ocean beaches from the end of Lake Ozette Road. This northern trail traverses 3.3 miles along a nearly continuous boardwalk over wetlands to Cape Alava, the westernmost point in the contiguous United States. At the end of the trail, explore the rocks on the shore to view petroglyphs carved by Native Americans many years ago.

Sand Point Trail—The southern trail to the coast from Lake Ozette Road crosses more wetlands on boardwalks, covering 3 miles before reaching the shore of the Pacific Ocean. For both this trail and the Cape Alava Trail, be sure to check the tide tables before setting out. For those who want to make a loop hike on the coast, walk the beach north from the end of Sand Point Trail to connect with the Cape Alava Trail and return to your car on that route.

## Mora and La Push

Third Beach Trail—Starting at LaPush Road, some 12 miles west of U.S. Highway 101, this sandy beach stretches 1.4 miles from the trailhead.

Second Beach Trail—Also on LaPush Road, about 14 miles west of U.S. Highway 101, you'll find the trailhead for Second Beach. This trail is 0.8 miles one-way, and it offers views of sea stacks offshore as well as tidepools for exploring at low tide.

Rialto Beach Trail—Besides a paved 0.1-mile path from the parking lot to a view of the beach, walkers can make a 1.5-mile, one-way jaunt north along the beach to Hole-in-the-Wall, a well-known and much-photographed rock outcropping surrounded by tidepools.

## Hoh Rainforest

Hall of Mosses Trail—A popular and easy three-quarters-of-a-mile trail through the rain forest, this route starts at the visitor center at the end of the Hoh River Road.

Spruce Nature Trail—This longer trail offers a 1.25-mile, round-trip glimpse of the dense vegetation of the rain forest.

## Kalaloch

Ruby Beach—The northernmost of seven trails to the beach near Kalaloch, the short walk down to Ruby Beach offers a sandy beach and views of the shoreline in an area that was once home to oil drilling rigs.

## Queets

Sams River Loop Trail—Walkers on this three-mile trail have a great chance of seeing Roosevelt elk in the morning or evening in one of the meadows that were once the sites of homesteads. The trail—which passes both the Queets and Sams Rivers—can be picked up either at the Queets Ranger Station or at the trailhead one mile east of the station.

## Quinault

Maple Glade Rain Forest Trail—A half-mile loop, this trail starts across the bridge from the Quinault Ranger Station and winds through the woods, with interpretive signs denoting the plant life along the route.

Graves Creek Nature Trail—Beginning at the Graves Creek campground, this one-mile loop trail travels through temperate rain forest.

## Staircase

Shady Lane Nature Trail—Walk across a bridge from the Staircase Ranger Station to start this three-mile, round-trip jaunt.

Staircase Rapids Loop Trail—Wander through virgin forest along the Skokomish River and cross the Staircase Rapids at the one-mile mark on this short trail that starts across from the Staircase Ranger Station.

## Dosewallips

Terrace Loop Trail—A 1.5-mile trail, this route begins and ends within 100 yards of the Dosewallips Ranger Station. It also offers access to the Dosewallips River.

> **Insiders' Tip**
>
> During the winter months, park interpreters offer guided snowshoe walks on weekends and federal holidays at Hurricane Ridge. Snowshoes are provided for a $2 donation.

# Gig Harbor

Hotels and Motels

Bed and Breakfast Inns

Restaurants

Shopping

The quiet harbor that would become Gig Harbor was familiar to local Native American tribes such as the Nisqually, but it didn't appear on the maps of European settlers until 1841. That was when the Wilkes Expedition mapped the lower reaches of Puget Sound and crewmen, using a captain's gig, stumbled upon the harbor and aptly named it Gig Harbor. Twenty-six years later, fisherman Samuel Jerisich and two other fishermen pulled into the inner harbor to spend the night, and they liked the area so much that they decided to make their home nearby.

Yugoslavian and Scandinavian immigrants moved into the region in the following years and helped turn the area from a sawmill town into one of the largest fishing cities in the state. At its peak, more than 70 commercial fishing boats set out every year from the harbor. The Skansie Shipbuilding Company built more than 180 purse seiners and cannery tenders that firmly placed Gig Harbor on the map.

Gig Harbor retains its marine influence today. The city of 6,500 people still has hosts of commercial fishing vessels that call the inner harbor home. But it is known for more than fishing. Gig Harbor is a center of the arts on the Kitsap Peninsula, as evidenced by the number of artists and galleries that populate the prime shopping space along the inner harbor. The city is also a popular bedroom community for people who commute to Tacoma and Seattle.

## Hotels and Motels

Hotel accommodations in Gig Harbor are spread across town from The Inn at Gig Harbor near Washington Highway 16 on top of the hill to The Maritime Inn in the heart of the former fishing village. We include four hotels and motels in this chapter, including one motel—the Westwynd Motel—near the neighboring community of Purdy. Most of the hotels have smoking and nonsmoking rooms, as well as at least one wheelchair-accessible room.

## Insiders' Tip

While planning your trip to Gig Harbor, take a look at the following Web sites for research and tips about the town: www.gigharbor.com and www.gigharborchamber.com.

# Price Code

Our price code reflects the average price of a double-occupancy room during the peak season, which runs from mid-May to mid-October. Room rates are usually discounted from late fall to early spring. The prices quoted do not take into account the state and local sales taxes.

$ . . . . . . . . . . . . . .under $60
$$ . . . . . . . . . . . . . .$60–$90
$$$ . . . . . . . . . . . .$91–$130
$$$$ . . . . . . . . . . .over $131

**Gig Harbor Motor Inn    $$**
**4709 Pt. Fosdick Dr. N.W., Gig Harbor**
**(253) 858-8161, (888) 336-8161**
**www.gigharbormotorinn.com**
The Gig Harbor Motor Inn isn't your typical inn. Set on 23 acres laced with walking trails and a duck pond, the inn is billed as a log cabin hidden in the trees, and guests in some rooms can watch ducks feeding just outside their windows. Guests can choose from rooms with either king- or queen-size beds. All rooms have cable TV, phones with data ports, small refrigerators, and coffeemakers. The inn offers both smoking and nonsmoking rooms, and pets are allowed with some restrictions. Each additional person over double occupancy adds $10 per night.

**The Inn at Gig Harbor    $$$**
**3211 56th St. N.W., Gig Harbor**
**(253) 858-1111, (800) 795-9980**
**www.innatgigharbor.com**
Located just off Washington Highway 16 on the hill above downtown, The Inn at Gig Harbor caters to a wide range of guests, from business travelers to honeymooners. The 64-room hotel opened in 1997, and in addition to standard rooms, it features deluxe, two-room Jacuzzi suites that cost around $200. All the rooms offer either queen- or king-size beds, along with cable TV, phones with data ports, air-conditioning, and coffeemakers. Two extended-stay suites offer kitchenettes, and some suites offer two phone lines so that computer users can check their e-mail and make calls at the same time.

Downstairs at the inn, guests can listen to live music in the lounge on Fridays and Saturdays, or opt for dinner in the on-site restaurant. Dinner dishes range from steak to seafood, chicken, duck, and lamb. An on-site exercise studio rounds out the inn's amenities. Pets are allowed in some rooms, with a non-refundable damage deposit of $15 and a $5 per night additional charge.

**The Maritime Inn    $$**
**3212 Harborview Dr., Gig Harbor**
**(253) 858-1818**
**www.maritimeinn.com**
In the mood for a Victorian inn? How about a marine theme? The Maritime Inn in downtown Gig Harbor features 15 rooms, many with different themes, along with a continental breakfast each morning between 8 and 11 A.M. Manager Kathy Franklin says the inn sees a large number of return guests due to its "bed and breakfast" feel, which offers a bit of intimacy and the feel of a small residence but with all the privacy of a hotel. Open since 1996, the inn, rated three diamonds by AAA, sits

in the heart of downtown, with some rooms offering a view of the inner harbor. Add $10 per night for each guest in the room over double occupancy.

All rooms at The Maritime Inn have queen-size beds with private bathrooms, cable TV, air-conditioning, phones, and ADSL service to connect to the Internet at high speed.

**Westwynd Motel at Gig Harbor     $-$$**
**6703 144th St. N.W., Gig Harbor**
**(253) 857-4047, (800) 468-9963**
**www.westwyndmotel.com**

Spacious rooms at reasonable prices are the trademark of the Westwynd Motel at Gig Harbor. Most of the rooms in the motel were once apartments with full kitchens and multiple rooms. As a result, the Westwynd Motel features eight single rooms, six one-bedroom suites, and ten two-bedroom suites. All of the rooms offer queen-size beds, satellite TV, and telephones—some with data ports. Suites add full kitchens. Guests can choose from smoking and nonsmoking rooms.

Well-behaved pets are allowed at the hotel at no extra cost, and there are no additional charges for more than two people staying in a room. The motel doesn't offer wheelchair-accessible rooms.

# Bed and Breakfast Inns

Most bed and breakfast inns near Gig Harbor are nestled around the historic downtown area, with a few notable exceptions. We include seven inns in this chapter, ranging from the historic Olde Glencove Hotel and The Rose of Gig Harbor to modern inns such as the Hawaiian-themed Aloha Beachside Bed and Breakfast.

The allure of a bed and breakfast inn lies with the fact that someone coddles you, makes sure you are comfortable and cared for, and cooks you a delicious, warming breakfast to help you on your way. Occasionally you may have to share a bathroom. These inns have a charm that few hotels can hope to capture. It's almost like home, but someone else does the cleaning and cooking!

Since the proprietors of bed and breakfast inns are opening their homes to strangers as well as trying to provide a restful atmosphere, most don't allow smoking, children under age 12, or pets. Some will allow pets and children by prior arrangement. If you are allergic to animals, you may want to check with your hosts to see if they have or allow pets. Most accept major credit cards, and some will ask for a credit card to hold the reservation.

Each bed and breakfast listed provides a special home-cooked breakfast. Some innkeepers serve breakfast in bed, others serve it family style in a formal dining room or breakfast nook. You may be treated to a secret family recipe such as yummy chocolate banana bread. Or maybe it will be a well-known breakfast favorite with a twist like a smoked salmon and brie omelette, baked cheese and chile casserole, French toast with homemade berry syrup, or even thick, comforting oatmeal with a dried fruit compote. You can also expect to see fresh fruit, toast, and homemade jam as well as gourmet coffee, tea, and fruit juice on every table. Most innkeepers will accommodate special-needs diets or serve breakfast earlier or later if arrangements are made in advance. No matter what the situation, find out when and where breakfast is served, as it's a special part of the bed and breakfast experience.

# Price Code

Our price code reflects the average price of a double-occupancy room during the peak season, which runs from mid-May to mid-October. Room rates are usually discounted from late fall to early spring. The prices quoted do not include state and local sales taxes.

$ . . . . . . . . . . . . . .under $65
$$ . . . . . . . . . . . . .$65–$95
$$$ . . . . . . . . . . .$96–$140
$$$$ . . . . . . . . . .over $141

**Aloha Beachside Bed and Breakfast**    $$$
**8318 SR 302, Gig Harbor**
**(888) 256-4122**
**www.alohabeachsidebb.com**

Enjoy a touch of Hawaiian hospitality on the waterfront along Henderson Bay. The two-bedroom, three-bath cabana owned and run by Greg and Lelaine Wong opened in 1997 with a heavy Hawaiian theme, inspired by Greg's Hawaiian birthplace and by Lelaine's time living in the 50th state. Each room features a queen-size bed covered with French linens. Guests who want to watch TV can do so in the common room, and each room offers a phone with data port. Children are welcome, but no pets are allowed. Visitors can still get their animal fix, if they want, by meeting the two resident dogs—Buster the beagle and Oreo the mutt that loves to swim.

When breakfast time rolls around, the Hawaiian theme continues with Kona coffee, Hawaiian juices such as mango or papaya, oatmeal with brown sugar, cinnamon, nuts, and dried fruit, and a main dish such as eggs benedict or an omelette followed by crepes with marionberries. Guests rave about the breakfasts and how huge they are, but as Lelaine Wong says, "In Hawaii, they don't stop eating when they are full, but when they are tired."

The inn charges an additional $35 per night for each guest over double occupancy.

**Directions:** From Gig Harbor, take Washington Highway 16 west to the Purdy exit to Washington Highway 302. At the stoplight, turn left and go over the Purdy Bridge and go one mile past the end of the bridge. About eight-tenths of a mile past the bridge, turn on your left-hand turn signal to slow traffic behind you. The driveway for the bed and breakfast inn is a 45-degree turn immediately past a gated, cobblestone entry. There is a small sign denoting the inn at the turn.

**The Fountains Bed and Breakfast**    $$$
**926 120th St. N.W., Gig Harbor**
**(253) 851-6262**
**www.fountainsbb.com**

Visitors to the single suite at the Fountains Bed and Breakfast inn can soak up the sunrise, watch deer in a nearby field, or simply kick back and watch a movie on the TV in the sitting room. Hosted by owner Meri Fountain, the inn, nestled in the trees, offers a queen-size bed, telephone, and coffeemaker, microwave, and a refrigerator stocked with soda.

Guests enjoy their breakfast in a formal dining room with dishes such as eggs Benedict or French toast stuffed with apples and walnuts.

*The boat-filled inner harbor makes Gig Harbor one of the best places for boat watching in the state.* PHOTO: ROB McNAIR-HUFF

The Fountains Bed and Breakfast accommodates a maximum of two people. Children are welcome, as long as the number of occupants for the house stays at two people. Pets are not allowed.

**Directions:** From Tacoma, go across the Narrows Bridge on Washington Highway 16 and take the City Center exit into Gig Harbor. Turn right at the end of the off-ramp and take Pioneer down the hill to the waterfront. Turn left onto Harborview Drive and follow the road around the harbor, turning right near the Beach Basket Garden Center. Go 1.1 miles past the tennis courts to the intersection with Crescent Valley Drive, then turn left. Go six-tenths of a mile to the fire station, then turn right onto Drummond and go up the hill. In seven-tenths of a mile, turn left onto Moller. Continue straight until you reach 120th Street and look for the bed and breakfast sign. The inn is in the three-story house on the bluff.

**Island Escape Bed and Breakfast   $$$**
**210 Island Blvd, Fox Island**
**(253) 549-2044, (877) 549-2044**
**www.island-escape.com**

Soak up the sunset as it slips over the Olympic Mountains to the west in the single suite at the Island Escape Bed and Breakfast on Fox Island near Gig Harbor. Owners and hosts Paula and Roy offer a romantic setting for no more than two people per suite. The suite is decorated with items from the hosts' travels around the world, with the living room set in Hawaiian decor, the bedroom decorated in authentic German style with hand-carved furniture, and Japanese items displayed in the hallway. The suite has a private entrance and deck with a hammock, and it offers a king-size bed and private bath with a Jacuzzi tub.

The hosts pamper guests at the Island Escape, with bedside chocolates, a bottle of chilled cider, massage on request, and a pass to a local health club as part of the stay. And when breakfast time arrives, the meal consists of homemade entrees, fresh fruit, juice, and freshly ground, brewed coffee.

**Directions:** From Tacoma, go across the Narrows Bridge on Washington Highway 16 and take the City Center exit into Gig Harbor. Turn left at the end of the off-ramp and follow the signs toward Fox Island. After crossing the Fox Island Bridge, go four-tenths of a mile and turn right onto Cove Road. Turn right again onto Island Boulevard. Go two-tenths of a mile and then turn left onto Griffin Lane (a gravel road). Stay to the left and the inn is the last house at the end of the drive.

**The Olde Glencove Hotel    $$**
**9418 Glencove Rd., Gig Harbor**
**(253) 884-2835**
**www.glencovehotel.com**

Offering a blend of history and romance, The Olde Glencove Hotel offers four rooms within the confines of the resort hotel that originally opened in 1896. Under the ownership of Larry and Luciann Nadeau, the inn runs as a bed and breakfast, as it has since 1980. The Nadeaus purchased the aging hotel in 1973 and spent seven years restoring it. During the restoration process, the hotel was placed on the National Register of Historic Places in 1978.

Today the Nadeaus offer four rooms to guests—the Tisnn Room, with a quiet sitting area and French doors onto a deck overlooking Glencove; the Ivy Room, set in green with an extra queen-size sofa bed; the Captain Winchester Room, with a large porch overlooking Glencove and a whole wall of books; and the Bride's Room at the top of a stairway overlooking a secret garden. Additional guests will be charged $10 per night. Most rooms have queen-size beds, TVs with VCRs, and an outlet for a phone. Children are welcome.

Breakfasts are hearty, opening with fruit such as cantaloupe, muffins, French toast, new potatoes, meat, and eggs. Menus are up to the cook, but the Nadeaus will work with guests to accommodate special diets if prior arrangements are made.

**Directions:** From Tacoma, go across the Narrows Bridge on Washington Highway 16 and continue west before taking the Purdy-Shelton exit toward Washington Highway 302. Turn left and cross the Purdy Bridge on WA 302, then go straight for eight miles to the town of Key Center. Turn left at the blinking light in town and drive to the bottom of the hill. Turn right on Glencove Road. The inn is at the end of the second driveway.

**Peacock Hill Guest House    $$**
**9520 Peacock Hill Ave., Gig Harbor**
**(800) 863-2318**
**www.virtualcities.com/wa/peacock.html**

Set on the hillside overlooking Gig Harbor and with views of Mt. Rainier in the distance, the Peacock Hill Guest House features two rooms—the 1,000 square foot Salish Suite, accented with Native American and Southwest decor, and the smaller Sedona Room, decorated in oak and hues of blue, green, and rose. Both rooms feature queen-size beds, private bathrooms, TVs, and phones. The grounds just outside the rooms are covered with a series of meditation gardens interlaced with walking paths, bridges, and a nearby outdoor spa.

Depending on the day of the week, breakfasts range from fresh fruit with home-made baked goods and egg dishes during the weekdays to Southwest-style cuisine on the weekend with vegetarian dishes such as breakfast enchiladas and burritos. Owners Steven and Suzanne Savlov will also work with guests who have special dietary needs if arrangements are made ahead of time.

Each additional guest will be charged $10 per night, and the guesthouse requires a two-day minimum to stay on summer weekends. Children under the age of 16 are not welcome.

**Directions:** From Tacoma, go across the Narrows Bridge on Washington Highway 16 and continue west to the City Center exit into Gig Harbor. At the end of the off-ramp, go straight onto Stinson Avenue and continue down the hill to Harborview Drive. Turn left onto Harborview Drive. After three-tenths of a mile, turn left onto Peacock Hill Avenue.

### The Rose of Gig Harbor Bed and Breakfast
**$$**
**3202 Harborview Dr., Gig Harbor**
**(253) 853-7990, (877) 640-7673**
**www.gigharborrose.com**

One of the newest bed and breakfast inns in the area, The Rose of Gig Harbor is nestled in the heart of downtown in a 1917 house that was once owned by pioneer Mitchell Skansi. Recently remodeled and opened in 1999, the inn once served as a place to buy tickets for ferries that could be caught in the harbor across the street to travel to Tacoma and other areas.

The Harbor Rose Room offers a view of the inner harbor along with a queen-size bed. The roomy Desert Rose Suite features a king-size bed and a view of the town framed by lush foliage outside the windows. The Sweetheart Rose Suite features a four-poster, cherry-wood bed and a view of the harbor along with a floral motif throughout the room. One of the smaller rooms, the Antique Rose Room overlooks the harbor and offers mission-style furniture throughout. And the final room, the Tea Rose Room, has a double bed set in country style, with floral wallpaper. Guests can also gather in the living and dining room for breakfast as well as to watch TV or simply relax by the fireplace. Children over the age of 12 are welcome.

The Rose owners, Nancy and Mort Altman, serve breakfast around 9 A.M., with such dishes as salmon and mushroom croissants, French banana pancakes with cream sauce, or cheese blintzes.

**Directions:** From Tacoma, go across the Narrows Bridge on Washington Highway 16 and continue west to the City Center exit into Gig Harbor. At the end of the ramp, turn right and proceed down Pioneer to Harborview Drive. Turn left at the bottom of the hill onto Harborview Drive, and the inn is on the left-hand side of the street.

### Water's Edge Bed and Breakfast    $$$
**8610 Goodman Dr. N.W., Gig Harbor**
**(253) 851-3890**
**www.thewatersedgebb.com**

Befitting its name, the Water's Edge Bed and Breakfast is a single suite nestled on the edge of the inner harbor. The 800-square-foot suite features a gas fireplace, a living and dining room, deep-water moorage just outside the door, and a deck with an outdoor spa. Owners Joanie and Paul Mann welcome guests to the house with a separate, private entrance, a TV and VCR, and a phone with a data port in case guests just can't live without their e-mail. The suite is a nonsmoking environment and children and pets are not welcome.

When guests rise in the morning they can gaze through the plentiful windows across the harbor and back at downtown Gig Harbor before venturing to the dining area for a breakfast that includes such items as baked oatmeal with fruit, breads, eggs Benedict, French toast, and new potatoes. The Mann's try to make everything with as many organic ingredients as they can find. The Water's Edge requires a two-night minimum on summer weekends.

**Directions:** From Tacoma, go across the Narrows Bridge on Washington Highway 16 and continue west to the City Center exit into Gig Harbor. At the end of the off-ramp, turn right onto Pioneer and go down the hill to the waterfront before turning left onto Harborview Drive. Follow Harborview Drive around the harbor until it intersects with Vernhardson/96th Street. Go right, then turn right again onto Crescent Valley Road. The inn is on the right-hand side of the road where it intersects with Goodman Road.

# Restaurants

Restaurant choices abound in Gig Harbor. From chain restaurants to intimate eateries with specialized menus, the city has something for nearly every taste preference.

Unless stated, all restaurants have ample on-site parking. Fish and seafood are almost a way of life around here, and most of our restaurants serve at least one specialty dish based on the bounty of Puget Sound and the Pacific. The last few years have seen a resurgence in small farms, many growing organically or specializing in heirloom varieties. Many of the restaurants in the area buy their produce from these farms so you know your salad will be fresh and delicious. We have tried to represent a wide variety of restaurants from the steak and seafood house to the homey, family-style diner to the ethnic cafe.

## Price Code

Our price code reflects the average price of a single meal excluding drinks, tips, and taxes. Unless noted otherwise, the restaurants accept most major credit cards. Many do not accept out-of-state checks, so ask your server to be sure your check will be accepted.

$. . . . . . . . . . . . . . under $10
$$ . . . . . . . . . . . . . . $10–$15
$$$ . . . . . . . . . . . . . $16–$20
$$$$ . . . . . . . . . . . over $21

**Green Turtle Restaurant    $$$**
**2905 Harborview Dr., Gig Harbor**
**(253) 851-3167**

A hidden gem along the waterfront, the Green Turtle Restaurant has earned rave reviews for its menu, which features Pacific Rim influenced dishes, including fish and beef. Each meal is served with fresh baked bread. The Green Turtle Restaurant serves dinners only, and it is closed Mondays and Tuesdays. Due to the limited seating and limited hours, reservations are recommended.

**Harbor Inn Restaurant    $$-$$$**
**3111 Harborview Dr., Gig Harbor**
**(253) 851-5454**

Nestled against the inner harbor downtown, the Harbor Inn Restaurant features an extensive wine list and homemade desserts in the same location it has occupied since 1975. The breakfast menu offers dishes such as the Dungeness crab omelette or salmon Benedict, while lunch is highlighted by salmon tempura and sandwiches such as the bay shrimp croissant. Seafood dominates the dinner menu as well, with standards such as steamer clams or spicy oysters plucked from Washington waters. The Harbor Inn also offers an inexpensive children's menu and tasty desserts, such as chocolate lovin' spoonful—a rich fudge pudding sandwiched between dark chocolate cake and drizzled with chocolate cream icing.

### Harbor Rock Café    $$
**6565 Kimball Dr., Gig Harbor**
**(253) 853-3977**

Try a Mountain Burger with a half-pound of beef cooked to your taste, bacon, lettuce, onions, tomatoes, sauce, and onion rings, or opt for a Philly steak wrap from the lunch menu at the Harbor Rock Café. The easy-on-the-budget cafe also offers sandwiches such as the grilled cheese with roasted garlic butter, or turkey and cranberry. Diners can stop in for breakfast, lunch, or dinner, and parents will be relieved to see the special kids' menu as well as beer and wine for the adults.

### J.T.'s Original Louisiana Bar-B-Que    $$
**4116 Harborview Dr., Gig Harbor**
**(253) 858-1070**

There are no alligators around, and the weather seldom gets as sultry as in Louisiana, but owners James and Elsie Turner bring the Big Easy flavor to Gig Harbor at J.T.'s Original Louisiana Bar-B-Que in the heart of downtown. From fried catfish to dinners with pork ribs, beef ribs, or barbecue chicken, J.T.'s offers finger-licking good food to the waterfront under the motto of "Where the Grand Ole South meets the Great Northwest." Diners can also buy ribs by the rack.

### Le Bistro Coffee House    $$
**4120 Harborview Dr., Gig Harbor**
**(253) 851-1033**

Wander into a Bohemian setting and pull up a seat at the bar to watch your meal

**Insiders' Tip**

Gig Harbor is one of the best boat-watching spots in Washington, but visitors can also rent boats in town. Call Gig Harbor Boat Rentals at (253) 858-7341 to line up a pleasure craft.

being cooked at the Le Bistro Coffee House in downtown. Contrary to the restaurant's name, there is more to Le Bistro than coffee, and you will find locals filling the seats throughout the day, munching on breakfasts such as crab eggs Benedict or Belgian waffles, or lunching on deli sandwiches, salads, and fresh soups like French onion. Le Bistro serves Starbucks coffee and also features delectable desserts such as the macadamia macaroon torte. The coffeehouse stays open late into the night as well.

### Moctezuma's    $$
**4803 Pt. Fosdick Dr. N.W., Gig Harbor**
**(253) 851-8464**

Experience a taste of Mexico at the top of the hill in Gig Harbor at Moctezuma's. Start the meal with a quesadilla, followed by a specialty of the house such as Moctezuma's Favorite Enchiladas—beef or chicken enchiladas smothered in a light red sauce topped with fresh chopped onions, oregano, and grated Parmesan cheese—or *mole poblano*, strips of chicken breast cooked in a sweet and spicy sauce made of chile pods, sesame seeds, peanuts, cinnamon, chocolate, and spices. Moctezuma's also offers dinner and lunch combination meals, and diners can top everything off with a serving of flan or deep-fried ice cream.

### Shorline Steak and Seafood Grill   $$–$$$
**8827 N. Harborview Dr., Gig Harbor**
**(253) 853-6353**

Have a hankering for steak or seafood? Venture to the far end of the inner harbor downtown and take a seat in the Shorline Steak and Seafood Grill. One of the older restaurants in town, the Shorline offers dishes such as pan-fried oysters, a halibut sandwich, or clam chowder. Diners can also opt for such appetizers as deep-fried artichoke hearts in a lemon-butter herb sauce. Aside from seafood, guests can dig into standard dishes from the grill, including steak or a surf-and-turf combination.

### Susanne's Bakery and Delicatessen   $
**3411 Harborview Dr., Gig Harbor**
**(253) 853-6220**

If you are looking for soup and a sandwich in the heart of downtown Gig Harbor, check out Susanne's Bakery and Delicatessen. The small restaurant opens early each morning, Tuesday through Sunday, offering muffins, cookies, and croissants. Proprietors Mike and Susanne Tunney also serve coffee. Deli sandwiches, soup,

## Insiders' Tip

To learn more about Gig Harbor while in town, stop by the Gig Harbor Peninsula Historical Society and Museum (4218 Haborview Dr.) to check out exhibits on local history and historical figures.

and ice cream are added to the menu in the afternoon, along with quiche.

### Tides Tavern   $$
**2925 Haborview Dr., Gig Harbor**
**(253) 858-3982**

Lunch and dinner are served along with views of the Gig Harbor waterfront at the Tides Tavern. Diners can stop by or even float up and tie to moorage along the shore, then head indoors for fish and chips, pizzas, and burgers.

# Shopping

### The Beach Basket/Christmas Shop
**4102 & 4103 Harborview Dr., Gig Harbor**
**(253) 858-3008**

The Beach Basket sells a little of everything. Kitschy tourist souvenirs on one display case, children's toys down the aisle, and fine collectibles in another section of the store. The shop carries Shannon Crystal, Precious Moments, and Mary Engelbreit figurines as well as nautical-themed decor. A women's clothing store also fills one end of the shop. Walk across the parking lot to the Christmas Shop to find two floors worth of Christmas goodies. The shop carries collectible nutcrackers from Steinbeck and Christian Ulbricht as well as hundreds of glass ornaments, nautical ornaments, Snowbabies, and more. If it's related to the winter holidays, chances are you will find it in this shop.

### Cecil & Bird
**8805 N. Harborview Dr., Gig Harbor**
**(253) 853-4515**
**www.cecilandbird.com**

Rubber stamps are taken to the state of art and beyond at Cecil & Bird. Located at the end of the inner harbor downtown, the stamp store offers a wide range of stamps, inks, and custom papers. The shop teaches classes for making specialized cards, picture frames, and other items. If it has to do with rubber stamps, you are likely to find it here.

### Contemporary Dolls & Gifts
**3026 Harborview Dr., Gig Harbor**
**(253) 851-1665**

Doll collectors and enthusiasts of other collectibles will love to browse in this gift shop. Owner Donna Lormor offers extensive collections of dolls from such notable designers as Madame Alexander and Lee Middleton, along with Ginny dolls, Susan Wakeen dolls, and Snowbabies. The shop is located in the heart of downtown.

### Ebb Tide Gallery of Gifts
**8825 N. Harborview Dr., Gig Harbor**
**(253) 851-5293**

Located next door to Gallery Row, the Ebb Tide Gallery presents the works of local artists with stained glass, watercolor and oil paintings, fiber art, and jewelry, all set against the backdrop of the inner harbor.

### Foxglove Herb Farm & Gift Shop
**6617 Rosedale St., Gig Harbor**
**(253) 853-4878**

Gardeners will delight in the gifts and plants available at the Foxglove Herb Farm & Gift Shop. Located just up the hill from town, the shop caters to herb growers and enthusiasts, with classes about how to grow a basic herb garden to how to create a lavender wand in the Foxglove University College of Creativity. The gift shop also offers fragrant candles and soaps by Votivo, hand and body lotion, and pottery.

### Gallery Row
**8825 N. Harborview Dr. #1, Gig Harbor**
**(253) 851-6020**

Local artists take center stage on Gallery Row—a working studio and gallery at the far end of the inner harbor in downtown. The gallery presents the works of eight artists, ranging from paintings and photography to Raku pottery and multimedia art. The studio section also offers classes in various mediums throughout the year.

### Harbor Gallery
**3177 Harborview Dr., Gig Harbor**
**(253) 851-8626**

Billed as having one of the most extensive collections of maritime art on the West Coast, the Harbor Gallery in the Anchorage Building in downtown Gig Harbor features original paintings, prints, sculpture, and glass works. The gallery also offers a unique collection of indoor fountains. Artists from the Pacific Northwest are represented alongside national and international artists.

### The Harbor Peddler
**3311 Harborview Dr., Gig Harbor**
**(253) 851-6795**

If you are looking to decorate your home with country motif or nautical items, or simply gift shopping for a friend, The Harbor Peddler is a good bet in the heart of downtown. The shop, co-owned by Candy Schuman and Debbie Lerew, features custom stoneware, candles, prints, and nautical-themed gifts.

### Mostly Books
**3126 Harborview Dr., Gig Harbor**
**(253) 851-3219**
**www.mostlybooks.com**

What would a quaint waterfront town be without an independent book store? Fortunately, Gig Harbor residents don't know the answer, thanks to Mostly Books. The small bookstore run by owner Jo Graffe has held a place in book lovers' hearts for more than 30 years. It features a wide selection of boating titles, befitting the heavy boating influence in town. It also holds a solid collection of works by Northwest writers, and a kids' books section to keep young readers up well past bedtime.

### The Preuit Collection and Framery
**3115 Harborview Dr., Gig Harbor**
**(253) 851-3792**

Extremely local art is at the heart of the Preuit Collection and Framery in downtown Gig Harbor. Nearly 85 percent of the art comes from artists within 25 miles of the city. Step inside the shop and you will be bowled over by works such as string and driftwood sails, numerous whale and dolphin sculptures, and photos and paintings. Owners Don and Pat Preuit choose all of the art represented.

### Rosedale Gardens
**7311 Rosedale St. N.W., Gig Harbor**
**(253) 851-7333**

Tour lush gardens full of native plants, trees, and flowers at the Rosedale Gardens. Billed as "Washington's first ever-

*Custom statuary and pottery works are available alongside the extensive plant collection at Rosedale Gardens.* PHOTO: NATALIE McNAIR-HUFF

changing tour gardens," the gardens opened in 1981. Aside from shopping in the nursery or from the extensive collection of garden art and sculpture, visitors are invited to have a picnic on the landscaped grounds or to let the kids enjoy the play areas. During the holiday season the gardens are laced with thousands of lights, and the gift shop is stocked with Christmas and holiday gear in addition to the garden and outdoor gifts offered year-round.

### Seasons on East Bay
### 3720 E. Bay Dr. N.W., Gig Harbor
### (253) 858-8892

It may take a little searching, but gift buyers and decorators will love Seasons on East Bay when they find it nestled against Wollochet Bay on the opposite side of the hill from downtown Gig Harbor. The shop offers a smorgasbord of gift items, from jewelry to pottery, picture frames, country decor, table decorations, and books. Around the Christmas season the store transforms into a winter wonderland with multiple Christmas trees and gifts from Noritake, Fitz & Floyd, Spode, and others.

### Vintage American Antiques
### 3102 Harborview Dr., Gig Harbor
### (253) 857-7347

A visit to this antiques shop is like a tour through the last two centuries of American home decor. The wares offered at Vintage American Antiques include American primitives, vintage toys, block letters from old printing presses, and an extensive library of architectural literature. The shop is located in the heart of downtown, across from the harbor.

# Port Orchard

The residents of Port Orchard like the small town feeling (population 7,255) and the convenience of nearby Seattle, just a short ferry ride away. In fact, Port Orchard and the other small communities around here almost act as bedroom communities to Seattle since so many of the residents catch daily ferries to work in the city.

As you approach Port Orchard you can look and look for orchards, but you won't find them. Port Orchard is actually named after H. M. Orchard, a member of Captain George Vancouver's *Discovery* crew. When Orchard discovered the area, it served as a fishing outpost for the Native tribes like the Suquamish, S'Klallam, and Chemukum. First named Sidney after one of the original white settlers, the name was changed to Port Orchard in 1890. Early business owners worked hard to bring industry to the Peninsula. In addition to the ubiquitous logging of this area, early settlers grew fruit and berries, raised chickens and cows, and worked in a pottery works. Those early city leaders can also claim credit for helping to attract the Naval Shipyard to nearby Bremerton, still the largest employer on the Kitsap Peninsula.

Many early residents helped build the shipyard. In those days hundreds of foot ferries crisscrossed Puget Sound, providing quick and simple, albeit not always safe, transportation to the small communities dotting the shore. The ferries were known as the Mosquito Fleet. Several boats ferried workers across Sinclair Inlet to Bremerton. Horluck Transportation still runs two of the original boats across the inlet. Boating and fishing remain an important part of life in Port Orchard as is evidenced by its waterfront park and large, full marina. The town also sponsors a yearly gathering of Chris Craft boat owners.

Port Orchard offers visitors a respite from the busy, workaday world. Enjoy a pleasant day of shopping on Bay Street and then take a walk along the waterfront park after a delicious dinner of fresh fish or juicy steak, or come for one of the yearly festivals: Fathoms O' Fun, The Cruz car festival, or Mosquito Fleet Festival.

## Hotels and Motels

Port Orchard does not have a lot to offer as far as accommodations, but the two hotels in the immediate area are both clean and comfortable. The Guest House Inn will be a convenient spot for those who want easy access to the freeway and nearby McCormick Woods Golf Course. If you prefer a view of the water and mountains, try the Holiday Inn Express in downtown Port Orchard. Both hotels offer smoking and nonsmoking rooms and have at least one room that is wheelchair accessible.

# Price Code

Our price code reflects the average price of a double-occupancy room during the peak season, which runs from mid-May to mid-October. Room rates are usually discounted from late fall to early spring. The prices quoted do not take into account the state and local sales taxes.

$ . . . . . . . . . . . . . .under $60
$$ . . . . . . . . . . . . . .$60–$90
$$$ . . . . . . . . . . . .$91–$130
$$$$ . . . . . . . . . .over $131

### Guest House Inn    $$–$$$
### 220 Bravo Terrace, Port Orchard
### (360) 895-7818, (800) 214-8378

The lobby of the Guest House Inn, a recently opened franchise, is decorated with golf memorabilia to reflect its convenient location five minutes away from three golf courses. Most rooms offer a single king bed or two queen beds in addition to a table or desk and two chairs. All rooms include cable TV, refrigerators, microwaves, hair dryers, and coffeemakers, as well as full bathrooms. The Inn also offers a few spa suites with a king-size bed, fireplace, and a two-person Jacuzzi tub. Or, if you need a more family-friendly situation, you may want to reserve the Family suite, which has a king-size bed for the grown-ups and a bunk bed in a separate room that is equipped with a separate TV and video games. When you wake in the morning you may want to partake of the continental breakfast or take a dip in the indoor pool before a stop at the Jacuzzi or exercise room. Children under 19 stay free in a parent's room, but for additional adults add $10 per extra guest per night. Small pets can also stay for an additional $10 per night. Non-smoking and wheelchair accessible rooms are available. If you get the late-night munchies, you can walk across the parking lot to eat at Shari's restaurant.

### Holiday Inn Express    $$
### 1121 Bay St., Port Orchard
### (360) 895-2666, (800) 465-4329

From your room at the Holiday Inn in downtown Port Orchard, you will enjoy a view of the mountains and Puget Sound, including the Naval ships docked in the bay. In addition to 64 rooms, the hotel houses a conference room. Amenities include laundry facilities, an outdoor spa, and a private beach with picnic tables and a BBQ grill. Some rooms offer refrigerators and microwaves, and there are four king Jacuzzi rooms. Non smoking and wheelchair-accessible rooms are available.

# Bed and Breakfast Inns

Since Port Orchard itself did not offer many bed and breakfast inns, we have also included two located in nearby Olalla, 8 miles away from downtown Port Orchard. No matter which establishment you settle on for your stay, we're sure you will have a special experience with these friendly and knowledgeable innkeepers. Make sure to ask them about what to do and where to go: They are true Insiders.

The allure of a bed and breakfast inn lies with the fact that someone coddles you, makes sure you are comfortable and cared for, and cooks you a delicious, warming breakfast to help you on your way. Occasionally you may have to share a bathroom. These inns have a charm that few hotels can hope to capture. It's almost like home, but someone else does the cleaning and cooking!

Since the proprietors of bed and breakfast inns are normally opening their homes to strangers as well as trying to provide a restful atmosphere, most don't allow smoking, children under age 12, or pets. Some will allow pets and children by prior arrangement. If you are allergic to animals, you may want to check with your hosts to see if they have or allow pets. Most accept major credit cards, and some will ask for a credit card to hold the reservation. If the inn does not accept credit cards we have noted that with the price code.

Each bed and breakfast listed provides a special home-cooked breakfast. Some innkeepers serve breakfast in bed, others serve it family style in a formal dining room or breakfast nook. You may be treated to a secret family recipe such as yummy chocolate banana bread. Or maybe it will be a well-known breakfast favorite with a twist like a smoked salmon and brie omelette, baked cheese and chile casserole, French toast with homemade berry syrup, or even thick, comforting oatmeal with a dried fruit compote. You can also expect to see fresh fruit, toast and homemade jam, as well as gourmet coffee, tea, and fruit juice on every table. Most innkeepers will accommodate special-needs diets or serve breakfast earlier or later if arrangements are made in advance. No matter what the situation, find out when and where breakfast is served, as it's a special part of the bed and breakfast experience.

# Price Code

Our price code reflects the average price of a double-occupancy room during the peak season, which runs from mid-May to mid-October. Room rates are usually discounted from late fall to early spring. The prices quoted do not include state and local sales taxes.

$ . . . . . . . . . . . . . .under $65
$$ . . . . . . . . . . . . . .$65–$95
$$$ . . . . . . . . . . . .$96–$140
$$$$ . . . . . . . . . . .over $141

**Childs House Bed & Breakfast**  **$$–$$$**
**8331 S.E. Willock Rd., Olalla**
**(253) 857-4252, (800) 250-4954**
**users.aol.com/childshse/BnB.htm**

You'll feel as if you were hidden in an enchanted forest when you stay at Childs House. Tucked into five acres of woods, including an acre yard, it is a popular place for weddings and other events.

Early risers will love the spectacular sunrise views. The house is decorated with an eclectic assortment of Victoriana and handmade quilts in the rooms and contemporary design in the rest of the

house. For a luxurious evening of relaxation-reserve the Lilac Room with a king-size bed, shower for two, and soaking tub. It is the only room with a television. The Rose room contains a queen-size bed and shares a bathroom with Primrose, which contains a full bed.

Susan Childs, the proprietor, also caters weddings held on the premises as well as other local events, and her breakfasts reflect her culinary skills. Every morning, along with fresh fruit, coffee, and tea, she serves a breakfast entree like stuffed French toast or a frittatta. Childs

House also offers guests the use of a large meeting room and allows small pets by prior arrangement.

**Directions:** According to the Childs House Web site, "From Highway 16 take the Mullenix exit east, at the second stop sign, turn right onto Orchard. Go exactly one mile south to Willock Road, turn left. Continue across Banner Road (stop sign) to the second set of mail boxes on the left. Enter the driveway and stay to the left. The driveway through the woods leads you right to us. From the Southworth ferry dock, travel west on Sedgewick Road (Highway 160) three miles. Turn left on Banner Road, just past North Banner Road. Go four miles to Willock Road, turn left. At the second set of mailboxes on the left, turn left and stay to the left."

**Reflections Bed & Breakfast**   **$$–$$$**
**3878 Reflections Ln. E., Port Orchard**
**(360) 871-5582**
**www.portorchard.com/reflections**

Housed in a two-story colonial set on a bluff overlooking Port Orchard Passage, Reflections Bed & Breakfast offers guests a restful stay in the lap of luxury. Jim and Cathy Hall, the proprietors, moved to Port Orchard from Boston and brought a collection of New England and Virginia antiques, which can be found in nearly every room of the house.

Two rooms share a bathroom, while another two each have a private bath. The Annette Room, which also serves as the honeymoon suite, has a private deck, a small sitting room and dressing alcove, as well as a relaxing soaking tub and shower in its private bathroom.

Guests who wish to relax in front of the TV or watch a movie may do so in the downstairs family room. Others may want to curl up with one of the books available in the library or play a board game in front of the fireplace in the formal living room.

Each evening guests are asked to collectively select the next morning's breakfast from a list of 10 to 12 entrees. All the guests have to agree, but we're sure nobody will be disappointed with such special treats as a smoked salmon and brie omelette, banana nut pancakes, roast beef hash with eggs, or a morning feast with a Southern or Mexican theme.

**Directions:** From Wash. 16 take the Sedgwick Road exit and head east to Jackson. Turn left onto Jackson and follow it until it becomes Olney and you reach the water. Turn right onto Beach Drive and stay on it for two miles until you reach Reflection Lane. Turn right on the private road. Reflections is the first house on the right.

**Still Waters Bed & Breakfast**
**$–$$, no credit cards**
**13202 Olympic Dr. SE, Olalla**
**(360) 876-8608, (253) 857-5111**

Cynthia Sailor, the proprietor of this peaceful retreat, has been opening her house to guests since 1992. Her house, built in 1963 to replace a family farmhouse that burned, is set on land that was established as farmland in 1898. She still tends to the pear, apple, and plum trees of the original orchard.

Still Waters offers three rooms decorated with wicker furniture and restored antiques, including two cast-iron beds. One room contains a queen-size bed and offers a private bathroom with a shower, the other two each contain a full bed and share a bathroom with a bathtub. While you stay, take time to walk around the five acres dotted with gardens, a gazebo, and the old orchard. Upon your return to the house, you may appreciate a soak in the hot tub under the stars or a chat with other guests in front of the sitting room fireplace.

To make your stay extra special, arrange for a relaxing massage, offered on the premises in the spa room. In fact, Cynthia offers a sweetheart special that includes a one-hour massage. Arrange for massages when you make your reservation.

Wake up to a hearty breakfast of German apple pancakes, eggs, or hot cereal served with fresh fruit, bread, and homemade jams. Cynthia is more than happy to accommodate special dietary needs.

**Directions:** From Wash. 16 turn right onto SE Burley–Olalla Rd. In about 0.2 mile you will reach Olympic Dr. SE.

# Restaurants

For a town as small as Port Orchard, you'll find a surprising number of restaurants. Of course you could settle for drive-through at McDonalds or grab a burger and root beer float at the A & W by the mall, but we suggest you try one of the specialty restaurants we have listed. Treat the kids to breakfast or dinner at the Family Pancake House or Myhre's. For a more upscale evening of fresh fish, crab, or steak, try Tweten's Lighthouse or Mary-Mac's. And for one of the most impressive sushi menus we've ever seen, try Hiro Sushi. Most of the restaurants we've listed for Port Orchard are located downtown close to the water on Bay Street or a side street, but we have also included a few special establishments that are a little more off the beaten path.

Nearly every town on the Kitsap and Olympic Peninsulas abounds with restaurant choices. Unless stated, all restaurants have ample on-site parking. Fish and seafood are almost a way of life around here, and most of our restaurants serve at least one specialty dish based on the bounty of Puget Sound and the Pacific. The last few years has seen a resurgence in small farms, many growing organically or specializing in heirloom varieties. Many of the restaurants in the area buy their produce from these farms so you know your salad will be fresh and delicious. We have tried to represent a wide variety of restaurants from the steak and seafood house to the homey, family-style diner to the ethnic cafe.

# Price Code

Our price code reflects the average price of a single meal excluding drinks, tips, and taxes. Unless noted otherwise the restaurants accept most major credit cards. Many do not accept out-of-state checks, so ask your server.

$ . . . . . . . . . . . . . .under $10
$$ . . . . . . . . . . . . .$10–$15
$$$ . . . . . . . . . . . .$16–$20
$$$$ . . . . . . . . . . . .over $21

**Bay Coffee Co.    $**
**807-B Bay St., Port Orchard**
**(360) 895-2115**
Tucked down a narrow boardwalk alley, this airy little cafe serves a mean cup of coffee and offers a good selection of teas. Early risers can breakfast on locally made bagels, muffins, and cinnamon rolls while

they learn to recognize the insignia flags of the local yacht clubs. For lunch, order a bowl of homemade soup or pick sandwich fillings from a long list of ingredients. Unless you have a hearty appetite, we suggest you order a half sandwich since the fillings are served on mini French bread loaves.

*Restaurants dot the shoreline behind Main Street in downtown Port Orchard.* PHOTO: NATALIE McNAIR-HUFF

### Beachhouse Grill    $–$$
**1604 Bay St., Port Orchard**
**(360) 874-0371**

It may not look like much, but the funky murals of the undersea world create an interesting atmosphere. Locals don't come here for the decor, though. They come for the barbecue and prime rib dinners. The Beachhouse Grill serves more meat than you could flip a bullwhip at: hamburgers, sirloin and New York steaks, filet mignon, salmon, shrimp, crab, chicken, pork and beef ribs . . . well, you get the idea. Lunchtime diners and those with smaller appetites may wish to order a deli sandwich, the Asian chicken salad, or a bowl of freshly made soup. Beer is served here, and reservations are accepted and recommended on summer weekends.

### Family Pancake House    $
**1034 Bethel Rd., Port Orchard**
**(360) 895-0545**

How about a late-night breakfast of Swedish pancakes with lingonberry but-ter, Crepes Suzette, and Very Berry French Toast topped with blueberries, strawberry compote, bananas, and whipped cream? Breakfast is served for breakfast, lunch, and dinner, and the offerings take up two full pages on the menu. Of course, in the pancake house tradition, you can also order sandwiches, burgers, and other American family favorites. Children will have fun coloring the kids' menu, and seniors may select from a discount menu. Beer and wine are available, and the restaurant is wheelchair accessible. The Family Pancake House is practically a Port Orchard tradition, having been here for 16 years. Friday and Saturday, the restaurant is open 24 hours. Monday through Thursday it opens at 5:00 A.M. and closes at 11:00 P.M.

### J.J.'s on the Bay    $$
**100 Harris St., Port Orchard**
**(360) 876-1445**

Sit back, take a sip of your iced tea, and relax with a view of the waterfront park and marina at J.J.'s on the Bay. Start your meal with steamers, cioppino, or a rock shrimp quesadilla. For your entree choose from mouth-watering treats such as a crab cake burger, baked stuffed shrimp, or the Caribbean Shrimp Barbi of marinated tiger prawns with a Jamaican-style fire sauce served on sticky rice. J.J.'s is wheelchair accessible.

**MaryMac's Restaurant and Bar** $$–$$$
**5155 McCormick Woods Dr. SW,**
**Port Orchard**
**(360) 895-0142**
**www.mccormickwoods.com**

You'll enjoy a pleasant view of the award-winning McCormick Woods Golf Course from MaryMac's beautiful and spacious dining room and patio seating area. Exposed beams and a stone fireplace add to the ambience as you eat dishes based on the contemporary fresh food cuisine that is becoming the signature of Washington's best chefs. Lunch on the popular Northwest Wild Greens & Chinese Noodle Salad with Chicken, spiked with a lemon grass and soy marinade and topped with a light peanut dressing. Or choose from the daily specials list—perhaps grilled salmon with wasabi vinaigrette or pasta tossed with hazelnuts and three cheeses in a garlic cream sauce. The dinners are equally delectable with entrees like medallions of turkey with a pistachio crust served with a sun-dried blueberry sauce, filet mignon, or fresh fish or shellfish from the specials menu. MaryMac's also serves a sit-down Sunday brunch to make sure you are properly nourished before your tee time. The restaurant accepts credit cards but not out-of-state checks, and it is wheelchair accessible. Reservations are recommended.

**The Morning Side Bread Company** $
**707 Bay St., Port Orchard**
**(360) 876-1149**

You'll be hard-pressed to keep walking past this bakery when you smell the scent of freshly baked, handmade bread. The shop may be just a hole in the wall, but it offers a full selection of breads from

# Insiders' Tip

Pick up drinks and sandwiches in Port Orchard, then head to nearby Manchester State Park to eat, and afterwards hike one of the many wooded trails or walk along the beach and watch the boat traffic on Puget Sound.

French and sourdoughs to ciabatta and caraway rye. Of course, who can pass up a freshly made glazed doughnut or cinnamon roll? Morning Side is closed on Sundays and does not accept credit cards.

**Myhre's Restaurant** $
**739 Bay St., Port Orchard**
**(360) 876-4634**

Myhre's is the oldest established restaurant in Kitsap County. It originally opened its doors in 1927. No matter what time of the day you visit, you will see a contingent of loyal customers enjoying breakfast, lunch, or dinner in the diner-style setting. Myhre's serves a typical collection of breakfast choices all day long, including the 222&2 of two pancakes, two eggs, two strips of bacon, and two sausage links. Of course, it also serves sandwiches and hamburgers, as well as steak and seafood for those who like to eat breakfast only in the morning. After dinner, you may wish to adjourn to the attached lounge for a drink. Myhre's does not accept out-of-state checks.

**Hiro Sushi** $$
**920 Bay St., Port Orchard**
**(360) 895-8591**

If you like Japanese food and sushi, you may have a hard time deciding what to order from the extensive menu at Hiro Sushi. Though the restaurant is too small for a tatami room, the food is 100-percent authentic. Bento, tempura, and combo platters complement the huge selection of sushi. Choose from over 50 types of sushi: maki, tekamaki, nigiri, and combo plates. For the novice sushi eaters who prefer their fish cooked, we suggest Tamago (egg), Ebi (shrimp), Anago (eel), or a California roll. Ask your server for recommendations as well. For a real treat, sit at the sushi bar and watch the chef prepare your meal. You may even add a few Japanese words to your vocabulary. Parking here is tight, but if you see an opening take it. Closed on Mondays.

### King's Fish & Chips, Teriyaki, Sushi    $
### 1044 Bethel Rd., Port Orchard
### (360) 895-4148

King's has been serving fish and chips and Japanese food since 1985. Don't let the dated, drive-in decor fool you. Restaurants around here don't stay in business this long if they don't serve good food. King's does that at a bargain. Crispy, golden fish and chips, shrimp, halibut, and calamari are just the start of King's menu. If you have a hankering for more exotic fair, try one of the teriyaki or noodle dishes. King's also has a limited sushi menu. For a nice sampling of all that the restaurant has to offer, try King's Combo Special #3. You'll get two gyoza (pot stickers), one piece of shrimp tempura, rice, a bowl of miso soup, chicken teriyaki or sweet & sour chicken, and three pieces of a California roll—all for around $5.

### Tweten's Lighthouse    $$-$$$
### 429 Bay St., Port Orchard
### (360) 876-8464

Ask an insider where to go for dinner on a special evening, and most likely the answer will the Tweten's Lighthouse. Come for lunch, and on a clear day you'll have a fantastic, panoramic view of the marina, the naval ships anchored in the bay, and the majestic, snow-capped Olympic Mountains. Tweten's is open every day of the year for lunch and dinner, and reservations are not required, but they are recommended, especially on a summer weekend. For a light lunch, try the Mediterranean chicken salad with lemon-grilled chicken, feta cheese, sun-dried tomatoes, artichoke hearts, and black olives tossed with pasta. Fresh seafood specials such as grilled salmon and halibut medallions, and sandwiches round out the lunch menu. The dinner crowd, mostly couples and small celebratory groups, feasts on steak, pasta, and seafood specials. You may want to start your evening off with a cocktail from the fully stocked bar and an appetizer of steamed clams or crab-stuffed mushrooms. And don't forget to check the dessert menu. Chocoholics will drool over the Mile High Chocolate cake, while those who consider chocolate passè might go for burnt creme or a cherry cobbler. Tweten's Lighthouse is wheelchair accessible.

### Victorian Rose Tea Room    $
### 1130 Bethel Ave., Port Orchard
### (360) 876-5695

This place exudes charm. From the pink, peak-roofed, gabled exterior to the flower print tablecloths, the Victorian Rose Tea Room almost seems a child's dream come true. On one side of this building you'll find Springhouse Dolls and Gifts. The other side, separated from the gift shop by display cases and lattice work, serves as the Tea Room. Quiche, eggs Benedict, crepes, and more are served for breakfast until 11:00 A.M. For lunch visitors may eat a proper tearoom lunch like Chicken Almond Salad, or perhaps a curry chicken or roast beef sandwich. Lunch is served until 3 P.M. at which time the afternoon tea of scones and specialty desserts is served. Wednesday through Saturday the Tea Room serves dinner. A traditional high tea is served by advanced reservation and payment on the fourth Saturday of each month. Banquet facilities and a meeting room are also available, and reservations for parties of five or more are recommended. The restaurant is wheelchair accessible, but space is tight on the gift shop side. The Victorian Tea Room would make a lovely location for a mother-daughter luncheon or a pleasant break from shopping.

# Nightlife

Downtown Port Orchard closes down between five and six each evening, but you'll still find plenty to do in the evenings. We suggest taking a walk in one of the local parks or driving to Manchester State Park for an evening picnic and a night of stargazing when it's clear and dry. Many taverns and pubs have live music on Friday and Saturday nights. You may elect to drive to nearby Gig Harbor or Bremerton for more selection. For a pleasant evening sipping beer in a smoke-free environment we suggest the Harborside Bar & Grill, or for a more quiet evening, check to see what's on stage at the Bay Street Play House or on the screen at the Plaza Twin Cinema.

## Bay Street Ale House
**807 Bay St., Port Orchard**
**(360) 876-8030**

Enjoy the popular turkey-havarti sandwich for lunch, a burger for dinner, or gnosh on a specialty pizza like the Bay Street Bleu Cheese pizza with smoked turkey, crumbled bacon, tomatoes, mozarella and bleu cheese. The Bay Street Ale House offers 16 beers on tap, many from local microbreweries. The Ale House is only open to the 21 and over crowd, but they offer a smoke-free atmosphere and occasionally live music on Saturday evenings.

## Bay Street Play House
**820 Bay St., Port Orchard**
**(360) 871-6610**

For 20 years the Performing Arts Guild of South Kitsap has been producing musicals and plays for the community. The stage productions range from mysteries and comedies to hard-hitting dramas like *Steel Magnolias*. Other recent productions include *One Flew Over the Cuckoo's Nest*, *A Midsummer Night's Dream*, *Sylvia*, *Oliver*, and *You're a Good Man Charlie Brown*. Call to reserve tickets or check the Web site (www.pagsk.org) for a production schedule.

## Harborside Bar & Grill
**714 Bay St., Port Orchard**
**(360) 874-9575**

Every Friday and Saturday night, the Harborside Bar & Grill is filled with the sounds of live music. Bands that play here range from Latin jazz to punk to blues. Join the locals for an open-mike night of entertainment every Thursday, or drop in to munch on hamburgers and quesadillas

or a rack of barbecued ribs. The bar serves a good selection of microbrews and has what may be the largest collection of liquor on the Kitsap Peninsula. Harborside is open for lunch and dinner and is wheelchair accessible. No on-site parking is available so park on the street nearby.

## J. A. Michaels Restaurant and Lounge
**715 Bay St., Port Orchard**
**(360) 876-6124**

If you're in the mood for some live local music, go to J. A. Michaels Wednesday through Saturday evenings. The lounge doors open at 7:30 P.M. A DJ plays the tunes when live music isn't scheduled.

## Plaza Twin Cinema
**822 Bay St., Port Orchard**
**(360) 876-7785**

Forget multiplexes with rocking chairs and too-loud sound systems. The Plaza Twin Cinema is a locally owned, two-screen movie theater that shows second-run movies right in downtown Port Orchard. Adults can watch for $4. Children 12 and under and seniors watch for $2.

## Insiders' Tip

Train buffs will have a blast riding the scale-model steam train run by the Kitsap Live Steamers. The train runs on the second and fourth Saturdays from April through October. Call (360) 871-6414 for more information.

*Downtown Port Orchard.* PHOTO: ROB McNAIR-HUFF

# Shopping

Bay Street, paralleling the waterfront, is downtown Port Orchard. Most of the shops we've listed here are located on Bay Street or one of the short side streets. We've branched out of downtown to include South Kitsap Mall—this is not your average mall—and for a couple of unique establishments like Springhouse Gifts. While Gig Harbor, just a few miles to the south, abounds with art galleries, Port Orchard abounds with antiques stores, including a large antiques mall. From May through October, make sure you stop by the Port Orchard Farmers Market, every Saturday 9:00 A.M. to 3:00 P.M. where you will find arts and crafts and locally grown produce, much of it organically grown.

**Antiques by the Bay**
**802 Bay St., Port Orchard**
**(360) 876-4397**

In addition to the craftsman and mission-style furniture owned by the store, four other merchants display an eclectic collection of antiques and memorabilia ranging from rhinestone jewelry to china and silver, glassware and pottery, Pez dispensers, and Star Wars collectibles. Make sure you check out the Hummel and doll collections, and boxes of buttons may snag the collector for a while.

**Armchair Books**
**South Kitsap Mall, Suite 202**
**(360) 874-8932**
**www.armchairbks.com**

With over 15,000 new titles in stock, Armchair Books claims to have the largest selection of books in South Kitsap County. One of the most pleasant and spacious shops in the mall, the bookstore makes for a pleasant place to stop and read a while. The shop also sponsors special events, book clubs, and author signings.

## The Beachcomber
**821 Bay St., Port Orchard**
**(360) 874-1781**

In addition to selling beer-brewing and winemaking supplies, this shop specializes in T-shirts, jackets, and hats imprinted with pictures and logos that represent Port Orchard and the Northwest, both humorous and serious.

## Bell, Book & Candle
**1140 Bethel Ave. Suite A, Port Orchard**
**(360) 876-7500**

While Washington's larger cities seem to lack in independently owned bookstores, the smaller communities provide many choices as exhibited by this comprehensive shop on Bethel Avenue across the parking lot from the Victorian Tea Room. Buy a cup of espresso at the in-house coffee shop and then browse the shelves for an art book, tome of history, or novel to read as you continue on your journey.

## Cubbyhole Toys
**804 Bay St., Port Orchard**
**(360) 876-3971**

Bring your kids or your inner child when you enter this cubbyhole. This colorful shop is filled with fun and educational toys. You'll find Playmobil figures, thought-provoking books and games, and a menagerie of stuffed critters here. Don't be surprised if the kids decide they're done shopping once they've found this shop.

## Crystal Garden
**100 Frederick, Port Orchard**
**(360) 895-3781**

Wander into this little shop down a short side street off of Bay St., and take a deep breath of the relaxing herb-scented air. In addition to selling a huge assortment of bulk herbs, Crystal Garden offers herbal-lore classes as well as lessons on tarot reading, candle making, and dream pillows. You might also enjoy browsing the collection of metaphysical art such as paintings of faeries and woodland creatures and goddess sculptures, most by local artists. Closed Sunday and Monday.

## Elegant Clutter
**South Kitsap Mall, Suite 301**
**(360) 876-6650**

Elegant Clutter is packed with everything you could want to decorate a house. American and European antique furniture hold collections of knickknacks from all over the world. Decorators could spend hours sorting through the prints, figurines, and art books displayed here.

## Forget Me Not Bouquet
**834 Bay St., Port Orchard**
**(360) 876-4466, (800) 432-0466**

The colorful whirligigs, windsocks, and flags lining the walk will draw you into this florist and gift shop. Once inside browse more windsocks and small collectibles. You can also buy cards or order flowers to be delivered to your hosts while you are here. Closed on Sunday.

## Gardenscapes Herbs and Perennials
**4556 Terrace Way SE, Port Orchard**
**(360) 871-7245**

Gardeners will delight at the specialized selection of perennials and herbs offered here. If you visit, make sure to check out the herb knot. Be warned though, you'll be sorely tempted to take a beautiful, overflowing hanging basket home with you.

## Jomar Books
**713 Bay St., Port Orchard**
**(360) 874-8284**
**www.jomarbooks.com**

The Kitsap Peninsula has a large population of militaryfolk due to the presence of the Naval ship yard at Bremerton and the submarine base at Bangor. Jomar Books has benefited from this presence by becoming a sort of clearinghouse for books on military history. Science Fiction fans will also find treasures hidden among the stacks, as will fishing fanatics.

## Olde Central Antique Mall
**801 Bay St., Port Orchard**
**(360) 895-1902**

The Olde Central Antique Mall's motto says "The only museum where everything's for sale!" That is certainly an apt description for this collection of furniture, glasswear, china, Americana, and other collectibles. With 50 antiques dealers represented in this two-floor space, any antiques hunter will find something that catches the eye. Visitors from all over like to stand and listen to the Empress Queen Piano with Mandolin and Bells.

### Radiant Energy
**738 Bay St., Port Orchard**
**(360) 895-9095**

When the incense is lit, you'll smell it half a block away, enticing you to enter the calmness of Radiant Energy. In addition to the requisite crystals and semiprecious stones, smudge sticks and incense, you'll find a nice selection of other metaphysical equipment. One wall is taken by bookshelves loaded with books on an assortment of topics from Reiki and the healing arts to journal writing, shamanism, and Wicca.

### Sanctuary Book & Gifts
**834 Bay St., Port Orchard**
**(360) 710-5945**

You can smell the scent of smudge sticks and incense even when you stand on the sidewalk outside of Sanctuary Books & Gifts. The store sells almost everything the spiritual seeker needs from journals to tarot cards, essential oils to books and candles. The shop also offers classes in journaling, aromatherapy, and more, in addition to providing spiritual consulting and angel card readings. The shop is closed on Mondays.

### Sidney Gallery
**202 Sidney Street, Port Orchard**
**(360) 876-3693**
**www.portorchard.com/sidneygallery**

Housed in the town's original Masonic Hall, the Sidney Gallery features art by new as well as established artists, with a substantial number of its artists representing the Northwest. Each month a new Northwest artist is featured. In addition, the gallery sells a variety of all-occasion gifts for all price ranges from wood carvings and blown glass to brass animal sculptures. While you browse, send the kids upstairs to the museum for a free journey through the history and culture of the Kitsap Peninsula.

### Sidney Village
**702 Bay St., Port Orchard**
**(360) 876-4622**

Gifts, gifts, and more gifts from kitschy to charming. You will find it all in the Sidney Village, a retail market where more than 50 merchants display their wares on individual units. You don't need to worry which merchant sells which item though, since you'll pay for everything at one register. Here you can take home a handmade wood-burl clock, a bowl full of wildflower potpourri, collectible dolls and ceramics, or a beautiful piece of jewelry crafted by a local artist. Don't forget to check out the irresistible cat rock paintings by Trudi Peek. Each cat is painted onto a rock collected from local beaches. Peek paints with watercolors to let the natural beauty of the rock add depth to the personality of her cats. You'd swear these tiny treasures should be squeaking out meows.

### Ship's Store
**110 Harrison Ave., Port Orchard**
**(360) 876-1260**

During the summer months, boat and ship lovers will surely want to take a Kitsap Harbor Tours tour of the shipyard. Each 45-minute tour is a narrated journey through military history with an up-close look at the ships anchored as part of the Navy's mothball fleet: aircraft carriers, nuclear submarines, warships. Buy tickets for the cruises here at the Ship's Store. While you wait, and through the winter, visit the Ship's Store for nautical-themed gifts. The store also offers an extensive collection of Navy-blue baseball caps embroidered with the names of the ships in the American armada from the USS *Arizona* to the USS *Independence* to the USS *Wisconsin*.

**South Kitsap Mall**
**1700 SE Mile Hill Dr., Port Orchard**
**(360) 895-2112**

Most malls are filled with big-time corporate stores, and while Kitsap County has one of those malls in Silverdale, the South Kitsap Mall is more of a mom and pop mall. It's filled with locally owned boutiques and gift shops like Elegant Clutter, Etc. and Silk Bouquet, a fun children's clothing store called Kids, and a couple of shoe stores and adult clothing stores. Quilters and crafters will get lost in Rochelle's Fabrics & Quilts, Rose Crafts and Create-A-Plate, and booklovers will revel at the selection in Armchair Books. Not all stores are open during all mall hours, but the mall doors are open Monday through Friday, 10 A.M. to 8 P.M., Saturday 10 A.M. to 6 P.M., Sunday 10 A.M. to 5 P.M.

**Springhouse Dolls & Gifts**
**1130 Bethel Ave., Port Orchard**
**(360) 876-5695**

This dollhouse is designed with adults in mind. Little hands could get in trouble quickly, but the inner child in you will delight at the hundreds of teddy bears and collectibles filling every corner and display case. The spaces that are not taken up by dolls are covered with collectible figurines like Precious Moments, tea settings, and Victoriana. When you've had your fill of looking and buying, sit down at the adjoining Victorian Rose Tea Room for lunch or afternoon tea.

**Yamamoto's Nursery, Landscaping and Hydroseeding**
**5767 Sidney Rd. SW, Port Orchard**
**(360) 876-1889**

This nursery has been owned by the Yamamoto family for 20 years. A specialty collection of Japanese iris is talked about by people throughout the region. The nursery also offers a selection of trees and shrubs alongside a beautiful koi garden.

*A statue pays homage to workers at the Bremerton Shipyard.* PHOTO: NATALIE McNAIR-HUFF

# North Kitsap Peninsula

Bound by Hood Canal to the west and Admiralty Inlet to the east, the Kitsap Peninsula is a land defined by water. Fittingly, the water-based military services of the United States Navy make their homes in the area, with the largest being the Puget Sound Naval Shipyard in Bremerton.

The North Kitsap area includes three main cities, Bremerton in the south, Silverdale a little farther north, and Poulsbo closer to the Hood Canal Bridge that links the Kitsap Peninsula and the Olympic Peninsula.

Bremerton, a city of more than 36,000 people, was originally built around the shipyards that occupy a major portion of the waterfront. The waterfront is also a transportation center, with ferry service connecting to Seattle, and visitors can check out the boardwalk that leads to the USS *Turner Joy*, a well-known Navy destroyer notable for its role as the trigger to U.S. ground troop involvement in the Vietnam War. The *Turner Joy* is open for self-guided audio tours. Up the hill in the city center, art galleries and eateries mingle with a few shops to define Bremerton as a growing center for the arts in Kitsap County. The recently renovated Admiral Theater draws patrons to the area with concerts, musical revues, and film festivals throughout the year.

Bremerton, which was named the Most Livable City in the United States for its size by *Money Magazine* in 1990, hosts an annual Blackberry Festival in September. And fans of the arts can venture downtown on the first Friday of each month for the First Friday Art Walk.

Bremerton's neighbor to the north, Silverdale, is a community of approximately 14,000 people located at the end of Dyes Inlet. Silverdale is home to the Kitsap Mall and a large number of strip-mall and big-box stores. The development of this retail core is largely credited to the arrival of the West Coast Trident Submarine Base in nearby Bangor in the 1970s.

Silverdale hosts a number of festivals throughout the year, including the Kitsap County Fair and Rodeo at the county fairgrounds in late August, the Silverdale Whaling Days festival in July, and the Silverdale Christmas tree lighting in the first week of December.

North Kitsap's next city heading north is the Nordic-themed town of Poulsbo. With a population of 2,600, Poulsbo is known for its connection to the waterfront along Liberty Bay and the variety of Scandinavian and specialty shops that draw tourists to Front Street downtown. Like so many other towns on the Kitsap and Olympic Peninsulas, Poulsbo, founded in the 1880s, started as a logging town.

The northern portion of the Kitsap Peninsula also holds a number of smaller towns. Be sure to check out towns such as Port Gamble, which once had the longest continuously running sawmill in the United States. Other towns include the small waterside burgs of Hansville and Kingston as well as the reservation settlements of Indianola and

Suquamish. Chief Sealth, the chief whom Seattle is named after, is buried in Suquamish. Before the white people came to the area, this peninsula was considered to be Suquamish territory. After the 1854 treaty between local tribes and the U.S. government, the Suquamish were relocated to the Port Madison Reservation on the northern tip of the Peninsula. In 1870 the U.S. military burned Ole Man House, an extremely old and large longhouse, in order to force the tribe to accept the white man's way of life. Then, in the early 1900s, tribal members were forced onto individual allotments and the government sold the remainder of the land, mostly prime waterfront acreage, to real estate developers. Every August the tribe celebrates the Chief Seattle Days, and a replica of Ole Man House can be seen in the Suquamish Museum (15383 Sandy Hook Rd., Suquamish).

# Hotels and Motels

Each of the major communities in the North Kitsap region offers an independent hotel, motel, or inn with comfortable accommodations for travelers. Whether you are en route to the Olympic Peninsula on the other side of Hood Canal, or if the Kitsap Peninsula is your final destination, any of the hotels and motels we include here should provide a comfortable place to spend the night. Unless otherwise noted, the hotels and motels all offer smoking and nonsmoking rooms as well as at least one wheelchair-accessible room.

## Price Code

Our price code reflects the average price of a double-occupancy room during the peak season, which runs from mid-May to mid-October. Room rates are usually discounted from late fall to early spring. Prices exclude state and local sales taxes.

$ . . . . . . . . . . . . . .under $60
$$ . . . . . . . . . . . . . .$60–$90
$$$ . . . . . . . . . . .$91–$130
$$$$ . . . . . . . . . .over $131

**Midway Inn    $–$$**
**2909 Wheaton Way, Bremerton**
**(360) 479-2909, (800) 231-0575**
**www.midwayinn.com**

Views of the Olympic Mountains and a selection of meeting rooms make the Midway Inn a popular lodging choice in Bremerton. The 60-room inn opened in 1984, and today it offers modern rooms with queen-size beds, cable TV, phones with data ports, and coffeemakers. Both smoking and nonsmoking rooms are available, and each room has a small sitting area with a table and chairs. The inn also has six rooms with king-size beds and

kitchenettes and one suite. Guests at the Midway Inn can partake of a continental breakfast served between 7 and 10 A.M. The inn charges $5 per night for each additional guest.

**Oyster Bay Inn    $$**
**4412 Kitsap Way, Bremerton**
**(360) 377-5510, (800) 393-3862**
**www.visitkitsap.com/oysterbayinn/index.html**

Most of the 62 rooms at the Oyster Bay Inn feature views of the bay, but regardless of the view, guests enjoy the resort-like setting of this hotel just off Kitsap

Way in Bremerton. The inn, built in 1984, offers refrigerators and microwaves in each room along with either queen- or king-size beds, cable TV, and phones with data ports. Guests can enjoy a continental breakfast each morning between 5 and 9 A.M. on weekdays and between 6 and 10 A.M. on weekends. The inn does allow pets for $25 per visit. Extra guests will be accommodated for $6 per night for each person. The Oyster Bay Inn also has one chalet available for guests who want more private lodging.

**Poplars Motel     $$**
**9800 Silverdale Wy. N.W., Silverdale**
**(360) 692-6126, (800) 824-7517**
**www.poplarsmotel.com**

For travelers looking for a centralized place to stay in the North Kitsap area, the Poplars Motel in Silverdale is a prime candidate. Located just a block south of the Kitsap Mall, the 52-room motel that originally opened in 1969 offers queen-size beds, cable TV, phones in each room, and coffee in the lobby. Guests who stay dur-

ing the summer months can use a seasonal outdoor pool, and a spa is available as well. The Poplars Motel serves a continental breakfast each morning between 6 and 10 A.M. Additional guests will be accommodated for an additional fee.

**Poulsbo Inn     $$**
**18680 WA Hwy. 205, Poulsbo**
**(360) 779-3921, (800) 597-5151**
**www.Amouse.net/poulsboinn/**
**welcome.html**

Located just three blocks from the waterfront and the Scandinavian-flavored shopping for which Poulsbo is so well known, the 72-room Poulsbo Inn offers convenient and affordable lodging complete with an outdoor pool open in the summer and a year-round spa. Guests at the inn can also pay extra to stay in an apartment with a full kitchen. Rooms at the Poulsbo Inn all feature queen-size beds, cable TV, phones with data ports, and coffeemakers. The inn also serves a continental breakfast between 6:30 and 9:30 A.M. each morning.

# Bed and Breakfast Inns

Bed and breakfast inns are scattered across the northern end of Kitsap Peninsula. We include a few of the prime inns here—one near Bremerton and the others near the tourism-driven waterfront town of Poulsbo or overlooking the Hood Canal.

The allure of a bed and breakfast inn lies with the fact that someone coddles you, makes sure you are comfortable and cared for, and cooks you a delicious, warming breakfast to help you on your way. Occasionally you may have to share a bathroom. These inns have a charm that few hotels can hope to capture. It's almost like home, but someone else does the cleaning and cooking!

Since the proprietors of bed and breakfast inns are opening their homes to strangers as well as trying to provide a restful atmosphere, most don't allow smoking, children under age 12, or pets. Some will allow pets and children by prior arrangement. If you are allergic to animals, you may want to check with your hosts to see if they have or allow pets. Most accept major credit cards, and some will ask for a credit card to hold the reservation. If the inn does not accept credit cards we have noted that with the price code.

Each bed and breakfast listed provides a special home-cooked breakfast. Some innkeepers serve breakfast in bed; others serve it family style in a formal dining room or breakfast nook. You may be treated to a secret family recipe such as yummy chocolate banana bread. Or maybe it will be a well-known breakfast favorite with a twist like a smoked salmon and brie omelette, baked cheese and chile casserole, French toast with homemade berry syrup, or even thick, comforting oatmeal with a dried fruit compote. You can also expect to see fresh fruit, toast and homemade jam, as well as gourmet coffee, tea, and fruit juice on every table. Most innkeepers will accommodate special-needs diets or serve breakfast earlier or later if arrangements are made in advance. No matter what the situation, find out when and where breakfast is served, as it's a special part of the bed and breakfast experience.

# Price Code

Our price code reflects the average price of a double-occupancy room during the peak season, which runs from mid-May to mid-October. Room rates are usually discounted from late fall to early spring. Prices exclude state and local sales taxes.

$ . . . . . . . . . . . . . .under $65
$$ . . . . . . . . . . . . . .$65–$95
$$$ . . . . . . . . . . .$96–$140
$$$$ . . . . . . . . . .over $141

**Brauer Cove Guest House**    **$$$**
**16709 Brauer Rd., Poulsbo**
**(360) 779-4153**
**www.brauercove.com**

One of the newest bed and breakfast inns on the North Kitsap Peninsula, Brauer Cove Guest House opened in 1999 and offers two rooms for its guests. The inn, set in an old farmhouse near the water and run by Catherine Jones, is open to children of all ages. One room offers a king-size bed and the other a queen-size bed, and both rooms feature views of the water. Guests also can use the outdoor spa, and athletic visitors and water lovers can head out on the bay in either a rowboat or canoe. Each room in the inn includes a television, and a phone is available in the sitting room.

At breakfast time, guests find an expanded continental breakfast menu that includes such items as coffeecake and pastries.

**Directions:** From WA Hwy. 3, take the exit for WA Hwy. 305 into Poulsbo. Continue on WA Hwy. 305 through the business district, and then take a right onto Johnson Road. Drive down the hill and take a left at the stop sign onto Lemolo Shore Drive. After a short distance, take a right onto Brauer Road. After a bend in the road, take a right onto a concrete easement road between tall pine trees. If you get to the stop sign, you have gone too far. The inn is the second house on the right, behind the tall hedge.

**Foxbridge Bed and Breakfast**    **$$**
**30680 WA Hwy. 3, Poulsbo**
**(360) 598-5599**
**www.sfox.com/foxbridge**

Located just outside of Poulsbo and close to the east side of the Hood Canal Bridge, the three-room Foxbridge Bed and Breakfast invites its guests to kick back, slow down, and enjoy the atmosphere of the inn, which is situated on five secluded acres. Guests are encouraged to browse through the Oxford room library, lined with walnut bookshelves filled with collector edition books, or head outdoors to fish for rainbow trout in the stocked pond on the property. Back inside the inn, each of the rooms offers a queen-size bed, and guests who want to watch TV can do so in a common room. Children 16 and older are allowed at the inn, but pets are not allowed. Breakfasts at Foxbridge start with a first course of fresh fruit, juice, and hot or cold cereal, followed by a second course of peach cobbler or apple crisp drizzled with maple cream sauce. The entree includes items such as smoked salmon quiche or peach praline French toast. The inn charges $20 per night for each additional guest staying in any one room.

**Directions:** From WA Hwy. 3 heading north, the right-hand turn to the inn is 0.1 mile past mile marker 59. From WA Hwy. 3 heading south, the left-hand turn to the inn is about 1 mile from the end of the Hood Canal Bridge, just past Baltic Lane.

### Illahee Manor Bed and Breakfast  $$$$
**6680 Illahee Rd. N.E., Bremerton**
**(360) 698-7555, (800) 693-6680**
**www.illaheemanor.com**

Stroll the 330-foot private beach or lounge in the Jacuzzi during your stay at Illahee Manor Bed and Breakfast along the Bremerton waterfront. The inn offers five rooms within the main house and two separate cabins—each comes with a full, three-course gourmet breakfast served each morning. The main house with its five suites is not open to children or pets, but guests interested in bringing the kids or pets can opt for one of the cabins. One cabin can sleep up to 10 people. All rooms in the main house offer queen-size beds. Guests who stay in the main house will have TVs and VCRs in their rooms along with robes and private bathrooms. The cabins also offer queen-size beds, and one cabin is wheelchair accessible.

Guests can also opt to have dinner in the relatively new restaurant at Illahee Manor. The restaurant serves dinners on Fridays only, with a five-course fixed menu accented with Northwest wines and local microbrew beers.

**Directions:** From WA Hwy. 3 entering Bremerton, take the Washington 304 exit toward Bremerton. Follow the signs directing traffic to the Seattle Ferry, and then merge onto the Navy Yard Freeway, WA Hwy. 304. Continue following WA Hwy. 304 as it winds through town, then at the intersection of Burwell and Washington Streets, turn left. (Right would take

## Insiders' Tip

For an extra dose of history, visit Point No Point, where the 1854 treaty was signed to halt the region's Indian wars.

you to the ferry.) Follow Washington Street two blocks to the Manette Bridge, then turn right and cross the bridge. At the end of the bridge, take an immediate right, then left onto 11th St. Follow 11th to the intersection with Trenton, then turn left onto Trenton and keep to the left. Take Trenton for two miles, then turn right onto Illahee Road. Take Illahee Road for about two miles along the shoreline. Just past 3rd St., turn right just past a blue Methodist Church sign on the right. The driveway leads right up to the inn.

### Murphy House Bed and Breakfast  $$–$$$
**425 N.E. Hostmark, Poulsbo**
**(360) 779-1600, (800) 779-1606**
**www.bbonline.com/wa/murphy**

Just up the hill from historic downtown Poulsbo, the five-room Murphy House Bed and Breakfast lures guests in with its views of Liberty Bay and the Olympic Mountains in the distance. The inn features a large common room with a fireplace, a library, and a game room—all available to guests. All five rooms, including a large suite with a king-size bed and two twin beds, offer sitting areas and private baths. Cable TV and a guest phone are also offered in the common room. The inn has been in operation since 1993. Rates for each additional person beyond double occupancy costs $25 per night. Pets are not allowed, but children over the age of 12 are allowed. Breakfast is served around 8:30 A.M. and includes coffee, juice, fruit, and a range of main dishes such as omelettes and potatoes.

**Directions:** From WA Hwy. 3, take the WA Hwy. 305 exit into Poulsbo. Continue on WA Hwy. 305 to the intersection with N.E. Hostmark St., and turn left onto Hostmark. The Murphy House is on Hostmark as the road proceeds down the hill toward downtown.

**Willcox House     $$$**
**2390 Tekiu Rd., Seabeck**
**(360) 830-4492, (800) 725-9477**
**www.willcoxhouse.com**

Set in the woods just above the Hood Canal, the Willcox House offers a high-end bed and breakfast inn experience. The five-room inn, which opened in 1989, does everything it can to help guests get away from it all. The house does not offer a television, but there is a movie theater in one room. Each room is elegantly decorated while maintaining a period feel reflecting when the house was built in 1936. The rooms have king- or queen-size beds, and an additional $30 per night is charged for each additional guest. One room includes a Jacuzzi. The Wilcox House welcomes children ages 15 and older, but pets are not allowed.

Breakfasts start with a buffet including pastries and fruit followed by a main entree such as crepes, waffles, or French toast. The inn also features dinners—prices not included in room rate. Dinners feature regionally influenced cuisine that is enhanced by an extensive wine list. Saturday dinners are four-course meals, while the rest of the week's menu is selected by the chef.

**Directions:** From WA Hwy. 3, take the Kitsap Way exit. Go west on Kitsap Way 1.4 miles to Northlake Way, then fork to the left. Drive 1.1 miles and then take a left again onto Seabeck Highway. Go 2.9 miles, then turn left onto Holly Road. Drive 4.9 miles before turning left at the sign for Seabeck-Holly Road. Go another 5.2 miles to Old Holly Road, then fork to the right. Go 200 yards and turn right at the mailboxes on Tekiu Road. Follow the road 1.2 miles and turn left at the cabin to reach the house.

# Restaurants

Whether you are in Bremerton, Silverdale, or Poulsbo, the eateries on the north part of the Kitsap Peninsula offer a wide range of dining options. Fish and seafood are almost a way of life around here, and most of our restaurants serve at least one specialty dish based on the bounty of Puget Sound and the Pacific. The last few years have seen a resurgence in small farms, many growing organically or specializing in heirloom varieties. Several area restaurants buy their produce from these farms so you know your salad will be fresh and delicious. We have tried to represent a wide variety of restaurants from the steak and seafood house to the homey, family-style diner to the ethnic cafe.

## Price Code

Our price code reflects the average price of a single meal excluding drinks, tips, and taxes. Unless noted otherwise, the restaurants accept most major credit cards. Many do not accept out-of-state checks, so ask your server.

$ . . . . . . . . . . . . . under $10
$$ . . . . . . . . . . . . . $10–$15
$$$ . . . . . . . . . . . . $16–$20
$$$$ . . . . . . . . . . . over $21

*Boat Shed Restaurant beckons diners to the Manette area in Bremerton.* PHOTO: ROB McNAIR-HUFF

**Bahn Thai     $$**
**9811 Mickelberry Rd., Silverdale**
**(360) 698-3663**

Savor zesty curry dishes and sip Thai iced tea inside the Bahn Thai Restaurant in Silverdale. Rated as one of the top eateries in the area, the restaurant features noodle dishes, vegetarian dishes, and a host of beef, pork, chicken, and seafood specialties—from orange beef with broccoli, onions, and carrots to Bahn Thai Fried Rice with prawns in yellow curry powder, pineapple, eggs, tomatoes, and onions. Bahn Thai is open for lunch and dinner, seven days a week.

**Benson's Restaurant     $$–$$$**
**18820 Front St., Poulsbo**
**(360) 697-3449**

A scrumptious Sunday brunch and a solid dinner menu are the highlights of Benson's Restaurant in Poulsbo. Dinners include penne pasta in a spicy tomato sauce with Italian sausage and ricotta cheese, as well as risotto with butternut squash topped with pesto grilled vegetables and oven roasted mushrooms. The brunch menu includes dishes such as Benson's Benedict—sourdough English muffins topped with ham, poached eggs, and smoked mozzarella cheese sauce served with a fresh fruit salad. Benson's is closed on Mondays.

**Boat Shed Restaurant     $$**
**101 Shore Dr., Bremerton**
**(360) 377-2600**

What was once a shop that sold live bait is today one of the premier restaurants in Bremerton. The Boat Shed, located in the Manette region of town, is set in a former boat shed. It features prime seafood dishes such as baked Australian lobster, herb crusted halibut, and mixed shellfish sauté in black bean sauce. The Boat Shed also offers burgers and sandwiches, in addition to salads and pasta, all served in a smoke-free environment. Wine and beer are served from the restaurant's lounge.

**Gazebo Café     $**
**18830 Front St., Poulsbo**
**(360) 697-1447**

Chef Tanya Mayda brings the taste of an Italian cafe to the main street of downtown Poulsbo. Grab a zesty basil panini, made with fresh basil leaves, provolone and Swiss cheeses, artichoke hearts, roma tomatoes, red onion, and a balsamic vinaigrette, all sandwiched between grilled organic focaccia bread. The cafe also serves soups, salads, pasta dishes, and daily specials.

**Golden Dragon     $$**
**18801 Front St. N.E., Poulsbo**
**(360) 779-7673**

Have a hankering for chop suey while touring Poulsbo? Stop by the Golden Dragon. The Chinese restaurant offers a wide range of tastes, from Mandarin and Szechwan dishes to a Cantonese a la carte menu. Diners can also choose a family-style combination dinner such as beef chow yuk, sweet and sour pork, almond chicken, and pork fried rice.

**J.J.'s Fish House     $$**
**18881 Front St., Poulsbo**
**(360) 779-6609**

Venture to J.J.'s Fish House in Poulsbo for entrees such as the Caribbean shrimp barbi or pan-fried yearling oysters. The casual, spacious restaurant even has a special children's menu. Under the ownership of Jeff and Judy Eagleson, the waterfront restaurant also serves pasta dishes such as clam linguine and burgers, some with a unique twist like the crab-cake burger.

**Just Your Cup O' Tea     $**
**305 Pacific Ave., Bremerton**
**(360) 377-9457**
**www.cup-o-tea.com**

Shop for bulk teas, herbs, and spices, or opt for a bagel sandwich at Just Your Cup O' Tea in downtown Bremerton. The store and cafe offers lunchtime meals along with pastries, quiche by the slice, and ice cream. Just Your Cup O' Tea

## Insiders' Tip

Two Native American tribes have reservations on the Kitsap Peninsula—the Suquamish and the Port Gamble S'Klallam. The Suquamish Tribe's former leader, Chief Sealth—for whom Seattle is named—is buried in the town of Suquamish behind St. Peter's Catholic Church.

remains open late for the First Friday Art Walks each month, but it is closed on Sundays.

**Larry & Kristi's Bakery     $**
**1100 Wheaton Wy., Ste. H, Bremerton**
**(360) 377-3296**

Larry & Kristi's Bakery bills its donuts as the best in Kitsap County. In addition to baked goods such as cookies and muffins, the bakery also serves soups and sandwiches from its location in the heart of Bremerton. The shop is closed on Sundays.

**Liberty Bay Bakery & Café     $**
**18996 Front St., Poulsbo**
**(360) 779-2828**

Owners Hans and Pat Ebke serve fresh-baked breads and pastries along with deli sandwiches and soup in their bakery and cafe at the northern end of Front Street. Check the reader board for the special of the day.

**New Day Seafood Eatery     $**
**325 N.E. Hostmark, Poulsbo**
**(360) 697-3183**

There is no shortage of seafood-dining in Poulsbo, but fish fans will want to consider a stop at the New Day Seafood Eatery. Located along the waterfront with outside dining during the summer, the restaurant offers standards such as fish and chips as well as unique dishes like the oyster burger or oysters and chips. The menu also includes kids' meals, and ice-cream desserts.

### Pete's Jersey Subs    $
**2100 E. 11th St., Bremerton**
**(360) 377-5118**
**www.petesjerseysubs.com**

Billed as having the best subs west of the mighty Delaware River, Pete's Jersey Subs features fresh bread topped with the highest quality meats and cheeses available. Try The Phil Bomb, two ½-pound cheeseburgers, three strips of bacon, and two eggs on an 11-inch roll, or opt for a simple pork roll sandwich. The proprietors, originally from New Jersey, serve the hot and cold sandwiches in a laid-back atmosphere. The restaurant is not open Sundays.

### Poulsbo Wine Cellar and Café    $$
**18825 Anderson Pkwy. N.E., Poulsbo**
**(360) 697-9463**

Looking for lunch or dinner in downtown Poulsbo? The Poulsbo Wine Cellar and Cafe may have just what you need. Located up a flight of stairs across the parking lot from the Liberty Bay Marina, the cafe serves lunch dishes such as The Russian, a plate of chilled smoked salmon, English cucumber slices, vine-ripened tomato, red onion, and boursin herb cheese. Dinner dishes include pork loin chop pesto oreganato, and grilled rib-eye. The cafe suggests that dinner reservations are a good idea Thursdays through Sundays.

### Poulsbohemian Coffeehouse    $
**19003 Front St., Poulsbo**
**(360) 779-9199**
**www.silverlink.net/pbch**

Coffee and art mingle in the appropriately named the Poulsbohemian Coffeehouse. Aside from some of the best lattes in town, the coffeehouse features all-you-can-eat soups, fresh bagel schmears, sandwiches, and dessert items such as double chocolate brownies.

### That's-a-Some Italian Ristorante    $$
**18881 Front St., Poulsbo**
**(360) 779-2266**

Since its opening in 1989, That's-a-Some Italian Ristorante has served primo Italian food and fine wines. The extensive wine list includes more than 250 different wines from Italy, California, and the Pacific Northwest. The dinner menu features house signature dishes such as Anaheim Chili Penne—fresh roasted garlic, and Anaheim chilies blended in a cream sauce with cumin, diced tomato, and marsala wine. The restaurant also serves traditional Italian pasta dishes, seafood, and specialty pizza. End the meal with spumoni ice cream, tiramisu, or cheesecake.

### Vege Restaurant    $–$$
**18713 WA Hwy. 305 N.E., Poulsbo**
**(360) 697-2538**

The Vege Restaurant offers a wide choice of vegetarian entrees for diners in Poulsbo who want to eat something other than the simple salads offered as veggie choices on other menus. Opt for the tasty Clay Pot Vegetarian, with napa cabbage, fried tofu, broccoli, mushroom, carrot, water chestnut, onion, and chicken ham—a chicken-flavored vegetable protein that has a texture similar to chicken—all smothered in a rich brown sauce. All of the dishes at the Vege Restaurant are modeled after recipes once served in the Imperial courts of Southeast Asia.

### Waterfront Bakery and Café    $
**3472 N.W. Byron St., Silverdale**
**(360) 698-2991**

Tasty breakfasts and lunches along with fresh baked goods are the highlight at the

Waterfront Bakery and Café in the old town area of Silverdale. Diners can opt to pick up cookies and pastries, or aim for a more substantial item like quiche or a deli-style sandwich. The bakery and cafe is closed on Sundays.

# Nightlife

**Manette Saloon**
**2113 E. 11th St, Bremerton**
**(360) 792-0801**

Listen to live music while sipping a microbrew in the Manette region of Bremerton. Just on the east side of the Manette Bridge, the saloon, owned by Brad and Becki Grade, is open seven days a week.

**Silver City Brewing Co.**
**2799 N.W. Myhre Rd., Silverdale**
**(360) 698-5879**

Right next to the Kitsap Mall, the Silver City Brewing Company serves six hand-crafted ales and lagers on tap, as well as seasonal brews in a bright, friendly atmosphere. Billed as a great spot for gatherings, the establishment also serves daily lunch and dinner, and kids can eat for free when accompanied by a paying adult on Sundays.

# Shopping

Browsing and buying opportunities in the North Kitsap area are split between the three major communities—Bremerton, Silverdale, and Poulsbo.

Bremerton's downtown core is dominated by art galleries and specialty stores. Even in outlying regions of the city, such as the small community of Manette, art takes center stage. We mention some of the most notable galleries in this section, but there are more to be found scattered downtown.

The same can be said for the unique downtown shopping offered in Poulsbo. Much more geared to tourists, Poulsbo carries its Norwegian and Scandinavian theme from one store to the next along Front Street. Art and antiques are a major influence, along with gift shops and bakeries. Understandably, with commercial fishing boats among the hundreds plying the waters alongside downtown, many shops also carry fishing and marine-related items.

The Kitsap Mall, filled with your run-of-the-mill mall shops, and strip malls that line the streets downtown dominate the shopping options in Silverdale, but there are some independent shops selling antiques, gift items, and baked goods near the old-town area near Waterfront Park on Dyes Inlet.

**Amy Burnett Fine Art Gallery**
**402 Pacific Ave., Bremerton**
**(360) 373-3187**

A wide range of art, from multimedia works and large sculptures to paintings and prints, covers the large gallery space at the Amy Burnett Fine Art Gallery. A central gallery in the downtown Bremerton art scene, the gallery, owned by Amy Burnett, also hosts musicians from time to time and takes part in the First Friday Art Walk that runs year-round. It is closed on Mondays.

**Artists' Edge**
**2009 Harkins St., Bremerton**
**(360) 377-2930**

Although a little off the beaten path, the Artists' Edge store in the Manette section of Bremerton is a center for art. Besides offering art supplies and framing supplies, the shop offers gallery space, with a new show each month featuring the works of Pacific Northwest artists. The store in Manette is one of three Artists' Edge locations on the Kitsap Peninsula. There are also stores in Silverdale and Poulsbo.

*Rock sculpture and ancient bonsai trees reflect on the huge pond at Elandan Gardens.* PHOTO: NATALIE McNAIR-HUFF

**Bad Blanche Collection**
**18890 Front St., Poulsbo**
**(360) 779-7788**

Bad Blanche offers an eclectic and unique assortment of antiques, reproductions, and contemporary art pieces for the home. Fountains, dining sets, and art installations, all displayed together, may make visitors decide to go home and redesign the front room for one special piece.

**Cargo Hold**
**18864 Front St., Poulsbo**
**(360) 697-1424**
**www.cargohold.com**

Ship models and all things nautical take center stage in the Cargo Hold in downtown Poulsbo. The shop, owned by Doug Owen, offers boating related gifts, from ship logs to knot displays, and wood-and-brass weather instruments.

**Elandan Gardens**
**3050 W. WA Hwy. 16, Bremerton**
**(360) 373-8260**
**www.elandangardens.com**

With trees dating from the times of King Arthur, Charlemagne, and William the Conqueror, Elandan Gardens near Bremerton is a must-see for garden fans. Set on a former garbage dump site in the small town of Gorst, Dan Robinson and his family began transforming the grounds in 1994, dumping up to 10 feet of topsoil on the site to create the current gardens. Visitors can view their work, walking through the display of Bonsai trees, some more than 1,000 years old, in the 2.5-acre garden. The collection of Bonsai trees is billed as the best in the West. The Robinsons also invite visitors to shop for antiques and gift items in the Elandan Gallery. There is a fee for walking the gardens, but browsing through the gift shop and retail nursery costs nothing—unless you buy something. Elandan Gardens is closed Mondays and the entire month of January.

**The Embossible Dream**
**511 4th St., Bremerton**
**(360) 373-4522**

Take a class or simply stop by The Embossible Dream to pick up rubber

# Close-up

## Kitsap County Closely Linked to Navy

Naval history has deep roots on the Kitsap Peninsula. Since the establishment of Bremerton's Puget Sound Naval Shipyard—Puget Sound's oldest naval installation—in 1891, five other naval facilities have come to the peninsula. This concentration of naval resources on the peninsula is one reason that the Puget Sound area has the third-highest concentration of naval bases in the United States.

The Puget Sound Naval Shipyard along the Bremerton waterfront dominates as the largest employer in the area. It started in 1891, when Lt. A.B. Wycoff purchased 190 acres of waterfront property from the Bremer family for $9,512. Although at times in the past the shipyard was a center for shipbuilding, today workers primarily overhaul existing ships and run nuclear vessels through the deactivation process. As repair work dwindles, the shipyard has also become home to more Navy ships and military personnel. The shipyard employs about 7,800 civilians, making it the largest Navy shipyard in the country.

Naval Station Bremerton is the newest Navy installation in the area. Created when a portion of the shipyard was split off in 1998, the station is the home port for the aircraft carrier USS *Carl Vinson* and four combat supply ships, including the USS *Sacramento*, the USS *Camden*, the USS *Rainier*, and the USS *Bridge*.

Farther to the north, the Naval Submarine Base in Bangor is home port for eight Trident nuclear submarines, all ready to be armed with nuclear missiles. The base occupies 7,676 acres on Hood Canal, and it is home to nearly 5,800 military personnel. Look carefully while visiting the Olympic Peninsula and Kitsap Peninsula and you may see the topside of one of these subs as they work the waters of the Strait of Juan de Fuca, Admiralty Inlet, and Hood Canal.

Near the submarine base is the Naval Undersea Warfare Center in Keyport. The center serves as a test bed for torpedoes, sonar gear, fire control systems, mines, and targets, but the center's primary mission is to maintain torpedoes for the naval fleet.

The last two facilities on the Kitsap Peninsula are the Fleet and Industrial Supply Center Puget Sound (which supplies materials to the other naval facilities in the area as well as to

stamping supplies. Located in the heart of downtown, the shop offers rubber stamps, ink, custom papers, and magazines about the hobby. Co-owners Kris Covarrubias and Miki Turowski also teach classes with tips for creating greeting cards and gifts. The store is closed Sundays, but it stays open late on the first Friday of each month to take part in the First Friday Art Walk.

**Granny & Papa's Antique Mall**
**19669 7th Ave., Poulsbo**
**(360) 697-2221**

A lot of antiques malls turn into giant junk piles, but that is not the case with Granny & Papa's. Granny, Judy Haag, keeps pretty tight control of the clutter, and demands that her fellow antiques dealers select high-quality items for display. As a result, the antiques mall, located in a strip mall just outside of the downtown core, avoids that cramped and cluttered feel and makes the treasures on display easy to see and find. We found a nice collection of Civil War-era artifacts, including a piece of African American folk art from the period. Look up front for fiesta wear and authentic tin soldiers. Another plus here . . . Papa, Al Haag,

facilities in Alaska) and the Naval Hospital Bremerton (which offers its services to military personnel, military retirees, and their families).

Altogether, the five facilities in Kitsap County result in the Navy spending about $1.4 billion each year in the county.

Visitors to the region can get glimpses of the Navy facilities along the Bremerton waterfront. Take a drive along WA Highway 304 on the waterfront into town. The road winds right past the Puget Sound Naval Shipyard. Once downtown, stop along the waterfront just north of the ferry terminal to take a self-guided audio tour of the USS *Turner Joy*, a retired Navy destroyer that played a pivotal roll in the United States getting involved in the Vietnam War. Also in town, check out the Bremerton Naval Museum (130 Washington Ave., (360) 479-7447), where a history of the Navy involvement in the area is unveiled along with the history of the Puget Sound Naval Shipyard.

Farther north and west in Keyport, you'll find the Naval Undersea Museum at the Naval Undersea Warfare Center ((360) 396-4148), which unveils a history of undersea warfare and submarines, along with an exhibit about the underwater environment. The museum charges no admission fee.

*Visitor's to the Bremerton waterfront can take a self-guided tour of Navy destroyer, the USS* Turner Joy. PHOTO: NATALIE MCNAIR-HUFF

repairs porcelain, bisque, pottery, and crystal.

### Hattie Lin's
### 3425 N.W. Byron, Silverdale
### (360) 307-9894

Browse antiques, from furniture to dolls, or pick up items for your home at Hattie Lin's on the Silverdale waterfront. Nestled near the downtown dock, the shop, owned by Sherril Huff-Menees and Lin Ulin, offers a number of large furniture pieces in addition to smaller antiques. Hattie Lin's is closed on Sundays.

### Imagine That!
### 18954 Front St., Poulsbo
### (360) 779-3345

Vintage beads from around the world are unveiled in a spacious store along Poulsbo's main street. Browse wall-to-wall beads interspersed with mounted butterflies. The store relocated to its present location in 1999, but owner Mary C. Chambers started selling beads from another location in 1991. In addition to loose beads and findings, shoppers can browse and purchase finished necklaces and earrings, or sign up for beading classes.

## Kitchen Karousel
**18846 Front St. N.E., Poulsbo**
**(360) 697-4006, (877) 449-9590**
**www.kitchenkarousel.com**

Kitchenware from around the world, and especially from European and Scandinavian countries, is offered seven days a week at Kitchen Karousel on Front Street. Owner Sharon Lucas brings items such as lefse griddles, rosette irons, and krumkake bakers to the United States, helping strengthen Poulsbo's connection to Scandinavia. The shop also sells teapots, cookie stamps, and even more standard cooking items like pots and pans.

## The Landmark Gifts & Collectibles
**18990 Front St., Poulsbo**
**(360) 779-2900, (888) 722-2901**

Scandinavian gifts such as Kharismakat Collectibles are featured in the display cases at Landmark Gifts & Collectibles. Collectible plates, ceramic cats, birds, and butterflies, as well as items such as Beanie Babies also fill the shelves of the shop owned by Doug and Shirley Hawley.

## Liberty Bay Books
**18881D Front St., Poulsbo**
**(360) 779-5909**

Best-selling books share shelf space with children's books, Native American related books, cooking titles, and Scandinavian related books at Liberty Bay Books, an independent book store in the heart of Poulsbo. The reader-friendly shop also features an espresso stand at the back of the store, as well as helpful staff members who can help place special orders for books that can't be found on the shelves.

## Los Andes
**435 Pacific Ave., Bremerton**
**(360) 479-8709, (877) 473-7886**
**www.losandesnet.com**

Los Andes brings parts of the culture of Peru to the heart of Bremerton. Handmade dolls, beads, alpaca coats and clothing, and other items are imported from the proprietor's homeland nestled in the Andes Mountains of South America. In addition to the imported goods offered in

> **Insiders' Tip**
> Before becoming a bedroom community and the retail center of Kitsap County, Silverdale was best known as a chicken farming area.

the store, shoppers can inquire about tours to Peru offered by another business associated with Los Andes. The proprietor is also more than happy to talk with visitors about his homeland and his adopted home of Bremerton.

## The Manette Book and Coffee House
**2110 E. 11th St, Bremerton**
**(360) 405-1881**

Travel to the east side of the Manette Bridge to dig into used books in Bremerton. The Manette Book and Coffee House features a large selection of literature and non-fiction, along with a section of collectible books and children's titles. The store is a resource for finding out-of-the-ordinary used books, and it gives generous credit for trading in your own used books. The book store is closed on Sundays.

## The Nordic Maid
**18954-C Front St., Poulsbo**
**(360) 779-9863**

Learn the true meaning of the Norwegian expression *uff da* and laugh at other Scandinavian jokes at The Nordic Maid. The shop that opened in downtown Poulsbo in 1996 offers European gifts, including trolls, gnomes, and Swedish-made table runners.

## Port Gamble General Store
**1 Rainier Ave., Port Gamble**
**(360) 297-7636**

At the center of historic Port Gamble, the general store is the place to stop. Established in 1853, today's Port Gamble General Store offers dolls and gift items, toys

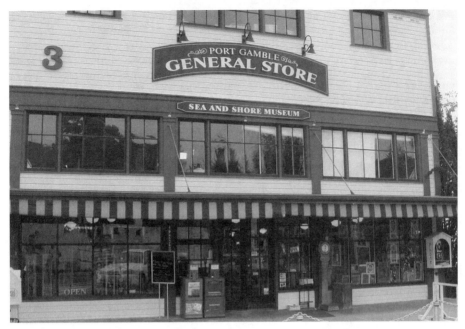

*The Port Gamble Store houses a cafe, a gift shop, and the Sea and Shore Museum.* PHOTO: ROB McNAIR-HUFF

for kids, Christmas ornaments, and a limited selection of clothing. Visitors will also find a selection of crystal and china dishes. And the building holds more than just the store. Venture to the back of the building for food and drinks in the cafe, or go upstairs and wander through the Sea and Shore Museum. Head downstairs to visit the history museum.

### Potlatch Gallery
**18830-B Front St., Poulsbo**
**(360) 779-3377**

Prints and paintings by Pacific Northwest artists are the main feature of the Potlatch Gallery on the main street in Poulsbo. The small gallery, owned by Simone and John Avery-Morrison, also offers a collection of jewelry and wood and stone works. The galley is closed on Sundays and Mondays.

### Raven Blues
**18827 Front St. N.E., Poulsbo**
**(360) 779-5662**

An eclectic mix of clothing and art comes together in the Raven Blues store in downtown Poulsbo. The shop offers a blend of products—women's fine clothing and accessories, painted furniture, jewelry, art clocks, and sculpture. Visitors will always see at least one raven and the resident cat.

### Rocambole Garlic Shop
**18804 Front St., Poulsbo**
**(360) 779-2415**

The Rocambole Garlic Shop bills itself as a garlic lover's dream come true. Shoppers can buy fresh garlic of all varieties, of course, but the store also features garlic roasters, garlic-related gifts and clothing, garlic-growing guides and cookbooks, and hot sauces to go along with those garlic-laden dishes. Shop owner Teresa Schultz opened the store in 1998.

### Rubber Soul
**18830A Front St., Poulsbo**
**(360) 779-7757**

Hobbyists can pick up rubber stamping supplies, from the stamps themselves to ink and custom papers, at the Rubber Soul in downtown Poulsbo. The shop offers classes throughout the year, including some geared toward children.

## Silverdale Antiques
**9536 Silverdale Way N.W., Silverdale**
**(360) 692-2462**

Set aside a chunk of time if you want to see everything in Silverdale Antiques. The large warehouse in the heart of Silverdale offers a wide selection of antiques, from sets of dishes to more than a dozen free-standing wood wardrobe closets covering wide price ranges. The store is a furniture lover's must-see. Collectors of old glass bottles will also enjoy browsing the collection in this shop run by owners Denis and Deborah Housen. Silverdale Antiques is closed on Mondays.

## Sluys Poulbso Bakery
**18924 Front St. N.E., Poulsbo**
**(360) 779-2798**
**www.sluysbakery.com**

Pick up a loaf of the widely-known "Poulsbo Bread," or taste test a specialty such as cinnamon apple bread or cinnamon orange bread at Sluys Poulsbo Bakery. Since it opened in 1966, the shop has tempted shoppers with Norwegian delicacies such as lefse, rosettes, or stöllen. Sluys also makes cookies and has gift items for sale.

## Terry's Antiques & Imports
**18881 A Front St., Poulsbo**
**(360) 779-2323**

Furniture such as dinner tables, sofas, and bed sets are featured at Terry's Antiques & Imports. The unique thing about this store, which has a distinct Southwest flavor, is the Whacky Studio—a corner of the store set aside and stocked with hats, masks, and funny glasses where customers can have their pictures taken. Once the picture has been shot, shop around among the collections of Southwest pottery.

## Verkstad Gallery
**18937 Front St., Poulsbo**
**(360) 697-4470**
**www.verkstadgallery.com**

The Verkstad Gallery fulfills the role of the artists' co-op in Poulsbo. Local artists sell a wide range of fine art pieces like photographs of local scenes, paintings in a myriad of media, and sculptures in wood, metal, and cloth. The Verkstad Gallery also represents some local crafters, including Gracie LaBombard's beautifully designed, hand-sewn European costumes made to fit the popular American Girl dolls.

# Port Townsend

Hotels and Motels

Bed and Breakfast Inns

Cottages, Cabins, and
Vacation Rentals

Restaurants

Nightlife

Shopping

Port Townsend, also known as the "City of Dreams," has so much to offer for a city of approximately 8,000 people that you could easily spend your entire vacation here, shopping at downtown boutiques, antiques stores, and art galleries, playing at Fort Worden—hike the beach, tour the officers' quarters, and pet sea slugs, driving to the top of nearby Mt. Walker, or kayaking around the bay. You could spend yet another day bird-watching at Kah Tai Lagoon Park, on Marrowstone Island, or at one of the small county or state parks in the area. You'll be treated to great music, art, poetry, or the sight of hundreds of boats on    the bay if you happen to be in town during one of the many festivals. A sampling of the annual festivals includes the Victorian Festival, Rhododendron Festival, Kinetic Skulpture Race, Port Townsend Film Festival, and the popular Wooden Boat Festival. Plus you can eat at a different restaurant for every meal and never run out of options. Port Townsend has nearly everything that a big city has to offer, including crowds and traffic jams during some of the more popular events and around the winter holidays. But, not many big cities feature such an amazing collection of original Victorian-era houses and office buildings, many of which have been transformed into luxurious bed and breakfast inns.

Captain George Vancouver took a spin through the area in 1792, noted the protected bay, and took the liberty of naming it after the Marquis of Townshend. The area was already in use however, although not as a permanent settlement. Area tribes, primarily the Klallam, used it as a seasonal camp. What is now Kah Tai Lagoon Park marks the portage point for crossing Quimper Peninsula to get to the Strait of Juan de Fuca, thus allowing them to avoid the treacherous waters at Point Wilson. White settlers built the first cabins on what is now Water Street in 1851. Within 30 years, Port Townsend had become a boomtown, and many people speculated that the city would be the railroad terminus and the shipping capital of the Northwest. With the boom came a flurry of building influenced by the popular Victorian styles of that age. Then, in the late 1890s, the boomtown went bust when all hopes of railway greatness were dashed. For years the houses languished in neglect, but at least they were not torn down. This chain of events left a unique collection of architectural treasures seen in the downtown commercial buildings and in the uptown houses. Port Townsend is registered as one of only three historic seaports on the National Registry, thanks in large part to the concentrated effort of the residents to preserve and refurbish the legacy.

Each year visitors are given the chance to peak inside many of the residences during the Historic Homes Tour. Of course, you'll also have a chance to see inside one if you stay in a Victorian bed and breakfast inn. Make sure you take the time to drive or walk self-guided tours that will take you by many of the historic homes, including the Starrett House, buildings such as the customshouse and courthouse, and through the equally historic Fort Worden.

Although a single military installation remains on the fort, the Point Wilson Lighthouse and U.S. Coast Guard Station, the 434-acre fort now serves as a park. Inside the park you'll find miles of accessible beach, lodging in converted officers' quarters, a campground, the marine science center, a theater, museums, and Copper Canyon Press, an independent publisher of contemporary poetry. Fort Worden hosts conferences and is home to Centrum (www.centrum.org), a non-profit organization dedicated to fostering the arts through education and exposure to the community. Centrum organizes writers' and artists' conferences, music festivals, and sponsors artist residencies. If you happen to be in town during one of Centrum's events, you are in for a rare treat indeed.

Visitors seem to fall in love with Port Townsend, and many return to retire, and more than a few have moved to Port Townsend with the hopes that fate would see to their livelihoods. The region boasts an incredibly diverse and rich arts community, and hardly a weekend passes without one arts-related event taking place in the city and its environs. We could write a book just about Port Townsend, and as a matter of fact, someone else has already done so. If you want to learn more about Port Townsend, drop by the Imprint Bookstore to pick up a copy of *City of Dreams: A Guide to Port Townsend* edited by Peter Simpson. Stop by the Visitors Information Center on Sims Way to pick up maps and guides for the tours we mentioned. The city also has an informative Web site: www.ptguide.com.

## Hotels and Motels

Although more people come to Port Townsend to stay in the Victorian bed and breakfast inns, the city contains more than a few hotels to accommodate the overflow. Some of the hotels are housed on the upper floors of the town's original office buildings and warehouses, one has taken over a castle, and others have been built much more recently. We have also included two hotels in the nearby resort town of Port Ludlow, which is about 20 minutes away by car. Unless otherwise noted, these establishments offer smoking and nonsmoking rooms and have at least one wheelchair-accessible room. No matter what time of year you plan to visit Port Townsend, we suggest that you make reservations at least a week in advance, more in the summer.

## Price Code

Our price code reflects the average price of a double-occupancy room during the peak season, which runs from mid-May to mid-October. Room rates are usually discounted from late fall to early spring. Prices exclude state and local sales taxes, around 10 percent for hotels and motels.

| | |
|---|---|
| $ | under $60 |
| $$ | $61–$90 |
| $$$ | $91–$130 |
| $$$$ | over $131 |

**Bishop Victorian Hotel    $$$**
**714 Washington St., Port Townsend**
**(360) 385-6122, (800) 824-4738**
**www.bishopvictorian.com**
During World War II this building served as housing for military personnel who were stationed here for aircraft landing training. Since then, the building has been refurbished and redecorated to offer nostalgic splendor with modern-day amenities like data ports. Today, William Morris, the Victorian decorator, would feel right at home in the Bishop Victorian Hotel. The ground-floor lobby features a

grand fireplace mantel, based on one Morris designed for the ship, *Olympic*, sister ship to the *Titanic*. Rich wall coverings, finely detailed Victorian-style chandeliers, and plush Oriental carpets complete the look.

None of the 15 suites looks exactly like another, although each contains a kitchenette with refrigerator, microwave, and workspace. Each room is also decorated with antiques and reproduction pieces, cozy down comforters, and a gas fireplace. Sleeper-sofas plus a dining table and chairs add comfort to each suite. Families will appreciate the third floor two-bedroom suite. The bedrooms are separated by a sitting room for added privacy, and the suite easily sleeps six. For a romantic weekend, book the front corner room with a soaking tub. A deluxe continental breakfast is served each morning on the upstairs landing. Visitors can also walk around the newly installed, landscaped gardens behind the hotel. The Bishop offers romantic and recreation packages and weekly or monthly rates. Guests also receive temporary privileges at the Port Townsend Athletic Club. Each additional guest will be charged $15. The hotel does not allow smoking, and no wheelchair-accessible rooms are available.

**Harborside Inn    $$**
**330 Benedict St., Port Townsend**
**(360) 385-6984, (800) 942-5960**

The Harborside Inn bucks Port Townsend's quaint and Victorian trend. Instead, the inn, which opened in 1990, features waterfront rooms and modern amenities like televisions and VCRs, microwaves, refrigerators, hair dryers, and data ports. Each sleek and comfortably spacious room includes a private patio and a water view in addition to a single king-size or two queen-size beds. Wheelchair-accessible rooms are available, and one suite with a king-size bed also includes a Jacuzzi tub. A year-round spa and seasonal pool offer recreational outlets. Boat Haven is conveniently located just across the street, and downtown Port Townsend is just a short walk away. A guest laundry is on the premises, and continental breakfast is served each morning in the lobby. Each additional guest will be charged $5 per night.

**Heron Beach Inn    $$$$**
**1 Heron Rd., Port Ludlow**
**(360) 437-0411**
**www.heronbeachinn.com**

Literally built over the water, Heron Beach Inn offers 37 luxury rooms with views of the Cascade and Olympic Mountains and Port Ludlow Bay. The private whirlpool tubs, plush bathrobes, and fireplaces in each spacious room add to the relaxing and romantic atmosphere. Mission-style furniture and down-filled duvets on thick European mattresses create a cozy retreat after a day filled with activities: The nearby marina rents kayaks and small boats, and the 27-hole Port Ludlow golf course is right down the road. Additional amenities include a complimentary video

## Insiders' Tip

Take a field trip to Fort Flagler State Park on the northern tip of Marrowstone Island. The 800-acre, former military stronghold now hosts a hostel, a campground, vacation rentals, and a museum. It's often deserted so you'll have the beach and trails to yourself for prime bird-watching, fishing, and clam digging. It also offers beautiful views of the mountains and the sunset.

*The Manresa Castle serves as a hotel and restaurant for travelers to Port Townsend.* PHOTO: ROB McNAIR-HUFF

library and VCRs, a volleyball court, croquet on the lawn, and board games in the sunroom or lounge. Three suites, each containing a sleeper-sofa, are also available, and all rooms include coffeemakers and refrigerators. For some extra special pampering, arrange for an in-room pedicure, manicure, aromatherapy session, or massage. A continental breakfast is served each morning in the sunroom, and seasonal Northwest cuisine prepared by Chef George Eubanks and his cooks is served each evening in the restaurant. Children under 17 stay free with a parent, and pets are welcomed. Additional adult guests will be accommodated for $35 per night. The inn is a nonsmoking establishment, and wheelchair-accessible rooms are available.

### Manresa Castle    $$
**7th & Sheridan Sts., Port Townsend**
**(360) 385-5750, (800) 732-1281**

The Manresa is perhaps the most famous building on this part of the Peninsula, complete with stories of hauntings. In the late 1800s, businessman and community leader Charles Eisenbeis built a 30-room Prussian castle for his beloved, Kate. The castle was built with locally made bricks, 12-inch thick walls, and finely detailed tiled fireplaces and woodwork. Charles died only 10 years after completion, and the castle stood empty for 20 years until it became a vacation convent and then a monastery. Since 1968 the Castle has served as a hotel. Each room is decorated with antiques and reproductions, and some have views of the bay. Room layouts vary from a single queen-size bed to a suite with king-size and queen-size beds. All rooms have private baths, but some of the bathrooms are a few steps down the hall, and two suites come with romantic, over-sized Jacuzzi tubs. Each morning the Manresa serves an ample continental breakfast for all of its guests. The Castle also houses a lounge and restaurant, which serves dinners and Sunday brunch. No wheelchair-accessible rooms are available.

**Port Ludlow Resort    $$$$**
**200 Olympic Pl., Port Ludlow**
**(360) 437-2222**
**www.portludlowresort.com**

The Port Ludlow Resort lodges its guests in condominium suites as well as individual guest rooms within the condominiums. Each condominium features a full kitchen, dining room, living room with fireplace, and one to four bedrooms. A private bathroom accompanies each of the bedrooms. Some condominiums also feature water and mountain views. The resort also offers special golf and getaway packages. During your stay, take advantage of the many recreational opportunities on the campus, including a playground, tennis courts, outdoor guarded pool, and plenty of waterfront for walking, picnics, and fishing. Of course, the 27-hole golf course is nearby and draws many people to the resort. The on-site marina also rents boats and kayaks to guests. Wheelchair-accessible condominiums are available.

**Olympic Hostel    $**
**272 Battery Wy.,**
**Port Townsend**
**(800) 909-4776**
**www.olympus.net/**
**ftworden/accommod.html**

Hostels provide basic accommodations at a great bargain, and that's exactly what you'll get at the Olympic Hostel at Fort Worden. A single night's lodging for an adult costs less than $20, and children under 18 stay free with a parent. This hostel is unique among hostels because, in addition to the men's and women's dormitories, it offers a few private rooms with queen-size beds and bunks or rollaway beds. Instead of spending the evening watching the televi-

sion, hostel guests often gather in the common rooms to talk, play games, or play the hostel's piano. Two more features make staying at the Olympic Hostel a unique hosteling experience: The second floor rooms have water views, and a free self-serve, all-you-can-eat pancake breakfast in the fully equipped kitchen gives lodgers a great start to the day. The hostel charges $2 for a set of linens, and your voluntary help in cleaning is appreciated. This hostel sees 1.5-million visitors each year, so reservations, especially in summer, are recommended.

**The Swan Hotel    $$$–$$$$**
**216 Monroe St., Port Townsend**
**(360) 385-1718, (800) 776-1718**
**www.theswanhotel.com**

James G. Swan spent years living with, researching, and writing about the first peoples of the Pacific Northwest. In 1859

*The Swan Hotel sits at the far end of Port Townsend.* PHOTO: NATALIE McNAIR-HUFF

he arrived in Port Townsend to launch a whaling business. Although that venture failed, he did serve in a few public positions, but his greatest fame came posthumously for his enormous collection of Native American artifacts, and for his anthropological, archeological, and scientific research. Today, this collection of cottages, guest suites, and a penthouse bears his name. Kitchenettes with microwaves and refrigerators, cable TV, and comfortable queen-size beds create a cozy retreat in each of the four cottages, great for a romantic interlude. If you want a little more space, reserve one of the one-bedroom suites. Each suite includes a queen-size bed plus a full kitchen, large bathroom, and a sleeper-sofa in the living room. The suites comfortably sleep four adults. The four-bedroom, multilevel penthouse includes a luxurious master-suite with a king-size bed and whirlpool bath. A large dining area, complete kitchen, living room, and two porches make the penthouse perfect for a family or group retreat. The second-floor suites and penthouse have impressive water views, and all rooms feature beautiful woodwork and a mixture of contemporary and antiques furnishings. A $15 charge will be added for each guest over double-occupancy. Pets can be accommodated in the cottages for $15 per night. Ask about the special recreation packages.

# Bed and Breakfast Inns

Port Townsend is well known for its beautiful and historic Victorian bed and breakfast inns. If you have a chance to stay in one, we highly recommend it. They offer a genteel touch that standard hotels and motels lack. Staying in some of the houses is practically a history lesson, and a few are rumored to be haunted. The proprietors of Port Townsend's bed and breakfast inns preserved the beauty of the original houses while providing the modern comforts and amenities that most of us are used to.

The allure of a bed and breakfast inn lies with the fact that someone coddles you, makes sure you are comfortable and cared for, and cooks you a delicious, warming breakfast to help you on your way. Occasionally you may have to share a bathroom. These inns have a charm that few hotels can hope to capture. It's almost like home, but someone else does the cleaning and cooking!

Since the proprietors of bed and breakfast inns are opening their homes to strangers as well as trying to provide a restful atmosphere, most don't allow smoking, children under age 12, or pets. Some will allow pets and children by prior arrangement. If you are allergic to animals, you may want to check with your hosts to see if they have or allow pets. Most accept major credit cards, and some will ask for a credit card to hold the reservation. If the inn does not accept credit cards we have noted that with the price code.

Each bed and breakfast listed provides a special home-cooked breakfast. Some innkeepers serve breakfast in bed, others serve it family style in a formal dining room or breakfast nook. You may be treated to a secret family recipe such as yummy chocolate banana bread. Or maybe it will be a well-known breakfast favorite with a twist like a smoked salmon and brie omelette, baked cheese and chile casserole, French toast with homemade berry syrup, or even thick, comforting oatmeal with a dried fruit compote. You can also expect to see fresh fruit, toast and homemade jam, as well as gourmet coffee, tea, and fruit juice on every table. Most innkeepers will accommodate special-needs diets or serve breakfast earlier or later if arrangements are made in advance. No matter what the situation, find out when and where breakfast is served, as it's a special part of the bed and breakfast experience.

# Price Code

Our price code reflects the average price of a double-occupancy room during the peak season, which runs from mid-May to mid-October. Room rates are usually discounted from late fall to early spring. Prices exclude state and local sales taxes.

$ . . . . . . . . . . . . . .under $65
$$ . . . . . . . . . . . . . .$65–$95
$$$ . . . . . . . . . . .$96–$140
$$$$ . . . . . . . . . . .over $141

**Ann Starrett Mansion   $$$$**
**744 Clay St., Port Townsend**
**(360) 385-3205, (800) 321-0644**
**www.starrettmansion.com**

The Ann Starrett Mansion captivates tourists with its many gables, gingerbread trim, and impressive turret. And that's just the outside. Once inside, the wonders continue to impress as one of the finest examples of Queen Anne architecture in the city. George Starrett, a wealthy contractor, built the house in 1889 as a wedding gift for his wife, Ann. As soon as you enter the house you see a unique and mysterious, hanging spiral staircase topped by a rare, eight-sided cupola bearing figures representing the four seasons and four virtues modeled after Ann. On the first day of each season, a beam of sunlight passes through a red, stained-glass window to highlight the figure representing the season. Guests can tour the house as part of their stay, but public tours are also available every day.

Every room in the house includes something special, from the intricately hand-carved wood trim to the wall frescoes and custom-designed friezes to the Belgian tapestry in the stairwell. Each bedroom and suite includes a comfortable seating area. Some have mountain and water views, and all are decorated with antiques. The mansion houses a total of nine suites and rooms, and two more suites are also housed in a separate cot-

*The Ann Starrett Mansion.* PHOTO: NATALIE McNAIR-HUFF

tage—the only accommodations where children are allowed, and the only ones that include televisions. All rooms and suites offer private bathrooms, some with bathtubs. Some of the tubs are also unusual: the second-floor cottage suite features a jetted tub in its bathroom, the Gable Suite in the main house lets guests soak sore muscles in an antique, round soaking tub, and the garden suite sports a bright red, clawfoot tub. A full breakfast is served each morning and features such dishes as New Orleans–style French toast stuffed with berries and cream cheese, German pancakes, and quiche. Breakfast is served in the dining room, but you can also have it delivered to your room if you talk to the innkeeper. Pets are not allowed here, and the mansion is a completely smoke-free environment. The Web site claims that "A $350 fumigation fee will be imposed if a room is smoked in." Additional guests will be accommodated for $35 per guest per night. Make your reservation well in advance.

**Directions:** From WA Hwy. 20/Sims Way, turn left onto Kearney at the traffic light. Stay on Kearney until you reach Lawrence Street; turn right. Take Lawrence past the uptown shops and Aldrich's grocery store, then turn right onto Adams Street. The inn will be on your left at the corner of Adams and Clay Streets.

### Annapurna Retreat & Spa    $$$$
**583 Adams St., Port Townsend**
**(360) 385-2909, (800) 868-ANNA**
**www.annapurnaretreat-spa.com**

When the stress of overwork and too much junk food wears you down, head to the Annapurna Retreat & Spa, named after the goddess of plenitude. A day at the inn starts with early morning yoga followed by a vegan breakfast. Breakfast may start with a fruit smoothie before proceeding with a fresh fruit or vegetable entree such as fruit "pizza," often prepared with produce harvested from the on-site organic garden. After breakfast you can relax with a meditation session in the garden or detoxify in the sauna or

steam room. Robin Sharan, the proprietor, intends for the inn to be a place of rest and healing. Toward those ends, the inn also offers healing therapies such as reflexology, colonics, massages, cranial-sacral therapy, and facials.

Decorated with a combination of Victorian-style reproductions and contemporary furnishings, the inn offers five guest rooms and a small cottage. Rooms include a small seating area and queen-size or full beds. Some are wheelchair accessible, and three share a bathroom. Two rooms, Rose and Lotus, can be rented together as a suite. Children are welcome, as are pets, for $15 per pet, by prior arrangement. A third guest can be accommodated for an additional $20. The Annapurna Retreat & Spa has a two-night minimum stay requirement, and they offer special packages for weekend and week long retreats.

**Directions:** From WA Hwy. 20/Sims Way, go straight through the traffic light at Kearney Street and take Water Street all the way through town. Make a left onto Monroe at the Swan Hotel. Turn left again onto Clay Street. The inn will be on the corner of Adams and Clay.

### Captain John Quincy Adams House    $$$
**1028 Tyler St., Port Townsend**
**(360) 379-8832, (888) 385-1258**
**www.captnjqadams.com**

Captain John Quincy Adams, the great-great-grandson of President John Quincy Adams lived in this house, which his son built in 1887. The house suffered years of neglect, abuse, and a close brush with destruction by fire. The current owners, Marshal and Selena Raney, purchased the house in 1998, restored it, and turned it into a bed and breakfast inn. The inn is decorated with antiques, including a Victorian pool table that came north from San Francisco. The inn offers three rooms and one extravagant suite, the Presidential Suite. The five-room suite occupies the third floor, and the suite's Master bedroom in the turreted section has a queen-size, four-poster bed. The den contains a TV and VCR, and a dormer includes two twin beds, perfect for a children's hide-away while the adults can enjoy the Jacuzzi tub in the bathroom.

The inn's standard rooms feel just as lush. The Lady Hamilton overlooks the rose garden and is decorated appropriately with bright floral prints. The room includes a sitting area with a large couch and a private bathroom with a bathtub and shower. The Victoria room, so named because the bed came from Queen Victoria's summer palace, features a view of the garden and a Victorian fainting couch. The private bathroom has a shower but no tub. Advertised as the house's "most private and romantic room," the Armada room features a large, marble-floored bathroom with a clawfoot tub and separate shower. A large sitting area and antique French bedroom set round out the amenities.

Additional amenities will make your stay feel even more special. Homemade dessert is served in the afternoon or after dinner, and coffee and tea are available at all hours of the day. Guests can also take a dip in the hot tub in the manicured garden. Each morning's breakfast starts with coffee or tea and fresh muffins or croissants followed by an entree such as polenta topped with eggs scrambled with cheese and sausage or bacon. Children over age 12 are welcome, but pets are not. Additional guests can be accommodated for $25 per night.

**Directions:** From WA Hwy. 20/Sims Way, turn left onto Kearney at the traffic light. Stay on Kearney until you reach Lawrence Street; turn right. Stay on Lawrence for 12 blocks and then turn left onto Tyler and follow it to the jog in the road at Blaine St. The inn is located on the right where Tyler starts to curve after the jog.

**Chanticleer Inn   $$$**
**1208 Franklin St., Port Townsend**
**(360) 385-6239, (800) 858-9421**
**www.northolympic.com/chanticleer**

Part of the allure of the Chanticleer Inn is the southern hospitality served up by your native-Texan hosts, Shirley and Pat-

### Insiders' Tip

Many bed and breakfast inns include guest journals in each room or in the main living room. Read through the journals to see what other people who stayed there did. You may find the perfect spot for a picnic, a recommendation for a lovely hike, or learn about the room's ghost.

tye O'Connor, a mother-daughter team. That combined with the lighter, Victorian country-home atmosphere makes for a unique stay. Of course, the delicious breakfasts add even more to the experience. When you stay here your morning will start off with some homemade granola and fresh fruit to be followed by a filling entree such as French toast or an egg casserole with feta, spinach, and mushrooms accompanied by coffee cake, cinnamon rolls, or another type of breakfast bread. The inn offers four rooms in the main house, each with a private bathroom. All of the rooms are papered in light colors and have cheery, lacy linens and down comforters on feather beds. The Virginia room features white wicker furniture, a lacy canopy over the bed, and a Jacuzzi tub. The Springfield Suite coddles guests with a king-size feather bed, a pleasant sitting area, and a private balcony with a view of the water and mountains.

The detached Carriage House sleeps up to four people, two in a private bedroom with a queen-size bed, and two on a sleeper-sofa in the living room. The charming retreat also offers a cozy fireplace as well as a TV with VCR, and a complete kitchen. Pets are not allowed anywhere at the inn, and children are allowed only in the Carriage House. A two-night minimum stay is required to reserve the Carriage House, and each guest over double-occupancy will be charged $15.

**Directions:** From WA Hwy. 20/Sims Way just after the Kearney traffic light, take the gentle left onto Washington Street and go up the hill. Stay on Washington for eight blocks and turn left onto Fillmore Street and go two blocks. The inn is on the corner of Fillmore and Franklin Streets.

### The English Inn Bed & Breakfast    $$$
**718 F St., Port Townsend**
**(360) 385-5302, (800) 254-5302**
**www.english-inn.com**

Each room at The English Inn is named for a poet: Rossetti, Keats, Longfellow, and Yeats. Each room features a view of the Olympic Mountains or of the on-site gardens. The Rossetti room is the largest room at the inn and includes a king-size bed with plantation-style furnishings and colorful walls and linens. It also features an in-room, clawfoot tub with a view of the mountains. The Yeats room also features an in-room clawfoot tub canopied with lace and a queen-size bed. A television is available to all guests in the common room, and a hot tub and garden gazebo beckon guests to the backyard. A buffet in the common room serves as a coffee bar and is kept stocked with fresh, locally roasted coffee, hot water, and baked goods. Each morning guests sit down to a breakfast of fresh-baked breads and pastries, breakfast meats, and an egg dish such as Mock Eggs Benedict—English muffins topped with eggs scrambled with Swiss cheese and ham.

The Italianate-style house was built by Henry Bash, the shipping commissioner, in 1885, and is close to Fort Worden, where visitors can hike, walk the beach, or stroll in the gardens. The inn is quiet since it is not located near the downtown core. Children over the age of 14 are welcome at the inn, and additional guests will be accommodated for $10 each night. The three dogs on the premises don't appreciate pets coming along, however.

**Directions:** From WA Hwy. 20/Sims Way just after the Kearney traffic light, take the gentle left onto Washington Street and go up the hill to Walker Street. Turn left onto Walker, which becomes Cherry Street. Take Cherry to F Street and turn right. The inn will be on the left side of the street just past Rose Street.

### Holly Hill House Bed & Breakfast    $$$
**611 Polk St., Port Townsend**
**(360) 385-5619, (800) 435-1454**
**www.hollyhillhouse.com**

You may want to stay at the Holly Hill House just so you can tour the garden filled with 185 rose bushes and bordered by a white picket fence. The garden also features a rare 100-year-old upside-down Camperdown Elm tree.

To take advantage of an impressive view of Admiralty Inlet and the Cascade Range in a spacious and genteel setting, reserve the Colonel's Room. It is the largest guest room in the house and features a king-size bed with a beautiful, stippled wood headboard that extends to the ceiling and ends in a fringed canopy. The room also offers an ample seating area, an extra twin bed, and a jetted bath in the en suite bathroom. Billie's Room shares the same view, visible from a cozy queen-size bed. Lizette's Room and the Morning Glory Room both feature views of the garden and flower printed linens and comforters on queen-size beds. Lizette's Room also has a spare twin bed. If you like to stargaze, then you may want to stay in the ivy-twined Skyview Room, which has a skylight to let moonbeams and sunlight in.

Each morning guests gather in the formal dining room for a candle lit, multi course breakfast—maybe the popular baked French toast—served on fine china and crystal. Your hosts also serve afternoon tea and pastries in the parlor. Children over 12 years old are welcomed, and an additional guest will be welcomed in

Lizette's or the Colonel's Room for an additional $10 per night. Smoking is allowed only on the porch, and your pets will need to stay elsewhere.

**Directions:** From WA Hwy. 20/Sims Way, turn left at the Kearney Street traffic light onto Lawrence Street. After 11 blocks turn right onto Polk Street.

### The James House     $$$–$$$$
**1238 Washington St., Port Townsend**
**(360) 385-1238, (800) 385-1238**
**www.jameshouse.com**

The James House, situated on a bluff overlooking the ferry terminal, opened as a bed and breakfast inn more than 25 years ago. It was the first in the Northwest, and it remains today as one of the more outstanding examples of what a bed and breakfast inn can be. Francis James, a customs agent, spent $10,000 on building the house in 1889. He was in his 70s when it was built, and he picked the location because it was a stone's throw away from the customshouse where he worked. As soon as you walk in the front door, you understand that you are walking into another age, another world. The parquet wood floor is composed of individual pieces of walnut, cherry, and oak that have been assembled with puzzle-piece precision. The hand-carved cherry staircase and cherry-toned wood doors and wainscoting all invite you to look, touch, and smell the past.

The twelve rooms are no less impressive. Most feature water views and private baths, and all contain unique antique furnishings, and a modern touch—data ports.

Each room includes a special surprise such as the window seat by the eyelid window in the Alcove Room, the hand-painted garland circling the Olympic View Room, the private second-floor deck that accompanies the Chintz Room, or the massive and intricately carved headboard, fireplace, and sitting room in the Bridal Suite. Two brick-lined, ground-level suites and the Gardener's Cottage contain cable televisions and sofa-beds or spare beds.

A filling breakfast greets guests each morning. Breakfast starts with juice, coffee, and fresh fruit. An egg dish such as quiche is served every day, as are scones and breakfast breads. After breakfast make sure you take a stroll through the gardens, which are gaining fame in town. Children over the age of 12 will be welcomed to the inn, but pets must stay elsewhere. Suites with extra beds will accommodate an additional guest for $20 per night. No smoking is allowed at the inn.

**Directions:** From WA Hwy. 20/Sims Way directly after the Kearney St. traffic light, turn left onto Washington Street and take it up the hill. The James House will be on your left looking over the street and the bluff to the ferry terminal below.

### The Old Consulate Inn     $$$$
**313 Walker St., Port Townsend**
**(360) 385-6753, (800) 300-6753**
**www.oldconsulateinn.com**

Although never technically an embassy, from 1908 to 1911 two rooms in this mansion indeed served as the official residence and office of the German Consul. The inn is also known as the F.W. Hastings House in honor of Senator F.W. Hastings, the man who built the house in 1889, and who was also the son of one of the original founders of the city. Hastings made his fortune from the trolley car company that he owned, but by 1904, after the trolley rails were removed from the city streets, his fortune began to dwindle.

Today, the house has been restored to its former glory, including an exterior paint job in the original brick red with white and green trim. The innkeepers have decorated the house with period antiques and reproduction furnishings, including a pump organ in the parlor. The game room sports a 1900-replica pool table, and more modern entertainment options such as a TV and VCR. Guests also can relax in the hot tub, which is enclosed in a gazebo. Each of the inn's eight rooms includes a private bath, some with tubs, and three suites also offer sitting rooms; all include king-size beds except the Alcove Mini Suite, which has a queen-size bed. Three rooms, including the Tower Honeymoon Suite and Harbor View, provide views of Admiralty Inlet or Port Townsend Bay, while another looks over the Olympics. The remaining rooms look over the gardens or the neighboring homes. The most spacious suite, the Master Anniversary Suite, actually takes up an entire side of the second floor and features the incredible water view plus a king-size, canopied bed, a wood burning stove, and a bi-level bathroom with a clawfoot tub.

Each morning, an incredibly large breakfast is served banquet style in the dining room. Sample cantaloupe drizzled with honey-celery syrup, a baked Greek puff with fall vegetables and four cheeses, and pound cake topped with peaches. Children over age 12 may stay at the inn, and additional guests can be accommodated on a roll-away bed for $40 per night. Smoking is allowed only on the porch, and pets must stay elsewhere.

**Directions:** From WA Hwy. 20/Sims Way directly after the Kearney St. traffic light, turn left onto Washington Street and take it partway up the hill and turn left onto Walker Street, which is the first street you will come to. The brick-red inn will be on the left side of the street.

**Quimper Inn Bed & Breakfast     $$–$$$**
**1306 Franklin St., Port Townsend**
**(360) 384-1060, (800) 557-1060**
**www.olympus.net/quimper**

Book lovers will rejoice at the shelves stuffed full of musty tomes that lend a special ambience to Quimper Inn. If you're a real book nut, rent the Library Room, with 1,200 books and a queen bed—a library ladder lets you reach the books on the top shelves. Harry & Gertie's Suite also offers a wall of books that separates its two rooms, one proffering a queen-size bed, the other made for reading in wing-backed chairs and a sofa or writing at the desk with a view of the nearby clock tower. Michele's Room was made for relaxing either in the queen-size bed fitted

in bay windows or in the clawfoot tub in the commodious bathroom. Two smaller rooms, Christopher's and John's, share a bathroom. Christopher's is stocked with more books and two twin beds while John's is purported to "possibly be the world's quietest room." The house has an interesting architectural history. The first part of the house was built in 1888, but after the crash of 1900, Gertie and Harry Barthrop bought and remodeled the house in 1904 to add a Craftsman flavor with window seats, dormers, and large house-wide front porches.

If you are able to resist the urge to read all night and can get up in the morning, your hosts, Sue and Ron will feed you a healthy breakfast that might include baked pears with raspberry sauce, melon with yogurt and granola, scones, and a fluffy souffle. Sue also enjoys the challenge of satisfying special dietary needs. While you eat breakfast, Sue and Ron will be happy to talk with you about a couple of their favorite topics: Sue loves all things French, and Ron is passionate about Porsches. Quimper Inn welcomes children over 12 years old, but does not allow pets or smoking.

**Directions:** From WA Hwy. 20/Sims Way just after the Kearney traffic light, take the gentle left onto Washington Street and go up the hill. Stay on Washington for seven blocks and turn left onto Harrison Street and go two blocks. The inn is on the corner of Harrison and Franklin Streets.

**Ravenscroft Inn     $$$**
**533 Quincy St., Port Townsend**
**(360) 385-2784, (800) 782-2691**
**www.ravenscroftinn.com**

You may be surprised to learn that Ravenscroft Inn is actually a new house modeled on the Colonial homes of Charleston, South Carolina. The large house fits right in with the historic homes of Port Townsend. Inside, the eight spacious rooms feature private bathrooms and a variety of special touches and comforts. For simple, secluded comfort, rent

The Bower or the Quincy Room with queen-size beds. For a taste of luxury, rent the rose-toned Fireside Suite with a canopied, queen-size bed, access to the veranda, and a view of Admiralty Strait, and, of course, a large, brick fireplace flanked by two wing chairs. To experience all that Ravenscroft has to offer, rent the ultra-luxurious Rainier Suite located on the top floor. Wake to a view of the bay and the mountains and read a book while sitting in a wicker rocking chair. At night, stoke the fire and crawl into the soaking tub with your sweetheart.

Each morning guests eat a gourmet, multicourse breakfast in front of the fireplace downstairs. A typical breakfast starts with a fruit frappe or a warm fruit dish such as poached pears, an egg dish like quiche, and breakfast breads or coffee cakes round out the offerings. Freshly brewed coffee and tea are always on hand as well. Ravenscroft Inn likes to provide peaceful and romantic retreats for adults so children and pets should stay elsewhere.

**Insiders' Tip**
Casual clothes are the norm around here. Few restaurants have dress codes, and most of the finest welcome diners in jeans and clean flannel.

**Directions:** From WA Hwy. 20/Sims Way, turn left onto Kearney at the traffic light. Stay on Kearney until you reach Lawrence Street; turn right. Take Lawrence for 15 blocks, which will take you past the uptown shops and Aldrich's grocery store, then turn right onto Quincy Street. The inn will be on your right, just past Clay Street

## Cottages, Cabins, and Vacation Rentals

If you prefer the simpler life than that offered by a bed and breakfast inn or hotel, look into some of these rental cabins and cottages. We feature vacation rentals that place you in the heart of nature or right near the heart of Port Townsend, although with the settings you'll be in you'd never know it. Most of these rentals can be secured by the night or the week.

**Ecologic Place**
**10 Beach Dr., Nordland**
**(360) 385-3077, (800) 871-3077**
**www.ecologicplace.com**

This is the place to go if you prefer to spend your time outside kayaking, walking on coastal tidelands, bird-watching, stargazing, or hiking in search of deer and elk. Located next to a wildlife preserve on Marrowstone Island, Ecologic Place is 10 acres of tide flats, woods, and grassy fields. Eight rustic cabins, all with water and mountain views, rent for around $100 per night, double occupancy; two of the smaller cabins rent for around $70. Each wood-stove-heated cabin has a bath-room with a shower and a full kitchen, including dishes, utensils, coffeemaker, and toaster. The cabins sleep between two and six people with a $25 per night charge for each additional adult and a $10 per night charge for each additional child over double occupancy. Due to the wild nature of the area, pets are not allowed, and smoking is allowed only outside.

**Fort Worden Accommodations**
**(360) 344-4434**
**www.olympus.net/ftworden/accommod. html**

In addition to offering a hostel and campground, Fort Worden has transformed its historic military barracks, officers' homes, and even a castle into rental accommodations for individuals and families, and three are wheelchair accessible. The homes have fully equipped kitchens (no microwaves) and most have fireplaces as well. They feature pressed-tin ceilings and are decorated with Victorian-styled reproductions. Most of the houses sleep between three and seven people, and the Madrona Vista sleeps 23 in 11 bedrooms. Fort Worden also offers a host of recreational opportunities: a large open field for playing games, miles of accessible beach and hiking trails, historic officers' quarters tours, rhododendron and Chinese gardens, even a marine science center where kids can pet creatures of the sea. Most of the houses rent for less than $150 per night, and some of the larger houses go for more than $250. Fort Worden hosts a lot of arts and education events so the houses fill quickly. If you want to stay in one, make your reservations early. Reservations can be made up to a year in advance.

### Old Church Inn
**130 Randolph Street, Port Hadlock**
**(360) 732-7552**
**www.olypen.com/inn**

Need some old-time religion? Then rent the Old Church Inn a few miles outside of Port Townsend in Port Ludlow. The church comfortably sleeps up to 10 adults, and two upstairs bedrooms with queen-size beds provide privacy. Restored wood floors and fir wainscoting provide a warm background for a large, comfortably furnished living room and dining room. An immense, fully equipped kitchen will make any gourmet cook feel right at home. Outside, guests can play games on the large, fenced yard or grill dinner on the gas barbecue, perhaps using a marinade with herbs from the herb garden. The church has two bathrooms, and a washer and dryer. Rent it by the day or week, but make your reservations early.

### Pilot's Cottage
**327 Jackson St., Port Townsend**
**(360) 379-0811**
**www.10kvacationrentals.com/pilots**

This charming, cedar shake cottage offers a quaint and comfortable retreat with a front-seat view of the yachts and wooden boats right across the street in the Point Hudson marina. It is also conveniently located within walking distance of the downtown shopping district, but you may decide to stay locked away in the cabin cuddling in bed or reading in front of the fireplace. Puget Sound shipping pilots built the cottage in 1936 as a place to stay while away from home. The cottage still makes a nice home away from home with a fully equipped kitchen and two bedrooms with queen-size beds. During the warmer months you may want to eat your meals on the front deck so you can keep your eye on the water and the boats passing by. The cottage rents by the week.

### Vienna Suites
**925 Water Street, Port Townsend**
**360-385-3007**
**www.the-belmont.com/viennasuites. html**

Cuddle with your sweetheart or bring the whole family when you stay in the Vienna Suites. The suites are located downtown on the third floor of one of the city's Victorian buildings. Each suite, essentially an apartment, is tastefully decorated with contemporary furnishings and includes living and dining rooms, two bedrooms with queen-size beds, a full bathroom, and a complete kitchen. The dining rooms contain tables that seat six, and televisions and VCRs are in the living rooms. The suites rent for around $100 to $130 per night and may also be rented for the week.

# Restaurants

Port Townsend has so many restaurants that no matter what you are in the mood for, you will find something to ease your cravings. Many of the restaurants rival those in Seattle for selection and quality. Northwest fusion cuisine makes creative dishes out of seafood and seasonal vegetables, and the ethnic restaurants will tantalize your palate with intriguing blends of spices. You can dress up or dress casual, head out for a romantic, candlelit dinner or just grab a quick lunch. For coffee, handmade chocolates, fudge, or an afternoon snack, stop by McKenzie's Coffee Company & Deli (221 Taylor Street). For soup and sandwiches plus freshly made bread and pastries find the Bread & Roses Bakery (230 Quincy Street). Take the kids to Elevated Ice Cream (673 Water Street) and the attached candy shop where they make their own ice cream, Italian ices, soda syrups, and candies. Nifty Fiftys Soda Fountain (817 Water Street) also makes a fun family stop where you can listen to table-top juke boxes while you eat burgers and slurp ice-cream floats.

Most of the restaurants in Port Townsend include at least one vegetarian entree, often made with locally harvested organic produce, and many prohibit smoking. We have highlighted the restaurants that we think offer something unique or special, or that we know are popular among locals and tourists. There are plenty more to choose from as well.

## Price Code

Our price code reflects the average cost of a dinner for one, excluding drinks, tips, and taxes. Unless noted otherwise, the restaurants accept most major credit cards. Many do not accept out-of-county or out-of-state checks, so ask your server,

$ . . . . . . . . . . . . . .under $10
$$ . . . . . . . . . . . . .$10–$15
$$$ . . . . . . . . . . . .$16–$20
$$$$ . . . . . . . . . . .over $21

**Ajax Café**    **$$$**
**Lower Hadlock Rd., Port Hadlock**
**(360) 385-3450**
**www.ajaxcafe.com**

The Ajax Café is downright funky and fun, and it serves great food to boot. You don't have to wear a tie here, but if you really want to, the restaurant keeps a zany collection of neck-cinchers and hats on hand; they go right along with the mismatched dishes and chairs. In addition to the items on the seasonal menu, the cafe serves a daily special, more often than not fresh fish—Alaskan halibut, line-caught salmon, tuna. Before your entree arrives, tempt your tummy with an appetizer like a shi-

itake mushroom and sweet onion tart with asiago flan in a pastry crust. Move on to an entree such as pan-fried oysters and crab cakes or Mediterranean Fisherman's Stew. Locals also visit for the steaks. In fact for five years running, diners voted that the restaurant has the best steaks.

Homemade ice cream, flan, fresh fruit tarts, and cheesecake may be featured on the dessert menu, so save room. Kids can order from a special menu, and adults will appreciate the wine and beer list. Thursday through Sunday, diners are treated to live music—blues, folk, and jazz, including the local wine seller and classical guitarist, Joe Euro. The Ajax Café is closed Mondays, and it is a smoke-free establishment. This used to be one of the area's best-kept secrets, but now the secret is out, so reservations are recommended.

### The Belmont    $$$–$$$$
**925 Water St., Port Townsend**
**(360) 385-98368**
**www.the-belmont.com/dmenu.html**

The Belmont opened in 1889 and soon became a popular restaurant and saloon. If you could travel back in time you would see it filled with merchants, ship captains, and sailors. Today, The Belmont serves fresh seafood along with other American favorites for lunch and dinner. Stop for lunch and eat on the deck overlooking the water. Lunch entrees include hot and cold sandwiches such as The Birdie, grilled chicken breast with Monterey Jack cheese, avocado, and cream cheese on peasant bread. You'll also find salads such as the Belmont Cobb Salad with chicken, shrimp, bleu cheese, bacon, egg, and tomatoes served on mixed greens, as well as pastas, hot chicken, and seafood entrees.

Start dinner with the rich and creamy Dungeness Crab and Artichoke Dip or pancetta-wrapped prawns served with a citrus Grand Marnier sauce and dried cranberries. It may take you a while to select your dinner entree with so many choices. The Northwest Seafood Sauté has a bit of everything: salmon, halibut, clams, mussels, and prawns. For something different, try the Whidbey Island Duck pan roasted with cherries and served with lemon zest and black pepper spaetzle. The Belmont also serves daily specials. On one summer day, one of our parents visited and was transported back to his childhood when he ordered salmon fish and chips. Beer and wine are served from the full bar in the lounge. Reservations are recommended during the summer months.

### Chimacum Café    $
**9253 Rhody Dr., Chimacum**
**360-732-4631**

Large, filling breakfast and home-style meals are the hallmark of this local favorite. Find the Chimacum Café if you have a hankering for country favorites such as baked ham, fried chicken, meat loaf, or chicken fried steak. They also serve a mean hamburger. Don't forget to save room for a milkshake or homemade pie. The café has repeatedly received the local vote for best pie in *The Leader's* Best Food contest.

### El Sarape    $
**628 Water St., Port Townsend**
**(360) 379-9343**

Venture into the brightly colored setting of El Sarape in downtown Port Townsend to feast on Mexican specialties such as carne asada, chicken en mole, or a combination meal like Los Tres—chile verdé, chile colorado, and a chile relleno. Open your meal with a quesadilla or Mexican pizza. The main courses feature seafood, vegetarian, and egg dishes, or burritos. Meals are served in friendly surroundings, with murals and paintings of parrots on the walls, along with Mexican ornaments. El Sarape serves lunch and dinner.

### Fountain Cafe    $–$$
**920 Washington St., Port Townsend**
**(360) 379-9343**

The Fountain Cafe doesn't take reservations, and it has only about half a dozen tables, but if you can wait to get in, do it. Located a few doors away from the town fountain, the cafe serves creative Northwest fusion dishes in a funky, somewhat Bohemian atmosphere. We find the appetizers and pastas hard to resist here. Try steamed clams and mussels or the Roasted Walnut & Gorgonzola Penne as a light meal. For something more substantial, try the Paella, Wild Mushroom Risotto, or one of the daily specials. The menu changes seasonally, so you'll always find something new, fresh, and imaginative. The Fountain Cafe also serves wine and beer, and incredible homemade desserts that change with the seasons and the moods of the chef.

**Harbormaster Restaurant    $$$–$$$$**
**200 Olympic Pl., Port Ludlow**
**(360) 437-2222**
**www.portludlowresort.com/Dining.htm**

The Harbormaster Restaurant features great water views as well as fresh Northwest cuisine for breakfast, lunch, dinner, and a lavish Sunday brunch. Traditional breakfast foods are featured alongside specialties like Eggs Ludlow, poached eggs on an English muffin topped with sautéed bacon, onion, sweet peppers, and hollandaise. Lunch features soups, salads, sandwiches, and light seafood entrees such as pan-fried oysters and shrimp quesadillas. Nightly dinner specials include fresh seafood and prime rib. Order an entree salad for a lighter meal such as blackened salmon served with mixed greens and an orange-ginger vinaigrette. Entrees such as sautéed tiger prawns or salmon stuffed with bay shrimp and jack cheese star in the evening. Ask your server to recommend a wine or beer to accompany your meal or head to the Wreckroom Lounge after dinner for some live music and drinks. The Harbormaster Restaurant is wheelchair accessible.

**Jake's Original Grill    $$–$$$**
**600 Sims Way, Port Townsend**
**(360) 385-5356**

Jake's doesn't look too promising from the outside, and its location on the hill into Port Townsend makes it easy to pass by. We made the mistake of ignoring it until three locals recommended it as a favorite place one day. We won't make that mistake again. Jake's serves dinners with that well-known Northwest flavor. One of the most popular items on the menu is the Stuffed Gorgonzola Burger. It's so popular that customers demanded its return when it was removed from the menu. Jake's takes a half-pound burger and stuffs it with gorgonzola before grilling it, topping it with caramelized onions and setting it on a bun baked fresh by the local Heliotrope bakery. Of course, you can't have a grill without featuring steaks, and Jake's features thick-cut T-bone, top sirloin, and New York steaks as well as seafood specials such as Dungeness crab cakes and a rich and hearty cioppino.

**Khu Larb Thai    $$**
**225 Adams St., Port Townsend**
**(360) 385-5023**

Khu Larb Thai, whose owners are from Thailand, features a wide range of popular and delicious Thai dishes. Start with an appetizer such as chicken satay—chicken pieces marinated in Thai spices and coconut milk—served with cucumber salad and a homemade peanut sauce. Entrees include a large selection of vegetarian dishes as well as pad thai—stir fried rice noodles with prawns, small sliced bean cakes, bean sprouts, and egg topped with ground peanuts. Beef, poultry, pork, and seafood dishes are highlighted as well, including the spicy seafood combination, which includes cod, calamari, scallops, prawns, and clams with Thai spices and curry. You set the spiciness from one to five stars. Khu Larb Thai is closed Mondays.

**Lanza's    $$**
**1020 Lawrence St., Port Townsend**
**(360) 379-1900**
**www.olympus.net/lanzas**

Take an Italian family, locally grown produce, and fresh seafood, and you get the food at Lanza's, a family-run restaurant in one of uptown Port Townsend's old brick buildings. Pizza is always a popular choice; in fact pizza is how Lanza's started. Vegetarians will appreciate many of the items on the menu, including the Greek Pizza with eggplant, feta, kalamata olives, and sun-dried tomatoes. Of course, you can also sit down to Fettucine Luna with smoked salmon in a feta-cream sauce or one of the house specials such as Pollo Bolognese, pasta topped with a chicken breast with prosciutto and provolone served with a marsala-cream sauce. If you have room, make sure you check the dessert platter for some sinfully delicious homemade desserts. Children can order from the bambini menu, and adults can drink wine and beer with dinner. Live music is featured Friday and Saturday evenings. Lanza's only serves dinner and is closed Sundays and Mondays.

**Lonny's Restaurant**
**2330 Washington St., Port Townsend**
**(360) 385-0700**
**www.lonnys.com**

To say that Lonny's competes with restaurants in Seattle may seem like a stretch, but it's not. Diners actually do make the trip from across the Sound just to eat at Lonny's, an intimate restaurant where the tables are set with white linen and the diners can watch Lonny Ritter and his chefs at work. If you leave the Peninsula without trying the oysters, you'll be missing out. If you plan on eating oysters at only one restaurant, we strongly suggest you try Lonny's sinfully delicious Oyster Stew. Exquisitely sweet, perfectly sized Dabob oysters are simmered in cream with pancetta, fennel, and leeks until just done.

Lonny's features locally harvested produce in the soups, appetizers, and entrees, including some creative vegetarian dishes such as a light, wild mushroom soup. Fresh fish and seafood are always on the menu. Prawn Curry with Penne Rigate is served with a spicy sauce that includes Thai curry and coconut milk. Grilled Lamb Sirloin and Grilled Duck Breast with Orange Coriander Glaze show off the chef's skills. Lonny's offers an extensive selection of wines to accompany your meal, and the full bar makes a great place to wait while your table is being prepared.

---

## Insiders' Tip

During the summer months, make sure you place a reservation if you really want to eat at a particular restaurant, especially on Friday or Saturday evenings.

---

Make sure you ask to see the dessert menu, although Lonny's Coco Halvah, a frozen delight, is always a good way to end the evening. And, if you ask nicely, your server will also arrange to let you share your entrees and soups so you can sample more dishes. Lonny's suggests making reservations. It is open for dinner seven days a week and is wheelchair accessible.

**Manresa Castle    $$–$$$**
**7th & Sheridan Sts., Port Townsend**
**(360) 385-5750, (800) 732-1281**
**www.manresacastle.com/restaurant. html**

If you've ever wanted to eat dinner in a castle, here's your chance. Experience four-course dining in the elegant setting of the Manresa Castle's luxurious dining room. Choose an appetizer such as Smoked Salmon Torte, followed by entrees like Curry Chicken Casimiri, with curry, jasmine rice, caramelized bananas, and traditional condiments, including chutney and chopped nuts. Or try mushroom bruschetta and top sirloin or salmon rosettes. When the dessert tray is brought around after dinner, you may have a hard time choosing from such items as cheesecake, chocolate hazelnut torte, chocolate mousse, and fruit salad with ice cream.

Sunday brunch opens with a bread basket, which offers a sample of muffins, pastries, and croissants. Main course menu items include French toast, cheese blintzes with blueberry sauce, and Swiss Roesti, a dish combining shredded potatoes, chopped onions and peppers, ham, and bacon, all topped with fried eggs. The Manresa serves dinner seven days a week from April to September, and Wednesday through Saturday the rest of the year. Sunday brunch is served every week. Reservations are recommended.

**Osamu Ocean Grill & Sushi Bar    $$**
**1208 Water St., Port Townsend**
**(360) 379-4000**
**www.OsamuOceanGrill.com**

Osamu is one of Port Townsend's newest restaurants. In an area crazed with fresh seafood, you can't get much fresher than sushi. You can order almost any type of sushi you can dream of from sashimi—raw pieces of fish—to nigiri, maki, and hand rolls. For the sushi-novice we suggest the Yasai-Maki and Spicy Tempura Shrimp Rolls. If you prefer to eat something warm, noodles are served in soups and pan-fried with a variety of ingredients.

**The Public House    $$**
**1038 Water St., Port Townsend**
**(360) 385-9708**
**www.thepublichouse.com/frame.html**

Pull up a seat at the bar or opt for one of the tables in the main dining area to enjoy grilled food, or drinks from the full bar, at The Public House. Inside the spacious restaurant with open-beam construction and an ornate pressed-tin ceiling overhead, diners enjoy the food and on some nights live acoustic music. Start your meal with an appetizer such as Chinese-style BBQ wings or coconut-crusted prawns, then move on to an open-faced portabello mushroom sandwich with gorgonzola cheese and caramelized onions on focaccia bread. Or try one of the house specials, such as the mixed grill gumbo with spicy Andouille sausage, grilled chicken, prawns, and dirty rice. Add a drink from the large selection of microbrew beers on tap and in the bottle, or from the wine list, and your meal is set. The Public House also offers a kids' menu, and desserts such as marion berry crumble a la mode or the espresso creme caramel will tempt you to squeeze in a bit more.

**Salal Café    $$**
**634 Water St., Port Townsend**
**(360) 385-6532**

Fans of savory breakfast combinations will dig the Salal Café. Voted the best breakfast in town several years in a row, the café features local produce, locally baked breads, and organic ingredients, when available. Specialty dishes such as a seafood sautée with shrimp, salmon, mushrooms, and onions in garlic butter with a red sauce and Parmesan cheese over potatoes bring customers back. The extensive breakfast menu also offers blueberry crepes, cheese blintzes, and a variety of scrambles, including the Dabob oyster scram, with oysters sautéed in garlic butter, and scrambled with three eggs, jack cheese, and red potatoes. Vegetarian and vegan dishes are also featured. The Salal Café is open for breakfast and lunch year-round, and dinners are offered on summer nights from Thursdays through Mondays (the dinner cook takes off to go skiing in the winter). Arrive early or expect to wait to eat breakfast on weekend mornings. If you can, eat in the solarium or on the deck to look over the gardens behind the block of buildings.

**Sentosa    $$**
**218 Polk St., Port Townsend**
**(360) 385-2378**
**www.thepublichouse.com/sentosa**

Feast on Japanese cuisine in the intimate setting of Sentosa. Specializing in sushi and pan Asian noodle dishes, Sentosa is set just off Water Street, in the same building as The Public House. Stop in for lunch or dinner for featured dishes such as Malaysian-style chicken and curry, or anise and chili braised beef with soba noodles. The sushi menu includes a number of nigiri, or handheld, sushi, maki sushi such as the Port Townsend Roll, or temaki, or hand roll, sushi such as blackened albacore tuna. Sentosa is a popular spot, so be advised to show up early for your meal or plan to wait for a seat. And be sure to check the list of creative daily specials.

**Shanghai    $$**
**265 Point Hudson, Port Townsend**
**(360) 385-4810**

Venture to Point Hudson, at the far north end of downtown, for a taste of Chinese cuisine in a town that once had a thriving Chinese population. Chef Lee, the head chef, has been serving Port Townsend's residents for more than 15 years. The Shanghai features Hunan and Szechuan dishes, all served without MSG, in either smoking or nonsmoking dining rooms. Diners can try one of the family-style dinners or opt for individual entrees such as kung pao chicken, mu-shu pork, or Shanghai Special Sesame Seeds Beef. The restaurant also offers fried rice, chow mein, and chop suey, as well as tasty sizzling rice soup. Shanghai will also box your food for an evening picnic at the park or deliver it to your hotel room if it is within the city limits.

**Silverwater Café    $$–$$$**
**237 Taylor St., Port Townsend**
**(360) 385-6448**

Voted one of the most popular restaurants in newspaper polls and the best seafood in town for four straight years, the Silverwater Café is a must-taste stop for diners. The café serves lunch and dinner, with specialties such as loin of lamb with rose petal sauce, seared ahi tuna, cioppino, and rotini gorgonzola. This is a favorite local hangout, with a full wine list, locally roasted coffee, and a selection of homemade desserts. The Silverwater also features a wide variety of vegetarian entrees. The friendly wait-staff and 1880s architecture simply add to the casual ambience. Reservations are recommended and are requested for groups of six or more.

**Tyler Street Coffee House    $**
**215 Tyler St., Port Townsend**
**(360) 379-4185**

You'll find more than stellar coffee, tea, espresso drinks, and pastries available at the Tyler Street Coffee House. The shop offers homemade soups, including clam chowder, potato soup, and white bean and broccoli soup. It also serves sandwiches and tasty tarts such as the savory cabbage tart with ham, tomatoes, and feta cheese. Everything is made right on the premises, so the specials change daily and with the seasons. The comfortable and welcoming atmosphere invites patrons to linger after the meal over another cup of coffee. The coffeehouse is closed Mondays and does not accept credit cards.

**Waterfront Pizza & The Upstairs    $**
**951 Water St., Port Townsend**
**(360) 379-9110**

If you smell pizza while walking along Water Street, your nose will soon lead you to the walk-up window at Waterfront Pizza. Order pizza by the slice downstairs, or wander to The Upstairs for sit-down dining. Create your own combination pizza by choosing ingredients from the menu upstairs, or opt for one of the special combination pizzas such as the Portuguese Delight, with linguica sausage, olives, mushrooms, and cheese, or the Very Veggie with mushrooms, olives, onions, green peppers, chiles, tomatoes, and sprouts. Waterfront Pizza also serves beer and wine.

**Wild Coho    $$$**
**1044 Lawrence St., Port Townsend**
**(360) 379-1030**

Seattleites may be mourning, but Port Townsenders are rejoicing. One of Seattle's top chefs, Jay Payne, formerly of Tulio and the Four Seasons, has defected across the Sound to take up the reins at Wild Coho. He and his wife, Christine, moved to Port Townsend to run their own restaurant in a familiar and friendly atmosphere. The restaurant has been around for a long time, but Jay and Christine have transformed it with a new coat of paint, new furnishings, and a drastically different, seasonal menu of items prepared with fresh seafood, locally grown meats, and locally grown organic produce. Dinner starts with a lagniappe compliments of the chef—a small tidbit like bruschetta whipped up that night just to give your appetite a little jump-start. To give your appetite more of a jump, or to halt your growling stomach, try an appetizer such as sweet potato gnocchi or split a surprising and flavor-packed salad of escarole with Parmesan, pickled red onions, candied lemon, and almonds. An inspired autumn risotto is paired with roasted pumpkin, crisp shallots, and sage, and the roasted duck is served on sage spaetzle drizzled with a cabernet grape sauce.

Wild Coho also serves brunch on Saturday and Sunday, which features breakfast favorites with a twist. Belgian waffles come topped with warm apple praline sauce, and omelettes feature wild mushroom and leek fondutto. Kids can even order yummy and curious dishes from a special section just for them. We're still scratching our heads at the "Chocolate-y Oysters with Burnt Pickles and Seaweed in a Mud Crust with Spicy Sawdust." It's a bargain at $5,000 a serving. Don't worry though, if you want dessert, Wild Coho serves infinitely more digestible desserts made daily. Wild Coho is closed on Mondays and Tuesdays.

# Nightlife

Of all the cities on the Peninsula, Port Townsend offers the most lively and varied nightlife. Although most of the shops close by 6 P.M., restaurants serving dinner often stay open until nine or ten at night. Many restaurants contain lounges that stay open until the last customer goes home or until last call, around 2 A.M. Port Townsend is full of musicians from the most amateur to professional. Rarely does a night go by that you can't find live music somewhere. Ask around or pick up *The Leader* to find out who's playing where.

If you happen to be in town on the first Saturday of the month, take advantage of the gallery walk. Most art galleries and some of the gift boutiques stay open late to show off the newly hung shows. You can also listen to short-story readings that night at the Pope Marine Park Building located next to the City Dock. If you want to dance, check out the events at the Palindrome Community Hall (1893 S. Jacob Miller Road), where during the winter months contra and square and swing dances are held for all levels.

**Maxwell's Brewery & Pub**
**126 Quincy St., Port Townsend**
**(360) 379-6438**

During the day, Maxwell's is a family eatery serving burgers, sandwiches, pasta, and seafood. But Maxwell's also brews beer on the premises, including ales, stouts, porters, and an intriguing Nut Brown with hints of chocolate and a thick body. Stick around the lounge in the evenings sipping one of these brews or a glass of wine, and listen to live music whenever someone shows up to play.

**The Rose Theater**
**235 Taylor St., Port Townsend**
**(360) 385-1089**

The Rose Theater has been lovingly refurbished and shows two first-run movies each week on two screens. The Rose is also one of the venues used for the Port Townsend Film Festival. Movies are shown twice a day Sunday through Thursday, with an additional late showing on Friday and Saturday. General Admission costs around $6, and admission for children under age 12 costs

# Close-up

## Messing about with Boats

Travel by sea has been one of the primary methods of moving from place to place as long as people have inhabited the Olympic Peninsula. Native Americans made canoes out of cedar trees. The first white explorers sailed in ships made of wood. The relationship between wood, water, and boats is never-ending, and the history of wooden boats lives on in Port Townsend thanks to the efforts of the Wooden Boat Foundation, the Northwest School of Wooden Boat Building, and the Maritime Education Alliance, which is a partnership between the school and the foundation.

The Wooden Boat Foundation formed in 1976 to "foster respect for self, community, and environment by providing a center for unique educational experiences through the exploration of traditional maritime skills." Its offices are located in Point Hudson, which is at the far end of Port Townsend.

The Wooden Boat Festival is the most visible and well-known foundation activity; it is also its primary fund-raiser. Held every fall near the beginning of September, the three-day festival draws boating fans from across the nation with its educational seminars, workshops, and demonstrations. Festival activities run the gamut from seminars on outfitting boats for open-water cruising to small boat and schooner races. Kids make and sail their own model boats, and boatbuilders, sail-makers, and carvers give demonstrations and sell their wares. More than 150 wood boats are displayed in the Point Hudson Marina, and more dock and anchor in Port Townsend Bay, many offering tours and cruises. Workshops are also presented during the week prior to the festival on topics that include blacksmithing, woodworking, sailmaking, and boatbuilding.

Educational programs are the heart of the foundation. A centerpiece of the program is The Townshend, a replica of the yawl carried aboard the Capt. George Vancouver's HMS *Discovery*, which he sailed into Puget Sound in 1792. The boat, built in 1992 by the Northwest School of Wooden Boatbuilding, serves as a floating classroom and museum for the Wooden Boat Foundation. The Townshend is also used in a summer youth camp designed to teach maritime skills and to expose students to the seldom-seen marine life of northern Puget Sound. The center presents courses on sailing, navigation, and other maritime arts for the beginner and the lifelong sailor. Some of the courses include live-aboard, hands-on cruises on open water.

Through the partnership forged to create the Maritime Education Alliance, the foundation works closely with the Northwest School of Boat Building. The school's mission is "to teach and preserve the skills and crafts associated with fine wooden boatbuilding and other traditional maritime arts with emphasis on the development of the individual as a craftsperson." In short, they teach students to repair and build wooden boats, from kayaks to schooners, from the ground up. The school is located just south of Port Townsend. It offers a six-month basic wooden boatbuilding program and a nine-month traditional boatbuilding program where students learn the fundamentals of boat design and the skills needed to craft seaworthy vessels made the old-fashioned way, but with an eye on new techniques and tools. Summer workshops are offered for those who don't have the time to dedicate to a longer program.

Port Townsend is proud of its maritime heritage, and citizens, businesses, and non-profit organizations have banded together to create the Northwest Maritime Center in order to preserve that heritage and the waterfront that nourishes it. The center is in the process of buying an "endangered" waterfront plot that was almost turned into a condominium complex and a resort. Public outcry stopped the development, and the center was developed to purchase the Thomas Oil property adjoining Point Hudson to establish the center and protect the working waterfront for tourists and residents. When the center is complete it will house a conference center, educational programs, and a maritime library and resource center.

*Boats of all shapes and sizes dot the Port Townsend waterfront during the annual Wooden Boat Festival in the fall.* PHOTO: ROB McNAIR-HUFF

These organizations certainly prove the dedication people around here have to preserving the maritime history and lifestyle, and they give visitors a unique opportunity to learn skills not readily found anywhere else.

For more information on these organizations, visit their Web sites:

Wooden Boat Foundation: www.woodenboat.org

Northwest School of Boat Building: www.nwboatschool.org

Maritime Education Alliance: www.maritimealliance.org

Northwest Maritime Center: www.nwmaritime.org

around $4. The Uptown theater also presents a single daily screening of a first-run movie. The Uptown is located at the corner of Lawrence and Polk Streets.

### Sirens
**832 Water St., Port Townsend**
**(360) 379-1100**
**www.sirenspub.com**

Sirens bills itself as a "Pub of Distinction," and we aren't going to tell you any differently. The pub is an adult-only establishment located on the second floor of one of Port Townsend's (yep, you guessed it) historic buildings on Water Street. The lofty height provides an impressive view of the bay while dining on the deck. Play a round of pool, sip a brew, and on Friday and Saturday nights, listen to live jazz and blues. If you're hungry, order a hamburger. For some more unique Pub fare, order the Sausage Sautée with locally made sausage sautéed in balsamic vinegar and Guinness, or the Caramelized Onion Marinara. Sirens opens at noon for the lunch crowd and serves dinner until 11 P.M.

### The Upstage
**923 Washington St., Port Townsend**
**(360) 385-2216**
**www.theupstage.com**

The Upstage offers a little bit of everything: local, regional, and nationally-known musicians and comedians, poetry readings, maybe a scene or two from a play, even lectures. Add a varied wine list, a round-up of microbrews, and some great grub, and you have the ingredients for a fun-filled evening. If you're looking for a snack, you can order a goat cheese-pesto salad sandwich or the TriTip Steak sandwich. If you're really hungry, order a flat bread pizza or the Garden Plate with marinated and grilled vegetables and a mound of couscous.

### Uptown Pub
**1016 Lawrence St., Port Townsend**
**(360) 385-1530**

The Uptown Pub is a simple tavern that serves burgers from the grill and pizzas from Lanza's, which is right next door, along with microbrews, big-brews, and wine. Stop by on Tuesday for the open-mic or on the weekends for some live tunes.

### Town Tavern
**Quincy & Water Sts., Port Townsend**

The Town Tavern doesn't have a listed phone number. Everyone knows where it is. The Town Tavern is where the locals hang out to play a game of pool or sip a beer. Don't be surprised if you hear a few heated debates while you're here.

### Key City Players
**419 Washington St., Port Townsend**
**(360) 385-7396**
**www.olympus.net/community/kcplay**

This community theater group produces comedies and dramas with a volunteer cast and crew. Recent productions include *Oleanna*, *The Mad Woman of Chaillot*, *On Golden Pond*, and *Little Shop of Horrors*. Visit the visitor information center or call the playhouse for a production schedule. Tickets cost around $10.

### Wheel-In-Motor Movie
**210 Theater Rd., Port Townsend**
**(360) 385-0859**
**www.rodeodrivein.com/wheelin**

And you thought the drive-in had gone the way of the dinosaur. Surprise! Built in 1952 by Ernie and Genevieve Thompson, the drive-in is still run by members of the same family. Thursday through Sunday nights during the summer months, you can line your car up, recline the seat, put the top down, and dig into a bucket of popcorn in anticipation of a good time. Treat the kids to a vanishing way of life, and you may dig up a few memories.

# Shopping

Downtown Port Townsend is practically a shopper's paradise. Forget the chain stores that have led to the "mallification" of America. These merchants run unusual gift boutiques, unique art galleries, and fun antiques stores. Although most of the shops are downtown along Water and Washington Streets, and on the streets connecting the two, don't forget to check uptown on Lawrence Street. There you'll find Aldrich's. If you're looking for more organic foods and whole foods, stop by the Food Co-Op (414 Kearney Street). Flagship Pavilion on Water Street houses an interesting mix of stores and a restaurant, including Old World Glass Studio, Puzzle Place, Bags by Sophia, Cheeks Bistro, and Stepping Stones Gallery, a working gallery that displays the works of local artists. Port Townsend is also a great stop for book lovers. For used books, check William James Bookseller (829 Water Street) and cross the street to Melville & Co. Used Books (914 Water Street), which has a sign hanging in the front window that boasts about the same old, opinionated management that has been running the shop for more than 20 years.

We have highlighted a handful of shops in Port Townsend, but this is only a sample of the many downtown shops.

### About Time
**839 Water St., Port Townsend**
**(360) 385-4795**
**www.abouttimefashions.com**

About Time bills itself as a shop that sells "fashions with a flair." Translated, that means they sell high-quality casual clothes with an international flavor and lots of natural fibers: beaded vests, patch-work skirts, dressy outerwear, knit separates, and silk-lined jackets.

### Abracadabra
**936 Water St., Port Townsend**
**(360) 385-5060**

At Abracadabra you'll find magical toys for the child in everyone. In addition to stuffed animals, puzzles, and games suitable for birthday parties, you'll find more adult-type gifts like fine journals, snappy jewelry, and inspirational and funky ceramic tiles.

### Aldrich's Market
**940 Lawrence St., Port Townsend**
**(360) 385-0500**

Aldrich's is Port Townsend's oldest store. It first opened its doors in 1865. Today it is a grocery store with that special touch like nearly every shop in Port Townsend. You have to see Aldrich's to understand how a community can be tied together by locally produced fruits, vegetables, meats, and fresh breads, sitting next to run-of-the-mill grocery store goods. You can also pick up a salad, cup of homemade soup, or sandwich from the in-house deli. Aldrich's even makes its own butter.

### Ancestral Spirits Gallery
**701 Water St., Port Townsend**
**(360) 385-0078**
**www.Ancestralspirits.com**

As you surely know by now, art plays an important role in the Northwest culture, and Ancestral Spirits Gallery displays the culmination of that artistic passion with prints, carvings, dolls, and masks created by Native American artists from across the nation. Of course, the primary collection consists of pieces by artists from the Northwest Coast First Peoples such as Haida, Inuit, Kwakwaka'wakw, and the Coast Salish. Even if you don't buy from this shop, you will learn something about the region's indigenous cultures.

### The Antique Company
**10894 Rhody Dr. (WA. 19), Port Hadlock**
**(360) 385-9522**

As you drive into Port Townsend on Washington Highway 19, also known as Rhody Drive, through Port Hadlock, don't pass by The Antique Company. This shop sells mostly furniture—a lot of furniture is displayed in this warehouse-size building. The pieces have been lovingly refinished when needed, but often they show the warm patina of well-preserved, original finishes. The collection consists mostly of Victorian, Arts & Craft, and Art Deco hutches, armoires, beds, tables, and desks with a nice representation of English, French, and German pieces rounding out the mix, all for reasonable and very competitive prices.

### April Fool and Penny Too
**725 Water St., Port Townsend**
**(360) 385-3438**
**aprilfoolandpennytoo.com**

Eclectic is the perfect descriptor for April Fool and Penny Too. This shop carries almost everything, including one of the most imaginative collections of hand-crafted miniatures for vignettes and doll-

### Insiders' Tip
Port Townsend sponsors many annual events from the Wooden Boat Festival to the Jazz Fest. Arrange shopping trips to coincide with or avoid annual events— many of the events draw large crowds.

houses: marble dining rooms, complete Victorian bedroom sets, and the tiniest perfume bottles around. The miniatures display takes up one entire wall of the large back room. Antique china, jewelry, home furnishings, and lace share the back room. The front of the shop houses display cases of beaded jewelry, glass ornaments, teapots, and Debbie Thibault figurines. April Fool and Penny Too also serves as home to a menagerie of animals, some stuffed and two live, Auzriel the queen kitty and Emily the puppy princess.

### Artisans on Taylor
236 Taylor St., Port Townsend
(360) 379-8098
www.andreaguarino.com/Studio.html

Artisans on Taylor is one of the city's smaller galleries, but Andrea Guarino, the gallery owner and a glass bead artist, has assembled a fun collection of locally produced artworks. Ceramic and wood bowls and plates hang on the walls over found-object collages and nature crafts while blown-glass sea shapes and vases top display cases full of beads, jewelry, and other small artworks.

### The Clothes Horse, The Northwest Man
910 Water St., Port Townsend
(360) 385-1414

This building actually houses three clothing stores. The Clothes Horse carries women's clothing from dresses and silk scarves to linen slacks and warm, plush jackets. Next door, The Northwest Man carries several lines of casual men's clothing, including the ubiquitous flannel shirt and blue jeans combo. If you prefer your clothes pre-worn, just walk downstairs to Fancy Feathers to find a consignment clothing store that carries high-quality used clothing.

### EarthenWorks Gallery
713 Water St., Port Townsend
(360) 385-0328

More than 300 artists are represented at EarthenWorks Gallery, including many Northwest artists. Tom Torrens' metal sculptures and gongs look great in the gar-

den or the front room. Glass and ceramic pieces likewise look nice set on a table or hanging on the wall. Visitors will also find plenty of one-of-a-kind necklaces, earrings, and bracelets. Exquisitely crafted wood boxes, bowls, and decoys fill a case near the rear of the store, and pictures and sculptures in nearly every media give collectors plenty to ponder.

### Folklore
810 Water St., Port Townsend
(360) 385-6550

Thomas Stammer, the proprietor of Folklore, served seven years as a member of the Peace Corps in Ecuador. Today he imports folk art and native crafts from Peru, Ecuador, Chile, and Guatemala. He buys the items straight from the artists and sells them in his shop, so the craftspeople actually receive fair trade for their goods. A case near the front of the shop is filled with jewelry and smaller items while Guatemalan bird weavings and other woven textiles hang from the walls. You'll also find hats, sweaters, jackets, and other handmade clothing.

### Forest Gems
807 Washington St., Port Townsend
(360) 379-1713
www.forestgemsgallery.com

You can't return home without taking a bit of the Northwest with you. Susan and Harvey Windle literally sell pieces of the Northwest. Harvey has been designing and creating wooden treasures since 1976, and he sells his works, along with the works of other Northwest woodworkers, in one space. Myrtlewood from the Oregon coast has been transformed into turned vases and bowls. Clocks and tables have been created from Redwood burls from Northern California. You'll also find puzzle boxes to hold smaller treasures, whale and bear sculptures, and a variety of relief carvings.

### The Imprint Bookstore
820 Water St., Port Townsend
(360) 385-3643

As you walk into The Imprint Bookstore, the first thing you'll see is a table loaded with books by Northwest writers next to a table filled with trail guides and regional guidebooks. If you get past these first two tables, the rest of the shelves will bring many pleasant surprises, including the collection of environmental and Native art books, a section dedicated to sailing and boatbuilding, and a great children's book room. If you like bargains, check the backroom clearance table. Also, don't forget to check the poetry section, which includes collections from Port Townsend's own Copper Canyon Press. We always find a couple of bags' worth of books when we visit.

## Maestrale
**821 Water St., Port Townsend**
**(360) 385-5565**

Walking into Maestrale feels a bit like you are walking into a Persian market. The shop is stuffed with imports from Indonesian wood carvings to Indian hand-carved cabinets to rugs from Iran and Afghanistan. The store also carries imported antiques and larger furniture pieces like bedframes and hutches.

## Mind Over Matter
**1012 Water St., Port Townsend**
**(360) 385-3851, (888) 385-3853**

When you're in need of a quiet place to meditate for a few minutes, find Mind Over Matter and retreat to the "secret" meditation room. Then, when you're more rested and refreshed, spend a few minutes browsing through the metaphysical books and Feng Shui items. Display cases filled with crystals and polished semiprecious gems, goddess sculptures, and spiritual art.

## Sandcastle
**840 Water St., Port Townsend**
**(360) 385-4616**

Can you handle more fun? Primarily a toy store for kids, Sandcastle carries Playmobil villages, Koosh games, and even old-fashioned yoyos. Doll and teddy bear collectors may find a few cuddly friends to take home, and Sandcastle also offers an excellent collection of creative stuffed animals and puppets.

## Summer House
**930 Water St., Port Townsend**
**(360) 344-4192**

The proprietor of the Summer House is a recent transplant to Port Townsend. When she arrived, she realized that quite a few crafters in the area were making great decorative items and furniture out of salvaged and found items. A paneled wood door becomes a desk, and windows paned with old glass become picture frames. If you like shabby chic or the look of a New England Summer House, you may find something to suit your fancy.

## Phoenix Rising
**696 Water St., Port Townsend**
**(360) 385-4464**
**www.phoenixrising-pt.com**

Phoenix Rising built and moved to its spacious new home just as the new millennium began. Crystals, semiprecious gemstones, and sculptures of goddesses, gods, and Buddhas sit in the windows and invite you into the store. Inside you'll find an extensive collection of metaphysical and spirituality books covering a wide range of subjects: creativity, Paganism, Wicca, Buddhism, yoga, ecology, and more. Many cards and gifts, including new age music CDs, tarot cards, candles, incense, and jewelry, are set among the books. Phoenix Rising also frequently hosts workshops, psychic readings, channelers, healers, and spiritual counselors.

## Port Townsend Antique Mall
**802 Washington St., Port Townsend**
**(360) 385-2590**

No matter what type of antiques you collect, you'll find more here. Plan on spending at least an hour browsing these two floors of antiques if you want to see it all. Upstairs, you'll find an impressive collection of clocks and fine china. One merchant presents a unique display of Japanese prints and collectibles next to another merchant's collection of Native American artifacts. Downstairs, amid more antiques, shoppers will get a unique history lesson about Port Townsend's

Chinatown, which used to occupy the part of town where the antique mall sits.

### Twigs
### 425 Water St., Port Townsend
### (360) 379-0301

Located at the very end of town, across from the Swan Hotel, you'll find a cute little corrugated metal building painted green with a host of plants climbing its sides. Go ahead, walk inside. You'll find a unique collection of old embroidered linens, writing boxes, home furnishings, and even a few pieces of jewelry. Don't forget to stop in next door at the Twisted Ewe to find handspun wool and cotton yarns for knitting and crocheting. Twigs is open April through January.

### The Wine Seller
### 940 Water St., Port Townsend
### (360) 385-7673, (888) 629-9463
### www.winespt.com

If your local vintner intimidates you, just visit The Wine Seller. It may very well be the most friendly wine shop ever. Joe Euro, the proprietor, has assembled an impressive selection of domestic and imported wines to satisfy all tastes and pocketbooks. In addition, with handwritten notes describing flavors and nuances, he makes it easy for shoppers to select a wine. The shop hosts wine tastings on the first and third Fridays of each month. If you need more help, feel free to ask Joe or a staff member for suggestions. Joe sells wine because he likes wine; it's not a status symbol for him, it's a pleasure. While you're in the shop, pick up a copy of Joe's CD—the acoustic guitar tracks make the perfect accompaniment to a good bottle of Pinot Gris.

## Insiders' Tip

During festivals and busy summer weekends, avoid parking tickets and struggling with the traffic. Instead, leave your car at the Haines Place Park-and-Ride by Safeway and ride the bus to downtown or Fort Worden.

# Sequim

**Hotels and Motels**

**Bed and Breakfast Inns**

**Cottages, Cabins, and Vacation Rentals**

**Restaurants**

**Shopping**

Ask any person in the valley, many of whom are retirees, why Sequim is home, and the answer will likely be, "The climate." Unlike the rest of the Peninsula, Sequim is the driest spot in Western Washington. The valley receives only 15 to 17 inches of rain per year, which pales in comparison to the 120-plus inches that Forks receives. Locals like to brag about the fact that the sun comes out for at least 15 minutes every day. In fact, a local ordinance guarantees that visitors will benefit from good weather. People from around the nation have settled in the Sequim-Dungeness valley as a place to spend their retirement years. The valley offers great fishing grounds, award-winning golf courses, and all the natural beauty of the mountains and the Strait of Juan de Fuca.

Until a few years ago, U.S. 101 bisected Sequim and made it a dangerous place for pedestrians. Today the highway skirts along the south edge of town, and the pedestrian-friendly downtown strip is starting to fill in with gift boutiques and art galleries. The nearby 7 Cedars Casino, run by the Jamestown S'Klallam Tribe, fills the nightlife bill with live entertainment and gambling. On the east end of town, the protected John Wayne Marina provides moorage for locals and visitors. By the way, the marina's name was not picked at random. John Wayne was a frequent visitor to the area, and he owned and donated the land on which the marina now sits.

Quite a few TV and movie stars still live in the valley. They all live on a former dairy farm, now known as the Olympic Game Farm (1423 Ward Road). Game Farm animals starred in early Disney animal movies *The Incredible Journey*, and the "Grizzly Adams" television series. Today the farm houses over 200 animals, including wolves, tigers, lions, zebras, and grizzly bears. The Game Farm is open for driving tours all year, seven days a week, and in the summer an additional walking tour lets visitors get even closer to some of the animals.

While you're in the valley, make sure to drive the scenic Dungeness Loop. The loop passes through the valley with its many farms and pastures and along the shore near the Dungeness National Wildlife Refuge, which encompasses the Dungeness Spit. The refuge and adjacent recreation area are good places to hike, camp, or picnic. For a pleasant, leisurely walk, go to the Dungeness River Railroad Bridge Park, which sits just to the west of the city. The bridge used to be part of the Milwaukee Road railroad line, but it has been transformed into a flat, wheelchair-accessible trail surrounded by cottonwood trees and evergreens. Both areas also offer prime bird-watching opportunities, so keep those binoculars and bird guides handy.

When pioneers first settled this valley, the dry climate worked against them until they installed the irrigation system. Since then, the valley has been home to large and small farms. Today many of the farms have been turned into residential areas, but a few micro-farms remain to grow a large portion of the produce—mostly organic—found in nearby markets and restaurants. Recently lavender farms have popped up in the valley. Lavender has become such a big deal here that a Lavender Festival is held every year on the third weekend in July. Lavender growers open their farms to guests to cut lavender bouquets or buy gifts and crafts made with the fragrant crop.

As soon as you reach town, stop by the Sequim-Dungeness Valley Chamber of Commerce to pick up coupons, brochures, and guides for a downtown walking tour and the Dungeness Loop driving tour. The visitor information center is on Washington Street at the east end of town.

Oh, and by the way, Sequim is pronounced skwim. It means "quiet water" in the Salish language.

# Hotels and Motels

As the Sequim-Dungeness valley has filled in with homes built by and for retirees, the golf courses have followed, and the golf courses attract tourists. The mild, dry climate also invites many tourists to use Sequim as a centrally located home base for further explorations on the Peninsula. In response to the tourism, hotels and motels continue to crop up in the city. Most of the lodging establishments within the city limits are on Washington Street, which until recently was U.S. 101. When the road was still the main highway, road noise would often interrupt sleep, but Washington Street is a lot less busy now.

## Price Code

Our price code reflects the average price of a double-occupancy room during the peak season, which runs from mid-May to mid-October. Room rates are usually discounted from late fall to early spring. Prices exclude state and local sales taxes, around 10 percent for hotels and motels.

$ . . . . . . . . . . . . .under $60
$$ . . . . . . . . . . . . .$61–$90
$$$ . . . . . . . . . . .$91–$130
$$$$ . . . . . . . . . .over $131

**Ramada Limited      $–$$**
**1095 E. Washington St., Sequim**
**(360) 683-1775, (800) 683-1775**
**www.sequimramada.com**

One of the nice things about the Ramada Limited is that it is quiet for a downtown hotel since it is set back off the road a bit. This is Sequim's newest hotel, and it boasts about its large rooms, especially the suites. Standard rooms, decorated with contemporary prints and colorful fabrics, offer two queen-size beds, cable TV, microwaves, refrigerators, data ports, and small seating areas. The King Suite features a king-size bed plus a sleeper sofa, separated by a half wall. Jacuzzi suites and queen suites, which can sleep up to six adults, are also available. Coffee can be found in the lobby, and each morning a deluxe continental breakfast is served at the breakfast bar. A guest laundry is also available. The indoor pool and hot tub offer year-round recreation, and kids stay free in a parent's room. Pets are not allowed, but additional adult guests will be accommodated for $10 per guest per night.

**Red Ranch Inn    $$**
**830 W. Washington Street, Sequim**
**(360) 683-4195, (800) 777-4195**
**www.redranch.com**

You can't miss the Red Ranch Inn as you drive along Washington Street. The bright red buildings practically jump onto the road in front of you. The 55 rooms offer queen-size or king-size beds and seating areas. Several suites offer kitchenettes and larger accommodations. All rooms have cable TV. The Red Ranch Inn offers several golf packages, and they are quite popular since the valley has perfect golf weather yearlong.

**Sequim Bay Lodge    $$**
**268522 U.S. Hwy. 101, Sequim**
**(360) 683-0691, (800) 622-0691**

The Sequim Bay Lodge is located outside of town between the city limits and the 7 Cedars Casino. In Sequim, these 54 rooms are the closest you'll get to luxury rooms unless you stay in a bed and breakfast inn. Large, clean, and modern, the rooms feature queen-size beds, coffeemakers, and cable TV. Several suites with kitchenettes and fireplaces are also available. Some suites also feature jetted bathtubs. Kids and golfers will want to play a few rounds on the nine-hole putting course, and the pool is always good on hot summer days. Extra guests will be charged $8 per night, and pets are welcomed for an additional $10 per night. For dinner, walk across the parking lot to the Xanadu Restaurant for a fine dining experience.

**Sequim West Inn    $$**
**740 W. Washington Street, Sequim**
**(360) 683-4144, (800) 528-4527**
**www.olypen.com/swi/**

Sequim West Inn is located just off of Washington Street near, appropriately enough, the west end of town. The motel offers clean rooms in a standard motel layout with one or two comfortable queen-size beds. Each room includes a refrigerator and microwave in addition to the remote-controlled television. Don't be surprised if you hear a little noise from the other rooms or from the roads, but it shouldn't be loud enough to be distracting. If you want more space, rent one of the cottages. Additional guests are accommodated in the standard rooms for $5 per guest per night. Pets are welcomed for an additional $7 per night. No wheelchair-accessible rooms are available.

# Bed and Breakfast Inns

The bed and breakfast inns in the Sequim-Dungeness area each offer a little something extra. Some feature incredible, filling, gourmet breakfasts. Others offer stunning views of the Dungeness Spit and the Olympic Mountains. A few have been decorated with special themes. And some offer all of the above. All of the inns that we've selected will make sure your stay in the Sequim valley is relaxing and special.

The allure of a bed and breakfast inn lies with the fact that someone coddles you, makes sure you are comfortable and cared for, and cooks you a delicious, warming breakfast to help you on your way. Occasionally you may have to share a bathroom. These inns have a charm that few hotels can hope to capture. It's almost like home, but someone else does the cleaning and cooking!

Since the proprietors of bed and breakfast inns are opening their homes to strangers as well as trying to provide a restful atmosphere, most don't allow smoking, children under age 12, or pets. Some will allow pets and children by prior arrangement. If you are allergic to animals, you may want to check with your hosts to see if they have or allow pets. Most accept major credit cards, and some will ask for a credit card to hold the reservation. If the inn does not accept credit cards we have noted that with the price code.

Each bed and breakfast listed provides a special home-cooked breakfast. Some innkeepers serve breakfast in bed while others serve it family style in a formal dining room or breakfast nook. You may be treated to a secret family recipe such as yummy chocolate banana bread. Or maybe it will be a well-known breakfast favorite with a twist like a smoked salmon and brie omelette, baked cheese and chile casserole, French toast with homemade berry syrup, or even thick, comforting oatmeal with a dried fruit compote. You can also expect to see fresh fruit, toast and homemade jam, as well as gourmet coffee, tea, and fruit juice on every table. Most innkeepers will accommodate special-needs diets or serve breakfast earlier or later if arrangements are made in advance. No matter what the situation, find out when and where breakfast is served, as it's a special part of the bed and breakfast experience.

# Price Code

Our price code reflects the average price of a double-occupancy room during the peak season, which runs from mid-May to mid-October. Room rates are usually discounted from late fall to early spring. Prices exclude state and local sales taxes.

$ . . . . . . . . . . . . . .under $65
$$ . . . . . . . . . . . . .$65–$95
$$$ . . . . . . . . . . .$96–$140
$$$$ . . . . . . . . . .over $141

**Dungeness Lodge Bed and Breakfast  $$$**
**1330 Jamestown Rd., Sequim**
**(360) 582-9843, (877) 294-0173**
**www.dungenesslodge.com**

Dungeness Lodge Bed and Breakfast features a low-bank waterfront and wonderful views of the bay and the sunsets. Each of the inn's four rooms offers mountain or water views, contemporary decor, private baths, and cable TV with VCRs. The Admiral's Suite, the largest of the suites, features a king-size bed, large private bath with soaking tub, and a private deck and hot tub. Guests are also invited to borrow a book from the library and pull up a seat in the vaulted great room, which boasts a wall of windows, perfect for bird-watching or taking in the view. Guests meet in the great room each morning for a hearty country breakfast. The resident black lab,

Ozzy, owns the grounds, so please leave your pets at home. The inn is a nonsmoking establishment.

**Dungeness Panorama     $$$**
**630 Marine Drive, Sequim,**
**(360) 683-4503**
**www.awaterview.com**

Guests of the Dungeness Panorama sleep in one of two private suites housed in a guesthouse. The suites feature queen-size beds, water and mountain views from private decks, gas fireplaces, kitchenettes stocked with coffee and tea, televisions, and CD players. Patricia Merritte, the proprietor, serves a crepe breakfast each morning in the guest dining room located on the first floor of the guesthouse. She stuffs the crepes with a variety of sweet and savory fillings, including smoked salmon, shrimp, and artichoke. Home-made breakfast cakes and breads accompany the crepes, and she'll even bring breakfast to your room. Patricia also invites guests to the main house to see the large collection of custom-designed furniture. Her father, a French designer, designed many of the pieces. Pets are not allowed at the inn, but children over the age of 12 are welcome. Additional guests will be accommodated for $15 per guest per night. Dungeness Panorama does not accept credit cards or allow smoking.

### The Greywolf Inn    $$–$$$
**395 Keeler Road, Sequim**
**(360) 683-5889, (800) 914-WOLF**
**www.greywolfinn.com**

Each room at the Greywolf Inn is decorated with a different international theme. The Marguerite Room features a king-size, French country sleigh bed along with two comfortable wing chairs, and a book-lined wall and fireplace. Families often rent the Marguerite Room and the smaller Miss Lillian Room because the two are connected by a door, and twin beds in the Miss Lillian Room make it a perfect hideaway for children. Large, canopied beds dominate the Nancy and Pamela Rooms. The Nancy Room is decorated with oriental furnishings, including a wood screen. Bird watchers may want to reserve the Kimberleigh Room, which is decorated with birdhouses, bird books, tree murals, and even a pair of binoculars for watching birds out the window. The Grey Wolf Inn is a prime location for wildlife-viewing. Located outside of town on five wooded acres, the quiet property often sees feathered and furred visitors such as elk, deer, woodpeckers, and many songbirds.

Guests often gather in the downstairs common room to read or play board games in front of the fire. An outdoor, covered, and sky-lit hot tub also beckons guests to soak away their worries under the stars. Each morning, Peggy and Bill Melang, the proprietors, serve a filling breakfast starting with fresh fruit, juice,

and coffee or tea. A main entree like French toast, a frittata, or quiche along with fresh breads and muffins completes the meal. Children are welcome at the inn, but two labs already greet guests, so leave your pets at home. Extra guests will be accommodated for $25 each night.

### Groveland Cottage Bed and Breakfast
**$$–$$$**
**4861 Sequim-Dungeness Way, Sequim**
**(360) 683-3565, (800) 879-8859**
**www.northolympic.com/groveland**

Guests of Groveland Cottage love to linger in the large great room after each morning's four-course breakfast. Originally built in 1886 as a family home, Groveland Cottage was remodeled to serve bed and breakfast guests, but the original twelve-foot-high ceilings, stained-glass sliding doors, and river rock fireplace still make guests feel like they are in a quaint country house. The Happy room and the French room both contain queen-size beds, and the Happy room also features a sky-lit whirlpool tub. The Waterfall room and Mr. Seal's room contain king-size beds and sitting areas, and the east-facing windows make them perfect for early risers who want to see the sunrise. Mr. Seal's room also comforts guests with a jetted tub, a queen futon sofa, and the best view in the cottage. All rooms include TVs with VCRs and private bathrooms. Families may want to reserve the Secret Room, actually a detached cottage, which offers a queen-size bed, full sleeper sofa, and a kitchenette.

Simone Nichols, your host and a caterer, serves a four-course, gourmet breakfast each morning. Before you depart, make sure to walk through the large garden full of flowers, fruit trees, and berry bushes. If you want a quiet place to read, take your book out to the gazebo and listen to the birds and bees. Children over the age of six are welcome. So are pets for an additional $10 per night, but only in the Secret Room. Additional guests will also be accommodated for an additional $15 per night.

*Toad Hall mural.* PHOTO: ROB McNAIR-HUFF

**Toad Hall Bed and Breakfast     $$$**
**12 Jesslyn Ln./Sequim Ave., Sequim**
**(360) 681-2534**
**www.toadhallbandb.com**

The children's book *Wind in the Willows* was the inspiration for this charming, adult-only bed and breakfast inn. Bruce and Linda Clark have created an enchanting retreat where murals starring the book's characters grace the walls. Badger's Lair, also the honeymoon suite, coddles guests with a queen-size, mahogany sleigh bed and a private jetted tub in the oak-paneled private bathroom. Ratty's Suite provides guests with a view of the wonderfully landscaped English garden. The suite also features a private sitting room with a sleeper-sofa, and a large private bathroom is just a step down the hall. Toad's Room is dominated by a large, carved, mahogany four-poster bed, but the spacious room still has space for a comfortable sitting area. Each room includes a TV and VCR, CD player, refrigerator, cozy down comforter, at least one pile of books, and a copy of *Wind in the Willows*, of course.

Downstairs, guests can gather for a chat or sit to sip sherry in the large living room, which is decorated with collectibles from around the world. Many of the items, such as the pictures of the royal family, come from England, Linda's homeland. Each morning Linda will start your day by delivering coffee or tea to your room before breakfast is served in the dining room. Breakfast always starts with fruit and cereal—creamy Scottish porridge or berries baked with granola. The main entree often includes English specialties such as bubble and squeak, and the traditional breakfast of bacon, eggs, sausage, grilled tomatoes, and mushrooms. Linda also serves fresh scones, her own blended coffee, tea, and juice with every breakfast. After breakfast, guests can walk around the gardens or sit down with a book on the wide porch that surrounds the house. During the summer, guests can also cut their own lavender bouquets from the lavender patch. Bruce and Linda like to offer quiet, private retreats for couples, so children should stay elsewhere, and Muppet, the housedog, also demands that your pets stay at home.

# Cottages, Cabins, and Vacation Rentals

These vacation cottages offer a little something extra, from panoramic views of the Strait of Juan de Fuca to little luxuries few of us indulge in at home. All may be rented by the weekend or week, and on weekdays many may be rented for a single night. Vacation cottages offer more privacy than hotels or bed and breakfast inns, and they often serve as creative or romantic retreats.

**Changes in Latitude Changes in Attitude Guest Cottage**
**150 Marine Drive, Sequim**
**(360) 683-7559, (877) 683-7618**

Relax with a group of friends or create a private and rejuvenating retreat for two when you rent this contemporary cabin, which sleeps up to four people. A gas fireplace, granite bathtub, and impressive views of the Strait of Juan de Fuca and the Dungeness Spit would be pleasure enough for most people. However, your hosts, by prior arrangement, will go the extra mile and stock the full kitchen with your favorite foods. Or, if you prefer to leave the cooking to someone else, your hosts can also pack a gourmet picnic or prepare a special dinner right in the cabin. If that's not enough pampering, you can also purchase a Spa Options Package to take advantage of professional massages, foot reflexology, or facials. Special packages need to be booked or arranged in advance, preferably when you reserve the cabin.

**Dungeness Bay Motel**
**140 Marine Drive, Sequim**
**(360) 683-3013, (888) 683-3013**
**www.dungenessbay.com**

A stay in one of these six cottages affords visitors with breathtaking views of Dungeness Bay to the north and the Olympic Mountains to the south. Each cottage offers a fully equipped kitchen with a dining table and chairs, as well as plenty of space to spread out and lounge about while you enjoy the views or read a book. Two cottages have bathtubs as well as showers and all are equipped with cable TV. A large pasture with barbecue grills and picnic tables make the area ideal for family outings, and the friendly hosts will be more than happy to help you plan your itinerary. Pets are allowed only by prior arrangement and only in one cottage, and all cottages are nonsmoking.

**Juan de Fuca Cottages**
**182 Marine Drive, Sequim**
**(360) 683-4433**
**www.dungeness.com/juandefuca/index. htm**

Enjoy a semi-private retreat with views of the Strait of Juan de Fuca and the Olympic Mountains when you stay in one of the six thoroughly equipped Juan de Fuca Cottages. Each comfortable unit includes a queen-size and a full bed and a complete kitchen as well as a sky-lit Jacuzzi tub in each bathroom. Guests can also watch one of over 200 classic movies from the video library if they decide they don't enjoy the offerings on the cable TV included in each cottage. For an extra shot of romance, stay in the Fireplace suite and curl up by the stone fireplace while you watch the sun set. Although none of the cottages meet the ADA requirements, there is one cottage that many wheelchair-bound guests use: There is one step into the cottage and bars installed in the bathroom with a wide door. Small pets are allowed only by prior arrangement, and expect to pay $10 for each additional guest.

# House and Cabin Rentals

In addition to the cottages listed above, the Sequim area also offers many house and cabin rentals from the refined to the rustic. Here are a few resources for finding an abode to suit your needs.

Brigadoon Vacation Rentals—www.northolympic.com/brigadoon, (360) 683-2255, (800) 397-2256

Vacation Rentals in Sequim—www.northolympic.com/rentals, (360) 683-3565, (800) 879-8859

Sunset Marine Resort—www.SunsetMarineResort.com, (360) 681-4166

# Close-up

## Dungeness Spit

One of the most popular tourist destinations on this part of the Peninsula, the Dungeness Spit draws hikers, bird-watchers, and lighthouse fans into the Strait of Juan de Fuca. The spit measures almost six miles long, which makes it the longest, naturally formed spit in the country. Some say it's the longest in the world. The spit sits at the mouth of the Dungeness River and at the base of steep sandstone bluffs. The rising tides crash against the bluffs and slowly erodes them. In fact, if you stand on top of one of these bluffs at high tide you can hear and feel pounding waves hitting the bluffs. The spit was formed as tidal action and waves shaped and mounded river silts, clay, and the eroded sandstone. High tides and storm surges continue to change the nature of the spit as pieces of driftwood are added to and removed from the pile topping the spit. The pieces of driftwood provide endless hours of entertainment as hikers climb over them, and families create forts with them.

On clear days visitors will be treated to a breathtaking view of Vancouver Island, Mt. Baker, and nearby Protection Island, another haven for birds. The spit offers plenty to see even on cloudy days. For a good day hike, pack a picnic lunch and a couple bottles of water, put on a few layers of clothes, and a pair of good hiking boots to make the 10-mile round-trip trek to the New Dungeness Lighthouse. The lighthouse was built in 1857 and was the first on the Strait of Juan de Fuca. Today the lighthouse is no longer active, but volunteer guides give daily tours. More of the spit lies beyond the lighthouse, but harbor seals inhabit it, and people are not allowed there.

Visitors are also prohibited from walking on the land side of the spit and on Graveyard Spit, a smaller spit on the south side of the Dungeness Spit. These areas are reserved for the birds and other wildlife. More than 200 species of birds have been spotted here, including bald eagles and other raptors, harlequin ducks, plovers, snow geese, scoters, and common murre. During the winter months, black brandts camp out in the small bay created by the Graveyard Spit. If you plan on hiking the entire length of the spit, make sure you check the tide tables so you do not get trapped on the end by a high tide. Local shops and the visitors information center will have tide tables available.

The spit's trailhead lies inside the Dungeness Recreation Area, 216 acres of grasslands and woods dedicated to camping, hiking, horseback riding, and bird hunting. If you don't have the time to hike the spit, grab some take out in Sequim and watch seagulls playing in the wind as you eat lunch on a bluff overlooking the spit. The recreation area has picnic tables scattered throughout, including several along the mile-long bluff trail. The 67-site campground fills quickly when it is open—February 1 to September 30—and reservations are not accepted, so show up early and cross your fingers. The campsites will accommodate RVs or a couple of large tents. A free dump site is provided, but there are no water or electricity hookups available.

During legal bird-hunting seasons, a 100-acre portion of the recreation area is open to hunting on Wednesdays, Saturdays, Sundays, and legal holidays. Shellfish, except for oysters, may also be collected from the beaches in the recreation area, but not on the spit. Hiking the spit is a bargain at $3 per family. Pets are not allowed on the spit or refuge, but leashed pets are allowed in the Dungeness Recreation Area.

A trip to the Dungeness Spit will make a memorable and enjoyable trip for the entire family. Nowhere else on earth will you find the same combination of elements meeting to create this special wilderness refuge.

*Cows have a prime view from this farm set on the bluff overlooking the Dungeness Spit near the former town of Dungeness.* PHOTO: NATALIE McNAIR-HUFF

# Restaurants

You may associate retirement communities with over-salted, over-cooked, bland, and colorless food. If that's what you want, you can surely find it here, but all of the restaurants we feature serve tasty, vibrant food. The local chefs have developed creative and often simple dishes that let the fresh flavor of the locally harvested produce and seafood shine through. The mild, sunny winters and cool summers make the Sequim-Dungeness Valley prime farmland. In the last few years some of the small area farms have begun the transition to organic farming. Most of the local restaurants get all or part of their produce from the local farms.

## Price Code

Our price code reflects the average cost of a dinner for one, excluding drinks, tips, and tax. Unless noted otherwise the restaurants accept most major credit cards. Many do not accept out-of-county or out-of-state checks, so ask your server.

| | |
|---|---|
| $ | under $10 |
| $$ | $10–$15 |
| $$$ | $16–$20 |
| $$$$ | over $21 |

### El Cazador    $–$$
### 531 W. Washington St., Sequim
### (360) 683-4788

El Cazador is a small, local Mexican chain. The chain's Sequim restaurant is located in a converted grain elevator that used to mark the end of town. The large and spacious restaurant fills to capacity on summer weekends with locals and tourists hungry for a taste of spice. For a combination taste of Mexico and the Northwest, try the Chile Relleno "a la Jorocha," a chile stuffed with cheese, shrimp, and crab, or the Conchita del Mar, a baked foil packet full of crab, prawns, and fresh vegetables in a special sauce. El Cazador also serves traditional Mexican dishes like enchiladas, tacos, burritos, and Carne Asada.. The restaurant is wheelchair accessible. Vegetarians will appreciate the tofu or spinach enchiladas and other special vegetarian dishes.

### Hi-Way 101 Diner    $
### 392 Washington St., Sequim
### (360) 683-3388

Decorated like a set from *Happy Days*, the Hi-Way 101 Diner makes a popular dinner spot for locals and tourists. Typical diner fare, such as hot turkey sandwiches, burgers, and the ever-present milkshake, are served in ample portions alongside more updated entrees like a barbecued pork loin sandwich and fish and chips. Kids will have fun sitting at the old-fashioned fountain bar. The diner is also a popular spot for chowing down on pizza.

### Hurricane Coffee    $
### 104 W. Washington St., Sequim
### (360) 681-6008

Take a break from shopping or stop in on your way to the Dungeness Spit to pick up a cup of coffee or espresso. Pastries and muffins help the coffee go down, and tea lovers will appreciate the ample selection of loose teas. Cafe tables and comfy sofas and chairs provide ample seating. Conveniently located at the intersection of Sequim's two busiest streets, Hurricane Coffee opens early and stays open late.

### Jean's Deli    $
**134 S. Second Ave., Sequim**
**(360) 683-6727**

Located in the original and historic St. Luke's church, Jean's Deli claims to serve "a little taste of heaven." Jean's serves fresh pastries, muffins, and bagels for breakfast, and coffee and espresso all day long. At lunch time Jean's serves homemade soups, salads, and unique deli sandwiches like the Canadian Wonder with Canadian bacon, Swiss cheese, avocado, lettuce, onion, and tomato, or the Summertime Dream, a sandwich with summer sausage and cream cheese topped with sprouts, tomatoes, and onions. Jean's Deli will package your meals to go, but it is closed on Sundays.

### Khu Larb Thai    $$
**120 W. Bell St., Sequim**
**(360) 681-8550**

After it's phenomenal success in Port Townsend, the owners of Khu Larb Thai took the plunge and opened a sister restaurant in Sequim. The residents of Sequim flocked to the restaurant for the spicy and flavorful, authentic Thai food. Khu Larb is a great place for Thai-food neophytes because the friendly wait staff will help select a balanced variety of dishes for spice wimps and spice lovers. You can determine the spice factor for most dishes. If you want to sample a mild dish, try the Beef with Oyster Sauce—thin strips of beef stir fried with fresh mushrooms in a sweet and savory sauce. Iron-tongued diners can brave a four-star Massamun Curry. Of course, all good restaurants on the Peninsula feature seafood, and Khu Larb's menu sports 18 seafood dishes. Vegetarians will find more than enough to satisfy.

### Oak Table Cafe    $
**292 W. Bell St., Sequim**
**(360) 683-2179**
**www.oaktablecafe.com**

The Oak Table Cafe serves some of the biggest and most creative breakfasts on the Peninsula. The breakfast menu spans three pages, but these aren't your everyday breakfasts. Fresh Potato Pancakes are served with applesauce and sour cream. Buttermilk pancakes get kicked up a notch with a whole host of ingredients baked inside—blueberries, pecans, bacon bits, apples and cinnamon, even chocolate chips. The Oak Table Cafe also serves crepes, German and Swedish pancakes, and all the traditional egg dishes, including gargantuan baked omelettes. The pièce de résistance however, is the baked Apple Pancake—a three-inch-high, baked pancake filled with fresh apple slices and crusted with cinnamon glaze. The homey wood interior of the restaurant makes this a comfortable place to relax over an after-breakfast cup of coffee. The Oak Table Cafe also serves soup, salads, burgers, and sandwiches for lunch. But really, go for the breakfasts, and you won't leave hungry.

### Paradise    $$
**703 N. Sequim Ave., Sequim**
**(360) 683-1977**

Paradise may not look like its namesake, but the food is good, and you'll find more than a few locals eating lunch and dinner

## Insiders' Tip

If you want to see the Peninsula but also want to remain as dry as possible, stay in Sequim and take day trips to see the sites. Sequim is the driest spot on the Peninsula, with an average rainfall of 15 to 17 inches a year.

here. The house-specials list features calf's liver grilled with bacon and onions, veal Oscar, and lamb chops. Seafood specials include pan-fried oysters topped with mushrooms, green peppers, and onion sautéed with wine and lemon.

For a good deal on basic fare, get one of the Early Bird Dinners, which are served from 11 a.m. to 6 p.m. Paradise serves wine and beer from its full bar in the lounge. The restaurant is closed on Mondays.

**Petals Garden Cafe    $$$–$$$$**
**1345 South Sequim Ave., Sequim**
**(360) 683-4541**
**www.petalscafe.com**

Eat lunch or dinner surrounded by flowers and the scent of dried herbs at Cedarbrook Herb Farm's on-site restaurant, Petals Garden Cafe. Petals serves fresh, simple meals prepared with locally harvested produce and herbs grown on the spot. Sit down to a lunch of a Thai prawn salad with marinated cucumbers and a sweet and sour dressing served over bean thread noodles; the Ploughman's Lunch of sausage, pickled onion, tomato, cheese, mustard, and a rustic bread served with an herb butter and chutney; or marinated portabello mushrooms with sun-dried tomato polenta. Wednesday through Saturday evenings, Petals also serves dinner. Try the impressive High Seas Tower, a literal tower of seafood including oysters, salmon, and prawns. Paella and pan-seared duck also star at dinner. Don't forget about dessert. The restaurant's signature desserts include Pavlova served with fresh fruit and the lavender cheesecake. Petals also serves a popular Sunday brunch and afternoon High Tea starts with fruit sorbet before proceeding to a tower of homemade pastries, scones, and other English goodies. Dinner reservations are recommended.

**The 3 Crabs    $$$–$$$$**
**11 Three Crabs Rd., Sequim**
**(360) 683-4264**

For more that 42 years, The 3 Crabs has been luring tourists to its oceanfront dining room to feast on piles and piles of Dungeness crab, seafood, and steaks. For an all-crab meal start with a crab cocktail and a cup of Dungeness Cioppino, and for your entree choose crab cakes, a whole Dungeness crab, or an open-faced crab sandwich. Seafood lovers will appreciate the Taste of Dungeness, a bucketful of crab, clams, mussels, prawns, cod, and scallops. The 3 Crabs also serves oyster and salmon specialties as well as large servings of the steak of the day. While you eat dinner, you will also be treated to a wonderful view of the Dungeness Spit and Lighthouse. The 3 Crabs also serves beer and wine to accompany its lunches and dinners. Reservations are recommended.

**Xanadu Restaurant    $$$–$$$$**
**268522 Hwy 101, Sequim**
**(360) 681-0928**

A short drive to the east of Sequim next to the Sequim Bay Lodge, you'll find Xanadu, one of Sequim's newest restaurants. Vaulted exposed wood ceilings, large picture windows, and a contemporary fireplace create a fresh, Northwest ambience to go with similarly fresh and unique Northwest cuisine. The meals here are big, so we suggest you come with an appetite. Start your meal with one of the creative appetizers like Spiced Fried Calamari.

On Friday and Saturday nights the place fills quickly with diners coming for the prime rib dinners, but the bleu cheese crusted or blackened filet mignon will also satisfy those who long for a cut of beef. Seafood specials are featured nightly, but fish dishes like crab topped halibut in a lemon-butter sauce are also on the permanent menu. Vegetarians will be happy to know that the chef will create a special vegetarian dish upon request. Xanadu also offers a nice selection of wines and beers, and the lounge includes a full bar. If you have room after your meal, ask to see the dessert menu for such sweet treats as créme brulee or wonderful chocolate creations. Reservations are recommended.

*The Cedarbrook Herb Farm draws shoppers from around the Peninsula.* PHOTO: NATALIE McNAIR-HUFF

# Shopping

Since the highway no longer cuts through downtown, several gift shops and art galleries have set up shop on Washington Street, the main drag through town. We have also included a couple of stores that are off of the main street. During the warmer months, Sequim farmers and crafters also sell their products on Saturdays at the Open Aire Market. Just walk to West Cedar Street and North Second Avenue to buy produce, nuts, lavender-scented gifts, and handmade crafts.

### Belle's Bakery
**181 W. Washington St., Sequim**
**(360) 683-5956**

What's a small town without a bakery? We don't want to find out. In Sequim, Belle's Bakery fulfills the role of town baker where Tuesday through Saturday, you can buy fresh-baked bread and yummy pastries. Stop by on your way out of town for a bagful of snacks.

### Blue Whole Gallery
**129 W. Washington St., Sequim**
**(360) 681-6033**
**www.bluewholegallery.tenforward.com**

More than 40 area artists display their works at the Blue Whole Gallery, an artist's cooperative. Each month the artists invite the public to a reception to see the newly hung show. Watercolors of local landscapes, acrylics, and oils of nature scenes, pottery, and metal sculptures are only a small sample of the items you'll find.

### Cedarbrook Herb Farm
**1345 Sequim Ave. S., Sequim**
**(360) 683-7733**
**www.lavenderfarms.com/cedarbrook/cb.htm**

Cedarbrook Herb Farm opened in 1967, making it the first public herb farm in the state. Today, in addition to the lavender that is now being grown all over the valley,

Cedarbrook carries over 200 varieties of herbs, and 50 varieties of lavender. Visitors to the farm can buy herbs fresh, dry, or potted and ready to take home to plant. In the farmhouse, now a retail shop, visitors will find gift baskets and herbal crafts such as lavender wands, sachets, wreaths, and dried flowers. Everyone in the family will have fun walking through the herb gardens, especially in summer when the bees are buzzing and the flowers are in bloom. And, if you're hungry, just step into the on-site restaurant, Petals Garden Cafe.

### Christmas Cottage
**126 E. Washington St., Sequim**
**(360) 693-1163, (888) 854-4646**
**www.christmas-cottage.com**

Sequim rarely sees snow, but in this shop, you can celebrate Christmas every day. This Christmas Cottage specializes in Department 56 ornaments and villages. If you're a collector, you may even find that retired piece you need to complete your village. The shop also carries nutcrackers, European glass and wood decorations, and other Christmas novelty items.

### Classy Creations
**138 W. Washington St., Sequim**
**(360) 683-1460, (800) 616-9380**

Figurine collectors may never leave Classy Creations. The bright, little shop sports shelf upon shelf filled with collectibles such as Dreamsicles, Fenton Glass, Har-

mony Kingdom, angels, and nature figurines. If little hands come along, you might want to keep an eye on them.

### Mad Maggi
**131 E. Washington St., Sequim**
**(360) 683-5733**

This clothing boutique specializes in upscale clothing for women of all sizes. A large display filled with trendy jewelry will give you another reason to linger. You can even go for a total makeover with new clothes and a new hairstyle: the Etta St. Salon is housed in the same space.

### Northwest Native Expressions
**1033 Old Blyn Hwy., Sequim**
**(360) 681-7828**

The Jamestown S'Klallam Tribe has two galleries near Sequim. This one is in the Tribal Center; the other is just down the road in the 7 Cedars Casino. Contemporary and traditional Northwest Native art works are attractively displayed at both galleries. Some of the most well-known artists of the region have pieces on display here. You'll find lithographs, prints, masks, cedar boxes, bowls, textiles, and jewelry.

### Over the Fence
**112 E. Washington St., Sequim**
**(360) 681-6851**

Gardeners will want to make sure to take a trip through Over the Fence. Willow arches, hardscapes, garden stakes, and a host of garden toys and tools will make you wish you had some dirt to dig in.

### Pacific Mist Books
**121 W. Washington St., Sequim**
**(360) 683-1396**

Let your kids lounge on the comfy and colorful critters in the children's nook while you browse the stacks. Pacific Mist Books stocks a varied collection, and has a particularly nice grouping of books about the Pacific Northwest and the environment. Fiction readers will have a grand time browsing the new releases collection. Bring a shopping bag along to carry home your finds.

## Insiders' Tip
Two nearby wineries are open to the public for tours and tastings: Lost Mountain Winery (730 Lost Mountain Road) and Olympic Cellars Winery (255410 U.S. Hwy. 101).

## Pondicherri
**119 E. Washington St., Sequim**
**(360) 681-4431**

Stepping into Pondicherri is like stepping into an Indian bazaar. All of the hand-made items sold here are custom-made for Pondicherri in a family-run factory outside of New Delhi. Pondicherri started life as a wholesale distributor of its imported textiles; the storefront opened in Sequim. More recently, another retail outlet opened in New York City as well. This place is a designer's dream. It is filled with cotton bedding, table linens, curtains, and pillows for the home. A few select women's clothing items such as sarongs, jackets, lightweight nightgowns, and skirts complete the collection. The bright Indian floral prints, damasks, jacquards, and metallic-woven fabrics will complement nearly any wardrobe or decor.

## Sunnyside Antiques
**132 E. Washington St., Sequim**
**(360) 582-9258**

If you're on the lookout for something a little on the different side, check out Sunnyside Antiques. Tom and Kristy, the shop owners, also service estate sales. As a result, they are able to keep their eyes open for some unusual pieces, and they avoid the junk. You'll find many old treasures tucked on the shelves and hanging from the ceiling—perfume bottles, teapots, clam baskets, brownie cameras—all waiting for someone to take them home. Sunnyside is closed on Sundays.

*Port Angeles Visitor Center offers glimpses of public art outside its doors.* PHOTO: ROB McNAIR-HUFF

# Port Angeles

**Hotels and Motels**

**Bed and Breakfast Inns**

**Restaurants**

**Nightlife**

**Shopping**

At the northern base of the Olympic Mountains, the area that would eventually become Port Angeles was first discovered by European explorers in 1791, when a Spanish ship captain sailed into the harbor formed by 4.5-mile Ediz Hook and the meandering shoreline. The captain named the city Puerto de Nuestra Señora de Los Angeles, or "Port of Our Lady of Angels."

Port Angeles started to become a city in 1862, when the customshouse moved to the area from Port Townsend. After getting off to a slow start and surviving a flash flood that washed away the customshouse, the town became the center of a utopian community for a time in the 1880s, and then began its long-term role as a mill town and deep-water harbor.

Today, Port Angeles is a city tied to the sea, with tourism running through its veins. It is the sole port of entry on the Olympic Peninsula, with daily car ferry and passenger ferry service to and from Victoria, British Columbia, Canada, through the ferry dock along the downtown shoreline. The city truly fits its tourism motto: Where the Olympics meet the sea.

Besides being a gateway into the United States, Port Angeles is the gateway to Olympic National Park. The park visitor center is just to the south of town on South Race Street. And those who continue to drive farther south into the heart of the park can go 17 miles from town to Hurricane Ridge. The ridge is the most popular destination in the park, drawing sightseers in the spring, summer, and fall. Winter activities such as downhill and cross-country skiing bring recreationalists to Hurricane Ridge in the snowy months.

In addition to the national park and the ferry terminal, Port Angeles draws visitors with tours of the Coast Guard Group Port Angeles air station facilities on Ediz Hook and boating in the Port Angeles Boat Haven. The Port Angeles City Pier, with its lookout tower at Hollywood Beach and the Arthur D. Feiro Marine Life Center nearby, also offers opportunities for fun and discovery. The town is in the process of expanding the five-mile Waterfront Trail that skirts the marina and harbor to eventually form a 10-mile trail corridor when it hooks up with the Olympic Discovery Trail at Morse Creek.

Festivals in Port Angeles draw crowds to food, crafts, and entertainment. Highlights of the annual schedule include the Juan de Fuca Festival in May, Arts in Action in July, and The Big Hurt—a multisport competition that combines a 12-mile mountain bike course, a 10k run, a 40-mile road bike course, and a 4.1-mile kayak course—in September.

## Insiders' Tip

During the late fall, winter, and early spring months, stop by the Olympic National Parks Visitor Center before heading up to Hurricane Ridge. Blizzard conditions often close the road, and the folks at the visitor center can keep you up to date on the road conditions.

# Hotels and Motels

As a point of entry into the United States—the only one on the Olympic Peninsula—Port Angeles is flush with hotels and motels. More than a dozen establishments are scattered across the city limits, and even more outside the city cater to tourists bound for Hurricane Ridge, elsewhere in the Olympic National Park, or even for someplace in the city.

Unless otherwise noted the hotels and motels listed here all offer smoking and non-smoking rooms as well as at least one wheelchair-accessible room.

## Price Code

Our price code reflects the average price of a double-occupancy room during the peak season, which runs from mid-May to mid-October. Room rates are usually discounted from late fall to early spring. The prices quoted do not take into account the state and local sales taxes.

$ . . . . . . . . . . . . . .under $60
$$ . . . . . . . . . . . . .$60–$90
$$$ . . . . . . . . . . .$91–$130
$$$$ . . . . . . . . . .over $131

**Aircrest Motel    $**
**1006 E. Front St., Port Angeles**
**(360) 452-9255**
**www.aircrest.com**

The family-owned and -operated Aircrest Motel offers 24 rooms along U.S. 101, close to the heart of downtown. A budget motel, the Aircrest offers rooms with a king- or queen-size bed, cable TV with VCR, phone, and plentiful parking. Guests staying for multiple nights can also use the courtesy van to ride to and from the ferry. Additional guests over double occupancy cost $5 per night, and pets are not allowed in the AAA-rated motel.

**Best Western Olympic Lodge    $$$–$$$$**
**140 Del Guzi Dr., Port Angeles**
**(360) 452-2993, (800) 600-2993**
**www.portangeleshotelmotel.com**

One of the premier hotels in Port Angeles, the Best Western Olympic Lodge offers 105 rooms on the eastern edge of town. Opened in 1992, the lodge is part of the Best Western hotel chain. Rooms include a king- or queen-size bed, cable TV, phones, air-conditioning, and a coffeemaker. Once you are settled into your room, wander down to the exercise room that is open 24 hours a day, or opt to kick back in the 10-foot Jacuzzi, or swim in the indoor, heated pool. Kids under age 12 stay free with their parents in the hotel that is rated three diamonds by AAA. Extra guests can stay in a room for an additional $10 per night, and there are six wheelchair-accessible rooms.

**Port Angeles Inn    $$–$$$**
**111 E. 2nd St., Port Angeles**
**(360) 452-9285, (800) 421-0706**
**www.portangelesinn.com**

Take in one of the best views of the city and the Port Angeles waterfront from the Port Angeles Inn. Perched on the hillside overlooking town, most of the rooms offer some kind of water view or a view of the Olympic Mountains to the south. Most rooms have queen-size beds, cable TV, phone, microwave, refrigerator, and a coffeemaker. The inn also offers an elevator to its upper floors, and there is a fax machine and copier available to guests on request. Each night's stay includes a continental breakfast. There is a $5 per night charge for an extra person in a room.

### Portside Inn    $$$
**1510 E. Front St., Port Angeles**
**(360) 452-4015, (877) 438-8588**
**www.portsideinn.com**

One of the larger hotels in town, the Portside Inn offers 109 rooms—including 9 suites and 2 mini-suites—to guests interested in staying near the heart of Port Angeles. All rooms offer queen-size beds, cable TV, phones, and coffeemakers. Each of the suites adds a microwave oven and refrigerator. Amenities at the inn include a seasonal outdoor pool and spa, guest laundry, and hair dryers in the rooms. Four rooms are designated for pets, and there are six wheelchair-accessible rooms. Extra guests can stay in a room for $10 per person per night. In the morning, guests are welcome to grab a free muffin in the lounge between 6 A.M. and 11 A.M. The inn is rated two diamonds by AAA.

### The Royal Victorian Motel    $$
**521 E. First St., Port Angeles**
**(360) 452-2316**

Since its expansion in 1992, the Royal Victorian Motel in downtown Port Angeles features 20 rooms at budget prices. Most rooms have microwaves and refrigerators in addition to a queen-size or double bed, cable TV, phone, air-conditioning, and free coffee in the lounge each morning. The motel charges $8 a night for additional guests in a room, and credit cards and cash are the only acceptable forms of payment. Nonsmoking rooms are not available.

### Uptown Inn    $$-$$$
**101 E. 2nd St., Port Angeles**
**(800) 858-3812**
**www.northolympic.com/uptowninn**

Another inn overlooking downtown, the Uptown Inn offers 51 rooms, most with views of the waterfront. All rooms offer a king- or queen-size bed, cable TV, phone, coffeemaker, and continental breakfast. Each room has its own refrigerator and decoration theme. In addition to a place to lay your head, the inn has a spa available for guests. Expect to pay an extra $5 per night for additional guests in a room, and small pets are allowed in one section of the inn for an extra $10 per night.

# Bed and Breakfast Inns

Many of the visitors to Port Angeles who plan on catching the ferry to Victoria, B.C., book a room in one of the city's many bed and breakfast inns. The inns that we list here are scattered from the east near Sequim to the west near the Elwha River with a few located within the city. Some have water views, and all that we include here offer the comforts associated with bed and breakfast inns. Two of the state's premier inns are included here as well—the incomparable Collette's and the luxurious and comfortable Domaine Madeleine.

The allure of a bed and breakfast inn lies with the fact that someone coddles you, makes sure you are comfortable and cared for, and cooks you a delicious, warming breakfast to help you on your way. Occasionally you may have to share a bathroom. These inns have a charm that few hotels can hope to capture. It's almost like home, but someone else does the cleaning and cooking!

Since the proprietors of bed and breakfast inns are opening their homes to strangers as well as trying to provide a restful atmosphere, most don't allow smoking, children under age 12, or pets. Some will allow pets and children by prior arrangement. If you are allergic to animals, you may want to check with your hosts to see if they have or allow pets. Most accept major credit cards, and some will ask for a credit card to hold the reservation. If the inn does not accept credit cards we have noted that with the price code.

Each bed and breakfast listed provides a special home-cooked breakfast. Some innkeepers serve breakfast in bed; others serve it family style in a formal dining room or breakfast nook. You may be treated to a secret family recipe such as yummy chocolate banana bread. Or maybe it will be a well-known breakfast favorite with a twist like a smoked salmon and brie omelette, baked cheese and chile casserole, French toast with homemade berry syrup, or even thick, comforting oatmeal with a dried fruit compote. You can also expect to see fresh fruit, toast and homemade jam, as well as gourmet coffee, tea, and fruit juice on every table. Most innkeepers will accommodate special-needs diets or serve breakfast earlier or later if arrangements are made in advance. No matter what the situation, find out when and where breakfast is served, as it's a special part of the bed and breakfast experience.

# Price Code

Our price code reflects the average price of a double-occupancy room during the peak season, which runs from mid-May to mid-October. Room rates are usually discounted from late fall to early spring. The prices quoted do not include state and local sales taxes.

$ . . . . . . . . . . . . . .under $65
$$ . . . . . . . . . . . . . .$65–$95
$$$ . . . . . . . . . . . .$96–$140
$$$$ . . . . . . . . . .over $141

**The Bowman of Port Angeles    $$$**
**210 1126 E. 7th, Port Angeles**
**(360) 457-4098, (877) 738-8956**
**www.thebowmanofportangeles.com**

Since opening in 1999, The Bowman of Port Angeles, run by Mark and Nancy Bowman, has become a popular bed and breakfast inn for travelers. The four-room inn is in a newer, craftsman-style home with views of the Strait of Juan de Fuca. Each room has its own name. The Lucille is a secluded upstairs room with a gas fireplace and an aerated tub for two, all set in a garden theme with views of the city to the west. The Jacob features dark wood accents and historic photos on the wall, with a separate sitting room attached. The last two rooms, the William and the Margaret, can be combined into one large suite referred to as the Bowman Suite. The rooms have views of the Port Angeles waterfront.

The Bowman welcomes children age 10 and older, but pets are not allowed since the resident cat Breyer may get a little jealous. Breakfast at the inn normally starts with homemade breakfast bread or cake, fruit, juice, coffee, and a gourmet entree such as sherry mushroom egg bake or pear pizza with cream.

**Directions:** Take U.S. 101 to Race Street. Turn left onto Race Street, then left onto 7th Street. Turn left again onto Chambers Street, then left into an alley on the east side between 7th and 8th Streets. The parking lot is at the end of the alley.

### Colette's Bed and Breakfast Inn    $$$$
**339 Finn Hall Rd., Port Angeles**
**(360) 457-9197, (877) 457-9777**
**www.colettes.com**

One of the premier bed and breakfast inns on the Olympic Peninsula, Colette's pampers its guests. Enter the 10-acre, secluded estate and step inside the great room with its 20-foot-high wall of windows with a view of the Strait of Juan de Fuca. Sit down for wine and cheese upon your arrival, then head off to one of the five deluxe suites—Iris, Spruce, Cedar, Lavender, and Azalea—all with king-size beds, Jacuzzi tubs for two, private decks with panoramic views, and complete entertainment centers. Colette's doesn't allow kids, and pets are not allowed either.

Guests dine on a five-course breakfast, with items such as fruit smoothies, homemade sorbet, fresh baked orange currant scones, or pumpkin muffins. Other courses include such dishes as quiche, a frittata, coffee, juice, or cereal.

**Directions:** From Port Angeles, go east on U.S. 101 for 7.2 miles from the ferry dock. Turn left onto Old Olympic Highway and drive 1.6 miles to Wild Currant Way and turn left. In 50 yards, turn right onto Gehrke Road, then in another four-tenths of a mile turn right onto Finn Hall Road. Colette's is three-tenths of a mile down the road on the left.

### Domaine Madeleine    $$$$
**146 Wildflower Ln., Port Angeles**
**(360) 457-4174, (888) 811-8376**
**www.domainemadeleine.com**

Stay in an atmosphere that combines French and Asian influences at Domaine Madeleine. Nestled on five acres, the five-room inn offers a level of privacy not normally found at a bed and breakfast establishment. Two of the five rooms are in the main house; another room with a private entrance is in an addition to the main house. The other two rooms are split up with one in the caretaker's house, where owners Jeri Wienhold and Paul Collier live, and another in a separate cottage. Four of the rooms—the Ming Room, the Monet Room, the Rendez-vous Room, and the Cottage—have Jacuzzi tubs in addition to king- or queen-size beds, TV, VCR, tape player with CD, and phone. Each room also has a fireplace.

Breakfasts at Domaine Madeleine start with items such as chicken crepes, gourmet seafood omelettes, or Fruits de Mer served with a leek and Pernod sauce. And meals are always accompanied by freshly brewed, custom-blended coffee. Items such as lemon or chocolate mousse, or fresh fruit tarts round out the meal. The inn, which opened in 1991, does allow children ages 12 and older to stay the night, but pets are not allowed.

## Insiders' Tip

U.S. Highway 101 takes quite a detour through Port Angeles. At the east end of town the highway splits into two one-way streets. Front Street skirts the shore and heads west. First Street takes visitors from Lincoln through town toward the east. The two streets meet at Lincoln, which takes visitors north and south before turning west toward Forks.

*The Clallam County Courthouse competes for space along the Port Angeles skyline with the Olympic Mountains south of town.* PHOTO: NATALIE McNAIR-HUFF

**Directions:** From Port Angeles, head east from the ferry dock on U.S. 101 for 7 miles. Turn left onto Old Olympic Highway for 1.4 miles before turning left onto Wild Currrent (just past the bridge). Go one block, then turn right onto Gehrke Road. In three-tenths of a mile, turn right onto Finn Hall Road and go two-tenths of a mile to the Domaine Madeleine sign, then left onto Wildflower Lane.

**Elwha Ranch Bed and Breakfast $$$**
**905 Herrick Rd., Port Angeles**
**(360) 457-6540**
**www.northolympic.com/elwharanch**

If you are looking for a bed and breakfast inn set against the Olympic National Park and the Elwha River, the Elwha Ranch will fit the bill. The ranch offers two suites and one log cabin. One suite is a one bedroom with a deck outside offering a view of the river. The other suite offers two bedrooms with a front sitting room, and a kitchenette. The cabin is nestled away from the main house for more privacy. The 96-acre ranch, owned by Margaret and Bob Mitchell, offers a TV and VCR, and a private bathroom in each of its lodgings. Children are allowed at the inn, but pets are not: A dog and six horses live at the ranch.

Breakfasts are served between 8 and 10 a.m., depending upon the wishes of the guests. The meal features a full country breakfast, with waffles or hotcakes, meat, eggs, and toast, along with juice and coffee.

**Directions:** From Port Angeles, take U.S. 101 west eight miles to Herrick Road. Look for the sign for the Elwha Ranch B&B and then take the next left onto Herrick Road. In one mile, take the first road to the left after the S-turn and look for the board fence and signs.

**Five SeaSuns Bed and Breakfast Inn** $$$
**1006 S. Lincoln, Port Angeles**
**(360) 452-8248, (800) 708-0777**
**www.seasuns.com**

With a room built around each of the four seasons, and one extra in the carriage house for good measure, the Five SeaSuns Bed and Breakfast Inn offers lodging set in a 1926 Dutch colonial home right along U.S. Highway 101. Each room in the inn owned by Bob and Jan Harbick offers a queen-size or double bed, set in a smoke-free environment with views of either the garden, the Olympic Mountains, or the Strait of Juan de Fuca. The inn welcomes kids ages 12 and older, but leave the pets at home, because Max the golden retriever may be jealous. Breakfast is served each morning at 8:30 A.M., with dishes such as Dutch babies, smoked salmon frittata, or smoked salmon off the grill in the summer. The Harbicks will also work with guests who are rushing to catch the ferry to Vancouver Island, so ask if you want a different breakfast time.

**Directions:** From the ferry dock in downtown Port Angeles, follow the signs for U.S. 101 west on Lincoln Street, up the hill past Safeway. The inn is on the corner of East 10th Street and Lincoln Street.

**Ocean Crest Bed & Breakfast** $$
**402 S. M, Port Angeles**
**(360) 452-4832, (877) 413-2169**
**www.northolympic.com/oceancrest**

One of the newer bed and breakfast inns in Port Angeles, Ocean Crest offers three rooms with water views and nearby beach access. The inn opened in 1997, and inn owners John and Barbara Evans offer good food and hospitality to guests in addition to rooms appointed with queen-size or double beds, a common room with a library, and the chance to converse with the owners and other guests. Kids of all ages are allowed at the inn, and pets are OK too. Guests can also say hi to Buster, the pomeranian. Breakfasts at the Ocean Crest are worked around guests' schedules, and they include such items as waffles, fruit, muffins, quiche, eggs Benedict, or oatmeal cereal cooked with apple cider and served with cream.

**Directions:** Take Marine Drive into town, then turn left onto Hill Street. Veer right at the top of the hill onto 4th Street. The inn is ahead one block on the corner of 4th and M Streets.

**Tudor Inn**
**1108 S. Oak, Port Angeles**
**(360) 452-3138**
**www.tudorinn.com**

Stay in one of the unique lodging establishments in Port Angeles, and one of the longest-operating bed and breakfast inns in the state when you stay at the Tudor Inn. Set in a 14-room English Tudor–style house built by a prominent Port Angeles dentist in 1910, the inn offers five guest rooms, all with a king- or queen-size bed. Two rooms have phones, and guests can watch TV in the common room. The house's history is depicted in photos scattered throughout the inn. Part of that history may appeal to football buffs, since the father of famed National Football League quarterback John Elway lived in the house for two years. The Tudor Inn welcomes kids ages 12 and older, but pets are not allowed.

Breakfasts at the inn are served at 8:30 A.M. The meals include such dishes as waffles or blueberry pancakes, eggs Florentine, fruit, meat, coffee, and juice.

**Directions:** Take U.S. 101 through town, then turn left onto Lincoln Street. Continue on Lincoln Street until turning right onto 11th Street. Follow 11th Street for two blocks to Oak Street. The inn is on the corner.

# Restaurants

Because Port Angeles is a port of entry, it sees quite a few tourists from all over the world. All those visitors need to eat, and the restaurateurs of the city are more than happy to satisfy that need. Port Angeles has far too many restaurants for us to list them all here, but we have selected a few. We tried to find something to satisfy every taste and every pocketbook. The restaurants listed here cover the range from home-style American to many of the ethnic restaurants that dot the city, including French, Thai, Chinese, and European.

## Price Code

Our price code reflects the average price of a single meal, excluding drinks, tips, and taxes. Unless noted otherwise, the restaurants accept most major credit cards. Many do not accept out-of-state checks, so ask your server.

| | |
|---|---|
| $ | under $10 |
| $$ | $10–$15 |
| $$$ | $16–$20 |
| $$$$ | over $21 |

### Bella Italia    $$–$$$
**117B E. First St., Port Angeles**
**(360) 457-5442**
**www.northolympic.com/bellaitalia**

Fresh seafood, a lengthy and impressive wine list, a smoke-free atmosphere, and great food have earned Bella Italia its reputation as a great place for family dining. Proprietor Neil Conklin places a lot of emphasis on fresh food, and he has taken special steps to use organically grown produce as much as he can. Daily specials often highlight seafood, and the Cioppino filled with shrimp, crab, mussels, and more, is always a wise choice. Comforting gnocchi, the traditional Italian potato dumpling, is served in a tomato-marsala sauce, and the Parmigiana de Melanzane is a filling dish of eggplant layered with marinara sauce, ricotta, and Parmesan cheese. Bella Italia also serves crisp-crusted specialty pizzas, and the kids' menu features dishes that children will snarf down. Wine lovers should be sure to ask about the reserve wine list. If you need assistance, your server will be happy to help you make your selection. Reservations are recommended.

### Bonny's Bakery    $
**215 S Lincoln St., Port Angeles**
**(360) 457-3585**

Housed in an old firehouse near the historic courthouse, Bonny's Bakery serves tender pastries, hearty breads, cinnamon rolls, muffins, and nearly every other baked good imaginable. In addition, you can order gourmet salads and comforting soups such as broccoli and cheese soup. If you want a full meal, order a sandwich—try the smoked salmon sandwich—or a piece of quiche. Dine inside or out, or just stop by for a cup of coffee or a latte.

**The Bushwhacker** $$–$$$
1527 E. First St., Port Angeles
(360) 457-4113

The Bushwhacker specializes in steak and seafood in a family-friendly atmosphere. A visit to the extensive salad bar is part of each dinner. There, in addition to salad greens and fresh dressings, you'll find homemade bread and a clam chowder that is loaded with clams and flavor. Choose your entree from the assortment of fresh, locally caught salmon, halibut, oysters, cod, clams, and crab. Meat eaters will want to come back again for prime rib, filet mignon, and aged steaks from corn-fed beef. The Bushwhacker has been serving area diners for more than 20 years and won *Pacific Northwest Magazine*'s award for Best Steak Restaurant. Children can order specially prepared dishes from the kids' menu, and adults can order wine or beer to accompany their dinners. The Bushwhacker also offers a lounge for after-dinner drinks.

**C'est Si Bon** $$$$
23 Cedar Park Dr., Port Angeles
(360) 452-8888
www.northolympic.com/cestsibon

The writer Raymond Carver used to eat at C'est Si Bon, a world-class restaurant that serves classic French cuisine. Norbert and Michéle Juhasz have created a luxurious and romantic setting for their guests. Chandeliers, white linens, and tables overlooking the rose garden lend elegance to the dining room. Norbert greets diners and assists them with their dinner and wine selections while Michéle works in the kitchen to perfect each meal. The couple's efforts impressed the reviewers at the *Los Angeles Times*, who once declared C'est Si Bon to be one of the best restaurants in the United States. Start your meal with the classic French onion soup served piping hot and crusted with melted cheese or escargots with garlic and shallot butter. For a classic French meal, try the Coquilles St. Jacques or Médallion au Beurre de Cassis, a cut of beef tenderloin

**Insiders' Tip**
If you want to take a good day hike, start at Hollywood beach and walk to the end of Ediz Hook and back. The trail skirts the waterfront, where you will see many shorebirds.

in a cassis sauce. Don't forget to save room for dessert and a taste of the ultimate chocolate mousse. C'est Si Bon is closed Mondays, and reservations are recommended.

**Chestnut Cottage Restaurant** $$
929 E Front St., Port Angeles
(360) 452-8344

A stone fireplace in the wood-paneled lobby greets diners at Chestnut Cottage. Stop by for breakfast or lunch in a casual atmosphere. The high, open-beamed ceilings add a cozy feeling in the dining room. Each item on the menu has a special little twist. Try one of the "Uncommon" Pancakes such as lemon pancakes with raspberry puree or the Fruited Porridge served with strawberries, blackberries, and blueberries. The adventurous lunch menu features a Fruited Belgian Waffle as well as specialty salads, sandwiches, and hot entrees. Vegetarians will appreciate the filling Haven Vegie Browns—hash browns topped with sautéed seasonal vegetables, melted cheese, avocado, tomatoes, and sour cream. Daily Fresh Sheets include seasonal dishes such as a smoked salmon omelette for breakfast and chicken enchiladas for lunch. Chestnut Cottage serves beer and wine and features scrumptious pastries and desserts. The restaurant is a smoke-free establishment.

*The 5-mile Waterfront Trail goes from Ediz Hook and winds past Hollywood Beach and the tower that overlooks Port Angeles harbor.* PHOTO: NATALIE McNAIR-HUFF

**Dupuis    $$$$**
**256861 U.S. Hwy. 101**
**(360) 457-8033**

On U.S. Highway 101 between Sequim and Port Angeles, you'll drive by a yellow and blue house with a sign on top that says Dupuis. The humble exterior belies the incredible magic inside. Too many people don't give Dupuis (pronounced Do-peas) a second look, but a recent visit by Barbra Streisand and James Brolin created quite a stir in the community. In 1920, Joe Dupuis turned his front room into a tavern where he served spaghetti and crab and later added casseroles to the menu. Since Joe's day, rooms have been added, but the wood-paneled front room with the original bar still welcomes diners and serves as the music rooms where patrons listen to live piano music. Today, owner Maureen McDonald runs Dupuis, and she takes great pride in how she has lovingly refurbished the restaurant while maintaining its homey ambience and traditional dishes.

Order one of Joe's original dinners from the "Authentic Entrees" menu. The featured Whole Dungeness Crab & Spaghetti dinner serves two and comes with ½ carafe of wine, soup or salad, garlic bread, and sherbet for dessert. Each of the three casseroles—El Coronado, The Supreme, and The Newburg—also features crab and shrimp. More seafood and aged steaks round out the menu. If you have room for dessert, you'll be treated to homemade wild blackberry pie or maybe a peach and berry cobbler. Dupuis serves dinner seven days a week, and recommends reservations.

**Dynasty Chinese Restaurant    $–$$**
**136 E. 1st St., Port Angeles**
**(360) 452-8687**

Dynasty is located on the corner of one of the busiest intersections in Port Angeles. The busy restaurant is almost always full of diners indulging in the hot, spicy, and savory Chinese dishes. House specialties include the sweet and popular Honey

Glazed Walnut Prawns and Sizzling Seafood Delight, prawns and scallops served with fresh vegetables and a white wine sauce. If you wish to taste a little bit of a lot of dishes, order one of the combination dinners, and rest assured that you won't see a lot of deep-fried food with gloppy, red sauce. Vegetarians will appreciate dishes such as the spicy Sizzling Szechwan Eggplant and the Mu Shu Vegetables. Dynasty is open six days a week for lunch and dinner, and it is also open on Sundays for dinner.

**Mom's Japanese Restaurant    $$**
**1617 E. Front St., Port Angeles**
**(360) 417-3929**

If you prefer your seafood raw and au natural, you'll find just what you want at Mom's Japanese Restaurant. There you can order all sorts of sushi as well as traditional dishes. The restaurant occupies a building that once housed a fast-food joint, but the addition of fish tanks and a few other amenities have transformed it into a casual, yet comfortable, place to eat. For a filling feast, and a taste of all the favorites, order the Makunouchi Bento. In addition to a few pieces of sushi, you'll also get tempura, teriyaki, and a few special side dishes. Mom's Japanese is closed Sundays.

**Port Angeles Crab House    $$$**
**221 N. Lincoln St., Port Angeles**
**(360) 457-0424**

Eat breakfast, lunch, or dinner overlooking Hollywood Beach and the city pier at the Crab House. Located on the waterfront side of the Red Lion Inn, the restaurant serves fresh seafood all daylong. Start your morning with Crab House Crab Hash or a more traditional breakfast entree such as waffles, pancakes, or an omelette. The lunch and dinner menus feature a lengthy list of seafood specialties such as Crab & Shrimp–Stuffed Rainbow Trout and Alder Planked King Salmon. For a special treat, order from the Fresh Catch menu, a selection of the freshest seafood either charbroiled with lemon and herbs or prepared "Hong Kong"–style and steamed in a Ponza broth. Steaks, entree salads, and pasta dishes round out the dinner menu, and sandwiches complete the lunch menu. We suggest you start your meal with a bowl of sinfully rich and delicious Fresh Dungeness Bay Crab Bisque. If you have a hard time making a selection from the extensive menu, an extremely knowledgeable and friendly wait staff will guide you. The Crab House also serves beer, wine, and mixed drinks from the lounge. Reservations for groups over six are requested.

**Thai Peppers    $$**
**222 N. Lincoln St., Port Angeles**
**(360) 452-4995**

Notes from customers line the tables at Thai Peppers, easily one of the hottest places in town. One of these notes says, "Of all the Thai restaurants in all the world, we have never had a more amazing dinner." This is a sentiment shared by

## Insiders' Tip

A lot of tourists miss out on the Port Angeles Fine Arts Center, which is the westernmost contemporary art museum in the United States. The center features an outdoor exhibition space as well as rotating exhibits in the gallery. Admission is free, and the gallery is located at 1203 E. Lauridsen Boulevard.

many who visit the restaurant to feast on perfectly seasoned Orange Beef, hot and spicy Red Curry Chicken, and the complex and crispy Sizzling Duck. The dark green walls are hung with traditional Thai decorations, and golden Buddhas watch over diners and create a casual atmosphere that invites diners to relax and have fun. To make a simple dinner into an adventure, start your meal with Chicken Saté or a bowl of Tom Kha Gai—chicken simmered with galanga and mushrooms in a hot and sour coconut milk soup. The ample vegetarian menu will please vegetarians, and many dishes can be made with tofu rather than meat. Thai Peppers is open seven days a week and is a completely nonsmoking establishment. Reservations are recommended and are requested for groups of six or more. Thai Peppers also prepares to-go meals so you can eat in your hotel room or on nearby Hollywood Beach.

**Toga's    $$$$**
**122 W. Lauridsen Blvd., Port Angeles**
**(360) 452-1952**

Chef Toga Hertzog trained as a chef in Germany's Black Forest, and then spent time cooking on cruise ships before returning to his hometown of Port Angeles with his wife, Lisa. Once home, he opened this gem of a restaurant located in a converted house on West Lauridsen Boulevard., which is also U.S. Highway 101. The cozy and intimate restaurant serves European specialties found few places in the state, let alone on the Peninsula. If you choose to eat at Toga's you are in for a spectacular treat.

Start the evening with the NW Smokehouse Sampler, a plate of applewood–smoked salmon, scallops, oysters, and prawns on a mixed greens salad with raspberry vinaigrette. You may have a hard time choosing your entree from the array of unusual dishes. If you want a traditional fondue, you'll need to make your reservations 24 hours in advance and specify the type of fondue that you want: Swiss cheese, seafood, or meatlovers. For something unique, order one of the Jagersteins—German for hunter's stone. A flat, super-heated stone will be brought to your table and your dinner will be cooked in front of you on the stone. We also suggest the melt-in-your-mouth German Sauerbraten or one of the fresh seafood entrees. And don't pass up dessert. The chocolate mousse will make you feel like you're eating in the halls of Valhalla. Toga's also features imported beer and an impressive wine list and strongly suggests reservations.

# Nightlife

During the summer months, Port Angeles looks like a hopping boom town. The city is dotted with pubs and taverns catering to those looking for a game of pool or darts and a pitcher of beer. You can find live music in some of the bars nearly every weekend of the year. So forget about staying in your hotel room clicking through the TV channels. Get out there and have some more fun.

**Lincoln Theatre**
**132 E. 1st St., Port Angeles**
**(360) 457-7997**

Head downtown to watch a movie at the three-screen Lincoln Theatre. The theater shows first-run movies on two main screens, and upstairs on a third screen it runs two more first- or second-run movies. For a wider choice of movies, you can also head to the Deer Park Cinema on U.S. Highway 101 at the east end of town.

**Oh Gallagher's Sports Pub**
**1605 E. Front St. #A, Port Angeles**
**(360) 452-0873**

This is the place to go if you want to take the kids with you. Video games and televisions line the walls. Family seating is separate from the bar so the kids can join Mom and Dad to watch the big game, nosh on burgers, and play a round of darts.

**Peak's Pub**
**130 S. Lincoln, Port Angeles**
**(360) 452-2802**
Stop by for a late dinner and a pitcher of beer, including an assortment of microbrews. The pub also offers dartboards and a pool table for patrons.

**Sirens Pub**
**134 W. Front St., Port Angeles**
**(360) 417-9152**
**sirenspub.com/west/index.html**
The original Sirens Pub in Port Townsend was so successful that a second pub has opened in downtown Port Angeles. The owners bill it as "a pub of distinction."

The combination of great food, a good selection of microbrews, beer, wine, and drinks, and live music every Friday and Saturday night makes Sirens unique among the local bar scene. All that, plus the fact that the pub is a nonsmoking establishment makes it an attractive place for a casual night of fun and relaxation.

**The Wreck**
**1025 E. 1st St., Port Angeles**
**(360) 457-9791**
The Wreck has been owned and run by the same family for more than 60 years. You'll find quite a few locals sitting here sipping a beer or playing video games, shuffleboard, pool, or darts. If you're thirsty, you'll be guaranteed to find something you like among the 113 beers offered.

# Close-up

## Port Angeles' Short Story Giant

Raymond Carver already earned much of his fame as one of America's most lauded short-story writers when he moved to the Port Angeles area late in his life. Just before his death in the summer of 1988, Carver, whose collections include *Where I'm Calling From*, *Cathedral*, and *What We Talk About When We Talk About Love*, moved to a house east of town and overlooking the Morse Creek Valley and the Strait of Juan de Fuca.

Carver was drawn to the area in 1979 thanks to his relationship with poet and writer Tess Gallagher. Gallagher's hometown of Port Angeles was an on-again, off-again home base for the couple. They lived in nearby Chimacum in the summer of 1979, and returned to the area in 1980 to live in a borrowed cabin outside Port Angeles. Carver continued to return to the area regularly over the next eight years to fish, to get away from the rigors of the writing world, and to relax.

Throughout this time, Carver wrote some of his best-known stories and books. He also wrote poetry and nonfiction during his stays on the Olympic Peninsula. A great Raymond Carver Web site (people.whitman.edu/~lucetb/carver/carver.cgi) offers a complete look at his work, along with a map depicting some of the places Carver and Gallagher used to hang out in Port Angeles, including the Port Angeles Library, the 3 Crabs Restaurant, Odyssey Bookshop, and the Port Angeles Boat Haven.

Carver passed away from complications of lung cancer on August 2, 1988. His grave can be found at the Ocean View Cemetery (3127 W. 18th Street). According to recent newspaper stories, people from all over the world visit Carver's grave, and visitors can sign and leave notes in a journal at the wind-swept gravesite that overlooks the Strait of Juan de Fuca. Tess Gallagher often writes back to those who leave notations in the journal, keeping the legacy of Carver and his work alive.

# Shopping

Port Angeles doesn't offer as much for the shopper as Port Townsend, but shoppers needn't despair either. Port Angeles boasts two excellent bookstores where browsers can wander for hours. You'll also find a number of gift shops, art galleries, and antiques shops both uptown on First Street and closer to the waterfront.

### Alley Cat Boutique
**121 ½ W. 1st St., Port Angeles**
**(360) 417-8097**

Alley Cat Boutique carries trendy women's clothing. Asked how she selects her lines, owner Tracie Hedin says she just picks what she likes. Tracie seems to like an eclectic assortment ranging from frilly to utilitarian. You'll find beaded skirts, leather pants, angora sweaters, and linen ensembles perfect for the office. Alley Cat is closed Sunday and Monday.

### Bergsma Showroom
**139 W. 1st St., Port Angeles**
**(360) 452-5080, (800) 923-5080**

When well-known painter Jody Bergsma was a teen, her aunt, Eileen Knight, encouraged her to enter her paintings in a Port Angeles art contest. Bergsma did, and she won. Soon she was selling her prints throughout the region, and today her pieces are sold around the world. Eileen Knight now runs this showroom and continues to be one of her niece's biggest fans, as you'll learn when you visit. In addition to Bergsma's prints of children and wildlife, the shop carries the Alaska prints of Rie Muñoz, works by other artists, and other home decor items.

### The Clallam Art Gallery
**The Landing Mall, 115 Railroad Ave.,**
**Ste. 206, Port Angeles**
**(360) 452-8165**

Hand-carved, painted gourds, large wood sculptures, and detailed dry-brush watercolor paintings are just a few of the things you will find in this artists' cooperative. Occupying a large space on the first floor of The Landing, the gallery serves as a showroom for local artists.

### The Corps Shop
**129 B. W. 1st St., Port Angeles**
**(360) 457-7041, (800) 457-7041**

The Corps Shop looks much more like a museum than a store, but nearly everything you see is for sale. Shop owner Robert Mingram, a former Marine, will be happy to regale you with stories of the service men and women who once owned what he now sells. Each display cabinet is set up like a vignette with mannequins dressed in Corps gear from past and present. This shop is worth going out of your way to see. The Corps Shop is closed on Sunday.

### The Country-Aire Grocery
**117 E. 1st St., Port Angeles**
**(360) 452-7175**

We haven't included many natural foods or grocery stores, but the Country-Aire has an incredibly large selection of whole foods, organic produce, and other specialty items. In addition, the shop has the cozy feel of an old-time general store, and the friendly staff will be glad to help you find what you need.

### Hegg & Hegg Smoked Salmon, Inc.
**801 Marine Dr., Port Angeles**
**(360) 457-1205, (800) 435-3474**
**www.heggandhegg.com**

If you want to take fresh seafood home with you, or if you want to send some to friends and family, visit Hegg & Hegg. The family-owned company carries much more than just smoked salmon. You'll find canned clams, shrimp, crab, sturgeon, and salmon, smoked and plain. You can also find fresh and frozen seafood as well. All can be shipped home for you. Hegg & Hegg has three retail outlets in Port Angeles: The Landing Mall, at the boat haven at

*Uptown Port Angeles.* PHOTO: NATALIE McNAIR-HUFF

the address listed above, and on U.S. Highway 101 at the east end of town.

### Odyssey Bookshop
**114 W. Front St., Port Angeles**
**(360) 457-1045**

Odyssey Bookshop is a book browser's delight. Open seven days a week, the store maintains a well-organized collection of new and used books. We were pleasantly surprised to find that many of the used books were published in the last few years. The shop's large size gives the owners enough space to display many of the books face out. That makes them extremely tempting.

### Olympic Stained Glass
**112 N. Laurel St., Port Angeles**
**(360) 457-1090**

Olympic Stained Glass is a working studio where you can buy beautifully elaborate pieces. You can also place custom orders. In addition to the stained glass, the shop carries a select assortment of imported gifts such as amber and gemstone jewelry and glass pieces from Seattle's Glass Eye studio.

### Port Book and News
**104 E. 1st St., Port Angeles**
**(360) 452-6367**

Wow! That's the first thing we said when we walked in to Port Book and News. One entire wall is occupied by the store's collection of over 2,000 magazines and periodicals. Even more impressive is that the staff knows the name of nearly every magazine there. Of course, shelf upon shelf holds an incredible assortment of books, including one of the largest selections of regional books that we've seen. When writers are in town, the shop hosts readings and signings, and they will special order a book if they don't have what you are looking for. Book lovers should definitely put this on their itineraries.

### Reigning Visions Artwork
**The Landing Mall, 115 E. Railroad Ave.,**
**Ste. 208, Port Angeles**
**(360) 452-8743**

Reigning Visions Artwork is at the back of the second floor of The Landing Mall. If you are in the mall, we recommend that you find the store, where you'll find an impressive collection of artworks by local artists. Detailed wood carvings by Bill Lohnes reflect the birds and other animals of the region, and the wood bowls and vases turned by Brandt Weaver reveal the fine grain of the wood. Gallery owner Melissa Penic also displays her paintings and art glass. Other pieces include intricately inlaid wood boxes by Joni Britt and soft sculptures, ceramics, basketry, and glassworks by a host of artists.

### Retroville
**133 E. 1st St., Port Angeles**
**(360) 452-1429, (877) 399-1429**
**www.retroville.com**

Go retro in a major way at Retroville, an antiques shop that bills itself as "Vintage Outfitters." One step into the shop and you will almost swear you walked through a time warp. The front of the store is filled with kitchenware from the 30s, 40s, and 50s. Lounge goods like ash trays, tumblers, and serving platters complete the scene. As you walk toward the back of the store you'll find a room full of vintage clothing such as Hawaiian print shirts and letterman jackets, as well as Bakelite bangles and beads. The back corner room is filled with household items like paintings and linens. Take your kids and let them see what it was like in the "olden days."

### Rose's Garden
**126 W. 1st St., Port Angeles**
**(360) 452-7397**

If you're looking for pink frills, angels, and Victorian-styled decorations, walk through Rose's Garden. The shop carries porcelain dolls, teapots, cat-related knick-knacks, and other small items just right for gift giving. To complete the gift theme, you'll also find fine art deco–style prints and greeting cards.

### Small Treasures Antiques
**129 W. 1st St., Ste. A, Port Angeles**
**(360) 452-3350**

Across the hall from the Corps Shop you'll find a space filled with antiques arranged in vignettes. Looking for kitchen gadgets? You'll find them in the kitchen and dining-room scene. You'll find tin cans, old glass jars, and other such items in the dry goods store. Additional scenes include a car repair shop, a magazine shop, a soda fountain, and a bedroom. Each scene is attractively arranged so that there is plenty of room to move around and look at everything.

# Juan de Fuca Highway

Hotels and Motels

Bed and Breakfast Inns

Restaurants

The Juan de Fuca Highway was named a National Scenic Byway in 2000, but long before that official designation by the U.S. Federal Highway Administration, the road has been a favorite of travelers. The route winds from the Elwha River in the east to Neah Bay in the west. Along its length, the Juan de Fuca Highway, also known and noted on maps as Washington 112, passes through a number of small communities, including Joyce, Pysht, Clallam Bay, Sekiu, and Neah Bay. But the road also passes through history.

The northwesternmost tip of Washington has always been known for fishing and its connection to the water, as well as for the Native American tribes such as the S'Klallam, Ozette, and Makah that have called the area home for thousands of years. European settlers claimed the Pacific Northwest as their own when Spain established a short-lived settlement in what would become Neah Bay in 1792, and shortly after the Spanish abandoned the area, it became part of the Oregon Territory in the early 1800s.

Long before Scandinavian settlers started to arrive in the late 1890s, more than 4,000 Native Americans lived in the area. The S'Klallam, the largest of area's tribes, lived and roamed between Discovery Bay near Sequim to present-day Clallam Bay. The Ozette and the Makah were coastal tribes, living near Ozette Lake, Cape Alava, and near present-day Neah Bay.

Today that heritage is noted at the Makah Cultural and Research Center in Neah Bay, which is open to visitors year-round, with exhibits and artifacts from an archeological site near Ozette. Five hundred years ago, most likely after a long stretch of rainy weather, a water-soaked hillside rushed down upon a Makah village. The residents had no hope of escape, and much like the ancient village of Pompeii, the village was perfectly preserved through the ages by the mud. Materials that normally degrade in the moist environment survived more than 500 years locked in a muddy tomb. Through the years, rain and erosion scoured away at the mud until the village was revealed to a passing hiker. Archeologists and tribal members descended on the site and began to excavate it. They discovered longhouses, fishing equipment, canoes, bark baskets, hats, clothing, and everything else that the tribe used for day-to-day survival. The artifacts recovered from that site are now seen only in the museum at Neah Bay. People travel from all over and make the long drive to Neah Bay just to visit the museum.

The Makah also pay tribute to their ongoing tribal traditions each August with the Makah Days festival. Most recently the Makah made international news when it fought for the right under its treaty with the United States to harvest a migrating gray whale, which it succeeded in doing in 1999. Gray whales migrate along the Olympic Peninsula twice each year, passing within a couple of miles of the coast near Neah Bay. As a traditional whaling people, the Makah people have killed gray whales and used their blubber and meat for sustenance. The tribe revisited its past in 1999 by whaling under provisions of its treaty with the United States.

Fishing and timber-harvesting drew immigrants to the area along the Juan de Fuca Highway. The towns of Clallam Bay, Sekiu, and Neah Bay have long been destinations for sport anglers, and much of the lodging along the route caters to the seasonal fishing crowd. The area is also becoming known for scuba diving. Landlubbers can enjoy one of the many trails accessible near the highway, such as the 1.5-mile round-trip walk to Cape Flattery, the northwesternmost point in the lower 48 states, or the 9.3-mile Ozette Lake/Cape Alava/Sand Point Trail along the coast.

Recreation also abounds along the highway. Many areas on the route offer tidepools for exploration during low tide, but be sure to stay aware of the changing tides while wandering the pools. A popular tidepool destination along the highway is just west of Joyce at the Salt Creek Recreation Area and campground.

# Hotels and Motels

Since the area along the Juan de Fuca Highway is known mostly for its scenery and access to fishing, lodging in the small towns along the route is pretty simple and made up of comfortable, rather than deluxe, accommodations.

## Price Code

Our price code reflects the average price of a double-occupancy room during the peak season, which runs from mid-May to mid-October. Room rates are usually discounted from late fall to early spring. The prices quoted do not take into account the state and local sales taxes, around 10 percent for hotels and motels.

$ . . . . . . . . . . . . . .under $60
$$ . . . . . . . . . . . . . .$61–$90
$$$ . . . . . . . . . . . .$91–$130
$$$$ . . . . . . . . . .over $131

**Curley's Resort and Dive Center    $$**
**291 Front St., Sekiu**
**(360) 963-2281, (800) 542-9680**
**www.curleysresort.com**

Located just across the street from the Strait of Juan de Fuca, Curley's Resort and Dive Center is a destination for boaters and divers who don't want to waste their time getting to the water. The resort offers 31 rooms in a hotel and three cabins. All rooms have either a queen-size or twin-size bed, cable TV, phone, and either a kitchenette or a full-sized kitchen. Small pets are allowed in some rooms, but guests are advised to call ahead to make arrangements for pets. There is a $10 per night charge for a pet in a room, and extra guests in a room cost $10 per night as well.

In addition to the rooms, the resort also features a full-service dive shop with gear for rent and for sale. The shop also rents kayaks.

**Silver Salmon Resort    $–$$**
**1280 Bayview Ave., Neah Bay**
**(360) 645-2388, (888) 713-6477**

This 11-room resort opened in the late 1980s in the heart of downtown Neah Bay. Guests can choose from rooms that have a full kitchen with a double or twin bed, or a nonsmoking room with double, twin, or queen-size beds. Rooms have sitting areas with a table and chairs. Pets are allowed in smoking rooms, and there is a $10 per night charge for more than two people in a room. Aside from the hotel, the resort also offers 18 spaces for RV parking.

## Insiders' Tip

Interested in seeing what the area along the Juan de Fuca Highway has to offer by checking the Internet? Then click to www.sekiu.com, the site for the Clallam Bay and Sekiu Chamber of Commerce.

**Straitside Resort**   $$
241 Front St., Sekiu
(360) 963-2100 www.straitsideresort.com

The Straitside Resort invites visitors with two rustic cabins, two suites, and three studio lodging rooms within a stone's throw of the Strait of Juan de Fuca. Recently remodeled, the resort is set up for computers, with data ports located near tables. All rooms have cable TV, coffeemakers, and showers. The rooms are decorated more like a bed and breakfast inn, with art displayed from owner Linda Palumbo's private collection. The resort also offers barbecues, tables, and flower gardens outside. Boaters will be happy to know that moorage is available in the summer. Guests are expected to make minimum two- or three-night stays during the summer months and fishing seasons, and there is a $10 charge for extra guests in a room.

**Van Riper's Resort**   $$–$$$
280 Front St., Sekiu
(360) 963-2334, (888) 462-0803
www.vanripersresort.com

Be sure to book your room well in advance before heading to Sekiu for a stay at Van Riper's Resort during the height of fishing season. The 16-room resort offers a wide range of lodging, from simple single rooms with a queen-size bed and shower to deluxe suites that offer full kitchens, multiple rooms, and enough space to accommodate up to 10 guests. All rooms offer phones, cable TV, and private baths in addition to refrigerators, microwaves, and coffeemakers. Visitors need to stay a minimum of two nights during weekends in the summer, and three nights on holiday weekends.

# Bed and Breakfast Inns

Bed and breakfast inns haven't made their mark yet along the Juan de Fuca Highway. Despite the scenery, there are only a few inns on the route. We include two in this chapter—one close to the start of the highway and the second in the heart of Clallam Bay.

The allure of a bed and breakfast inn lies with the fact that someone coddles you, makes sure you are comfortable and cared for, and cooks you a delicious, warming breakfast to help you on your way. Occasionally you may have to share a bathroom. These inns have a charm that few hotels can hope to capture. It's almost like home, but someone else does the cleaning and cooking!

Since the proprietors of bed and breakfast inns are opening their homes to strangers as well as trying to provide a restful atmosphere, most don't allow smoking, children under age 12, or pets. Some will allow pets and children by prior arrangement. If you are allergic to animals, you may want to check with your hosts to see if they have or allow pets. Most accept major credit cards, and some will ask for a credit card to hold the reservation. If the inn does not accept credit cards we have noted that with the price code.

Each bed and breakfast listed provides a special home-cooked breakfast. Some innkeepers serve breakfast in bed, others serve it family style in a formal dining room or breakfast nook. You may be treated to a secret family recipe such as yummy chocolate banana bread. Or maybe it will be a well-known breakfast favorite with a twist like a smoked salmon and brie omelette, baked cheese and chile casserole, French toast with homemade berry syrup, or even thick, comforting oatmeal with a dried fruit compote. You can also expect to see fresh fruit, toast, and homemade jam, as well as gourmet coffee, tea, and fruit juice on every table. Most innkeepers will accommodate special diets or serve breakfast earlier or later if arrangements are made in advance. No matter what the situation, find out when and where breakfast is served, as it's a special part of the bed and breakfast experience.

# Price Code

Our price code reflects the average price of a double-occupancy room during the peak season, which runs from mid-May to mid-October. Room rates are usually discounted from late fall to early spring. The prices quoted do not include state and local sales taxes.

| | |
|---|---|
| $ | under $65 |
| $$ | $65–$95 |
| $$$ | $96–$140 |
| $$$$ | over $141 |

**A Hidden Haven Bed and Breakfast**
**$$–$$$**
**1428 Dan Kelly Rd., Port Angeles**
**(360) 452-2719, (877) 418-0938**
**www.ahiddenhaven.com**

Since opening in 1999, owners Chris and Jodi Jones have welcomed guests to their three-room inn, which is set on 20 acres near the Elwha River. Each of the three rooms features a theme centered on the inn's secluded setting. The Garden room is the largest, with a private entrance and private bath, in addition to a patio that overlooks a pond. The upstairs Otter room features a private deck with views of forest and a deer pasture, and shares a bathroom with The Wild Bird room, which is the smallest and offers a view of the forest and deer pasture. All of the rooms have queen-size beds, and the Joneses charge an additional $20 per night for each extra guest in a room. Kids are allowed at the inn by prior arrangement, but pets are not allowed.

Outside the inn, the 20-acre property has plenty of room for all the resident animals, such as peacocks, rabbits, fallow deer, and wild birds. The inn is becoming a favorite of birders.

A Hidden Haven offers a full country-style breakfast, with dishes such as pancakes, French toast, scrambled eggs, or hash browns.

**Directions:** From Port Angeles, take U.S. Highway 101 west to Washington Highway 112. Turn right onto WA 112 and continue westward, over the Elwha River and to Dan Kelly Road on the left. Go 1.5 miles on Dan Kelly Road to reach the inn.

**Winters Summer Inn Bed and Breakfast**
**$$**
16651 WA Hwy. 112, Clallam Bay
(360) 963-2264
www.northolympic.com/winters

Take in views of the Strait of Juan de Fuca from the back deck or from one of the rooms at the Winters Summer Inn Bed and Breakfast. The inn, which opened in 1993, touts its rural setting where traffic and jet noise are replaced by windswept rain and the sounds of other guests getting away from the world. Set in a renovated 106-year-old house, the inn's rooms include the Master Suite, with a queen-size bed, private bath, private entrance, and a Jacuzzi, and the Queen Room, which features a private half-bath and a queen-size bed. There is a $10 charge for extra occupants in a room, and pets and children are welcome at the inn. The Studio Suite, which is located in a separate building, has a private entrance, fireplace, king-size bed, a pool table, a full kitchen, and a multi level deck with views of the Strait of Juan de Fuca and the Clallam River. The Studio Suite can sleep up to

## Insiders' Tip

Despite being located so close to the coast, Ozette Lake is the largest natural body of freshwater in Washington.

eight people, and breakfast is not included for those who stay in the suite.

Breakfasts at the Winters Summer Inn include items such as a garden scramble (scrambled eggs and vegetables), omelettes, blueberry pancakes, and fresh fruit. The inn is also a gallery featuring works by local artists.

**Directions:** From Port Angeles, take U.S. Highway 101 west past Lake Crescent to the intersection with Washington Highway 113 at Sappho. Turn right onto WA 113 and drive into Clallam Bay. Follow the road through town to the sharp 90-degree turn to the left. The inn is the fifth building on the right after the turn.

# Restaurants

Diners have limited choices along the Juan de Fuca Highway, with each small town offering one or two restaurants during the peak summer season and even slimmer pickings in the winter months. But not to worry, the restaurants on the highway offer large portions of comforting food, and plenty of locally caught fish and shellfish.

## Price Code

Our price code reflects the average cost of a dinner for one, excluding drinks, tips, and taxes. Unless noted otherwise, the restaurants accept most major credit cards. Many do not accept out-of-county or out-of-state checks, so ask your server to be sure your check will be accepted.

$ . . . . . . . . . . . . .under $10
$$ . . . . . . . . . . . . .$10–$15
$$$ . . . . . . . . . . . .$16–$20
$$$$ . . . . . . . . . .over $21

**Joyce Café    $–$$**
**50530 WA Hwy. 112, Joyce**
**(360) 928-1012**

Stop in for a hearty breakfast or a filling dinner from the varied menu at the Joyce Café. Breakfasts include such standards as steak and eggs, French toast, or omelettes. The lunch menu adds favorites such as the 18 Wheeler burger, a ¾-pound burger on a homemade bun with all the toppings. Lunch also includes items such as the BLAT (bacon, lettuce, avocado, and tomato), or popcorn shrimp. And if you are heading through Joyce in the evening, try the veal Parmesan, tempura cod and chips, or sautéed beef tips with mushrooms and onions. Top off your meal with a slice of delicious homemade pie.

**The Breakwater    $$–$$$**
**15582 WA Hwy. 112, Sekiu**
**(360) 963-2428**

The Breakwater offers seafood, steaks, and burgers served with a view of the bay and the Strait of Juan de Fuca from its perch along the highway in Sekiu. Specialties include the Dungeness Crab Louie, or the captain's plate with oysters, prawns, fish, scallops, and clam strips. The restaurant also offers beer, wine, and cocktails.

**Makah Maiden Cafe    $$**
**Bay View Ave., Neah Bay**
**(360) 645-2924**

Recently remodeled, the Makah Maiden Cafe has the distinction of being one of the best places to eat in Neah Bay. Stop in for the most popular dishes, such as a halibut steak or fish and chips. For a unique treat, call at least 24 hours in advance to arrange a meal of salmon cooked the traditional Makah way on a cedar stake in front of a pit fire. In addition to seafood, diners can try a variety of sandwiches, steaks, and salads. A trip to the cafe is like a trip to a history museum with historic photographs lining the walls and servers who will gladly tell you the tribe's history and stories. Large groups are advised to make reservations.

# Forks

Rain and logging are synonymous with the community of Forks. Located in one of the rainiest places in the U.S., Forks registered 162.14 inches of rain in 1997. Even the city's name is associated with water. The city sits near the point where three rivers—the Bogachiel, the Calawah, and the Sol Duc—merge before rushing into the Pacific Ocean as the Quillayute River.

Shortly after becoming a city based largely on agriculture in the 1870s, Forks made a transition to become a center of commercial logging. Logging companies still own huge tracts of land along U.S. Highway 101 as it winds toward and through the town of more than 3,500 people, but logging is no longer the heart and soul of the city. Environmental concerns and protection for the Western spotted owl in the 1980s resulted in drastic cutbacks in commercial logging, especially on lands that make up the Olympic National Forest just east of town. And although huge clear-cut areas are still visible on the hillsides around town, commercial logging companies have been forced into a waiting period before they can cut second- and third-growth fir trees planted on company-owned tree plantations around the city.

Today the residents of Forks make their living promoting the benefits and beauty of the same forests they once leveled, all the while retaining ties to logging with popular tourism attractions such as the Forks Timber Museum and the nearby Forks Loggers Memorial, which pays tribute to area loggers who have died. Tourists can even line up a free guided tour of area sawmills.

Forks also serves as a gateway to recreation in the areas around the city. The town is close to the world-famous, moss-covered Hoh Rainforest, and Forks is close to ocean beaches such as Rialto Beach, and Second and Third Beaches near the Native American village of LaPush—a fishing village that dates back more than 800 years. To the south sit scenic Ruby Beach and Kalaloch Beach. All of these beaches are also part of the Olympic Coast Marine Sanctuary, a 3,300-square-mile sanctuary that stretches from Copalis in the south to Cape Flattery in the north.

Since the drop in logging, Forks has also redefined itself to cater to artists and art-related tourism. Formed in 1993, the Olympic West Arttrek offers a guide to businesses that offer unique art, antiques, crafts, gifts, and pottery. Be sure to pick up an Arttrek pamphlet at the Forks Visitor Center, right next to the Forks Timber Museum on the south end of town.

If you come to Forks seeking festivities, plan a trip in mid-April to take in RainFest, or stop next to the Thriftway store down-

*Logging dominates the history of Forks.* PHOTO: ROB McNAIR-HUFF

town on Fridays and Saturdays between April and October for the Forks Farmers' Market. Later in the year, taste the logging heritage of Forks in late September and early October during Hickory Shirt & Heritage Days, or stop in during November for the Forks Wine and Cheese Event.

## Hotels and Motels

Despite Forks' small size, the town sports quite a few hotels and motels. Why so many hotels in such a small place? Simple—with the scenic beaches and the world-famous Hoh Rainforest just a few minutes down the road, Forks is a gateway to the north coast.

All of the hotels and motels lie along U.S. Highway 101 (the main strip through Forks), and they range from the most modern accommodations, such as the Forks Motel and the Dew Drop Inn, to older and cozy confines such as Bagby's Town Motel.

## Price Code

Our price code reflects the average price of a double-occupancy room during the peak season, which runs from mid-May to mid-October. Room rates are usually discounted from late fall to early spring. The prices quoted do not include state and local sales taxes.

| | |
|---|---|
| $ | under $60 |
| $$ | $60–$90 |
| $$$ | $91–$130 |
| $$$$ | over $131 |

**Bagby's Town Motel    $**
1080 S. Forks Ave., Forks
(360) 374-6231, (800) 742-2429
www.bagbystownmotel.com

Words like cozy, friendly, and comfortable frequently roll off the tongues of visitors in reference to one of Forks's oldest motels, the Bagby's Town Motel. Owners Norm and Jan Bagby offer 17 rooms, each with cable TV, private baths, showers, and small desks, right along the main street through Forks. There are no in-room telephones, but a pay phone is available in the activity room.

In addition to indoor amenities, Bagby's features a garden with picnic tables and a barbecue. Bagby's also goes out of its way to make guests feel welcome with free coffee in the activity room, fresh flowers in the guest rooms each day, and a separate shower available for hunters and campers who are passing through town.

**Dew Drop Inn    $–$$**
100 Fernhill Rd., Forks
(360) 374-4055, (888) 433-9376
www.dewdropinnmotel.com

The newest motel in Forks, the Dew Drop Inn offers 23 rooms and a friendly attitude, but if you want to line up a room in the summer, think ahead. The motel, which was built and opened in 1996, fills up quickly in summer months. Located along the main street through town, the inn offers rooms with king- or queen-size beds, sitting areas with tables, cable TV, and in-room phones with data ports. Lodging for additional adults in a double-occupancy room costs $6 per night. Since it is such a new motel, wheelchair-accessible lodging is available. The inn also allows pets for an additional $10 per night. Smoking and nonsmoking rooms are offered.

**Forks Motel**    $$
**351 Forks Ave. S., Forks**
**(360) 374-6243, (800) 544-3416**
**www.forksmotel.com**

Family-owned since its start in 1955 and remodeled in 1999, the Forks Motel along U.S. Highway 101 offers 73 deluxe rooms, all with queen-size beds and contemporary decor representative of the area. The room options range from mini-suites with microwaves and refrigerators to rooms with two bedrooms, and all rooms offer phones and cable TV with remotes. The motel also offers a single Jacuzzi suite and one wheelchair-accessible unit. There are smoking rooms available as well. In addition to the room amenities, guests can head outside in the summer months to enjoy a heated swimming pool. Lodging for each additional person in a room costs $5 per night. Pets are also allowed, with size restrictions, for $5 per night.

**Olympic Suites Inn    $$**
**800 Olympic Dr., Forks**
**(360) 374-5400, (800) 262-3433**
**www.olympicgetaways.com/olympic**
**suites**

The most recently renovated hotel in Forks, the Olympic Suites Inn received a thorough makeover in 2000. It offers 33 rooms that the owner, Edward Boyd, describes as essentially being condominiums—one- and two-bedroom suites with microwaves, refrigerators, cable TV, and in-room phones with data ports. Twenty-eight of the rooms offer full kitchens, and a guest laundry is available as well. Guests can enjoy the French country-style decor while sipping in-room coffee, and all rooms offer either king- or queen-size beds. Each additional guest over double occupancy will pay an additional $5 per night. Pets are also allowed, with restrictions.

The Olympic Suites Inn is one of the few Forks hotels located outside town. It is just north of town, near the well-known Smokehouse Restaurant, just one block off U.S. Highway 101.

**Pacific Inn Motel    $$**
**352 S. Forks Ave., Forks**
**(360) 374-9400, (800) 235-7344**
**www.pacificinnmotel.com**

Spacious rooms and a friendly staff are trademarks of the Pacific Inn Motel. Located along U.S. Highway 101 downtown, the 34-room motel offers its guests queen-size beds, cable TVs with remotes, kitchenettes with microwaves and refrigerators, and air-conditioning. Guests can also use the on-site laundry facilities.

The Pacific Inn offers smoking and non smoking rooms, and two wheelchair-accessible rooms. Expect to pay $5 for each additional guest beyond double-occupancy. Credit cards are accepted, but checks are not.

# Bed and Breakfast Inns

Forks may not seem like a town that would hold a lot of bed and breakfast inns, but thanks to the lack of accommodations in the area during the summer months, bed and breakfast inns fill a definite need. The local inns also offer conveniences such as easy connections with fishing guides and hiking organizations in the region.

We include seven bed and breakfast inns in this chapter, ranging from places along the Sol Duc River north of town to the Hoh Humm Ranch south of town near the Hoh River. There are other inns in the area as well, but these are the cream of the crop.

The allure of a bed and breakfast inn lies with the fact that someone coddles you, makes sure you are comfortable and cared for, and cooks you a delicious, warming breakfast to help you on your way. Occasionally you may have to share a bathroom. These inns have a charm that few hotels can hope to capture. It's almost like home, but someone else does the cleaning and cooking!

Since the proprietors of bed and breakfast inns are opening their homes to strangers as well as trying to provide a restful atmosphere, most don't allow smoking, children under age 12, or pets. Some will allow pets and children by prior arrangement. If you are allergic to animals, you may want to check with your hosts to see if they have or allow pets. Most accept major credit cards, and some will ask for a credit card to hold the reservation. If the inn does not accept credit cards we have noted that with the price code.

Each bed and breakfast listed provides a special home-cooked breakfast. Some innkeepers serve breakfast in bed, while others serve it family style in a formal dining room or breakfast nook. You may be treated to a secret family recipe such as yummy chocolate banana bread. Or maybe it will be a well-known breakfast favorite with a twist like a smoked salmon and brie omelette, baked cheese and chile casserole, French toast with homemade berry syrup, or even thick, comforting oatmeal with a dried fruit compote. You can also expect to see fresh fruit, toast and homemade jam, as well as gourmet coffee, tea, and fruit juice on every table. Most innkeepers will accommodate special needs diets or serve breakfast earlier or later if arrangements are made in advance. No matter what the situation, find out when and where breakfast is served, as it's a special part of the bed and breakfast experience.

# Price Code

Our price code reflects the average price of a double-occupancy room during the peak season, which runs from mid-May to mid-October. Room rates are usually discounted from late fall to early spring. The prices quoted do not include state and local sales taxes.

$ . . . . . . . . . . . . . .under $65
$$ . . . . . . . . . . . . .$65–$95
$$$ . . . . . . . . . . .$96–$140
$$$$ . . . . . . . . . .over $141

**Bear Creek Homestead Bed and Breakfast**
**$$**
**2094 Bear Creek Rd., Port Angeles**
**(360) 327-3699**
**www.northolympic.com/bch**

Located on 16 acres that were originally homesteaded in 1891, the Bear Creek Homestead Bed and Breakfast offers three rooms and a secluded, outdoors atmosphere for its guests. The history of the homestead is unveiled in the pictures hanging in each room. All the rooms include private bathrooms and either king- or queen-size beds, depending upon which room you choose. Outside the home, guests can walk the farm, where owners Sherry and Larry Baysinger raise horses, llamas, chickens, and goats. The inn doesn't allow guests to bring their own pets, however. Children over the age of 12 are allowed.

Breakfasts at Bear Creek Homestead start with homemade breads, jam, muffins, and a variety of main dishes such as Dutch babies and egg dishes, all served between 7 and 9 A.M.

In addition to the inn, the homestead also offers a horse-packing service called the Sol Duc Valley Packers. Guests can request a horse-riding experience as part of their stay, especially during the off- season when the horses aren't busy carrying

A few miles west of Forks, along the north edge of Rialto Beach, you'll find one of the best tidepooling areas along the Washington coast. Check the tide tables for low tide and walk the beach north toward Hole in the Wall.

gear into the nearby forests for hiking expeditions.

**Directions:** From Forks, take U.S. Highway 101 east toward Port Angeles. Go 15 miles from Forks and turn left off U.S. 101 onto Bear Creek Road. Go to the end of the road.

**Brightwater House Bed and Breakfast   $$**
**440 Brightwater Dr., Forks**
**(360) 374-5453**
**www.northolympic.com/brightwater**

The Brightwater House Bed and Breakfast is a destination for fly fishers as well as travelers simply passing through the area. The four-room inn features 3,500 feet of low-bank riverfront on the Sol Duc River—perfect for fly fishing—nestled on 60 acres that were homesteaded in 1882. Owners Richard and Beth Chesmore purchased the property in 1990 and opened the inn in 1992.

Throughout the Brightwater House, the walls are adorned with fly-fishing gear, custom-tied flies, and other fishing memorabilia. The Chesmores work with their guests to make sure that their getaway is carefree by helping line up area fishing guides and scheduling the hearty breakfasts around guest schedules. The breakfasts include such things as fruit, croissants, quiche, and a variety of egg dishes such as fritattas.

The Brightwater House offers four rooms to its guests. Most beds are queen-size, and all of the rooms offer seating areas in addition to sweeping views of the prairie and the nearby Sol Duc River.

Lodging for each additional guest over the standard double-occupancy costs $10 per night, and pets are allowed in two of the units for an additional $10 per night. Children over the age of eight are welcome.

**Directions:** From Forks, take U.S. Highway 101 north to the intersection with Washington Highway 110. Turn left onto WA 110 and go three miles before turning right onto Quillayute Road. Continue down Quillayute Road until you cross a bridge over the Sol Duc River, then take the first left after the bridge.

**Hoh Humm Ranch Bed and Breakfast   $**
**171763 U.S. Hwy. 101, Forks**
**(360) 374-5337**
**www.olypen.com/hohhumm**

The Hoh Humm Ranch Bed and Breakfast is an animal lover's paradise. Set on a 200-acre ranch that houses cattle, goats, sheep, llamas, and a host of wild animals such as deer, the three-room inn is located within a country farmhouse owned by Bob and Mary Huelsdonk. There is an additional $10 per night for guests beyond the standard double-occupancy. The inn allows children, and kids under the age of 16 can stay for free with their parents. Well-behaved dogs can also stay for an extra $5 per night. Each room offers a queen-size bed, but the three rooms share a bathroom. Guests can also watch TV in a common room, where a phone is available for visitors as well. Each morning, guests sit down to a hearty farm breakfast of eggs, potatoes, corn bread, sausage, and main dishes such as Dutch babies.

The inn opened in 1997, but the ranch and farmhouse have been in the family's hands for more than 60 years. The property was originally purchased from a logging company.

**Directions:** From Forks, go south on U.S. Highway 101 for 20 miles. The ranch is located about 100 yards off the highway just past milepost 172.

**Manitou Lodge Bed and Breakfast**   **$$$**
**813 Kilmer Rd., Forks**
**(360) 374-6295**
**www.manitoulodge.com**

A great room measuring 40 by 30 feet with an enormous fireplace and vaulted ceilings the trademark of the Manitou Lodge. Located just down the road from the Mora campground and Rialto Beach, it is arguably the western most bed and breakfast in the contiguous United States. The lodge opened in the 1970s, largely as a fishing and hunting destination and gradually changed to the eight-room lodge that it is today. Owners Lynn and Ed Murphy, who have run the lodge since 1997, offer rooms and a hearty breakfast. An additional guest can be accommodated for $20 per night, and pets are allowed in the cottage, which has a separate entrance, for $10 per night. Children over the age of five are welcome as well.

Manitou is known for its forested ambience and the great room that greets guests when they first walk into the house. The house sits on a 10-acre site, and visitors will find three dogs and two cats to greet them on the grounds. When breakfast time rolls around (between 8 and 9:30 a.m.), guests can feast on large meals including fresh fruit and main dishes such as Belgian waffles, omelettes, or stuffed French toast.

**Directions:** From Forks, take U.S. Highway 101 north and then turn left onto Washington Highway 110. After traveling eight miles on WA 110, turn right onto

**Insiders' Tip**

While planning your trip to the west end of the Olympic Peninsula, be sure to check out the Forks Web sites: www.forkswa.com and www.forks-web.com.

WA Spur 110 and cross a one-lane bridge over the Sol Duc River. Kilmer Road is 0.5 mile down WA Spur 110. Turn right onto Kilmer Road, then proceed approximately one mile and look for the lodge on the left.

**Miller Tree Inn Bed and Breakfast**   **$$**
**654 E. Division St., Forks**
**(360) 374-6806, (800) 943-6563**
**www.millertreeinn.com**

Combine homestead history and more than 15 years of experience in the bed and breakfast business, and the Miller Tree Inn Bed and Breakfast earns high honors in Forks. Located near the heart of town, the inn is set in a 1914 farmhouse that has been restored to its original luster from when it was part of the original Peterson homestead. Owners Bill and Susan Brager offer seven rooms, including one suite with a full kitchen. Each room is decorated with a farmhouse theme, and each features either a king- or queen-size bed. Children ages seven and older are accepted, and pets are not allowed.

The Miller Tree Inn recently earned a two diamond rating from AAA. The experience is topped off by a huge, farm-style breakfast featuring fresh fruit, cereal, and a pastry bar followed by a main entree such as blueberry French toast or gingerbread pancakes with lemon sauce. Before departing, guests can lounge on the huge

*James Island is a sea stack located at the mouth of the Quillayute River.* PHOTO: NATALIE McNAIR-HUFF

porch or opt to soak in the large, eight-person hot tub on the back deck. The inn is a nonsmoking establishment, but guests can smoke outside.

**Directions:** From downtown Forks, proceed along U.S. Highway 101 to the only stoplight in town, then turn east onto Division St. at the light and go one-third of a mile to 654 E. Division St.

**Misty Valley Inn Bed and Breakfast**    **$$**
**194894 U.S. Hwy. 101, Forks**
**(360) 374-9389, (877) 374-9389**
**www.mistyvalleyinn.com**

Fans of Washington's state flower will want to book space at the four-room Misty Valley Inn Bed and Breakfast during the rhododendron blooming season. The modern, 6,000-square-foot stone and cedar house is surrounded by gardens that feature 26 types of rhododendrons, 56 types of roses, and a large selection of native plants and trees—all nestled on a ridge in the rain forest. Since opening in 1989, the inn, run by owners Jim and

Rachel Bennett, has earned a reputation for its hospitality and for the three-course gourmet breakfasts that feature such tasty dishes as a Washington apple soufflé, Irish waffles with orange sauce, or Moroccan omelettes.

Guests can choose from among three rooms with queen-size beds and one suite with a king-size bed. Children ages 12 and older are welcome, but pets are not allowed. Additional guests over double-occupancy pay an additional $25 per night. Another highlight of the inn is the outdoor spa, located right next to the rose garden. After enjoying the spa, visitors can stop to admire the view of the Sol Duc River valley.

**Directions:** From Forks, go north on U.S. Highway 101 until you cross two bridges and come up onto a straight stretch of the road. You should see a large road sign on the west side of the road and a blue lodging sign directly across from the driveway. Turn right into the driveway, and then take the left part of the split driveway. At the head of the driveway is a lighted sign. If you go past mile marker 195, you missed the driveway.

### Sol Duc River Lodge Bed and Breakfast $$
**206114 U.S. Hwy 101, Forks**
**(360) 327-3709**

The atmosphere at the Sol Duc River Lodge Bed and Breakfast entices guests of the three-room lodge to sit down, kick back with a good book, and soak up the homey ambience. The lodge, which opened in 1998, is run by Gloria and Jeff Sahar. It features a spacious living room with open beam ceilings and a large fireplace. Another room offers a pool table, an entertainment center with satellite TV, and a view of the river that gives the lodge its name. The rooms include one with a king-size bed and its own private bathroom, and two others that share a bathroom on the lodge's second floor. It costs another $15 per night to add a third person to a room. Children ages 12 and older are welcome, but pets are not allowed.

Breakfasts at the Sol Duc River Lodge can be arranged to the guests' schedule. After coffee and juice, the hearty meal features a variety of main courses, such as wild berry pancakes or salmon omelettes.

**Directions:** From Forks, go north on U.S. Highway 101 for 13 miles. The lodge is located just off the Sol Duc River along the highway.

## Cabins and Rentals

### Olson's Vacation Cabins
**2423 Mora Rd., Forks**
**(360) 374-3142**
**www.forks-web.com/bp/olsons.htm**

Enjoy a private getaway in one of the cabins offered by Olson's Vacation Cabins. Each cabin can accommodate between four and six people, and has a full kitchen. Set in a four-acre meadow along the Quillayute River, the cabins also allow pets and guests can use a hot tub on the premises. The rates are around $50, depending on the cabin.

## Restaurants

Despite its small size, Forks offers a modest selection of dining opportunities, from hamburgers to prime rib and lots of seafood. We include four restaurants in this chapter. All are along U.S. Highway 101.

## Price Code

Our price code reflects the average price of a single meal excluding drinks, tips, and taxes. Unless noted otherwise, the restaurants accept most major credit cards. Many do not accept out-of-state checks, so ask your server to be sure your check will be accepted.

$ . . . . . . . . . . . . . .under $10
$$ . . . . . . . . . . . . . .$10–$15
$$$ . . . . . . . . . . . .$16–$20
$$$$ . . . . . . . . . . . .over $21

**Golden Gate Chinese Restaurant**   $$–$$$
80 W. A St., Forks
(360) 374-5579

From homemade shaven noodles to more standard Chinese cuisine, the Golden Gate offers a wide range of food, all made without MSG. Diners can opt for one of four dinner combinations or choose individual entrees such as Shanghai Hand Shaven Chow Mein, Shanghai Special Fried Rice, or standard dishes like Mu Shu Pork. The Golden Gate is closed on Sundays.

**Raindrop Cafe**   $$
111 S. Forks Ave., Forks
(360) 374-6612

If you have a hankering for a gourmet hamburger in the heart of Forks, pull up a chair at the Raindrop Cafe. The restaurant bills itself as serving "Country home cooking with a touch of gourmet." Try the Raindrop burger, with pepperjack cheese, ham, Swiss cheese, bacon, guacamole, and onion, or the Blackened Fish Sandwich. The restaurant also offers salads such as a Hawaiian Chicken Salad.

Dinner is highlighted by steaks, seafood such as poached dill cod, and simple dishes like fish and chips. Follow up with ice cream, homemade desserts, and malts. The cafe is open seven days a week.

**Northwest Pizza Express**   $
86 Forks Ave. N., Forks
(360) 374-4343

Fresh pizza on homemade, traditional crust is the specialty at Northwest Pizza Express. Owners Greg and Lorri Gagnon offer dine-in, take-out, and delivery pizza seven days a week. Dine on standard combination pizzas such as the Hawaiian with Canadian bacon and pineapple, or opt for a unique creation such as the Chicken Fajita pizza with barbecue sauce, grilled chicken, cheddar cheese, onions, green peppers, and tomatoes. If you want something other than pizza, choose from a menu of sandwiches on fresh, homemade bread.

**Smoke House Restaurant**   $$$
193161 U.S. Hwy 101, Forks
(360) 374-6258

Smoked salmon and a large salad bar make the Smoke House a popular destination along the north coast. Whether you choose the alder smoked salmon, prepared Native American-style from the on-site smokers, or prime rib in portions from regular to large to giant, the Smoke House food is sure to fill your stomach. The restaurant offers a full range of seafood such as a seafood sauté with scallops, cod, salmon, and prawns sautéed with mushrooms, onions, and broccoli in a wine sauce and accompanied by smoked salmon. Or if you prefer selections from the broiler, try top sirloin charbroiled to your specifications.

Aside from the main courses, the Smoke House Restaurant offers a full lounge for evening entertainment. The restaurant is open seven days a week.

# Shopping

Most people travel to Forks and use the town as a base camp for their outdoor explorations in the nearby Hoh Rainforest, along the Pacific Ocean, or on one of the rivers that helped give the town its name. But Forks has more to offer than lodging. Visitors can find shopping along the main road through town—U.S. Highway 101—as well as on a few side streets. A few art galleries, antiques stores, and a bookstore are among the offerings within the city. We have also traveled beyond city limits to include an outdoors shop on the road to the Hoh Rainforest.

## Country Living Store
### 711 S. Forks Ave., Forks
### (360) 374-6500

Stop in the Country Living Store to peruse a hodgepodge collection of antiques, candles, specialty toiletries, and collectible items. The shop also features a collection of handmade knives and wooden toys. Leather goods and some clothing round out the offerings.

## Peak 6 Adventure Store
### Hoh Rainforest Rd., Forks
### (360) 374-5254

What better place for a wide collection of outdoors gear than at the gateway to the Hoh Rainforest? Peak 6 Adventure Store sits just outside the entrance to Olympic National Park on the Hoh River, offering everything from gift books and jewelry to the latest backpacks, sleeping bags, and tents. The shop also offers local arts and crafts. It is open seven days a week.

## The Errant Elk
### 37 N. Forks Ave., Forks
### (360) 374-8608
### www.manitoulodge.com

Explore Native American art from nearby tribes and find one-of-a-kind jewelry six days a week at The Errant Elk. Located along Forks' main drag, the shop offers a wide range of Native crafts—bark baskets, beadwork, and wood carvings—all at reasonable prices. Besides the items featured in the downtown store, shoppers can also drive to the Manitou Lodge outside town to see additional artwork.

## The Fern Gallery
### 11 N. Forks Ave., Forks
### (360) 374-4300

Fans of unique birding, yard, and garden supplies will enjoy a varied shopping experience at The Fern Gallery. As the name reflects, the store along the main street in Forks features original art by Northwest artists, offered alongside collectibles, cards, and a wide range of gift items. The store is closed on Sundays.

## Tinker's Tales & Antiques
### 71 N. Forks Ave., Forks
### (360) 374-9433
### www.tinkers-tales.com

Imagine a hybrid combining a coffee shop, a bookstore, and an art gallery all under one roof, and you'll have a good idea of what Tinker's Tales & Antiques offers shoppers. Espresso Elegante is the first thing visitors see at the front of the store, offering specialty coffee for shoppers who can check out the latest magazines or browse the collection of art and antiques along the shop walls. And visitors can walk all the way to the back of the store to check out the art in the "Alley Studio," featuring art by local artists such as Susan Gansert Shaw. The store is open seven days a week.

## West Wind Gallery
### 120 Sol Duc Wy., Forks
### (360) 374-7795

Like so many towns around the Olympic Peninsula, Forks wouldn't be complete without an art co-op. The West Wind Gallery fulfills the role with a rotating stock of art from nearly 50 local artists—woodcrafts, paintings, multimedia art, and jewelry—much of it reflecting regional seascapes and mountain scenes. The gallery also offers on-site framing. It is closed on Sundays.

> **Insiders' Tip**
> Check your gas tank in Forks before heading south. Forks is the last major town along the west side of the Peninsula until you reach the Grays Harbor area.

# Ocean Shores

Ocean Shores is the city that tourism built. A former cattle ranch, the land that would become Ocean Shores was developed in 1960 to be a major seaside destination, and it has lived up to the plan. The town of just more than 3,000 people is a hub of beachside activity in the summer, and even in the off-season it draws storm watchers and kite flyers. Nearly 3 million people visit Ocean Shores every year.

Approximately six miles long and two miles wide, Ocean Shores is the largest town along a 22-mile section of the Washington coast known as the North Beach area. Besides being surrounded by the Pacific Ocean to the west and Grays Harbor to the east, the town contains nearly 23 miles of canals. The North Beach area continues up the coast toward the small communities of Ocean City, Copalis Beach, Pacific Beach, and finally Moclips in the far north. The roads end at Taholah.

Popular activities in the area include bird-watching at places such as the Oyhut Wildlife Area near the Ocean Shores Environmental Interpretive Center (open from Memorial Day to Labor Day) at the far south end of Ocean Shores, hiking, kite flying, and horseback riding on the shoreline. A number of stables keep horses along the beach in Ocean Shores.

## Hotels and Motels

With the exception of the busiest summer weekends, travelers should have no trouble driving into Ocean Shores and finding a room at one of more than a dozen hotels and motels in the area. Hotels and motels are scattered from the far southern tip of Ocean Shores northward to Ocean City, Copalis Beach, Pacific Beach, and Moclips. Visitors can call a universal reservations line, (888) 702-3224, to make reservations for hotels, motels, bed and breakfast inns, and resorts.

## Price Code

Our price code reflects the average price of a double-occupancy room during the peak season, which runs from mid-May to mid-October. Room rates are usually discounted from late fall to early spring. Prices exclude state and local sales taxes, around 10 percent for hotels and motels.

$ . . . . . . . . . . . . . .under $60
$$ . . . . . . . . . . . . .$60–$90
$$$ . . . . . . . . . . .$91–$130
$$$$ . . . . . . . . . .over $131

**The Discovery Inn Condominiums    $$**
**1031 Discovery Ave. S.E., Ocean Shores**
**(360) 289-3371, (800) 882-8821**
**www.oceanshores.com/discovery**

Catering to families and travelers interested in a more secluded stay in Ocean Shores, The Discovery Inn Condominiums offers 24 rooms with second-floor views of the inner harbor. The inn is located just minutes from downtown. Open since the 1960s, it is highlighted by eight suites, essentially one-bedroom apartments with fireplaces and full kitchens. Most of the rooms offer kitchens or kitchenettes, and all of the rooms feature queen-size beds, cable TV, in-room phones, and coffeemakers. Aside from the rooms, guests can also use the heated outdoor pool, take advantage of the spa, check out the game room, or saunter down to the private dock on the inner canal for some fishing. Pets are allowed for an additional $10 per night.

**The Grey Gull    $$$**
**647 Ocean Shores Blvd. N.W.,**
**Ocean Shores**
**(360) 289-3381, (800) 562-9712**
**www.thegreygull.com**

The Grey Gull brings more than 30 years of lodging experience to the Ocean Shores waterfront. Guests can choose from 37 rooms, ranging from standard rooms to suites, or a penthouse that is one-of-a-kind in town. Many guests come back year after year to the rooms, which include full kitchens, cable TV, phones, and data ports. Each room in the Grey Gull is decorated differently, but all have either king- or queen-size beds and fireplaces. Each room also has a private patio facing the waterfront. An outdoor pool, spa, and sauna further pamper guests. Smoking and wheelchair-accessible rooms are available. Pets are allowed for an additional $10 per day.

**Linde's Landing    $$**
**648 Ocean Shores Blvd. N.W.,**
**Ocean Shores**
**(360) 289-3323, (800) 448-2433**
**www.lindeslanding.com**

Formerly known as the Gitchee Gumee Motel, Linde's Landing is a recently remodeled hotel geared to families. The hotel offers 64 rooms, ranging from simple, single-bed rooms up to rooms that can sleep five people. Town house suites sleep up to eight people. All rooms have king- or queen-size beds with cable TV, telephones, and many rooms have partial views of the ocean across the street. Most rooms include a comfortable sitting area with a sleeper-sofa, and all are tastefully decorated with cozy quilts and comforters. Guests can bring pets along to some of the rooms, for an additional one-time fee of $20. And once everyone is settled into their rooms, they can take a dip in one of two swimming pools—one inside and one outside. Many rooms also offer full kitchens.

**Ocean Crest Resort    $$**
**4651 WA Hwy. 109, Moclips**
**(360) 276-4465, (800) 684-8439**

Enjoy breathtaking sunset views from the edge of a 100-foot bluff at the Ocean Crest Resort in Moclips. Located at the north end of the North Beach area, the 40-plus-year-old resort offers 45 units split between six different buildings. Half of the rooms offer queen-size beds, and the others king-size beds. Kitchen suites, complete with utensils and dishes, are available. All rooms include cable TV, phones, coffeemakers, and use of the indoor pool, weight room, or sauna. The destination resort includes such amenities as an on-site massage therapist, a restaurant, a lounge, and a gift shop. If a walk along the beach is on the agenda, take the long, private staircase down the bluff to the surf. A two-night minimum stay is required on weekends.

**The Polynesian Resort**    **$$$**
**615 Ocean Shores Blvd. N.W.,**
**Ocean Shores**
**(360) 289-3361, (800) 562-4836**
**www.thepolynesian.com**

Check out the heart of Ocean Shores while staying in a condominium at The Polynesian Resort. Rooms at the Polynesian offer ocean views, fireplaces, and full kitchens as well as access to the on-site indoor pool, spa, sauna, and game room. Guests also get access to the private park next door with a basketball court, volleyball court, picnic tables, and play area for kids. The ocean beach is just a short walk away through the dunes. The resort has non smoking and pet rooms available, and additional guests can stay in a room for $10 per night. Rooms also include continental breakfast Mondays through Fridays, and dinner is available at the on-site Mariah's Restaurant.

**Quinault Beach Resort & Casino**    **$$$$**
**78 WA Hwy. 115, Ocean Shores**
**(360) 289-9466, (888) 461-2214**
**www.quinaultbchresort.com**

The newest major hotel on the Washington coast is not really a hotel at all. The Quinault Beach Resort & Casino opened in June of 2000. Owned by the Quinault Indian Tribe, the hotel boasts 159 rooms and 9 suites. All rooms offer queen- or king-size beds, large screen TVs, in-room movies and video games, two telephones, and high-speed Internet access. Extra-large, two-sink vanities make evening and morning preparations a breeze, and the gas fireplace and complimentary bathrobes let guests relax in luxury. Most rooms also feature views of the Pacific Ocean. Aside from the gambling entertainment in the casino and the on-site spa with massage, aromatherapy, and various body treatments, guests can also enjoy an indoor pool.

**Sand Dollar Inn**    **$$–$$$**
**53 Central Ave., Pacific Beach**
**(360) 276-4525**
**users.techline.com/sandlrin**

Known for having some of the best views on the Washington coast, the Sand Dollar Inn in Pacific Beach offers eight rooms and eight cabins for guests in a setting that has been in use since it opened in 1947. Under the ownership of Pam Rasmussen, the inn contains one- and two-bedroom lodgings within a stone's throw of the Pacific Ocean. Each room offers a full kitchen, cable TV, and queen-size beds. The rooms don't have telephones. The inn charges an extra $5 per night for additional guests in a room, and pets are allowed for $5 per pet, per night. Guests can also enjoy an outdoor hot tub and gas barbecue grills.

## Insiders' Tip

If you are interested in wildlife, head to the southern end of Ocean Shores to the Damon Point area. Damon Point, a 300-acre area, is home to more than 200 species of migratory and residential birds, wildlife, and marine life. It marks the western point of the fourth largest estuary on the Pacific Coast—Grays Harbor.

# Bed and Breakfast Inns

Ocean Shores hasn't caught onto the bed and breakfast inn craze quite yet, so the options for staying in an inn are limited in this tourist town. Travelers set on being pampered at a bed and breakfast inn are encouraged to reserve space at one of the two inns listed here with as much advance notice as possible.

## Insiders' Tip

Before visiting Ocean Shores, check out what is happening this weekend on the local chamber of commerce Web site: www.oceanshores.org

The allure of a bed and breakfast inn lies with the fact that someone coddles you, makes sure you are comfortable and cared for, and cooks you a delicious, warming breakfast to help you on your way. Occasionally you may have to share a bathroom. These inns have a charm that few hotels can hope to capture. It's almost like home, but someone else does the cleaning and cooking!

Since the proprietors of bed and breakfast inns are opening their homes to strangers as well as trying to provide a restful atmosphere, most don't allow smoking, children under age 12, or pets. Some will allow pets and children by prior arrangement. If you are allergic to animals, you may want to check with your hosts to see if they have or allow pets. Most accept major credit cards, and some will ask for a credit card to hold the reservation. If the inn does not accept credit cards we have noted that with the price code.

Each bed and breakfast listed provides a special home-cooked breakfast. Some innkeepers serve breakfast in bed, others serve it family style in a formal dining room or breakfast nook. You may be treated to a secret family recipe such as yummy chocolate banana bread. Or maybe it will be a well-known breakfast favorite with a twist like a smoked salmon and brie omelette, baked cheese and chile casserole, French toast with homemade berry syrup, or even thick, comforting oatmeal with a dried fruit compote. You can also expect to see fresh fruit, toast and homemade jam, as well as gourmet coffee, tea, and fruit juice on every table. Most innkeepers will accommodate special-needs diets or serve breakfast earlier or later if arrangements are made in advance. No matter what the situation, find out when and where breakfast is served, as it's a special part of the bed and breakfast experience.

## Price Code

Our price code reflects the average price of a double-occupancy room during the peak season, which runs from mid-May to mid-October. Room rates are usually discounted from late fall to early spring. Prices exclude state and local sales taxes.

| | |
|---|---|
| $ | under $65 |
| $$ | $65–$95 |
| $$$ | $96–$140 |
| $$$$ | over $141 |

**Beach Avenue Bed and Breakfast** $$
47 Beach Ave., Pacific Beach
(360) 276-4727
www.pacificbeachwa.com/Bus/Babb/
babb.html

**Silver Waves Bed and Breakfast** $$
982 Point Brown Ave. S.E.,
Ocean Shores
(360) 289-2490, (888) 257-0894
www.users.techline.com/silverwave

Travel to the Beach Avenue Bed and Breakfast for a touch of Hollywood on the Washington coast. Paul and Miriam Groesse own the inn, which opened in 1997. Each room in the three-room establishment is named after a movie that Paul's father, a three-time Oscar winner, worked on. One of the Oscars won by Paul's father is housed at the inn. Ask to stay in the Music Man, Pride and Prejudice, or Lili. Each room offers a queen-size bed, TV and VCR, desk, and coffee table. One room has a futon that folds out to sleep two guests. There is an additional charge of $5 for an extra person in the room. Kids are allowed, but the proprietors advise making arrangements for children before your arrival. Guests at the inn can rise for the 9:30 A.M. breakfasts of juice, fruit, omelettes, muffins, and scones. Miriam cooks the breakfasts, putting her 25 years of restaurant cooking experience to work.

In addition to the bed and breakfast, the owners also offer a guest cottage with a full kitchen. Breakfast is not included with the cottage. Pets are allowed in the cottage only, at an additional rate of $5 per night.

**Directions:** From Ocean Shores, take WA Highway 109 north toward Pacific Beach. Turn onto Beach Avenue in 10 miles to find the inn.

Overlooking the grand canal as it winds its way through Ocean Shores, just a short distance from the ocean, Silver Waves Bed and Breakfast features four rooms and a separate cottage. Open since 1998, the inn, owned by Reggie and Gae Whitehurst, offers king- or queen-size beds, depending on the room. The inn is decorated with a combination of contemporary and reproduction furniture, and light colors and floral prints predominate. Each room has satellite TV service, and guests who want to watch movies can do so on the TV and VCR in the great room. All rooms are nonsmoking, but an outside area has been set aside for smoking. Kids are OK at the inn, and pets are allowed in the cottage only, for an additional $10. There is a $10 charge for additional adults in a room.

Breakfasts are served around 9 A.M. in the sunroom overlooking the canal. Gae does the cooking, serving a full breakfast with fruit compote, either scones, biscuits, or coffee cake, and a main course, which ranges from pumpkin pancakes, French toast, or a Dutch baby with a side of bacon or ham.

**Directions:** From Ocean Shores, take the main street, Point Brown Avenue, south for four miles past the city center toward the marina. The inn is on the left-hand side of the road.

# Cottages, Cabins, and Vacation Rentals

If you are interested in a more casual stay in Ocean Shores, you can choose one of the many vacation homes and chalets that dot the beach and line the canals around town. These houses are self-contained, without the amenities of bed and breakfast inns or hotels. Most have full kitchens and are fully stocked and ready for your use. You just bring along food and friends. We include two vacation rental services below.

**Ocean Shores Vacation Rentals**
**759 Ocean Shores Blvd. N.W., Ocean Shores**
**(360) 289-3211, (877) 319-3211**
**oceanshoreswashington.com**

These rentals range from fully furnished one- and two-bedroom oceanfront condominiums to town houses and houses in and around town. All of the units—21 in all at the end of 2000—are privately owned, and most are within walking distance of the beach. Smokers and pets are welcome in some units, and many include a hot tub, deck, or sunroom.

**At the Beach Family Vacation Rentals**
**659 Ocean Shores Blvd. N.W., Ocean Shores**
**(360) 289-4297, (800) 303-4297**
**www.ricksbeachhouses.com**

Choose from two ocean view condos or 13 houses near the beach in locations from Ocean Shores to Moclips through At the Beach Family Vacation Rentals. Condos are available in Chalet Village near the heart of downtown Ocean Shores, while the beachfront houses are scattered throughout town and northward. Most of the houses include hot tubs, as well as full multimedia rooms with TV, VCR, and stereo. Some units allow pets for an additional nightly fee of $10. And many of the homes can accommodate larger groups of five to eight people.

## Insiders' Tip

If you want to dig razor clams when the season is open, make sure you have a license. Stop by the chamber of commerce or ask at your hotel for more information on where to purchase a license and where to dig.

# Restaurants

Most of the restaurants in the greater Ocean Shores area take advantage of the close proximity to the sea. Menus include some of the freshest seafood around alongside standards such as steak. A number of ethnic restaurants serve the tourists who venture to town, with Mexican, Chinese, Japanese, and Irish food among the offerings. Most restaurants don't require reservations, although they are recommended for large parties.

In addition to standard restaurants, during the summer months visitors can partake of hot dogs and other foods from street vendors.

## Price Code

Our price code reflects the average cost of a dinner for one, excluding drinks, tips, and taxes. Unless noted otherwise, the restaurants accept most major credit cards. Many do not accept out-of-county or out-of-state checks, so ask your server.

| | |
|---|---|
| $ | under $10 |
| $$ | $10–$15 |
| $$$ | $16–$20 |
| $$$$ | over $21 |

*Hundreds of kites fill the sky over Ocean Shores during the annual kite festival each June.* PHOTO: ROB McNAIR-HUFF

**Alec's By the Sea    $$–$$$**
**131 Chance Ala Mer N.E.,**
**Ocean Shores**
**(360) 289-4026**

Stop by for grilled Willapa Bay Oysters or a steaming serving of bouillabaisse with garlic bread at Alec's By the Sea. The restaurant, located just off the main intersection in town, serves burgers, chowder, steaks, and seafood for lunch and dinner in a friendly, casual atmosphere. Alec's opened in 1994. Aside from the food, the restaurant also serves beer and wine, and there is a full bar in the lounge.

**Dugan's Pizza    $$**
**690 Ocean Shores Blvd. N.W.,**
**Ocean Shores**
**(360) 289-2330**

Hand-tossed pizza for dining in, take out, or delivery is the specialty of Dugan's Pizza. Try the Dugan's Special, with pepperoni, Canadian bacon, salami, mushrooms, and black olives, or build your own custom pizza. The restaurant also serves sandwiches such as the meatball sub, or pasta dishes such as spicy Italian spaghetti or lasagna. Those who dine-in can watch TV or check out the video arcade while waiting for their meal.

**Emily's Restaurant at Quinault Beach Resort**
**$$$**
**78 WA Hwy. 115, Ocean Shores**
**(360) 289-9466**

Take a break from gambling for a stellar meal at Emily's Restaurant. Located within the Quinault Beach Resort, Emily's features local delicacies such as a Dungeness Bay crab pot—a whole crab on a bed of clams, mussels, corn on the cob, and broth—or alder planked salmon served with a honey and cider glaze, with fresh apples and sweet onions. The restaurant features a wide selection of fine wines by the glass, and most tables have great views of the Pacific Ocean.

**Galway Bay Irish Restaurant & Pub**   **$$**
**676 Ocean Shores Blvd. N.W. #3,**
**Ocean Shores**
**(360) 289-2300**
**www.galway-bay.com**

Drink in the Irish pub atmosphere and savory smells of dishes such as shepherds pie—steak, onions, carrots, potatoes, and a layer of colchannon—being cooked in the kitchen at the Galway Bay Irish Restaurant & Pub. Try a dish like the steak and Baileys, a New York steak grilled and then smothered in a sauce of Baileys Irish Cream served with a delicious mini-loaf of fresh-baked soda bread. The menu also features Irish strew, beef and Guinness, salads, and pizza. Stop by in the morning for sausage rolls or a traditional Irish breakfast with porridge, eggs, rashers, bangers, hash browns, toasted soda bread, and sliced tomatoes. The pub, which serves families in a dining room separated from the bar, also features live Celtic music on Friday and Saturday nights.

**The Home Port Restaurant**   **$$–$$$**
**857 Point Brown Ave., N.W.,**
**Ocean Shores**
**(360) 289-2600**

If you are looking for breakfast in Ocean Shores, one of the traditional eateries in town is the Home Port. Try an omelette such as the Dungeness crab with cheddar and Monterey jack cheeses, or opt for waffles or pancakes. Lunches feature items such as razor clams, locally harvested off the beach when in season, grilled, and seasoned with tartar sauce and lemon on the side. The dinner menu adds to the seafood offerings, with dishes such as lobster, salmon, clams, scallops, and two captain's plate combinations. The Home Port also serves beer and wine, and there is a full bar in the lounge.

**Las Maracas**   **$$**
**729 Point Brown Ave., Ocean Shores**
**(360) 289-2054**

Bring a big appetite for Mexican food when you visit Las Maracas. Open your meal with an appetizer such as a quesadilla, then dig into one of the house specialties such as chile verde or huevos rancheros. Las Maracas also offers orders to go.

**Mariah's at the Polynesian**   **$$–$$$**
**615 Ocean Shores Blvd. N.W.,**
**Ocean Shores**
**(360) 289-3315**

Across the parking lot from the Polynesian Resort, Mariah's serves seafood, pasta, and burgers in a cedar-lined setting. Start with an appetizer such as Dungeness artichoke dip, with crab, garlic, and Parmesan served warm with herb-crusted baguettes. Then choose a main course such as the first mate's plate, with salmon, halibut, prawns, scallops, and oysters, lightly breaded and deep fried. Mariah's also offers steaks, and anyone interested in a drink can stop over in the lounge.

**Mike's Seafood**   **$$**
**830 Point Brown Ave., Ocean Shores**
**(360) 289-0532**

Some of the freshest fish in town is served and sold at Mike's Seafood. The restaurant section of the shop features dishes such as cioppino with crab, clams, prawns, and cod in a San Francisco–style soup base. Diners can also test the smoked salmon, which is smoked on-site, or opt for a crab from the live tank for

## Insiders' Tip

Driving on the beach is allowed along much of the North Beach area. Stop by the Ocean Shores Chamber of Commerce office downtown for a map of accessible areas. Pedestrians on the beach need to be aware of drivers.

absolute freshness. The restaurant also offers fresh cheese-stuffed tortellini with crab or shrimp. Families will also like the fact that Mike's offers a kids' menu.

**Our Place    $**
**676 Ocean Shores Blvd. N.W.,**
**Ocean Shores**
**(360) 289-8763**

Order breakfast and lunch all daylong at Our Place. The breakfast menu features three-egg omelettes, pancakes, and egg combination dishes, with traditional sides such as ham, corned beef hash, or seasoned home fries. Lunch items include burgers, grilled sandwiches, and salads. The shop is also well known for its donuts and pastries.

# Shopping

As a tourist destination, Ocean Shores offers a number of shops to satisfy the shopping urge. Most shops are located downtown, either along Point Brown Avenue or along Ocean Shores Boulevard. The offerings range from souvenir shops to art galleries, with a few antiques shops mixed in for good measure. And more than any other town around the Olympic Peninsula, Ocean Shores features the latest and greatest in kite flying, with three stores offering everything from trick kites to simple rigs ready for the kids to fly as soon as they hit the beach.

**A Plus for Us**
**201 W. Chance Ala Mer Blvd., Ocean Shores**
**(360) 289-0906**
**www.aplusforus.com**

Forget about size twos, A Plus for Us sells clothes made for ample proportions. You'll find casual clothes, dresses, and cruise wear in sizes 1X to 6X. The clothes are well made, and you're guaranteed to find something unique here. If you are looking for cruise wear in standard sizes, walk next door to Fay's Too for sweat-shirts, blouses, sweaters, and slacks suit-able for the seashore.

**CC Loon Gallery and Gifts**
**899 Point Brown Ave. N.W., Ocean Shores**
**(360) 289-2985**

Browse lighthouse collectibles, Mary Engelbreit plaques, and cards at the CC Loon Gallery and Gifts. Photography lovers will want to check out the collection of framed photos, some by local artists.

**Cloud Nine**
**380 Damon Rd., Ocean Shores**
**(360) 289-2221**

Stop by Cloud Nine to browse the collec-tion of kites, windsocks, and other wind toys as well as souvenirs, shells, T-shirts, and saltwater taffy. This is the first store to greet visitors before they turn onto the main street through Ocean Shores or head straight onto beach access.

**Cottage By the Sea Antiques & Collectibles**
**810 Point Brown Ave., Ocean Shores**
**(360) 289-9046**

Fine antique furniture, including armoires and desks, are nicely arranged alongside a 1930s gas tank inside this collectibles shop. Take the time to browse both sides of the store to see the collection of die-cast toys, art, and pictures.

**Cutting Edge Kites and Cutting Edge**
**Toys & Games**
**676 Ocean Shores Blvd. N.W.,**
**Ocean Shores**
**(800) 379-3109, (360) 289-5682**
**www.cuttingedgekites.com**

Kites of every size, color, and design are the focus of this store, located just across the street from the beach. Kites range from simple models that can fold up into a small pouch that can be stuck in a pocket to the high-end trick kites that can make you the envy of the kite-flying crowd. If kites aren't your flavor of toys, then check out Cutting Edge Toys and

Games located a few steps away from the kite shop. Dolls, bendable figures, board games, spinning tops, and other toys are the focus here. The store also sells Groovy Girls and other name-brand toys.

### First Cabin
**676 Ocean Shores Blvd. N.W., Ocean Shores**
**(360) 289-9070**
**www.1stcabin.com**

Maritime-themed gifts and housewares have been a fixture at First Cabin since 1995. The shop also features candles, enamel wall hangings, and crystal perfume bottles among its offerings. Weather instruments, pottery, and custom textiles round out the gift items. If you can't find what you are looking for, be sure to ask the friendly staff for assistance.

### Flying Cats
**114 E. Chance Ala Mer Blvd., Ocean Shores**
**(360) 289-2287**

Gifts and accessories, including Flower Ferries, soaps, incense, teapots, and jewelry, are featured in the retail side of this two-part shop. Next door, stop in for a vanilla latte or custom cooking items in the coffeeroom and tearoom.

### Gallery Marjuli
**865 Point Brown Ave., Ocean Shores**
**(360) 289-2858**

Asian art and stunning works by local artists are displayed side-by-side with glass and ceramic works at the Gallery Marjuli. Owned by Julie Bitar and Marj

McBride, the shop also sells unique gifts such as pendulums, art supplies, and home decorating supplies.

### Galway Bay Trading Company
**676 Ocean Shores Blvd. #3, Ocean Shores**
**(360) 289-3955**
**www.galway-bay.com**

Irish-themed gifts and clothing fill this shop near the Galway Bay Irish Restaurant & Pub. Teapots and finely decorated cups and saucers sit next to imported teas and biscuits. Tartans, plaids, and woolen blankets, cloaks, and hats promise to keep you fashionably warm while books on the clans and Irish history will expand your horizons.

### Murphy's Candy and Ice Cream
**Chance Ala Mer Blvd., Ocean Shores**
**(360) 289-0927**

Satisfy a serious sweet tooth at Murphy's. The shop features homemade ice cream in an array of flavors, either served at the 1950s-style soda fountain, or in pints or quarts to go. The shop also sells homemade fudge, homemade chocolates, and saltwater taffy. If sweets aren't your cup of tea, you can try the specialties at the espresso bar or order a burger and fries.

### Ocean Shores Antiques
**817 Point Brown Ave. N.W., Ocean Shores**
**(360) 289-9840**

Ocean Shores Antiques brings together collectibles and oddities under one roof in a converted house in the heart of

## Insiders' Tip
Notice the odd tsunami evacuation route signs along many roads in the North Beach area. They mark the quickest way to head to higher ground in the event of a tsunami, or tidal wave. Emergency officials suggest that when you feel the ground shake from an earthquake in Ocean Shores, head inland to higher ground immediately. And don't return to the beach until officials give an "All clear" notice.

*A handlful of horseback riding outfits rent their horses to tourists on the beach.* PHOTO: ROB McNAIR-HUFF

Ocean Shores. Be sure to check the Star Wars room, stuffed with goodies related to the movies, as well as the comic book collection, glass collection, and dolls. The store also buys antiques.

**Ocean Shores Kites**
**172 West Chance Ala Mer N.W.,**
**Ocean Shores**
**(360) 289-4103**
**www.oceanshoreskites.com**

Beginner and expert kite flyers will find something of interest in Ocean Shores Kites. The store bills itself as having the largest selection of single-line, diamond kites in town, as well as a wide selection of inexpensive kites for kids. The shop also offers windsocks, banners, games, and toys.

**The Scurvy Dog**
**172 W. Chance Ala Mer, Ocean Shores**
**(360) 289-2414, (877) 684-6545**
**www.thescurvydog.com**

Located in the Shores Mall, The Scurvy Dog is a great place to browse collectibles such as Anheuser Busch steins, Matchbox cars, Harbour Lights, and a wide range of paintings by Thomas Kinkade. The shop also offers bath accessories from Crabtree & Evelyn, along with jewelry and shells.

*Lady Liberty greets visitors to Many Moons in Grays Harbor.* PHOTO: ROB McNAIR-HUFF

# Grays Harbor

Hotels and Motels

Bed and Breakfast Inns

Restaurants

Shopping

One of the two major inlets along the Washington coast, Grays Harbor is most known for its lumbering and fishing history. At one point in its past more lumber was harvested each year in Grays Harbor County than in any other county in the United States.

Logging regulations and environmental protections have slowed the pace of cutting in the forests surrounding the deep-water harbor over the last two decades, forcing a shift in the region's economy toward tourism. But the remaining forests in the nearby Willapa Hills to the south of the bay and in the Olympic National Forest to the north still offer a glimpse of the bounty of Douglas fir trees that lured generations of loggers to the region.

British explorer Captain Robert Gray first sailed into the waters of Grays Harbor in 1792 aboard the brigantine *Lady Washington* . What he found was a 12-mile-wide and 17-mile-long estuary that covers more than 200 square miles rimmed with mudflats, marshes, and ever-present Douglas fir trees.

Now the shores of Grays Harbor are dotted by former fishing villages, cities, and tourism destinations. The region's two largest cities, Aberdeen and Hoquiam, are home to more than 33,000 people.

Grays Harbor pays homage to its history through some of the major attractions in the area. A 170-ton, full-scale replica of the *Lady Washington* makes its home at the Grays Harbor Historical Seaport in Aberdeen, where the Chehalis and Wishkah Rivers converge near State Route 12. Visitors can tour the ship between 10 A.M. and 5 P.M. daily when it is in port.

A trio of historical museums also add to the tourism value of Grays Harbor. The Aberdeen Museum of History (111 East 3rd Street) offers glimpses of how life once was lived in the area, with rooms set up to depict a barbershop, a blacksmith shop, a doctor's office, a bedroom, a kitchen, a barn, and a mercantile store with a post office and switchboard. Admission to the museum is free, and it is open on weekends in the winter and Wednesdays through Sundays in the summer. The Polson Museum (1611 Riverside Avenue, Hoquiam) shows exhibits of Grays Harbor history along with items from the original owner of the 26-room mansion, timber heir Arnold Polson. The museum is open Wednesdays through Sundays in the summer, and on weekends from September to June. Admission is $2 for adults, $1 for students, and $5 for families.

Visitors to the area can also tour Hoquiam's Castle, a bed and breakfast inn on the hillside overlooking Hoquiam (515 Chenault Avenue). The nineteenth-century Victorian-style home is open daily for tours, with prices around $4 for adults, and $2.50 for children between the ages of 5 and 12.

Another event that draws people to the area takes place each spring, when millions of shorebirds descend on the Grays Harbor National Wildlife Refuge just west of Hoquiam. The Grays Harbor Shorebird Festival near the end of April marks the migration.

## Insiders' Tip

Grays Harbor is the largest and deepest natural harbor on the West Coast of the United States.

# Hotels and Motels

The three major towns in Grays Harbor each offer lodging opportunities. Montesano, as the smallest of the towns, is most notably appointed with bed and breakfast inns, while the twin cities of Aberdeen and Hoquiam hold the four hotels and motels mentioned here.

## Price Code

Our price code reflects the average price of a double-occupancy room during the peak season, which runs from mid-May to mid-October. Room rates are usually discounted from late fall to early spring. Prices exclude state and local sales taxes.

$ . . . . . . . . . . . . . .under $60
$$ . . . . . . . . . . . . . .$60–$90
$$$ . . . . . . . . . . . .$91–$130
$$$$ . . . . . . . . . . .over $131

### Olympic Inn Motel    $$
**616 W. Heron St., Aberdeen**
**(360) 533-4200, (800) 562-8618**

Looking for comfortable, clean lodging in the heart of Aberdeen? Check the Olympic Inn Motel. It offers 55 rooms with queen- and king-size beds, cable TV, phones, refrigerators, and microwaves. The Olympic Inn has three wheelchair-accessible rooms. Visitors with pets can keep them in selected rooms for between $5 and $10 extra per night. Extra guests can stay in a room for $10 per night over the normal rate. Guests can eat a continental breakfast between 6:30 and 10 A.M.

### Nordic Inn Motel    $$
**1700 S. Boone St., Aberdeen**
**(360) 533-3224, (800) 442-0101**

The Nordic Inn Motel and Convention Center in Aberdeen stands out as the major convention space in Grays Harbor. Built in the mid-1960s, the hotel offers 40 rooms year-round and 54 rooms during the peak summer season. Rooms are available in economy, standard, and executive formats. All rooms feature queen- or king-size beds, cable TV, and phones, and standard and executive rooms also offer coffeemakers. Rooms have sitting areas with a table and chairs. The inn also offers one wheelchair-accessible room during the summer months. The Nordic Inn does not accept personal checks.

### Thunderbird Motel    $$
**410 W. Wishkah St., Aberdeen**
**(360) 532-3153**

Established in 1957, the Thunderbird Motel offers 36 rooms in the heart of Aberdeen. Rooms at the Thunderbird feature queen- and king-size beds, tables and chairs, refrigerators, microwaves, and ceiling fans. The rooms also have cable TV and coffeemakers. Pets are allowed in some rooms, and two rooms are wheelchair accessible.

**Westwood Inn    $$**
**910 Simpson Ave., Hoquiam**
**(360) 532-8161**

One of the largest hotels in Grays Harbor, the Westwood Inn offers 65 rooms in the heart of Hoquiam. The inn, which opened in the 1970s, has both smoking and non-smoking rooms, all with either one queen- and one king-size bed or two queen-size beds. Rooms all offer cable TV with HBO, phones, and tub and shower combinations. Twelve rooms include full kitchens with separate bedrooms, making them more like apartments than hotel rooms. The inn also has guest laundry facilities. Pets are allowed, with small animals adding $5 per night to the bill and larger animals adding $10 per night.

## Insiders' Tip

Check the weather reports before heading to Grays Harbor. Storms rolling in from the west off the Pacific Ocean dump a major load of rain in the Grays Harbor area before rising up and over the Olympic Mountains.

# Bed and Breakfast Inns

Some of the most historic buildings in Grays Harbor serve as bed and breakfast inns— from Hoquiam's Castle Bed and Breakfast and the Lytle House Bed and Breakfast next door, to The Cooney Mansion just south of Aberdeen. Each of the five inns highlighted here has something special to offer guests, whether it be antiques or details about the special history of the house.

The allure of a bed and breakfast inn lies with the fact that someone coddles you, makes sure you are comfortable and cared for, and cooks you a delicious, warming breakfast to help you on your way. Occasionally you may have to share a bathroom. These inns have a charm that few hotels can hope to capture. It's almost like home, but someone else does the cleaning and cooking!

Since the proprietors of bed and breakfast inns are opening their homes to strangers as well as trying to provide a restful atmosphere, most don't allow smoking, children under age 12, or pets. Some will allow pets and children by prior arrangement. If you are allergic to animals, you may want to check with your hosts to see if they have or allow pets. Most accept major credit cards, and some will ask for a credit card to hold the reservation. If the inn does not accept credit cards we have noted that with the price code.

Each bed and breakfast listed provides a special home-cooked breakfast. Some innkeepers serve breakfast in bed, others serve it family style in a formal dining room or breakfast nook. You may be treated to a secret family recipe such as yummy chocolate banana bread. Or maybe it will be a well-known breakfast favorite with a twist like a smoked salmon and brie omelette, baked cheese and chile casserole, French toast with homemade berry syrup, or even thick, comforting oatmeal with a dried fruit compote. You can also expect to see fresh fruit, toast, and homemade jam, as well as gourmet coffee, tea, and fruit juice on every table. Most innkeepers will accommodate special-needs diets or serve breakfast earlier or later if arrangements are made in advance. No matter what the situation, find out when and where breakfast is served, as it's a special part of the bed and breakfast experience.

# Price Code

Our price code reflects the average price of a double-occupancy room during the peak season, which runs from mid-May to mid-October. Room rates are usually discounted from late fall to early spring. Prices exclude state and local sales taxes.

$............. under $65
$$ ............. $65–$95
$$$ ........... $96–$140
$$$$ .......... over $141

**The Abel House**    **$$**
**117 Fleet St. S., Montesano**
**(360) 249-6002**

Located near the Grays Harbor County Courthouse near downtown Montesano, the Abel House bed and breakfast inn features a mix of Victorian style and all the modern conveniences. In addition to the five guest rooms, each appointed with a king- or queen-size bed, the inn offers a guest lounge with a pool table and games and those who make reservations ahead of time can enjoy afternoon tea. Each room is decorated with a Victorian theme. The rooms also contain TVs and VCRs, and guests can check the library of videos for films to watch during their stay.

The Abel House serves a full country breakfast, with juice, fruit, bread, and main courses ranging from waffles to sausage and eggs with hash browns. The inn does not allow pets, but kids are welcome.

**Directions:** From Washington Highway 12, take the Main Street exit into Montesano. Go north on Main St. to Broadway Street East. Turn left onto Broadway St. East, then take the next left onto Fleet Street. The Abel House is on the right-hand side of the street.

**Aberdeen Mansion Inn Bed and Breakfast**
**$$–$$$**
**807 N. M St., Aberdeen**
**(360) 533-7079, (888) 533-7079**
**www.aberdeenmansionbb.com**

Built in 1905 by one of the area's lumber barons, the Aberdeen Mansion Inn Bed and Breakfast offers five rooms inside the turreted house with a nautical theme. The master suite is a spacious 500 square feet, with wood floors, a crystal chandelier, and a bathroom, once the maid's work room, with both a tub and a two-headed shower. The suite and two of the rooms have their own bathrooms, while the other two share a bathroom. All of the rooms include TVs and VCRs, and guests can check the video library for something to watch during their stay. In addition to the main house, a carriage house offers a full kitchen with two guest rooms and a common room, and it is the only part of the establishment open to visitors with children.

The Aberdeen Mansion serves a two-course breakfast, with fruit, bread, yogurt, and a main course such as stuffed French toast with meat on the side. Pets are not allowed at the inn.

**Directions:** On the corner of West 5th Street and North M Street, the inn is most easily reached by following the signs on U.S. Highway 101 for the "Historic Aberdeen Mansion."

**The Cooney Mansion Bed & Breakfast   $$**
**1705 5th St., Cosmopolis**
**(360) 533-0602, (800) 977-7823**
**www.cooneymansion.com**

Once known as the Spruce Cottage, this huge, 10,000-square-foot inn just south of Aberdeen in Cosmopolis, has only been a bed and breakfast inn since 1982. But the building itself is on the State and National Historical Registers, as it dates from 1908. The Cooney family once owned the largest sawmill in the world, and the family built the house in a mission- and arts-and-crafts style, with spruce paneling in some rooms. Some of the fixtures in the house, such as the bathtubs, came around the horn of South America by ship before being installed in the inn.

The inn keepers offer five rooms with private baths and three with shared baths. The rooms have queen- or king-size beds and offer all the amenities that bed and breakfast inn guests would expect. Breakfasts at the mansion are best classified as lumberjack breakfasts served family style, with three courses including fruit, juice, pastries, and entrees such as Lumber Baron Potatoes or a breakfast turnover with ham, cheese, and onions.

The Cooney Mansion does not allow pets, but children over the age of 12 are welcome. There is a $25 per night charge for extra guests in a room, and the inn doesn't accept checks.

**Directions:** Driving west into Aberdeen, take a left and follow the signs for Cosmopolis and Raymond on U.S. Highway 101. Upon entering Cosmopolis, follow the signs for Cooney Mansion and turn right onto C Street. At 5th Street turn left and drive up the hill to the mansion.

**Hoquiam's Castle   $$$**
**515 Chenault Ave., Hoquiam**
**(360) 533-2005, (877) 542-2785**
**www.hoquiamcastle.com**

One of the newest bed and breakfast inns in Grays Harbor is housed in one of the best-known historic buildings in the area—Hoquiam's Castle. The inn served as a museum until May of 2000, when the owners decided to open five rooms with

*Hoquiam's Castle is open for tours and it serves as a bed and breakfast inn.* PHOTO: ROB McNAIR-HUFF

private baths for overnight guests. Built in 1897, the castle is decorated in period furnishings, from furniture to clothing on display to the mirrors on the walls. Since the castle sits on the hillside above Hoquiam, some of the rooms do offer views of the harbor, the garden on the castle grounds, and Lytle House Bed and Breakfast Inn next door. Besides the view and antiques inside, each room has either a queen- or king-size bed, and while TVs are not available in each room, those who want to watch a show can stop by the den on the third floor to view TV. Hoquiam's Castle allows children 12 and older to stay, but guests are not allowed to have their pets stay in the inn along with them. There is a $15 per night additional charge for extra guests in a room.

Breakfasts at the castle are served until 9:30 AM at each guest's convenience, except for Sunday brunch. The menu usually includes fruit, muffins, scones, granola, yogurt, and main courses such as an herbed omelette or crepes. At 9 PM, guests can also enjoy tea, coffee, and sherry along with home made desserts.

Hoquiam's Castle is also open for daily tours, between 11 AM and 3 PM. Tours begin every hour on the hour, and they last about 30 minutes. The tour costs $4 for adults, $3 for seniors, and $2.50 for children between the ages of 5 and 12. Guests can also choose to have tea before or after the tour for a package price of $10.

**Directions:** Once in Hoquiam, follow the signs to get on WA Highway 109 heading toward Ocean Shores. Drive two blocks after starting down WA 109 and turn right onto Garfield Avenue. Take this to the top of the hill to Chenault Avenue and Hoquiam's Castle, and park either in the driveway or on the street below.

**Lytle House Bed & Breakfast     $$$**
**509 Chenault Ave., Hoquiam**
**(360) 533-2320, (800) 677-2320**
**www.LytleHouse.com**

Music lovers will enjoy a stay at the Lytle House Bed and Breakfast inn. Built around 1900, it was once owned by Hoquiam's grocer-turned-lumber-baron, Joseph Lytle. Open as an inn since 1984, it features a grand piano built in 1847 that guests are invited to play in the music room, as well as two parlors—one holding a TV and one appointed with reading lamps. The inn has eight guest rooms. Children are allowed to stay, but pets are not. There is no need for pet lovers to feel dismay though. They can wander outside to pet the English Angora rabbit, Tangles, or say hi to one of the three cats or the dog that call the Lytle House home.

Rooms at the Lytle House have queen-size beds, with two rooms containing additional twin beds as well. The rooms don't have their own TVs, but guests can view TV in the parlor. Breakfast is held each morning between 7:30 and 9 A.M., scheduled at the guests' convenience. The menu includes such main courses as omelettes, Dutch babies, or three differ-

*Lytle House Bed and Breakfast.* PHOTO: ROB McNAIR-HUFF

ent kinds of French toast. Meals are also served with fruit and a choice of teas or coffee. Guests may elect to sit at individual tables or at the large, family-style dining table.

**Directions:** Once in Hoquiam, follow the signs to get on WA Highway 109 heading toward Ocean Shores. Drive two blocks after starting down WA 109 and turn right onto Garfield Avenue. Take this to the top of the hill to Chenault Avenue and turn left to find parking for the Lytle House.

# Restaurants

Fitting with its history as an area full of lumbermen, restaurants in Grays Harbor tend to serve hearty portions of home-style cooking, with dishes ranging from steak and potatoes to fresh seafood from regional suppliers.

## Price Code

Our price code reflects the average price of a single meal excluding drinks, tips, and taxes. Unless noted otherwise the restaurants accept most major credit cards. Many do not accept out-of-state checks, so ask your server.

$ . . . . . . . . . . . . . .under $10
$$ . . . . . . . . . . . . . .$10–$15
$$$ . . . . . . . . . . . . .$16–$20
$$$$ . . . . . . . . . . . .over $21

**The Bee Hive Restaurant    $$**
**300 S. Main St., Montesano**
**(360) 431-1249**

Dine in a family atmosphere on Main Street at the Bee Hive Restaurant. Started in 1934 in a tent on the same corner where the restaurant stands today, the Bee Hive offers hearty breakfasts, sandwiches, and burgers for lunch, and steaks and seafood for dinner. For breakfast, try the Bee Hive Skillet—eggs with chopped green onions and ham scrambled in and topped with cheddar cheese and served with hash browns and toast. If you wander by for lunch or dinner, try the Dungeness crab–stuffed mushrooms before digging in to pasta, steak, or seafood.

**Bridges Restaurant    $$$–$$$$**
**112 N. G St., Aberdeen**
**(360) 532-6563**

Located just off the main drag and on the west end of the bridge over the Hoquiam River, Bridges Restaurant specializes in prime rib and steak, as well as regional specialties such as seafood. Check out the Steak Bridges, a center-cut filet with crab meat, sautéed mushrooms, bacon, and hollandaise sauce. Bridges also serves fresh oysters grown locally just for them, along with razor clams and other seafood dishes. If steak or seafood don't tickle your fancy, choose from their selection of burgers, salads, chicken entrees, or sandwiches. Bridges Restaurant also serves wine and cocktails.

**Duffy's Family Restaurants    $$–$$$**
**1605 Simpson Ave., Aberdeen**
**(360) 532-3842, (360) 532-8288**

Duffy's is so popular in Grays Harbor that the restaurant has three locations, all along the main drag through Aberdeen and Hoquiam. In addition to the location above, the restaurant is also at 1212 E. Wishkah Street in Aberdeen (360-538-0606) and at 825 Simpson Avenue in Hoquiam (360-532-1519). Duffy's serves family-style food, with dinners featuring seafood, pasta, and prime rib, and breakfasts including razor clams and eggs, hot cakes, and ten types of omelettes. The lunch menu includes burgers and cold sandwiches, and homemade pies are ready and waiting after any meal, including wild blackberry, apple, walnut, or cream pies. Duffy's is wheelchair accessible.

**El Rancho Family Mexican Restaurant    $$**
**216 S. Main St., Montesano**
**(360) 249-5500**

Dig into authentic Mexican cuisine at the El Rancho Family Mexican Restaurant in Montesano. El Rancho, which also has restaurants in Ocean Shores, Elma, Hoquiam, and Seattle, serves house specialties such as tacos al carbon—two soft tacos filled with either marinated beef or chicken served with sour cream, guacamole, rice, and beans. Start your meal with a quesadilla or taquitos rancheros appetizer, and be sure to save room at the end of the meal for a Mexican dessert such as sopapillas—quartered flour tortillas deep fried to a golden brown and

> ## Insiders' Tip
>
> A replica of the *Lady Washington*, the eighteenth-century brigantine that first explored Grays Harbor in 1792, makes its home in the Grays Harbor Historical Seaport in Aberdeen. It is open for tours between 10 A.M. and 5 P.M. daily when the ship is in port.

then drizzled with honey, cinnamon, and sugar.

**Savory Faire    $$**
**135 S. Main St., Montesano**
**(360) 249-3701**

This restaurant may look small from the outside, but step inside and you can tell you are in a place devoted to good food. Try an omelette, scramble, or French toast on the breakfast menu, or stop by for lunch and dig into a Caesar salad, or one of the cold sandwiches. You might want to try the soup of the day or the black bean chicken chili. Savory Faire also sells gift items and wine. The establishment is closed on Saturdays and Sundays.

# Shopping

Bring your car and prepare to wander throughout each of the major cities in Grays Harbor to shop. Thanks to the sprawling nature of Aberdeen and Hoquiam, there is no true shopping district in either town. Montesano, as the smallest of the three cities, does have more centralized shopping.

In this section we list the independent shops and antiques stores that are unique to Grays Harbor. There is more shopping in the area though. Stop by the Southshore Mall for more standard fare from stores such as Staples, Emporium, Factory 2-U, Ace Hardware, and Wal-Mart.

**Country Tyme**
**316 Main St. S., Montesano**
**(360) 249-5588**

Wander into this gift shop and home decor store to browse a wide array of collectibles in the heart of Montesano. Country Tyme features lighthouses, Boyds bears, Precious Moments, and a selection of Yankee candles. Shoppers can also stop by around the holidays for seasonal items.

**The Gift Haus**
**601 W. Wishkah, Aberdeen**
**(360) 532-8261**

Collectibles such as Hummel figurines and Boyds bears are among the items featured at The Gift Haus. The shop also has a bridal registry, where the soon-to-be-wed can select kitchen items and flatware they want to receive. The shop also sells coffee tables.

**Grand Heron**
**200 E. Heron Ave., Aberdeen**
**(360) 532-5561**

Antique furniture and home decor items are the highlights at the Grand Heron. The shop specializes in gifts and decorating accessories, such as pillows, tassels, and small furniture.

**Judy's Antiques & Collectibles**
**401 W. Market, Aberdeen**
**(360) 532-4359**

Owners Leonard and Judy Carney buy and sell paper dolls, records, trade tokens, and old books in their Aberdeen shop, which is open every day except Wednesdays. The shop also offers Grays Harbor area memorabilia and antique jewelry.

**Keepsake Cottage**
**519 N. Maple, Aberdeen**
**(360) 532-1863**

Looking for kitchen gadgets from years past? Then stop by Keepsake Cottage. The shop, owned by Christy and Rovena Brooks, also offers other antiques and

> ## Insiders' Tip
> Hoquiam is home to Olympic Stadium, a 6,000 seat wooden stadium built as a New Deal WPA project. The stadium is still used today for athletic events.

collectibles, such as cookie molds and linens. The first room features an incredible assortment of kitchen gadgets.

**La Vogue Department Store**
**623 Simpson Ave., Hoquiam**
**(360) 532-2310**

Practically a museum to department store shopping, La Vogues has modern goods for sale right next to "state-of-the-art" toys and household items from the 1950s and 1960s. As if that mix isn't enough to pull people in the doors of this unique store, there is also a bike shop on the premises. If you are a fan of shopping and history, this store is worth a visit. One life-long area resident describes shopping at La Vogue as the quintessential Grays Harbor experience.

**Many Moons Antiques & Desirables**
**2701 Simpson Ave., Hoquiam**
**(360) 538-1809**

Antiques and decorating items from Asia are the specialty at owner Donna Shine's unique shop in Hoquiam. Well known to drivers who pass by because of the Statue of Liberty light outside the front door, Many Moons also features a selection of books, Oriental fans, and select furniture items. Shine's philosophy about what she sells in the shop is basic: She buys the wares simply if she likes them.

*Thousands of shore birds descend on the Grays Harbor National Wildlife Refuge each spring.* PHOTO: ROB McNAIR-HUFF

**Out on a Whim**
**208 S. Broadway, Aberdeen**
**(360) 537-9905**

Stop by Out on a Whim to buy cards, jewelry, locally made beaded and metal toys, hair clips, purses, and photo frames.

**People's Emporium Antiques**
**2200 Simpson Ave., Hoquiam**
**(360) 532-9129**

Since opening in 1991, People's Emporium Antiques has served up local antiques such as fishing creels, handcrafted stick furniture, and depression glass. The two-floor shop also sells old comics and a wide array of furniture. The shop is closed on Mondays and Tuesdays.

**Insiders' Tip**

Public art plays a large roll in Grays Harbor. The county holds more than 40 murals depicting the history of the area.

# Shelton

Hotels and Motels

Restaurants

Shopping

Since its formation as the only incorporated city in Mason County in 1889, Shelton has seen its fortunes rise and fall along with the nearby timberlands that are the lifeblood of the local economy. Now a community of 7,700 people, Shelton remains tied to forestry, with the Simpson Timber Company providing the bulk of employment in town. The town and its surrounding areas are also tied to the sea, with businesses in nearby Oakland Bay and Hood Canal shipping shellfish to restaurants around the Pacific Northwest and beyond.

Mason County is home to more than 48,000 people, and it is one of the fastest growing counties in Washington.

Fitting with its logging heritage, Shelton hosts the annual Forest Festival Parade and other timber-related activities on the first weekend of each June. Other annual events include the Mason County Fair on the last weekend of July, and the Oysterfest in September, each held at the Mason County Fairgrounds in Shelton. To pick up a current calendar of events and a free map, stop by the Shelton-Mason County Chamber of Commerce. It's located in the Peninsula Railway Caboose #700, which is right in front of the post office on Railroad Avenue and is on the National Register of Historic Places.

## Hotels and Motels

Lodging options are pretty limited in Shelton and the surrounding area. We include two hotels in this chapter.

## Price Code

Our price code reflects the average price of a double-occupancy room during the peak season, which runs from mid-May to mid-October. Room rates are usually discounted from late fall to early spring. The prices quoted do not take into account the state and local sales taxes.

$ . . . . . . . . . . . . . .under $60
$$ . . . . . . . . . . . . .$60–$90
$$$ . . . . . . . . . . .$91–$130
$$$$ . . . . . . . . . .over $131

**Shelton Inn Hotel     $**
**626 Railroad Ave., Shelton**
**(360) 426-4468, (800) 451-4560**

Located downtown and within walking distance of everything on Railroad Avenue, the Shelton Inn Hotel offers 30 rooms including two with complete kitchens. Each room has a queen-size bed, cable TV, telephone, air-conditioning, and a coffeemaker. And from June to September, guests can use the outdoor swimming pool. The Shelton Inn Hotel does allow pets in some rooms for an additional $7 per night, and there is also a $7 charge for an extra person in a room.

**Shelton Super 8 Motel     $$**
**6 Northview Circle, Shelton**
**(360) 426-1654**

Since opening in 1992, the Shelton Super 8 Motel has offered thirty-eight rooms to the traveling public. Each room includes a queen-size bed, cable TV, phone, air-conditioning, and refrigerator, along with a complimentary newspaper in the morning and coffee in the lobby. The motel offers two wheelchair-accessible rooms, and pets are allowed in some rooms for a one-time charge of between $15 and $25 per visit (depending on the size of the pet). The motel charges $7 per night for additional guests in a room.

## Insiders' Tip

For the first 10 years of its existence, the county that contains Shelton was known as Sahewamish County.

# Restaurants

Shelton is a lumber town, and logging and working in a mill is hard work. Loggers burn a lot of calories wielding a chain saw, and when it's time to eat they're pretty hungry. You won't leave these restaurants hungry. Most of the restaurants in Shelton serve country-style dinners such as chicken fried steak and roast beef, but you'll also be able to feast on oysters and fresh seafood. Shelton also has two premiere restaurants, Xinh's Clam and Oyster House is known across Western Washington, and Steven's Fine Dining is where folks eat when they want to dress up.

# Price Code

Our price code reflects the average price of a single meal excluding drinks, tips, and tax. Unless noted otherwise, the restaurants accept most major credit cards. Many do not accept out-of-state checks, so ask your server.

$ . . . . . . . . . . . . . .under $10
$$ . . . . . . . . . . . . .$10–$15
$$$ . . . . . . . . . . . .$16–$20
$$$$ . . . . . . . . . . .over $20

**El Sarape**    $$
318 Railroad Ave., Shelton
(360) 426-4294

Sit down to a meal of traditional Mexican dishes in this roomy restaurant. The walls are decorated with sarapes, hats, and frescoes, and the food is filling and spicy. Try one of the house specialties, such as the enchiladas sonora—two chicken enchiladas, one covered in mole sauce and the other in chipotle sauce served with rice and beans—or the fiesta dinner, a char-broiled New York steak served with an enchilada, rice, and beans. The restaurant also features some unique seafood dishes such as the seafood chimichanga that is stuffed with shrimp, crab, and halibut. Vegetarians will appreciate the selection of meat-free dishes. In addition to the specialties, El Sarape serves traditional Mexican lunch and dinner items.

**Hattie Rose Café**    $$
405 W. Railroad Ave., Shelton
(360) 426-4113

Pull up a painted chair and sit down to one of the tables covered with vintage linens at the Hattie Rose Café. The cafe serves breakfast pastries as well as omelettes, salads, and hot and cold sandwiches. Try the Big Juicy Brie Burger with onion jam or the sausage linguine. The cafe also serves homemade soups. You'll feel just like you're eating in Grandma's kitchen.

**Hungry Bear Steak House**    $$–$$$
102 W. Railroad Ave., Shelton
(360) 426-1101

Steaks and seafood share center stage on the menu for the Hungry Bear Steak House in downtown Shelton. All steaks, from the 12-ounce New York to the 20-ounce rib eye are served with sautéed mushrooms, soup, salad, and potatoes. Alternatively, diners can choose from a seafood menu including deep-fried prawns, scallops, or clam strips. The menu also features the giant bivalve, the geoduck, in addition to hot sandwiches and burgers. For breakfast you can order

the Hangtown Fry to get your daily serving of oysters, or settle for more typical breakfast fare including eggs, pancakes, and French toast. You may enter the Hungry Bear hungry for breakfast, lunch, or dinner, but the huge servings will ensure you don't leave that way, and if you have room left for dessert, try one of the homemade fruit pies.

**Kobe Teriyaki**    $$
118 W. Alder, Shelton
(360) 432-0533

Get a taste of authentic Japanese teriyaki in downtown Shelton at Kobe Teriyaki. In addition to the standby chicken or beef teriyaki, diners can sample yakisoba or tempura dishes. Kobe also serves sushi in its simple store-front restaurant. Kobe Teriyaki is closed on Sundays.

**Ming Tree Café**    $$
423 W. Railroad Ave., Shelton
(360) 426-4423

Sample a wide range of fried rice or the pan-fried noodles at the Ming Tree Café downtown. The restaurant also features egg foo young and chow mein, but the menu doesn't stop there. Traditional American cuisine such as pork chops, steak, seafood, and burgers also share space at the Ming Tree. The Ming Tree Café doesn't accept credit cards.

**Steven's Fine Dining   $$$**
**203 W. Railroad Ave., Shelton**
**(360) 426-4407**

Step into a setting appointed with antiques and dig into a meal such as the Dungeness Bay Casserole, made with mushrooms, bacon, scallops, crab, and cream cheese, at Steven's Fine Dining. Steven's also offers a variety of appetizers, including crab and artichoke dip, oyster stew, or French onion soup. Cap the meal with a glass of wine, an Italian soda, or something from the full-service bar. Steven's Fine Dining is Shelton's most formal restaurant, but it still provides a comfortable and relaxed atmosphere.

**Timbers Restaurant   $$**
**628 W. Railroad Ave., Shelton**
**(360) 426-8757**

Fans of old-fashioned American food will eat up the atmosphere and menu items at the Timbers. The restaurant, located next door to the Shelton Inn, offers steaks, ham, chicken, and seafood. Try the chicken fried steak, or an open-faced oyster sandwich. Or, if you are in the mood for breakfast, try the stuffed potatoes with bacon, onion, tomato, mushrooms, and cheese. The Timbers also features homemade soups, and those of drinking age can have a cocktail, beer, or wine.

**Xinh's Clam and Oyster House   $$$**
**221 W. Railroad Ave., Shelton**
**(360) 427-8709**

Widely regarded as one of the best seafood restaurants in Western Washington, Xinh's specializes in oysters—pan-fried oysters, oyster stew, baby oysters topped with black beans and bacon, fresh Pacific oysters, and oysters on the half shell. Not in the mood for oysters? Then try one of the dishes featuring clams, mussels, prawns, or catfish. Diners can also opt for chicken curry or thin sliced beef with black bean sauce. Be sure to check the appetizer menu for items such as Thai crab cakes or fresh egg rolls.

## Insiders' Tip

At one point in time, three railroads operated in Mason County, all working to transport timber from the woods to the mills.

# Shopping

Shelton is a small town, and the prospects for shopping are limited, but an afternoon on Railroad Avenue will provide you with a few diversions. Take a break from shopping to wander through the Mason County Historical Museum.

**Frontier Antiques**
**317 S. First St., Shelton**
**(360) 426-7795**

Furniture, tools, and jewelry share this extensive space with the ever-present overseer, Bullwinkle the moose. The walls are hung with paintings, prints, and other wall art in addition to several other stuffed animal heads. As you wander deeper into the shop you'll find china and

even more furniture, dolls, games, and books. The shop, owned and operated by Joseph and Annette Kiser, specializes in taxidermy and lighting.

**Lynch Creek Floral**
**331 W. Railroad Ave., Shelton**
**(360) 426-8615**

Browse the selection of cards for all occasions or pick up gift items such as tea cups

*Bronze art works cover the grounds outside and are sold inside the Kimberly T. Gallery outside Shelton.*

PHOTO: ROB McNAIR-HUFF

and teapots, candles, or potpourris along with your flowers at Lynch Creek Floral. You can sit and sip an espresso made on the spot while you wait for your flowers to be arranged. The shop is closed on Sundays.

**Kimberly T. Gallery & Sculpture Garden**
**50 W. Fredson Rd., Shelton**
**(360) 427-3857, (888) 821-0372**
**www.thebronzeworks.com**

Bronze sculptures take center stage at the Kimberly T. Gallery & Sculpture Garden alongside Highway 101. Since it opened in 1995, the gallery that is part of The Bronze Works has served as a repository for fine art. Stop by on a Tuesday or Thursday to watch art being made before your eyes during one of the bronze pours, where artisans pour molten bronze into molds to create new works. Then browse the finished art in the sculpture garden outside or wander into the gallery to buy a piece. Visitors are invited to take a self-guided window tour of the foundry or to ask questions about the "lost wax" process used to create the molds for the bronze sculptures.

**Old Town Hobby**
**221 W. Railroad Ave., Shelton**
**(360) 432-1026**

From artist's supplies to model kits and games, Old Town Hobby has something for the hobbyist and kid in all of us. Located across from the red caboose on Railroad Avenue, the shop also features Matchbox collectibles, rubber stamps and ink supplies, and kites. Old Town Hobby is closed on Sundays and Mondays.

**Railroad Avenue Antique Mall**
**321 W. Railroad Ave., Shelton**
**(360) 432-8893**

High-quality furniture such as hutches and dining sets share space with vintage trunks and quilts among the antiques and collectibles at the Railroad Avenue

# Close-up

## Log Rush!

When the first white explorers sailed around the Olympic Peninsula they remarked about the denseness of its forests. When the first settlers built their cabins on the shores they found it difficult to battle the forest to find a clearing for building their cabins. Once the Olympic Peninsula was covered shore to shore in thick, nearly impassable forests. Only the highest reaches of the Olympic Mountains and the low shorelines were free of trees. Trees fed, clothed, and sheltered the Native Americans, who were the first loggers. They cut down trees and used fallen trees to build their dugout canoes, and they split long lengths of cedar to make siding for their longhouses.

By the time the Peninsula was inundated by the white settlers, the country was in dire need of good timber. The Eastern forests had long ago been decimated by settlers, and the wood-hungry nation had over logged the forests of the Midwest as well. So when word spread about the gigantic and plentiful evergreen trees blanketing the Peninsula, there was a veritable rush on the forests. Loggers and lumbermen came from all over to set up logging operations and erect mills on the shores of Puget Sound. Logging and lumber production made most of the Peninsula's towns, including Shelton, where the Simpson Lumber Company sits at the end of the town's main street.

By 1853 two rudimentary commercial sawmills had been erected on the northeast tip of the Peninsula—one at Port Ludlow and the other by the first residents of Port Townsend. They were antiquated water-driven affairs that seemed to be down for maintenance as often as they were cutting logs into lumber. Then in September 1853, Cyrus Walker, a representative of the Pope and Talbot Company—a prosperous New England lumber company—opened the first "high-speed" steam mill on the northwestern corner of the Kitsap Peninsula at Port Gamble. The mill cut 15,000 feet of lumber each day, and earned more than $70,000 in its first year. After that, there was no looking back. The log rush was on, and mills started popping up everywhere as the trees started disappearing. It seemed as if the trees would last forever.

Loggers and mill workers worked long days in dangerous conditions. Many men lost their arms to saw blades or their lives to logs flying through the air. The early loggers did everything by hand in a drawn-out process. First, brush cutters went into the woods to clear the undergrowth. Next, the loggers moved in to cut the giant trees. They set springboards near the base of the tree and then used axes—crosscut saws arrived on scene in the 1870s—to cut huge notches into the trees; the notches were large enough that a full-grown man could lie or sit in the empty space. Then, the loggers would set the springboards on the opposite side of the tree and chop or saw until the tree began to crack. A shouted "Timber-r-r" rang through the woods before the tree came crashing down. Then the limbers moved in to trim all the branches off before the logs were cut into manageable lengths and the bark was peeled so the log would move more easily over the skid road. The log was then hitched to a team of oxen and dragged to the water, where it was stored before a steamboat dragged the raft of collected logs to the mills. Logging has changed since then—Caterpillars have replaced oxen, chain saws have replaced axes, and log trucks carry the logs to market—but it is still dangerous.

As the loggers cut more and more, the increasing hunger for wood was so fierce that President Grover Cleveland set aside two-thirds of the Peninsula's trees in a timber reserve. Later, President Theodore Roosevelt turned part of the reserve into the Olympic National Park. The trees in the park will never be logged, but the trees in the reserve have been extensively logged. With each passing decade, the logging increased. Logging rates jumped after the railroads were built, and lumber production increased by astronomical rates during both world wars. By the 1980s most of the trees between the shores and the mountains had been logged and replaced by a ragged patchwork quilt of clear-cuts, stump forests, second-growth monoculture forests, and a few remaining patches of old-growth, virgin timber. Most of the giants were gone, and a little owl, the northern spotted owl, had lost most of its habitat and was in danger of extinction. Environmentalists rallied around the owl. Loggers, mill workers, and log truck drivers rallied around their jobs as they continued to reach for the last of the big trees. Logging on the Peninsula has slowed down due to a lack of resources and increased regulation, but the logging has not stopped. Environmentalists continue to try to protect the few remaining stands of virgin forest while the lumber companies continue to try to purchase rights to log on public lands and log the second- and third-growth plantation forests. This battle for the last of the old-growth giants is a battle that is sure to continue even though the log rush has ended.

Antique Mall. Aside from the extensive and well-organized collection of antiques, the mall also sells pizza by the slice or whole, cinnamon rolls, coffee, and espresso.

### Wildlife Attractions—A Nature Store
### 221 W. Railroad Ave., Suite C, Shelton
### (360) 426-4926

If you are looking for a creative outdoor project to do with kids or for supplies for your birdfeeder, Wildlife Attractions is a must-see on Railroad Avenue. The shop offers books, posters, and tapes on local wildlife. And be sure to check the variety of nesting boxes, birdbaths, and feeders.

> **Insiders' Tip**
> Need to get something done on a Sunday? Be sure to call ahead to make sure that the shop you want to visit is open.

*A great blue heron watches for fish along the eastern shore of Hood Canal.* PHOTO: ROB McNAIR-HUFF

# Hood Canal

Hotels and Motels

Bed and Breakfast Inns

Restaurants

Shopping

Originally named Hood's Channel by Captain George Vancouver in 1792, Hood Canal is not actually a canal. Before the last Ice Age, it was a river valley. Glaciers deepened the valley, and as they receded, an ice-dammed lake formed over the valley and much of the Kitsap Peninsula until the ice dam melted. As the last Ice Age ended, the sea level rose and water filled the fjord that is Hood Canal.

The Twana, the region's first inhabitants, settled along the small rim of land between the Olympic range and the water. Later, the Salish moved in along the south end of the canal. Today, their descendants live at the southern most tip of the canal on the Skokomish Reservation, which was allotted in the 1855 treaty of Point No Point.

Below the warm, protected waters of Hood Canal lies one of the world's richest and unique oceanic ecosystems, much to the delight of anglers, shellfish gatherers, and scuba divers. Divers from around the world brave the depths to see the giant Pacific octopus, wolf eel, colorful anemones, nudibranch, scallops, crab, and starfish. Those who prefer to stay above the water also enjoy the bounty of the sea as they fish for salmon or cod, drop crab pots, or gather shrimp, clams, oysters, even the infamous geoduck (pronounced gooeyduck), one of the world's biggest clams. The world's largest oyster hatchery, Coast Seafoods Company in Quilcene, ships oysters around the world. Hood Canal oysters are renowned for their sweet, delicate flavor, otherwise known as perfection. Birds also find the area to be a pleasant winter home, and seals, sea lions, and the occasional otter live here year-round. On one morning drive to the south end of the canal, we saw five great blue heron, a bald eagle, a golden eagle, two otters swimming along the shore, harlequin ducks, plovers, several ravens and crows, and so many salmon jumping that we lost count.

Kayaking may be one of the best ways to see the wildlife, but two drier locations on the canal offer prime wildlife-viewing spots. On the east side, near Belfair, stop at the 135-acre Hood Canal/Theler wetlands and walk along the 3.5 mile, wheelchair-accessible trail. Just north of Brinnon on the west side of the canal, stop at Seal Rock for easy beach access, another wheelchair-accessible trail, and impressive views of Mt. Rainier. To get a glimpse of one of the most amazing views in the region, drive to the top of Mt. Walker. Those in good hiking condition can also hike a challenging four-mile trail to the summit. On a clear day you can see forever, or at least all the way to Seattle to the north, and across the Olympic range to the west and south. Make the drive in May and early June for a floral display of the state flower, the rhododendron.

The wonders of the area don't stop at the shoreline. Mountain bikers will find several trails on U.S. Forest Service land, and just west of Hoodsport, Lake Cushman features fishing, boating, and more scuba diving. Alternatively, make your way to the Olympic National Park to camp or hike along the Hamma Hamma, Dosewallips, and Duckabush Rivers as well as at Staircase near the headwaters of the Skokomish River. Several scenic waterfalls are also tucked along the route.

Although most people come to Hood Canal for the recreational outlets, the Olympic Music Festival also draws crowds on weekends from late June to early September. Music lovers from every corner of the state gather in an old barn to listen to musicians from around the world.

We have organized the listings in this chapter beginning with establishments located at the south end of the canal and heading north. To reach the towns of Union and Belfair, go east on Washington Highway 106, which also leads to the Kitsap Peninsula.

# Hotels and Motels

Hood Canal is a recreation destination. Campgrounds and RV parks far outnumber hotels and motels. As a result, in the summer and on weekends during fishing season, lodging may be hard to find, especially if you don't have reservations. If you are unable to find a room during your trip along the canal, we recommend driving to Shelton to the south or Port Townsend or Sequim to the north. Unless otherwise noted, all hotels listed here offer smoking and nonsmoking rooms as well as at least one wheelchair-accessible room.

## Price Code

Our price code reflects the average price of a double-occupancy room during peak season, which runs from mid-May to mid-October. Room rates are usually discounted from late fall to early spring. Prices exclude state and local sales taxes.

$ . . . . . . . . . . . . . .under $60
$$ . . . . . . . . . . . . . .$60–$90
$$$ . . . . . . . . . . .$91–$130
$$$$ . . . . . . . . . .over $131

**Alderbrook Inn    $$$**
**7101 WA Hwy. 106, Union**
**(360) 898-2200, (800) 622-9370**
**www.alderbrookresort.com**

A stay at the family-friendly Alderbrook Inn, originally a logging camp, is an adventure waiting to happen. Spend your day walking one of the many trails on the 525-acre campus, play a round of golf, or a game of tennis, volleyball, or horseshoes. Finish the day with a swim in the indoor pool or soak away your worries in the Jacuzzi. The 1,200-foot dock provides plenty of space for fishing or crabbing, and outdoor swimming, as well as ample moorage if you choose to arrive by boat, or rent one from the inn. Sometimes it can be hard to find fine dining on Hood Canal, but Alderbrook has taken care of

that problem with a waterfront restaurant tucked among the trees. Of course the inn also offers a wide selection of recently remodeled, spacious, and comfortable rooms: courtyard rooms, waterview rooms, and waterfront rooms and suites. For larger groups, the inn offers two-bedroom cottages with complete kitchens and large common rooms. Each cottage easily sleeps at least six adults. The inn also serves as a Christian retreat and conference center, so advanced reservations are recommended during the summer months. Children sleep free in a parent's room, but additional adult guests will need to pay $10 per night. Alderbrook Inn is a completely smoke-free establishment.

**Bayshore Motel    $**
**306142 U.S. Hwy. 101, Brinnon**
**(360) 796-4220, (800) 488-4230**

The Bayshore Motel is located above the Brinnon Senior Center, so at least you won't have to put up with music blaring past midnight, but you may hear a bit of road noise from the highway. Don't expect lush accommodations or a continental breakfast. Instead, you will find clean and spacious rooms with a retro-70s feel and a pleasant view. Rooms on the highway side of the motel have a fine view of Hood Canal. Rooms to the rear look over a private farm and red barn to the Olympics. Each room contains one or two queen-size beds, a table and chairs, a built-in desk and vanity, and cable television. Pets are accepted by prior arrangement. The motel has no wheelchair-accessible rooms.

**Glen-Ayr Canal Resort    $$**
**25381 U.S. Hwy. 101, Hoodsport**
**(360) 877-9522, (800) 367-9522**

When you stay at the Glen-Ayr Canal Resort, you'll have the privilege of digging clams and collecting oysters from a private beach, access to a private boat pier, and the company of the RVers who are also staying at the resort. On Tuesdays and Thursdays during open seasons, Glen-Ayr allows guests to gather 30 clams and 10 oysters. Each of the 15 rooms contains one or two queen-size beds and a full bathroom, plus cable TV and a table and chairs. The kitchenette suites each accommodate four people in two queen-size beds. During your stay you may want to relax in the spa or join others in the clubhouse for a game of cards or a chat in front of the fire. And because Glen-Ayr serves RVs, it also has a coin-op laundry room. Glen-Ayr asks that guests stay a minimum of two nights on weekends from March to mid-November and three nights on holiday weekends like Labor Day. Pets are allowed on the grounds but not in the motel. Additional guests may stay for an additional $10 each per night. Moorage is available by advanced reservation.

> ### Insiders' Tip
> The many trails and public beaches along Hood Canal call visitors to them. Keep hiking shoes, a first-aid kit, water, and high-energy snacks in the car or packed in a daypack so you will be ready for a short hike at a moment's notice.

**Quilcene Hotel    $**
**11 Quilcene Ave.**
**(360) 765-3868**
**www.quilceneinn.com**

Originally built in 1917 by Rose Bailey, the Quilcene Hotel claimed early fame as a resting place for loggers, hunters, and travelers. Each Saturday diners also flocked to the inn for fried chicken dinners. Today the nine-room hotel still exudes old-time charm, and at a bargain. Telephones and televisions have been removed from all the rooms, but in the sunroom downstairs, all guests may meet to chat or watch cable TV or an old movie. Guests also adjourn to the sunroom each morning to munch on a continental breakfast of muffins, orange juice, tea, and coffee. All upstairs rooms share two bathrooms, one with a claw foot bathtub. The red room, the only room located on the first floor, has a queen-size bed and a private bath. Families may want to reserve rooms six and eight, which have a door connecting them. Room six contains two double beds while room eight contains a single queen-size bed. Rooms one, three, and seven also hold queen-size beds, while room two contains two twin-size beds, room four a king-size bed, and room five a double bed. Depending on which room you choose, you'll either have a view of Mt. Walker and the Quilcene

Range or of the old maple tree in the backyard. All rooms are nonsmoking and are not wheelchair accessible.

**Sunrise Motel & Resort    $$**
**24520 U.S. Hwy. 101, Hoodsport**
**(360) 877-5301**

The Sunrise Motel & Resort takes fresh seafood to a new extreme, with an outdoor barbecue for guests to cook crabs caught off the back side of the motel, which hangs over Hood Canal. The 66-room resort is well known for its recreational amenities—an on-site underwater park for scuba divers, an air station, crabbing with free use of crab pots for guests, and boat moorage.

Sandwiched between U.S. Highway 101 to the west and Hood Canal to the east, each room offers a great water view. The main difference between the rooms is the presence of kitchens. Rooms without kitchens cost approximately $10 less than those with kitchens. There is a $10 per night fee for each additional guest.

# Bed and Breakfast Inns

The bed and breakfast craze still hasn't hit Hood Canal, although most of the other communities on the Peninsula offer a plethora of choices. Still, we found a few cozy places for the weary traveler who wants all the comforts of home.

The allure of a bed and breakfast inn lies with the fact that someone coddles you, makes sure you are comfortable and cared for, and cooks you a delicious, warming breakfast to help you on your way. Occasionally you may have to share a bathroom. These inns have a charm that few hotels can hope to capture. It's almost like home, but someone else does the cleaning and cooking!

Since the proprietors of bed and breakfast inns are opening their homes to strangers as well as trying to provide a restful atmosphere, most don't allow smoking, children under age 12, or pets. Some will allow pets and children by prior arrangement. If you are allergic to animals, you may want to check with your hosts to see if they have or allow pets. Most accept major credit cards, and some will ask for a credit card to hold the reservation. If the inn does not accept credit cards we have noted that with the price code.

Each bed and breakfast listed provides a special home-cooked breakfast. Some innkeepers serve breakfast in bed, others serve it family style in a formal dining room or breakfast nook. You may be treated to a secret family recipe such as yummy chocolate banana bread. Or maybe it will be a well-known breakfast favorite with a twist like a smoked salmon and brie omelette, baked cheese and chile casserole, French toast with homemade berry syrup, or even thick, comforting oatmeal with a dried fruit compote. You can also expect to see fresh fruit, toast, and homemade jam, as well as gourmet coffee, tea, and fruit juice on every table. Most innkeepers will accommodate special-needs diets or serve breakfast earlier or later if arrangements are made in advance. No matter what the situation, find out when and where breakfast is served, as it's a special part of the bed and breakfast experience.

# Price Code

Our price code reflects the average price of a double-occupancy room during the peak season, which runs from mid-May to mid-October. Room rates are usually discounted from late fall to early spring. Prices exclude state and local sales taxes.

$ . . . . . . . . . . . . .under $65
$$ . . . . . . . . . . . . .$65–$95
$$$ . . . . . . . . . .$96–$140
$$$$ . . . . . . . . . .over $141

**Brinnon Flats Bed and Breakfast    $**
**80 Brinnon Ln., Brinnon**
**(360) 796-4935**

A big, white house surrounded by rhododendrons and open fields, Brinnon Flats is a cozy, homey place to stay with your sweetheart or family. The two guest rooms, both on the ground floor, share a bathroom. Kate Marsh, the innkeeper, invites guests to join her in the dining room for a chat, and a heartening breakfast, or in the living room, where guests may use the TV and VCR. She recommends that guests bring their favorite videos with them. The blue room contains a double bed, while the rose room contains a queen-size bed and features large, picture windows that keep the room airy and bright. Both rooms are decorated simply with family furniture, some antique and some not. Filling breakfasts feature entrees such as cornmeal pancakes with blackberries or chicken sausage with apples, and Kate always keeps a jar of her homemade jams, jellies, or apple butter open. Pets are not allowed since the resident dog and cat like to keep the house to themselves. Leave the cigarettes in the car because smoking is not allowed.

**Directions:** From U.S. Highway 101 turn west by the Halfway House Restaurant onto Brinnon Lane. Brinnon Flats is the first house on the right. If you drive past the post office, you've gone too far.

**Elk Meadows Bed & Breakfast    $**
**3485 Dosewallips Rd., Brinnon**
**(360) 796-4886**
**www.northolympic.com/elkmeadows**

Situated on 20 acres near the Dosewallips trailhead, Elk Meadows Bed & Breakfast offers a peaceful stay in a contemporary ranch-style home. Each of the two queen bedroom suites has a private bathroom and a view of the valley. Don't be surprised to wake to see cougar or bear walking by, or to see a field full of elk or deer. In the winter, curl up next to the Russian stone fireplace to read a book or talk with your hosts. In the summer, lounge on the deck or walk around the on-site commercial nursery.

Each morning you will be greeted by a full country breakfast. Your hosts will even pack boxed lunches and snacks for day hikes and clam-digging excursions. For an extra-special evening, weather permitting, arrange for an evening campfire by the riverside. Elk Meadows does not welcome children under age 14, pets, or smoking.

**Directions:** From U.S. Highway 101, turn east onto Dosewallips Road, which is right on the north side of the Bayshore Motel. Drive 3.4 miles on the road until you see the "Baisch" mailbox on the right, turn left onto the Elk Meadows' and drive.

**House Boats for Two  $$$$**
**Pleasant Harbor Marina,**
**308913 U.S. Hwy. 101, Brinnon**
**(360) 796-3440, (800) 966-5942**
**www.houseboats4two.com**

Technically, House Boats for Two isn't a bed and breakfast inn since guests make their own breakfasts, but if romance on the water sounds great to you, this is the place to stay. Docked at Brinnon's Pleasant Harbor Marina, these houseboats are well suited to romantic getaways and celebrations like anniversaries and honeymoons, so leave the family at home. If you rent houseboat number two, you'll get a glimpse of the personal poems and cards sent between the proprietors, Elaine and Jade Michaels. Each houseboat offers a cozy getaway for two adults. Children, pets, extra guests, and smoking are not allowed. That means that you and your sweetie will have all the privacy you desire while you enjoy the bay, the rain, and the sounds of nature.

A queen-size berth accompanied by a galley stocked with a welcome package is only a small part of the luxuries offered. Relax in the evenings or on a lazy Sunday morning in plush bathrobes while you cuddle in front of the fireplace. Or perhaps you'd prefer watching a complimentary movie or listening to the stereo, both part of the entertainment center in each houseboat. Relax in the marina's spa or, from April through October, take a dip in the pool. If you prefer a more private watery interlude, fill the tub and turn on the jets in the full-sized jetted tub in your bathroom. Order pizza or stock the galley with goods from the marina's grocery store. You can even buy gifts for that special person at Linda's Gift and Video. House Boats for Two can also arrange for special treats like flowers and birthday cakes if arrangements are made in advance.

**Directions:** If you are traveling north on U.S. Highway 101, look for mile marker 309 and turn right 0.1 mile past the mile marker. If you are traveling south, turn left into the marina 0.9 mile past mile marker 309.

**Selah Inn Bed & Breakfast  $$$**
**130 NE Dulalip Landing, Belfair**
**(360) 275-0916**
**www.selahinn.com**

Fresh flowers and chocolates in each room and afternoon tea hint at the many luxuries available at the upscale Selah Inn Bed & Breakfast. Housed in a contemporary Northwest-style lodge, the inn's Shoreline Room is decorated with nautical art that complements the plush green carpet and Shaker-style queen-size bed and desk. All four rooms have private baths and comfortable sitting areas. For the ultimate in luxury, reserve the King Room, which has a canopied king-size bed, private deck, and a view of the water, plus a Jacuzzi tub and comforting fireplace. During the day you may want to chat in front of the stone fireplace in the living room or curl up with a book and a cup of tea in the library. Each morning sit down to a full breakfast, which is served on fine china at individual tables set with linens. Pat and Bonnie, the innkeepers, like to talk to their guests about what they like to eat before determining the breakfast menu. In addition to coffee, juice, and breakfast breads, the meal starts off with some crunchy granola and always includes a special entree like eggs Benedict or perhaps pancakes and sausage. Guests also are invited to enjoy a gourmet dinner at the inn, all prepared by Bonnie. Dinners must be arranged in advance, and the price of dinner is not included in the room rate. Children are welcomed only in the two cottages on the grounds, but not the main house. Goldie, the resident yellow lab, likes guests to keep their pets at home. The inn is non-smoking.

**Directions:** From U.S. Highway 101 take WA Highway 106 east to Belfair. Follow the signs in Belfair that lead to WA Highway 300 and head west about four miles and once you have passed Belfair State Park take the first left onto Beck Road. Stay on Beck Road until you reach Dulalip Landing and turn left toward the beach. Follow this road to the inn.

# Restaurants

If you want hearty portions, great shellfish, and family-style dining, you'll enjoy the restaurants along Hood Canal. The world-famous geoduck (pronounced gooeyduck) clam, which may grow up to 16 pounds and often live well more than 100 years, can be found as a special dish on some of the menus. Oysters, the specialty of the canal, are sautéed, steamed, fried, and folded into omelettes. Reservations are not required at most of these restaurants.

## Price Code

Our price code reflects the average price of a single meal excluding drinks, tips, and taxes. Unless noted otherwise, the restaurants accept most major credit cards. Many do not accept out-of-state checks, so ask your server.

$ . . . . . . . . . . . . . .under $10
$$ . . . . . . . . . . . . .$10–$15
$$$ . . . . . . . . . . . . .$16–$20
$$$$ . . . . . . . . . . .over $21

**Alderbrook Inn    $$$**
**7101 WA Hwy. 106, Union**
**(360) 898-2200, (800) 622-9370**
**www.alderbrookresort.com**

The Alderbrook Inn actually offers two restaurants. The Waterfront Restaurant serves dinner and Sunday brunch while The Brook Café serves lighter, more moderately priced meals in a casual setting. For lunch, try the Micro Brew Battered Halibut & Chips or one of the cold or hot sandwiches offered at the cafe. In the evenings, enjoy fine dining while you look over Hood Canal to the Olympic Mountains. The restaurant's menu changes seasonally, but guests will always find fresh seafood among the offerings. Perhaps you'll choose to start the evening with locally harvested oysters on the half shell before digging into some lobster and Dungeness crab cakes served with a blackberry and red pepper sauce. For a feast of near epic proportions, order the captain's platter—fried scallops, prawns, oysters, and clams. Those who prefer red meat may elect to try a prime cut of aged beef.

And, to finish the evening, you may want to split a piece of cheesecake or some tiramisú. The Alderbrook Inn and restaurants are alcohol-free.

## Halfway House Restaurant    $
### 41 Brinnon Ln., on U.S. Hwy. 101, Brinnon
### (360) 796-4715

Locals fill the Halfway House Restaurant seeking the comfort of homemade soups like cream of chicken noodle and homemade desserts like the marion berry cobbler. In addition to the standard diner-style entrees, guests may also pick the nightly specials, which change each week. Specials include such savory dishes as a corned beef and cabbage boiled dinner, chicken fajitas, beef potpie, or a prime rib special served with three oysters on the half shell or a shrimp cocktail. All specials include soup or salad, a homemade roll, and dessert. Of course, those homemade soups also go well with sandwiches and burgers at lunch. Halfway House also serves large portions of traditional breakfast dishes like pancakes, eggs and bacon, and omelettes.

## Skipper John's Seafood & Market    $
### 23490 U.S. Hwy. 101, Hoodsport
### (360) 877-5661

You can certainly find fancier and more expensive restaurants with haute decor and trained servers, but if you want seafood and only seafood, this is the place to eat. Start with a crab or oyster cocktail then feast on a combo plate with three oysters and ten shrimp. Skipper John's also offers seasonal specials like the delectable ½ crab and three oysters, a deal at around $8. If someone in your party really doesn't like seafood, they can order chicken strips or the chicken teriyaki, but it would be a shame to miss out on this treasure trove of fresh, local seafood. After you've had your fill, make sure you check out the market section and take home a pint of oysters, a few salmon steaks or smoked salmon, or even a few crab from the live tanks.

## Tidewater Restaurant    $$
### 27061 U.S. Hwy 101, Hoodsport
### (360) 877-6450

Sip a glass of wine from the nearby Hoodsport winery while you eat at the Tidewater, a comfortable and welcoming restaurant along U.S. Highway 101. We're sure the Merlot will go well with a dinner of rib eye steak, and will even hold up to the baby back ribs. Or try the Gerweirztraminer with the First Mate combination—cod, oysters, clam strips, and prawns. End your meal with a piece of mixed berry pie. The Tidewater also serves lunches, salads, burgers, sandwiches, and fish and chips for lunch as well as a traditional assortment of breakfast dishes, which includes Super Browns, potatoes with onions, bacon, and topped with cheese.

## Insiders' Tip

You'll need a license if you want to fish or gather shellfish. Two-day combination licenses are available at many local sporting shops, and children under age 14 may fish without a license when accompanied by a licensed adult. Know the rules and regulations. For more information, visit the Washington Department of Wildlife's Web site, www.wa.gov/wdfw/fishcorn.htm.

# Close-up

## Bridges Over Troubled Waters

For centuries, the only way to travel to the Olympic Peninsula was to fight through dense forest or go by boat. Scheduled and unscheduled boats delivered people, livestock, dry goods, and housewares from Seattle and to the small logging communities that dotted the canal, and even after roads were built, ferries carried cars across the channel. The first bridge to connect the Kitsap and Olympic Peninsulas took more than three years to build and was not completed until 1961. It was an engineering wonder that spanned around 1.5 miles and floated on water up to 340 feet deep.

However, as advanced as that technological wonder was, the bridge that connects the two areas today is actually the second bridge built. You see, Washington State has an interesting history with its bridges—they have an uncanny habit of sinking.

On February 13, 1979, nature and faulty engineering gave a nasty Valentine's Day present to the state. The winds that night gusted to 120 miles per hour, with a sustained average speed around 85 miles per hour. The bridge shimmied and writhed on the high tide frothed even higher by the winds. Although the center span was opened in order to alleviate the pressure, the bridge simply could not take the stress. Several cables anchoring the bridge to the ocean floor snapped, and the pontoons keeping the bridge afloat broke loose, filled with water, and sank. The western span of the bridge soon followed the pontoons into the water.

It took three and one half years to rebuild the western half of the bridge. The residents and tourists were again required to wait for ferries or to take the long way around the canal. The new and improved William A. Bugge Bridge, also known as the Hood Canal Floating Bridge, finally reopened in October of 1982. High, sustained winds of 40 miles per hour or higher still close the bridge to traffic so that the middle draw span may be raised, in order to prevent a repeat of the original mishap.

Of course, Washington also claims ownership of a more well-known bridge mishap: the infamous Galloping Gertie, also known as the Tacoma Narrows Bridge. It too was an engineering marvel, a mile-long suspension bridge that spanned the swift flowing Narrows between Tacoma and the Kitsap Peninsula. Completed in 1940, the bridge lasted only four months before it too fell into the water.

From the very first crossing, residents knew that something wasn't right with the bridge. A person standing on one end of the bridge could watch approaching cars rise and fall on harmonic waves that crested along the bridge deck. Even the slightest wind made driving the span an adventure as the road also began to undulate side to side as well as up and down. Nobody was sure how the bridge would act in the high winter winds.

Then, on November 7, 1940, a 42-mile-per-hour wind set the bridge to galloping and twisting and groaning. As the bridge deck rose and fell and curled around, the cables snapped under the stress, and concrete sections fell one by one into the water far below. Newsreels of the bridge collapse are still featured on television shows. The new Narrows Bridge opened in 1950. The addition of open frets on the walls and deck of the bridge, plus additional support struts made the new bridge much more stable.

So far, both bridges are still standing. Although, as a safety precaution, both bridges are closed during high winds and other inclement weather.

The Hood Canal floating bridge spans about 1.5 miles to connect the Kitsap and Olympic Peninsulas.
PHOTO: ROB McNAIR-HUFF

**Twana Roadhouse    $**
**294793 U.S. Hwy. 101, Quilcene**
**(360) 765-6485**

Catch breakfast, lunch, or dinner at Twana Roadhouse. The spacious restaurant's friendly wait staff serves summer tourists and locals year round. Typical breakfast offerings include omelettes, pancakes, eggs, and biscuits and gravy. For lunch you can dine on the Timberman's Grilled Beef sandwich with grilled roast beef, green pepper, mushrooms, and onions all topped with melting cheddar cheese and served on a hoagie roll. Or for something lighter choose a fresh salad or a basket of fish and chips. For dinner you may want to sink your teeth into one of the specialty pizzas like the Lumberman's with pepperoni, sausage, Canadian bacon, mushrooms, black olives, and onions. Kids can even pick from a selection of pint-sized dishes.

# Shopping

People don't visit Hood Canal to go shopping. However, a few gift-shop gems have opened their doors along U.S. Highway 101. In addition, every few miles you'll find a store or stand that sells clams, oysters, and crab in season. If you love seafood, don't pass up the chance to stop at one of these shops. Many will package and express mail fresh fish and shellfish for you.

**The Daisy Pot**
**6960 WA Hwy. 106, Union**
**(360) 898-2424**

The shop may only be about the size of a daisy pot, but don't let that fool you. It is filled with treasures for your house, many of them older than you. Although small antiques stores can feel crowded and cluttered, this collection of antiques and French country gifts is well displayed, even though space is limited. The shop specializes in vintage rugs, linens, tablecloths, and dishes. A few select pieces of furniture, mostly chairs, benches, and mirrors, complete the collection. Quilt collectors will want to check the small collection of well-preserved quilts.

**Hoodsport Winery**
**23501 U.S. Hwy. 101, Hoodsport**
**(360) 877-9894**
**www.hoodsport.com**

Taste award-winning wines or stop by to find out about the wine-making process at the main location for the Hoodsport Winery. The winery opened in 1979, at a time when there were just 16 wineries in Washington. There are now more than 100 wineries in the state.

Visitors to the winery can enjoy free tastings of up to three wines. The winery specializes in traditional Vinifera wines— Chardonnay, Merlot, and Johannisberg Riesling—as well as fruit wines such as raspberry, rhubarb, and loganberry. In addition to tastings, visitors can buy wines at a discount—5 percent for four bottles, 15 percent on six bottles, and 20 percent on a 12-bottle case. The store also features wineglasses and other wine-related goodies. The Hoodsport Winery is open daily, except on holidays.

**Hood Sport 'n Dive**
**27001 U.S. Hwy. 101, Hoodsport**
**(360) 877-6818**
**www.hood.hctc.com/~hsd**

Scuba divers flock to Hood Canal, and Hood Sport 'n Dive is one of the full-service dive shops that dot the canal. In addition to selling gear, the shop fills air tanks, repairs gear, and rents scuba equipment, underwater cameras, and Cobra dive kayaks. As if that's not enough, the dive shop also provides exclusive access to the Sund Rock Marine Preserve. If you need a place to stay, ask about the bunkhouse.

**The Picket Fence**
**294773 U.S. Hwy. 101, Quilcene**
**(360) 765-3620**

Located barely off of U.S. Highway 101, The Picket Fence invites visitors to linger for a few moments while they enjoy the locally made handicrafts. After years of running a gifts and crafts business out of her home, the proprietor, KaraLee Monroe, decided to open this little shop where she sells hand-crafted gifts from angel pins to quilted pillows to flour sack towels to wooden wall hangings, all in the finest country tradition. She also hosts a special open house during the winter holidays.

**The Silver Wren at Alderbrook**
**7061 WA Hwy. 106, Union**
**(360) 898-4200**

No, The Silver Wren at Alderbrook does not sell birds, although you might find a sculpture or painting of one here. Instead, the little shop on the side of the highway sells some unique, upscale housewares, including carved and molded candles, lacquered chopstick sets, paintings and metal sculptures, even a bit of jewelry. In addition to the Northwest influence found in a lot of the region's gift shops, the Silver Wren has added just the right dash of Oriental spice.

**Walker Mountain Trading Post**
**300103 U.S. Hwy. 101, Brinnon**
**(360) 796-3200**

Originally built in 1929 as a restaurant and tavern, this wood-frame building, heated by an ancient wood stove, now houses antiques from the same era. Hazel Munday's aunt ran the store for 15 years before she retired and Hazel took over the family tradition of selling depression-era antiques and knickknacks. One room is

A panoramic view of the Olympic Mountains and the Quilcene Range from atop Mt. Walker. PHOTO: NATALIE McNAIR-HUFF.

dedicated to kitchen equipment, glass-ware, doilies, and hand-embroidered flour sack towels. Another is filled with the tools familiar to loggers and mill workers. Glass collectors won't want to miss the cubbyhole filled with medicinal and cobalt bottles. The rest of the shop is filled with everything but the kitchen sink.

### Waterwheel Gift & Gallery
**6960 WA Hwy. 106, Union**
**(360) 898-4438**

Just next door to the Daisy Pot, Water-wheel Gift & Gallery displays the works of local artists, collectible gifts, and local wares in a farmers' market–style setting. In the summer, flowers and potted plants brighten the corners and windows. A large collection of plush animals, includ-ing Ty beanie babies, Woolies, teddy bears, and finger puppets will keep the kids entertained while adults browse paintings, photographs, and framed

poems, all produced by local artists. If you stop on a Friday, bread day, you can also buy freshly baked bread made by a local baker. Make sure to buy a jar of honey to drizzle on the bread.

### Whitney Gardens & Nursery
**306264 U.S. Hwy. 101, Brinnon**
**(360) 796-4411**

For a visual feast, make sure you visit Whitney Gardens & Nursery in the late spring when the rhododendrons, azaleas, magnolias, and other spring-blooming trees put on the best show of the year. The nursery is a popular destination for gar-deners and tourists from all over, and after touring the 6.8-acre display garden you will understand why. The nursery grows over 1,000 varieties of rhododen-drons and azaleas as well as an extensive collection of exotic and native plants, and they will ship your plants home for you. There is a small fee to tour the gardens, but shopping at the nursery is free, of course.

# Relocation

Real Estate

Education

Healthcare

Retirement

Worship

"We wanted to get out of the rat race."
"I love being outside, kayaking, hiking, camping."
"It's the weather."
"I love the storms."
"It's just so beautiful here."

Those are just a few of the answers we heard when we asked people why they moved to the Olympic or Kitsap Peninsulas. People move here because of what is, and isn't, here. Don't plan on moving to the Peninsula to become a millionaire—odds are it won't happen. But, if you value outdoor recreation, small communities full of friendly people, and a slower pace of life, this might be the right place for you. However, if you crave warm, dry days, cloudless skies, and the bustle of city life, or if you want the convenience of 24-hour grocery stores just a few minutes away, you might want to reconsider. Clouds create a dark curtain most days from October to May, and the west side of the Peninsula gets drenched with rain. In fact, some people in the Pacific Northwest suffer from a winter depression called Seasonal Affected Disorder (SAD), that is due to the dark, short, gray winter days. You will find some respite from the clouds and rain around Sequim, which sits in the rain shadow cast by the Olympic Mountains.

Some people around here say we have two seasons, the rainy season and the rainier season. It's a little-known secret though that the weather is phenomenal in the summer, never too hot and never too cold—although you'll still get wet on the west side around Forks. If you crave variety in your weather, you'll never get bored in the spring or fall. As we say nearly every other day, "Wait five minutes, and the weather will change."

You won't find any major cities on the Peninsula, and it will take you a few hours to get to Seattle, Tacoma, or Olympia from most of the Peninsula. Nevertheless, although there are only a handful of incorporated cities, each has its own unique atmosphere, and you'll still see cell phones, be able to hook up to the Internet, and of course, this being Washington, you'll find good coffee everywhere.

The people here have the same concerns about their communities as the rest of the nation does. Although minorities are not well represented on the Peninsula—more than 90 percent of the population is white, with minority populations most strongly represented by Native Americans and Asians—cultural awareness and history are important to the residents. Education is a high priority in all of the communities, and you'll be pleased to know that the crime rate on the Peninsula is quite low. Hospitals and healthcare options are adequate in most cities, although they are sparse on the ocean side of the Peninsula. But overall, the quality of life is good, and you'll find plenty of opportunities to enjoy the arts and the outdoors. If you are civic-minded you'll find plenty of opportunities to volunteer with civic groups, environmental groups, and arts organizations.

Before you make the move, you should think about how you are going to make a living. The unemployment rate on the Peninsula is higher than the state average. In 1999, the state had a 4.7 percent unemployment rate, compared to 5.0 for Kitsap County, 5.9 for Jefferson County, 7.4 for Clallam County, 6.0 for Mason County, and 8.1 for Grays Harbor County. The per capita income on the Peninsula is also lower than the state average, which was $30,391 in 1999; 1998 figures reflect that Kitsap, Grays Harbor, and Clallam Counties fall in the $20,000 to $23,000 per capita range, while Mason County falls in the $16,000 to $20,000 range, and Jefferson County reaches into the $23,000 to $25,000 range.

Adding to that is the fact that much of the work on the Peninsula has a cyclical nature—unlike wheat, a crop of trees takes between 50 and 100 years to mature, and fish runs are not always consistent. Seasonal work increases in the summer as the tourist season picks up, but few seasonal jobs will give you enough income to live through the rest of the year. Good jobs can be found, but the opportunities vary by community. Also, if you live on the Kitsap Peninsula you have the option of driving to or taking the ferry to Seattle or Tacoma, although the prospect of a long and hectic commute to and from work, not to mention the added expense, is not always a pleasant thing to consider. Another option is to start your own business. Starting a business in Washington is not a difficult prospect as far as the paperwork goes. It generally takes businesses a year or so to become established, so it's a good idea to make sure you have enough money in reserve to see you through. The state offers some resources to help small-business owners through such agencies as the Business Assistance Center (edd.cted.wa.gov/bac) or the Washington Small Business Development Center (www.sbdc.wsu.edu).

Washington residents do not pay a state income tax, but a state retail sales tax is paid on most items. In 2000, the state rate was 6.5 percent, but city and county taxes generally raised the tax to 8.2 percent. Property taxes vary by region, amenities, and location, and school levies and other taxes are also assessed on property to help pay for services and school programs.

We continually hear stories about people who visited the Peninsula and then returned home only to sell the house and pack before returning to the area for good. These people are teachers, doctors, shopkeepers, woodworkers, and retirees. The ocean, mountains, and rivers offer so many riches that people simply fall in love. If you fall in love too, we hope this chapter will help smooth the transition to your new home.

# Real Estate

How do you want to live? What type of house or neighborhood do you prefer? Do you want to live within walking distance of the stores or do you want to live up in the hills?

When you start looking on the Peninsula, you'll find a variety of housing options, from golf course communities and planned communities to old Victorian neighborhoods to manufactured homes to sparsely developed tracts. If you want a house with a view or on the waterfront, expect to pay considerably more. You'll even find vacant plots for sale, and affordable vacation houses. Price ranges vary considerably from $300,000 view homes and million dollar mansions to $40,000 vacation cabins.

Before you settle on that house in the woods, where the nearest store is 30 minutes away, think about your lifestyle. If you currently live in the city with quick and easy access to services, stores, healthcare, and schools, you might want to think about how your life will change, especially if you have children who need to be driven to and from school activities.

If you want to build, you'll need to take a few things into consideration, such as finding out how much it costs to have utility lines run to your land. Of course, you can try living off the grid by using wind power and solar cells if your building site has suitable exposures. You'll also have to make sure the land is suitable for a septic tank, and think about where your water is going to come from if you can't get city water. Real estate agents and contractors will be able to help you figure out all of those issues, but you still need to keep them in mind when you find what you think is a great deal.

In most communities you'll be able to find apartments and houses to rent without any problem. The best way to find an apartment is to pick up the local newspaper and look through the listings. However, if you can't do that before moving to town, you may want to contact one of the realtors. Many also manage rental properties, and if not, they can help you find a property management company. Alternatively, look in any community phone book under property management.

**Northwest Real Estate**
**www.nwrealestate.com**

This is the Web site for the Multiple Listing Service. When you visit, you'll find agent and office listings, real estate news, and information about realtor associations. You'll also be able to search the listings for houses based on area, number of rooms, price, and whether it has a view or is on the waterfront.

**Washington Association of Realtors**
**504 East 14th Ave., Ste. 200;**
**P.O. Box 719, Olympia**
**(360) 943-3100, (800) 562-6024**
**www.warealtor.com**

The Washington Association of Realtors is a professional organization for realtors. Although the association won't recommend individual realtors, it will give you information about finding a realtor for the area in which you are interested. You will also be able to find information on new laws and developments that may impact real estate purchases.

## Gig Harbor

Gig Harbor is right across the Narrows Bridge from Tacoma. Many of the 6,500 residents work in the Tacoma area and some commute to Seattle in carpools or by riding the Southworth ferry to West Seattle. In fact, only 32 percent of the residents work in the Gig Harbor area, with 31 percent working in Tacoma and the rest working in Seattle and surrounding areas. The Gig Harbor area sprawls east to the Key Peninsula and west over a series of tiny peninsulas, islands, and bays. The area offers plenty of recre-

> ### Insiders' Tip
> Beware buyers' remorse. Don't buy a house when you are on vacation—your judgment may be slightly clouded.

ational opportunities, including three golf courses and a driving range, boat ramps, and hundreds of coves that make great places for kayaking and canoeing. Gig Harbor is a culturally rich community with a plethora of resident artists and arts organizations.

Gig Harbor—or The Harbor—experienced explosive growth in the 1980s and 1990s, and a second bridge across the Narrows is planned to help accommodate the increased traffic. Most recently Gig Harbor, which is part of Pierce County, has focused on sustainable growth while trying to maintain its environmental assets and the small town ambience. The real estate market in Gig Harbor is still hot and new homes frequently show up on parceled plots. Homes in the area don't come cheap, with a median income of $54,935; new homes cost $190,000. It's still possible to build new homes in the area, but there are some strict restrictions and building codes. Many houses feature waterfront access or views of the bay and the Olympics or Mt. Rainier.

*Historically known for its fishing industry, Gig Harbor is now a popular center for recreational boating.*
PHOTO: NATALIE McNAIR-HUFF

**Gig Harbor Realty**
**3118 Harborview Dr., Gig Harbor**
**(253) 851-9134**
**www.gigharborrealty.com**

For more than 40 years, Gig Harbor Realty has been a part of the Gig Harbor community. As a result, its 18 agents know the area inside and out, and two-thirds of them have won awards for sales. Gig Harbor Realty offers personalized service to help you find the home that you really want.

**Windermere Real Estate/Gig Harbor**
**5801 Soundview Dr., Ste. 101, Gig Harbor**
**(253) 851-7374**

According to one of its agents, Windermere Real Estate/Gig Harbor has the "lion's share of listings" for the area. Six of the 40 agents who work out of this branch have been recognized as top sellers in the region. The relocation services provided by Windermere through its main

office were recently ranked first in the nation by *National Relocation and Real Estate* magazine. In addition to standard residential homes, commercial real estate, and vacant plots, the office specializes in premiere property sales.

> ## Insiders' Tip
> If you buy a vacation home, think about renting it as a vacation getaway for others while you are at home. Several companies around the Peninsula offer vacation property management services for homes, cabins, and condominiums.

# Port Orchard

Like Gig Harbor to the south, Port Orchard enjoys moderate weather with a rare skiff of snow and a long growing period of around 200 days. This small community with approximately 7,300 residents features a new, state-of-the-art marina, and a lovely waterfront that is frequently the scene of community celebrations and concerts. Five nearby golf courses include McCormick Woods, which is also a planned community. The Puget Sound Naval Shipyard in Bremerton is the primary employer for Port Orchard, and approximately 20 percent of the residents travel to Seattle and Tacoma for work. Tourism is a growth industry, and the community is seeking to attract technology-based and light-manufacturing businesses to diversify its economic base.

Port Orchard is the county seat of Kitsap County, which has an estimated population of 230,000. The average price for houses in the area is $144,665 in 2000, but the price varies considerably by location. For instance, a house on the west side of Washington Highway 16 may go for $150,000 while a similar house on the east side of the highway might go for as much as $185,000 simply because of location and the water and mountain views.

**Coldwell Banker Park Shore Real Estate**
**4235 S.E. Mile Hill Dr.; P.O. Box 108,**
**Port Orchard**
**(360) 871-2332**
**www.cbparkshore.com**
Backed by the powerful relocation services and resources available through Coldwell Banker, Park Shore Real Estate specializes in residential homes and land. Park Shore has been selling homes in the area for more than 20 years. Its agents have a thorough knowledge of the area, and they sell homes throughout the Kitsap Peninsula.

# North Kitsap Peninsula

Bremerton is the largest town in Kitsap County with approximately 39,000 residents. That number is projected to grow to 69,000 by 2010. Recent efforts to revitalize downtown Bremerton have started to take hold, and the area now boasts a boardwalked waterfront with several museums and art galleries. The jewel of the arts district is the refurbished Admiral Theatre, where entertainers from across the nation perform. In 1990, *Money Magazine* declared Bremerton the number-one place to live in the country, and in 1997 *Reader's Digest* rated it as the fourth-best place in the country to raise a family. Although the Kitsap Mall is in Silverdale, the city itself is quite small with approximately 12,000 people. The community of Poulsbo offers the unique atmosphere of a Norwegian village and is a popular tourist spot. It's also known as one of Seattle's bedroom communities since so many people ride the ferry to work there.

More than 10,000 people, civilians, and military personnel are employed at the Puget Sound Naval Shipyard and the Pacific Fleet Supply Center. The average annual income in the area is around $40,000, and home prices range from $80,000 in some regions to $200,000 and more in others. However, the average price is between $140,000 and $150,000. Plenty of homes offer mountain or water views or are located on the waterfront.

## Insiders' Tip
Get a free welcome packet when you move to Kitsap County. Call the Kitsap Greeters at (360) 275-2255 or (888) 382-6934 or visit the Web site at www.kitsapgreeters.com.

**Prudential Northwest Real Estate/Poulsbo**
901 Lincoln Rd., Poulsbo
(360) 779-5566
www.pnwre.com/poulsbo

Prudential Northwest Real Estate has offices throughout the Kitsap Peninsula and in parts of Mason County. Fifteen agents and realtors work out of the Poulsbo office. They are all experienced and quite familiar with Poulsbo, and can help you find a new home on the waterfront, tucked into the hills, or even that perfect piece of land where you can build your own home.

**Reid Real Estate**
3330 Kitsap Wy.; P.O. Box 4420, Bremerton
(360) 697-4275
www.reidrealestate.com

Reid Real Estate is a family-owned company that sold its first houses in 1967. Since then it has grown to be a regional presence with five offices on the North Kitsap Peninsula in Belfair, Bremerton, Port Orchard, and Silverdale. The company has approximately 100 agents focusing on a variety of real estate specialties, including commercial, property management, land, and residential.

## Port Townsend

Port Townsend is the county seat of Jefferson County. Approximately 8,000 people live in Port Townsend, although the surrounding region includes small villages like Chimacum with 1,200 people and Port Ludlow with 1,600 people. Port Townsend residents are civic minded and are active volunteers. An eclectic collection of boatbuilders, artists, poets, writers, shopkeepers, retirees, and former Seattlites have banded together to create a charming atmosphere of open-mindedness and innovation. Port Townsend is well known for its well-preserved and historic Victorian homes. You can always find a few of the old homes on the market, although newer homes are not rare. For brand-new homes in a planned community complete with golf course, clubhouse, groomed trails, and resort-style living, and a popular retirement spot, check out nearby Port Ludlow. According to Susan Stenger-Meyer of John L. Scott Real Estate, in 2000 the average sale price of a three-bedroom home in the Port Townsend area was $188,000.

**John L. Scott Real Estate/Port Townsend**
2219 W. Sims Wy., Port Townsend
(360) 385-4115

John L. Scott's Port Townsend office boasts a number of award-winning realtors, including the recipient of the Top Overall Production Award and the 1998 Jefferson County "Realtor of the Year." The agency has been selling homes in Jefferson County for more than 16 years, and the agents pride themselves on their ability to match people to the homes of their dreams. Twenty full-time agents who specialize in all types of property can even help you select homes from afar.

**Windermere Real Estate/Port Townsend**
1220 Water St., Port Townsend
(360) 385-9344, (800) 776-9344
www.windermereporttownsend.com

Seventeen full-time agents are waiting to help you find a new home or a vacation home in Port Townsend and Jefferson County. The agency has been open since 1991, and the agents pride themselves on knowing why Port Townsend is so special and why people are drawn to the area. Their specialties include beach retreats, acreage, and recreational communities in addition to more standard residential properties.

> **Insiders' Tip**
> Get a Red Ribbon Welcome in Port Townsend. The welcome package includes offers from local businesses, maps, and an introduction to the town. Call (360) 385-7749.

# Sequim

Sequim is perhaps the most popular retirement spot in Western Washington. From our informal study, it is certainly the most popular retirement spot on the Peninsula. In fact, the median age in Sequim is 51. As a result the housing market here is fairly competitive. On average, new homes cost $140,100, while resale homes cost around $120,000. Rentals average around $600 per month. What makes Sequim such a popular retirement spot? The weather. Sequim lies in the rain shadow and averages a low 16 inches of rain per year. People here brag that they see the sun nearly every day, and it never gets too hot or too cold. In 1997 *Fortune* magazine selected Sequim as one of the top retirement communities in the country. The Sequim-Dungeness valley, which has a population of around 25,000, used to be filled with farms, but more recently those farms have been parceled into lots for new houses.

**John L. Scott Real Estate/Sequim**
**1190 E. Washington St.;**
**P.O. Box 1737, Sequim**
**(360) 684-4131, (800) 998-4131**

The John L. Scott/Sequim branch claims to be the leading agency in eastern Clallam County. Twenty-five full-time agents include lifetime residents as well as newcomers who moved to the area especially for the community and the climate. The agency focuses on the needs of the buyer, and spends time with each client to determine the client's requirements for a new home. Some agents specialize in waterfront homes, others in acreage, and all have plenty of experience working to help people find their retirement homes.

**Windermere Real Estate/Sequim**
**990E E. Washington St., Sequim**
**(360) 683-6867, (800) 366-6867**
**www.northolympic.com/winsequim**

Whether you live in Sequim and are looking for a new home or you're just in town for a weekend and think you might like to look around, the 25 agents at this Windermere office will be happy to work with you. The agents take pride in their personal relationships with their clients. All of the agents are experienced and many are longtime residents of the Sequim-Dungeness valley. The agency is open seven days a week and also manages rental properties.

# Port Angeles and Juan de Fuca Highway

With the Strait of Juan de Fuca providing views to the north and the Olympic Mountains rising steeply to the south, the residents of Port Angeles rarely grow bored of looking out their windows. The city averages 25 inches of rain each year and enjoys an extended growing season that makes gardeners very happy. The city features a popular waterfront, complete with wheelchair-accessible trail and a lookout tower at the public pier where you'll often see people fishing or jigging for squid. Port Angeles is also where you can catch the ferry to Vancouver Island, Canada, and as a result, the city is filled with hotels and great restaurants. Other than tourists, the city, which has a population of about 20,000, attracts artists, recreation fanatics, and retirees. The average price of a new home in the area is $127,000, while the price for a resale house is about $20,000 less.

Clallam County, which includes Port Angeles, Forks, Sequim, and the smaller communities of Joyce, Clallam Bay, Sekiu, and Neah Bay, has an estimated population of around 68,000. The area west of Port Angeles is much more rural, and as a result houses cost less. But there are fewer services available in those areas, the average income is lower, and jobs are harder to find. Neah Bay, Sekiu, and Clallam Bay experience seasonal business trends due to tourism and fishing. The area is a popular destination for sport fishers and hikers. The primary employer along the Juan de Fuca Highway is the Clallam Bay Corrections Center. If you move to the west end, you'll definitely want to make sure you have a job or alternate source of income before doing so.

**Coldwell Banker Uptown Realty**
**330 E. 1st St., Ste. 1, Port Angeles**
**(360) 417-2799, (800) 292-2978**
**583 W. Washington St., Ste. A, Sequim**
**(360) 683-6000, (800) 282-2853**
**www.uptownrealty.com**

Established in 1979, Coldwell Banker Uptown Realty has two branches: one with 10 agents in Sequim and one with 26 agents in Port Angeles. The agency sells 26 percent of the properties in the county, and a whopping 46 percent in Port Angeles. They offer relocation services through Coldwell Banker and specialize in residential and commercial properties. They also offer a land department if you want to buy acreage.

**John L. Scott Real Estate/Port Angeles**
**1126 E. Front St., Port Angeles**
**(360) 457-8593, (800) 446-8115**
**www.jlspa.com**

The 10 agents and broker at John L. Scott/Port Angeles claim to be the "funnest bunch in town." They also have some of the top producers in the region, but they all think that buying a new house should be fun and hassle free so they focus on the buyer's needs. They have been affiliated with John L. Scott for seven years and specialize in Internet sales and residential properties.

## Forks

The economy in Forks peaked in the 1980s when logging hit fever pitch and then took a nosedive in the 1990s when the trees were gone and conservation efforts kicked in. The area is still struggling to regain some sense of economic balance, and attracting tourists plays a major role in that effort. Forks is a small community with approximately 3,500 people living within the city limits. You'll find loggers, anglers, artists, and retirees in the local cafes. The top three employers in the area are the Clallam Bay Corrections Center, Forks Community Hospital, and the Quillayute School District. If you love the rain, Forks is the place for you. It averages 117 inches of rain each year, but the temperatures are mild, and there are plenty of recreational activities nearby on the beaches and rivers as well as in the mountains. Homes in the area range from double-wide manufactured homes sold for around $50,000 to ranch houses on more than 100 acres for $500,000, and everything else in between.

**Lunsford and Associates, Inc.**
**121 Campbell St.; P.O. Box 779, Forks**
**(360) 374-3141**
**www.lunsfordrealestate.com**

If you want to buy on the west side of the Peninsula from Clallam Bay to Kalaloch, turn to Lunsford and Associates. It is practically the only full-service real estate firm in the area. Eight licensed realtors take the time to get to know you while showing you around town. For more than 20 years, Lunsford agents and brokers have been matching people to houses and neighborhoods, and they sell the majority of the real estate in the area. They'll help you find a new home, land, or a vacation home.

## Ocean Shores

Ocean Shores was originally a cattle ranch, but in the 1960s a group of investors decided to turn the sandy peninsula into a resort destination. Folks are more likely to buy a vacation home or time-share condominium in Ocean Shores. There are no major industries in town apart from tourism, which is seasonal. Weather watchers love living in Ocean Shores though, since the sandy beach offers perfect views of incoming storms and many houses have unobstructed views of the ocean. It rains quite a bit in Ocean Shores, but the temperatures are moderate, and the summers tend to be cool but dry. Of the 3,500 residents, approximately half are retirees. You can find a small vacation home for around $60,000 although on average, homes cost around $130,000 and go as high as $300,000.

**John L. Scott Real Estate/Ocean Shores**
**711 Point Brown Ave., Ocean Shores**
**(360) 289-1000, (800) 562-6670**

Since 1979 these agents have been helping people find homes in the Ocean Shores area. The company recently changed associations to John L. Scott from Century 21. Through John L. Scott they offer relocation services and have the backing of all the resources available through the company. The branch specializes in second homes and vacation properties, although any of the 12 realtors will be more than happy to help you find a new primary residence as well.

## Grays Harbor

Trees made Grays Harbor the lumber capital of the world in the early 1900s. In fact, Aberdeen was the rip-roaringest town in the West with murderers, hoodlums, lumber barons, and loggers flocking to the city on their days off. It's not so happening anymore. Since the demise of logging and lumber, the area's fortunes have followed, and the economic downturn was accelerated when the two nuclear power plants at nearby Satsop were mothballed. The unemployment rate in the county is high, but service and tourism may be the solution. Approximately 68,000 people live in Grays Harbor County, which includes Aberdeen with 16,700, Hoquiam with 9,000, and smaller towns such as Cosmopolis with 1,500 people and Montesano with 3,600. The area still retains many of its original buildings, and arts-and-craft and mission-style homes are often found on the market. On average, houses sell for around $93,000, but you can find them for less and for a lot more.

**Coldwell Banker/First Harbor Real Estate, Inc.**
**110 W. Market St., Aberdeen**
**(360) 532-2610, (800) 448-0508**

Whether you want a home in Aberdeen, Hoquiam, Montesano, or anywhere else in Grays Harbor, you can see any of the 14 agents at this agency. They have been selling single-family homes, multifamily complexes, and commercial real estate in the area since 1985. Several agents are regional top sellers.

**Price & Price Real Estate**
**120 W. Pioneer St., Ste. 1, Montesano**
**(360) 249-4651**

According to the broker, Price & Price Real Estate has sold half of the houses in town two or three times since the company started selling houses in the 1940s. Most of the three agents and the broker were born and raised in the area, and they pride themselves on their intimate knowledge of the community and the market.

## Shelton

Shelton is the only incorporated city in Mason County, which extends halfway up Hood Canal and onto the southwest corner of the Kitsap Peninsula. Simpson Timber Company produces lumber and plywood and is the main employer. In fact Simpson dominates downtown Shelton with the plant sitting at the end of the main thoroughfare. Approximately 7,700 people live in Shelton, and on average, homes cost between $110,000 and $124,000. You may have difficulty renting in the area, however, since the rental market is pretty tight. As for buying, you'll find homes with acreage and waterfront views as well as homes on small lots near city center.

**Windermere Real Estate/Himlie Inc.**
**920 Railroad Ave., Shelton**
**(360) 426-2646, (800) 281-2740**

Windermere Real Estate/Himlie Inc. is the oldest established real estate company in the region. Himlie Inc. has been selling homes in the area since the 1960s. The agency has 14 licensed agents with more than 100 years of collective experience, and several are area natives. Agents specialize in waterfront homes, homes with acreage, and commercial real estate in addition to standard residential properties.

## Hood Canal

Hood Canal has never been an overly populated region; however, there were hopes at one point that the railroad-that-never-was would bring prosperity to the region. The communities that dot the canal are all small—Quilcene and Brinnon each claim around 1,300 residents—but their populations temporarily swell during the summer tourist season and when the salmon are running. House prices vary widely from inexpensive non-waterfront homes for around $60,000 to $70,000 to small vacation cabins for $15,000 to huge waterfront retreats for $200,000. Main industries on the canal include oyster farms and tourism. So why do people move to the area? To retire and retreat from the crowds while enjoying spectacular scenery and moderate, albeit wet, weather.

**Coldwell Banker/Settlers Real Estate**
**P.O. Box 247, Brinnon**
**(360) 796-4900, (800) 962-6401**
**www.cbsettlers.com**

Six agents offer a wide range of experience selling homes from Hoodsport to Quilcene. Some agents are lifetime residents while others are new to the area. Settlers has been selling homes in the area for more than 15 years, and they specialize in prime waterfront real estate, resort properties, and new homes.

**Windermere Real Estate/Hood Canal**
**Quilcene Business Center, P.O. Box 700, Quilcene**
**(360) 765-3450, (800) 676-3450**
**www.hoodcanal.com**

Experienced agents will help you find a vacation cabin or a new place to call home. The resources of Windermere Real Estate support six agents, most with more than 10 years of experience. This branch specializes in waterfront properties, second homes, and land purchases.

# Education

In 1993, the state legislature and the superintendent instituted a set of Essential Academic Learning Requirements (EALRs) that every school district must achieve. Before EALRs, each school district separately developed its goals and learning plans. Since the EALRs were launched, each school district has been striving to meet them. Districts continually reevaluate their programs and introduce new curricula in order to satisfy the requirements.

The state's educational motto is "Partners in preparing each student for the twenty-first century." In order to do that, the state has listed a few primary goals. The first goal is for students to learn to "read with comprehension, write with skill, and communicate effectively and responsibly in a variety of ways and settings." Other goals center on learning and applying mathematical and scientific skills as well as learning civics, history, and geography, and participating in the arts. The state wants children to learn how to solve problems with the skills they learn rather than just memorize facts and follow directions. In this way, the students will be better prepared to apply their knowledge to careers and continuing education.

Washington State also offers the Running Start program for high school students. Students can take courses for free at local community colleges. Course credits simultaneously apply toward high school graduation and college credit.

You will also be able to find private schools in most of the cities on the Peninsula. Cities like Gig Harbor and Port Townsend offer several private schools, some Christian-based and some not. Home schooling is another alternative. Most districts provide support for home schooling families in the form of textbooks, curriculum suggestions, testing, and the opportunity to use school labs and attend some classes.

Many districts also offer preschool for disabled and low-income students with remaining spots reserved for tuition-based clients. These programs are not large enough to satisfy all of a community's demands for preschool and childcare, however, so we have included a section listing childcare referral and evaluation services.

Peninsula residents benefit from a number of state-run community colleges. A few of the colleges have branch campuses in the smaller, surrounding towns. Each college listed here is accredited by the Northwest Association of Schools and Colleges. Credits and degrees earned at these colleges are accepted across the state and nation. Washington's community colleges offer certificates of completion in professional and technical fields as well as Associate degrees. Students can even earn four-year degrees through partnerships with four-year colleges and universities, and some partnership programs also offer Masters degrees in select disciplines.

# Public Schools

**Office of Superintendent of Public Instruction**
**P.O. Box 47200, Olympia**
**(360) 753-6738**
**www.k12.wa.us**

Visit the superintendent's Web site to get the inside scoop on Washington's schools. You'll find detailed information on the EALRs, certificates of mastery, assessment, testing, and plans for the future of Washington's schools.

**Peninsula School District**
**14015 62nd Ave. NW, Gig Harbor**
**(253) 857-6171**
**www.peninsula.wednet.edu**

The Peninsula School District serves 9,500 students in the Gig Harbor area. The district is known for its creative and innovative programs as well as high SAT test scores. Assessment tests of the fourth and eighth graders placed them in the 60th percentile, which ranks them among the highest in the nation, and among the top 20 in the state. Reading is stressed as the key to success, and the district's goal is to ensure that every student can read by third grade. The district also focuses on computer education with an average classroom ratio of one computer for every five students. However, each student in the fourth grade has access to a computer. Extracurricular activities are plentiful and all students are encouraged to get involved in sports, music, drama, and civic programs. One of the most telling signs that Gig Harbor's Peninsula School District is an exceptional district is the fact that 70 percent of its graduates go on to college.

**South Kitsap School District**
**1962 Hoover Ave. S.E., Port Orchard**
**(360) 876-7300**
**www.skschools.org**

Eleven thousand students from Port Orchard and unincorporated areas of south Kitsap County attend South Kitsap School District's 10 elementary schools, 3 junior high schools, and the high school. Emphasis is placed on the basics of language arts, math and sciences, social studies, art, health and physical education, as well as citizenship. Approximately 60 percent of graduates go on to technical instruction or college. The district has more than 4,000 active volunteers who help in the classrooms, on field trips, and on sports activities.

## Bremerton School District
134 N. Marion Ave., Bremerton
(360) 478-5151
www.bremertonschools.org

In addition to the basic education programs that focus on reading, communications, math, science, social studies, and the state's EALRs, the Bremerton School District has developed a number of special programs. One such program is its magnet middle school designed with gifted students in mind. The "school within a school" concept allows groups of students to work with a pod of teachers who teach all subjects. Younger gifted students benefit from the Challenge Program, and high school students can take advanced placement courses as well as attend classes at Olympic College as part of the state's Running Start program. The district's ROTC program is ranked as an Honor School, which allows administrators to nominate several students to the Naval academies. The district also maintains multiage classrooms, tutoring programs, an alternative high school, and the Kitsap Peninsula Vocation Skills Center. The entire city of Bremerton is proud of the high school's state-of-the-art, 1,200-seat performing arts center.

## North Kitsap School District
18360 Caldart Ave. N.E., Poulsbo
(360) 779-8704
www.nksd.wednet.edu

Nine schools serve the students of the North Kitsap School District, which serves the Poulsbo, Suquamish, and Kingston areas. The district includes six elementary schools, two junior high schools, and one high school. The district focuses on the core basics of reading, writing, and communication to meet the state EALRs. Special programs also emphasize integrated studies such as a fourth-grade program where students interview community elders in order to learn respect and about life 50 years ago. High school students participate in Running Start and Tech Prep, a program similar to Running Start but in the vocational fields, through a partnership with Olympic College. The district also offers an alternative high school and a program for home school students.

## Central Kitsap School District
P.O. Box 8, Silverdale
(360) 692-3111
www.cksd.wednet.edu

The educators of Central Kitsap School District say that their "highest priorities are student achievement, the efficient use of our resources, and providing a safe and caring learning environment." To those ends, the district has a few special programs, including a magnet school for gifted junior high school students, advanced placement classes for high school students, and a Montessori program for younger students. The advanced placement courses cover 10 subjects and enjoy high enrollment with more than 750 students enrolled in 2000. Central Kitsap also offers programs to support home school students, and access to technology and the Internet is stressed as one of the keys to communication for all students. The district has seen increasingly higher test scores over the last few years, and its assessment scores are above state and national averages. Central Kitsap serves more than 13,000 students at its 13 elementary schools, three junior high schools, two high schools, and single secondary school, which offers a unique cross-grade learning plan for each student. The district also offers an alternative junior high and an alternative high school.

## Chimacum School District
91 W. Valley Rd.; P.O. Box 278, Chimacum
(360) 385-3922
www.chimacum.wednet.edu

The Chimacum School District serves students who live around Chimacum, Port Ludlow, and Port Hadlock. Chimacum's first school was built in 1915 and served the community until it burned in 1943. A new building was constructed on the same spot. Approximately 1,500 students attend Chimacum's schools, including its primary school (K–2), elementary school, middle school, high school, and alternative high school.

High school students are encouraged to participate in extracurricular activities, including sports and clubs ranging from the hiking club to the National Honor Society to the award-winning band that once performed in the Rose Bowl during halftime. A special partnership program helps home school students, and multiage classrooms offer special benefits and long-term relationships between students and teachers for some third, fourth, and fifth graders. Elementary school students also participate in a special program called Chimacum Choice where students choose enrichment classes, which take place on select Fridays during the second half of the year. Classes include art, drama, dance, science, sports, and business courses.

**Port Townsend School District**
**450 Fir St., Port Townsend**
**(360) 379-4502**
**web.ptsd.wednet.edu**

Five schools serve the approximately 1,800 students of the Port Townsend School District: two elementary schools, a junior high, a high school, and Mar Vista, an alternative high school. An Individualized Choice Education (ICE) program assists home school students. One of the ways that the district acknowledges different learning styles is through the Talented and Gifted (TAG) program that starts in the fourth grade. The district also offers a Birth to Three program for infants with developmental and health concerns and preschool for 3 to 5 year olds of all abilities. Two more unique programs include OPEPO and a mentoring program. OPEPO (Optional Education PrOgram) enrolls approximately 50 students in a two-classroom, multiage school where children each learn at their own pace and work with community members including parents, artists, and a children's theater. OPEPO focuses on teamwork, personal responsibility, problem solving, and applied learning. Community members also participate in the mentoring program with high school juniors who participate in a sort of internship for a semester to earn high school credits.

**Sequim School District**
**503 N. Sequim Ave., Sequim**
**(360) 683-6303**
**www.sequimschools.wednet.edu**

Like the other districts in the state, Sequim's curriculum focuses on the disciplines that will satisfy the state mandated EALRs. The district also provides some special services, such as the partnerships offered for home school students as well as special vocational programs in the high schools that focus on commercial cooking, law and justice, and multimedia. The district has two elementary schools, Helen Haller Elementary and Greywolf Elementary, a middle school, and a high school. The high school features a recently remodeled performing arts center, which is well used by the choir and bands. The district also offers enrichment classes for students and the community. Enrichment courses include such courses as Genealogy, Landscaping, and Norwegian for adults and art, drama, and Spanish for all ages.

## Insiders' Tip

If you like lutefisk, move to Poulsbo. Every year, residents eat 1,600 pounds of the Norwegian specialty. They even celebrate it with a lutefisk dinner at the Sons of Norway Hall.

**Port Angeles School District**
**216 E. 4th St., Port Angeles**
**(360) 457-8575**
**www.pasd.wednet.edu**

The Port Angeles School District covers 330 square miles, with much of that land located within the Olympic National Park. Six elementary schools provide a strong foundation based on the educational building blocks of reading, writing, and mathematics. Special enrichment programs are also offered at the elementary level with an orchestra program and specialists in music, the arts, and physical education. Two middle schools enroll more than 600 students each, and the high school serves approximately 1,500 students. The high school offers sports programs and has an award-winning music program that includes an orchestra, concert band, choir, swing choir, marching band, and various ensemble groups. Overall, the district has more than 5,000 students.

**Cape Flattery School District**
**P.O. Box 109, Sekiu**
**(360) 963-2329**
**www.capeflattery.wednet.edu**

The Cape Flattery School District serves the communities of Sekiu and Clallam Bay as well as the Makah Tribe in Neah Bay. In Neah Bay, residents attend Neah Bay School or the Neah Bay Junior/Senior High School, which has approximately 200 students. An elementary school, a middle school, and a high school also serve the students in the Clallam Bay/Sekiu area. The district's mission is to "ensure that each student be given the opportunity to gain the knowledge, skill, and self-esteem necessary to become a contributing member of society." The Neah Bay schools also focus on providing students with the skills to live in a multicultural world so that they learn to value their cultural background; programs focusing on the Makah culture and history are included in the curriculum. The district also runs Eagle Crest High School, which serves the incarcerated teens of the Clallam Bay Corrections Center.

**Quillayute Valley School District**
**P.O. Box 60, Forks**
**(360) 374-6262**
**www.forks.wednet.edu**

The appropriately named Puddle Jumpers call Forks Elementary School their home. Elementary school students study a core curriculum of reading, language arts, and math with satellite courses in social studies, music, art, health, and physical education. After they grow up a bit they attend Forks Middle School for an integrated block studies approach before heading to Forks High School.

Most people wouldn't think a rural school district would be as technologically advanced as this one is, but for two years in a row, it was named one of the Top 100 Wired Schools by *Family PC* magazine. Forks High School is a charter member of Virtual High School, a nationwide network of distance-learning courses taught by teachers and attended by students from as far away as Maine. The Quillayute Valley district serves as the hub for the Washington Virtual Classroom, where schools collaborate on research projects and classes. In this way, even a small district such as this can incorporate more classes and disciplines.

The district also offers an alternative high school, a home school partnership program, and a Technology Lab that offers classes designed to help students master the skills needed for five computer-related career paths. Team sports include volleyball, running cross-country, wrestling, basketball, track, fastpitch softball, baseball, and of course football.

**North Beach School District**
**729 Point Brown Ave. N.W; P.O. Box 159,**
**Ocean Shores**
**(360) 289-2447**
**users.techline.com/nbeachhs**

North Beach School District is a small district with approximately 680 students attending two elementary schools (Ocean Shores Elementary School and Pacific Beach Elementary) and North Beach Junior/Senior High School. Multiage

*A huge bear carving greets visitors at the entrance to Hoquiam High School.* PHOTO: ROB McNAIR-HUFF

classrooms are offered for some grades, and many of the courses focus on integrated studies and local culture. The district also offers an integrated preschool for eligible students.

**Hoquiam School District**
**305 Simpson Ave, Hoquiam**
**(360) 538-8200**
**www.hoquiam.k12.wa.us/index.html**

Nestled right next to Aberdeen, the Hoquiam School District has one K to 1st school and three elementary schools, a middle school, and a high school. The district's mission is "to provide a quality learning experience for all students, emphasizing accountability, achievement, and lifelong learning." The staff continually examines assessment scores and developing new curriculum and teaching methods to improve student performance and meet the state EALRs. The district also operates an integrated preschool for children between three and five years old, and an alternative program exists at the

high school. Approximately 2,100 students attend school in Hoquiam.

**Aberdeen School District No. 5**
**216 N. G St., Aberdeen**
**(360) 538-2000**
**www.asd5.org/index.htm**

The Aberdeen School District opened its doors in a rough and rowdy community in 1884. The city has mellowed since then, and education is one of the highest priorities. More than 4,000 students attend the district's six elementary schools, Miller Junior High School, and Aberdeen High School. The district also offers an alternative high school called Harbor High School. Parents and community members play an important role in the schools as volunteers and classroom aids for the 500 teachers and staff members. Computer training starts early here, in preschool in fact, and teachers receive technology training in order to keep them up-to-date on the latest advances in computer hardware and software. The district strives to

*A sandstone embankment on the beach north of Ocean Shores casts its evening reflection.* PHOTO: ROB McNAIR-HUFF

meet the EALRs of course, and it also places a lot of emphasis on learning strategies, cultural awareness, problem solving, and skills that lead to lifelong learning.

**Montesano School District**
**302 N. Church, Montesano**
**(360) 249-3942**
**www.monte.wednet.edu**

Three schools—Beacon Elementary, Simpson Elementary, and Montesano Junior-Senior High School, serve students in the Montesano area. The district focuses on reading as a key to learning and success. High school students can participate in a wide variety of after-school activities, including Knowledge Bowl, Military Club, and the Dead Artist's Society. Multiage classrooms in the elementary schools mean that children work with the same teacher for two or three years. Such programs let the teacher work with each student's strengths and allow students to work at their own paces. The district also provides a preschool for children of all abilities between the ages of three and five.

**Wishkah Valley School District**
**4640 Wishkah Rd., Aberdeen**
**(360) 532-3128**
**www.wishkah.wednet.edu**

This is a tiny district serving a rural community about 12 miles north of Aberdeen. The district enrolls approximately 250 students from kindergarten through 12th grade and has been serving children in the area since the 1920s. The district still focuses on the basics, with the goal of ensuring that each student is accepted into college or is able to start a vocational career right out of high school.

**Shelton School District**
**207 N. 9th St., Shelton**
**(360) 426-1687**
**www.shelton.wednet.edu**

Approximately 4,200 students attend Shelton School District's six schools: Bordeaux Elementary School, Evergreen

Elementary School, Mountain View Elementary School, Shelton Middle School, Shelton High School, and Bordeaux Choice High School, the district's alternative school. The high school also enrolls students from Mason County districts that do not have their own high schools. The district focuses on the EALR basics in order to encourage lifelong learning and teach individual responsibility.

### Brinnon School District
**46 School House Rd., Brinnon**
**(360) 796-4646**

Brinnon School District is one of the tiniest in the state with only 71 students from kindergarten to eighth grade. Several multiage classrooms serve all the students and primarily focus on reading and the basics in math, science, social studies, and physical education.

### Quilcene School District
**294715 U.S. Hwy. 101; P.O. Box 40, Quilcene**
**(360) 765-3363**
**www.quilcene.wednet.edu**

Just north of Brinnon, the Quilcene School District serves a larger student body of approximately 300 students from preschool through 12th grade. The district emphasizes the basic building blocks in its curriculum so that children understand their world and gain the lifelong learning skills they will need to be competitive. The high school offers some unique extracurricular programs such as the Shellfish Club, which is a student-managed oyster culture business. Students can also participate in Knowledge Bowl, French or Spanish Club, even the Golf Club. Other extracurricular sports include football, volleyball, basketball, softball, and baseball.

## Colleges

### The Gig Harbor Peninsula College Center
**3993 Hunt St., Gig Harbor**
**(253) 851-2424**
**www.tacoma.ctc.edu/ghc**

Tacoma Community College operates this Gig Harbor Peninsula College Center. Tacoma Community College has offered classes to area residents since 1970, but it was only in 1995 that the center moved to its current 13,000-square-foot space on a 10-acre parcel. The building is already used to capacity and classes are held in community spaces such as the high school. Students on this side of the Narrows Bridge appreciate being able to attend class without having to drive across the bridge each day. The courses offered range from credit courses applied toward associate degrees, professional and technical courses, and worker retraining programs to noncredit continuing education courses for community members. High school students can also attend Center classes as part of the Running Start program. Many courses, including the popular computer software courses, are offered in the evenings and on weekends.

### Olympic College
**1600 Chester Ave., Bremerton**
**(360) 478-4506, (800) 259-6718**
**www.oc.ctc.edu**

Nearly 7,000 students attend classes at Bremerton's Olympic College and its satellite campus in Shelton and the extension campuses at Subbase Bangor and North and South Kitsap high schools. The main campus encompasses 30 acres in Bremerton and includes an art gallery, the Automotive Technology Center, student computer labs, and a multicultural center. Its Business Relations Center helps students acquire work experience through employment and internships and in turn it benefits local businesses by helping with recruitment, employee testing, and tax workshops.

The college offers one- and two-year certificates as well as Associate in Art and Sciences and Associate in Technical Arts degrees. An affiliation with Virginia's Old

Dominion University offers 17 bachelor degree programs and 6 graduate degree programs, including Masters degrees in business administration and education. Accredited degree programs are offered in nursing. The college also offers community enrichment and leisure programs, including art, language, landscaping, and even Feng Shui, classes as well as guided activities such as rafting, bird-watching, and skiing. Students can also take Adult Basic Education, GED preparation, and English as a Second Language courses.

**Peninsula College**
**1502 E. Lauridsen Blvd., Port Angeles**
**(360) 452-9277**
**www.pc.ctc.edu**

Founded in 1961, Peninsula College's main campus is nestled against the Olympic Mountains and overlooks the town of Port Angeles. Olympic National Park and nearby beaches and forests serve as a natural and practically free laboratory for science courses and as a giant playground for recreational activities and classes.

The college offers college-transfer Associate degrees, one- and two-year certificates as well as free adult basic education, GED preparation, and English as a Second Language courses. The liberal-studies degrees feature programs in English, the humanities, math, social sciences, and the natural sciences. The 23 professional technical programs include information technology, massage therapy, nursing, business administration, automotive technology, and fisheries. The college also features a Microsoft Training Center as well as international exchange and study programs to England, China, and Bolivia.

Peninsula College also offers two extension campuses. Students at the East Jefferson County Extension in Port Townsend (360-385-4605) can earn an Associate of Arts degree by attending evening classes in a three-quarter, four-year program. Academic continuing education and community service courses and professional development seminars are also offered in Port Townsend as well as the Forks Extension Site (360-374-3223). Students can use the on-site computer lab, at both locations.

Unlike most community colleges in the state, Peninsula College also offers a co-ed residence hall that is capable of housing up to 86 full-time students. For students who are unable to travel to the main campus or one of the extensions, Peninsula College offers TeleLearning courses through interactive television, videos, and the Internet. For students who wish to pursue advanced degrees, the college offers degree programs with the University of Washington, City University, Washington State University, and Western Washington University.

Community members also enroll in continuing education courses as well as attend the public lectures, readings, and entertainment events offered at the college. High school students can attend classes as part of the Running Start Program. All told, approximately 8,000 students enroll in courses at the college and its extensions.

> ## Insiders' Tip
> Know your speed limits to avoid getting a ticket. The speed limit on most city streets is 25 mph, 20 in school zones. It varies from 50 to 60 mph on U.S. Highway 101, 50 mph on WA Highway 19 and WA Highway 20, and 60 mph on WA Highway 104.

**Grays Harbor College**
**1620 Edward P. Smith Dr., Aberdeen**
**(360) 538-4050, (800) 562-4830 ext. 4050**
**www.ghc.ctc.edu**

Grays Harbor College incorporated as a private college in 1930 and became a publicly funded school in 1945. Like all community colleges in the state, the college offers courses in adult basic education, English as a second language, GED preparation, worker retraining, and continuing education courses. Courses are also provided to inmates of the Stafford Creek Corrections Center. Certificates of completion are offered in a variety of training programs and several Associate degrees are offered.

Students who want to enter the workforce as soon as possible may want to work toward an Associate in Applied Science, Associate in Technology, or the Associate in General Studies, which gives students a chance to take classes in several disciplines to create a sort of integrated studies approach. Those who plan on moving on to a four-year degree will want to focus on an Associate in Arts or an Associate in Science. Bachelor degrees are available through partnerships with Evergreen State College, which offers a Bachelor of Arts in Liberal Arts, and Washington State University, which offers Bachelor of Arts in Elementary Education as well as Bachelor of Arts in Agriculture, Business, Criminal Justice, Human Development, or Social Science. Distance-learning courses are available in some programs.

# Childcare

**Child Care Resource & Referral of Kitsap County**
**105 National Ave. N., Bremerton**
**(360) 405-5827**

This agency serves all the communities of the North Kitsap Peninsula from Kingston and Suquamish south to Bremerton and even Port Orchard. Call for childcare referrals and help in evaluating childcare providers. The agency also provides resources and training for childcare workers and provides parents with helpful resources as well.

**Parent Line**
**301 Lopez, Port Angeles**
**(800) 300-1247**

Serving Clallam and Jefferson Counties, Parent Line provides childcare referrals and resources to help parents decide which type of care is best for their children. In addition, the service works with local businesses to make sure that quality childcare is available where it is most needed.

**Coastal CAP CCR&R**
**117 E. 3rd St., Aberdeen**
**(360) 533-5100**

In addition to providing resources and support for parents, this community service can give you childcare referrals based on your location and requirements. The agency also works with parents, businesses, community organizations, and childcare providers to see where more childcare options are needed.

**Family Support Center**
**P.O. Box 784, Olympia**
**(360) 754-9297**
**www.familysupportctr.org**

Twelve childcare-related organizations work together at the Family Support Center. The center serves parents, children, and childcare workers in Mason, Thurston, and Lewis Counties. In addition to providing childcare referrals, its member agencies also work in crisis counseling, parent education, and childcare training.

# Healthcare

The Olympic and Kitsap Peninsulas are served by six hospitals and several clinics. Our hospitals provide a variety of services including oncology, radiology, obstetrics, and surgical care. You'll also be able to access hospice services and home healthcare through many of the hospitals. Bremerton actually has two hospitals, but since the Naval hospital is restricted to military personnel and their family members, we have not listed it here. Much of the area is extremely rural and hospitals often serve large areas. For instance, Forks Community Hospital serves residents in west Clallam and Jefferson Counties from Neah Bay down to Kalaloch. The next nearest hospitals are in the Grays Harbor area to the south and to the west in Port Angeles. The Port Townsend hospital serves the Hood Canal residents who live in Jefferson County, while the residents of Mason County go to Shelton.

Each of the Peninsula's hospitals offers 24-hour emergency service, and some offer level III trauma centers. Some also operate community clinics in surrounding towns or offer outreach programs to the most rural areas. If you are in immediate need of assistance, dial 911 to contact police, fire, and paramedic services.

We also have a number of walk-in urgent care clinics scattered around the Peninsula. They, along with a few appointment-only and outpatient clinics, are listed in the Clinics section of this chapter. In many cities you'll also be able to find natural healthcare practitioners who use homeopathic and naturopathic techniques, as well as massage therapists, acupuncturists, and aromatherapists. If you need further assistance finding a healthcare practitioner, refer to community phone books or call the chamber of commerce for referrals.

## Hospitals

**Harrison Hospital**
**2520 Cherry Ave., Bremerton**
**(360) 792-6505, (800) 281-4024**
**www.harrisonhospital.org**

Harrison Hospital is a 297-bed facility that serves Bremerton and north and central Kitsap Peninsula. The hospital features an emergency room with a level III trauma center and an urgent care clinic. Specialties include obstetrics and gynecology, cardiology, oncology, rehabilitation, and a full surgery unit that serves more than 1,000 people each month. Harrison also offers home healthcare, and in conjunction with Hospice of Kitsap County, it offers Companions in Care to help those who are terminally ill. Harrison Hospital also runs an urgent care clinic in Port Orchard and a secondary campus in Silverdale (1800 N.W. Myhre Rd.), which features women's and children's services, outpatient surgery, and an emergency room.

**Jefferson General Hospital**
**834 Sheridan St., Port Townsend**
**(360) 385-2200, (800) 244-9912**
**www.jgh.org**

Residents of Port Townsend and east Jefferson County are cared for at this 37-bed hospital. In addition to acute care and surgical support, the hospital features a critical care and intensive care unit equipped to handle up to eight patients as well as a 24-hour emergency room, and a helipad used by Airlift Northwest to transport patients to Seattle when needed. Specialty services include cardiac rehabilitation, respiratory care, rehabilitation services, home healthcare and hospice, and a four-room birth center. The hospital also offers community education programs through brown bag lunch lectures every Monday and a variety of support groups, from an Alzheimer's support group to a group for people living with cancer or chronic conditions such as fibromyalgia and diabetes.

*The Jefferson General Hospital sits on the hillside overlooking Port Townsend.* PHOTO: ROB McNAIR-HUFF

**Olympic Memorial Hospital**
**929 Caroline St., Port Angeles**
**(360) 417-7000**
**www.Olympicmedical.org**

Olympic Memorial first opened its doors in 1951, and it has grown to be the largest employer on the Olympic Peninsula with approximately 1,000 employees. Specialty care provided at the hospital includes cardiac and coronary care, endocrinology, orthopedic surgery, nuclear medicine, advanced radiology, and oncology. Internal medicine, ob/gyn, and rehabilitation services are also offered at the hospital. The 126-bed facility includes a level III

trauma center. An additional facility is operated in Sequim (777 N. 5th Ave.), and there are plans to expand the Sequim center to include a rehabilitation area. With an annual budget of more than $5 million, the hospital is constantly adding to its services as well as expanding into surrounding communities.

**Forks Community Hospital**
**530 Bogachiel Wy., Forks**
**(360) 374-6271**
**www.forkshospital.org**

The Forks Community Hospital serves approximately 11,500 residents on the west side of the Peninsula through several community clinics, a community outreach program, the 17-bed inpatient facility, and a 36-bed skilled nursing, long-term care facility. The hospital provides support for general surgery, and other services include radiology, mammography, and obstetrics. The community is also served by a volunteer ambulance service. The West End Outreach program features a mental health program with adult and child day treatment as well as chemical dependency and family violence intervention programs. Community clinics operated by the hospital include the Bogachiel Clinic, the Fork's Women's Clinic, and the Clallam Bay Medical Clinic.

**Grays Harbor Community Hospital**
**915 Anderson Dr., Aberdeen**
**(360) 537-5000**

Yes, the singer Kurt Cobain was born in this hospital. Yes, they know which room. No, it's not a museum, it's still a hospital, and according to one of the administrators, it is the busiest on the Peninsula. The hospital has a 259-bed capacity over two campuses. The main campus offers a level III trauma center, coronary intensive care, obstetrics, cardiology, pulmonology, oncology, and a pain clinic. The east campus, located at 1006 North H Street, houses the 16-bed inpatient chemical dependency clinic and a 60-bed acute skilled nursing facility as well as the busi-

ness offices and the home health agency. The hospital also maintains an urgent care center at the Anderson Drive campus that is open to walk-in patients until 8 P.M.

**Mason General Hospital**
**901 Mt. View Dr. Bldg. 1; P.O. Box 1668,**
**Shelton**
**(360) 426-1611**
**www.pugetsoundwa.net/MGH/index. html**

This 68-bed facility serves the residents of Mason County with an intensive care unit, a 24-hour emergency room, and physicians who work in 22 specialties, including neurology, obstetrics and gynecology, pulmonology, cardiology, and internal medicine. The hospital also includes an on-site oncology facility. Physical and respiratory services are available, as are in- and outpatient surgery facilities. The hospital also runs the North Mason Medical Clinic in Belfair and Oakland Bay Pediatrics in Shelton.

# Clinics

**Gig Harbor MultiCare Urgent Care**
**4700 Pt. Fosdick Dr. N.W., Gig Harbor**
**(253) 851-8182**

The emergency room at Tacoma General Hospital across the Sound is Gig Harbor's nearest trauma center, but patients with non-life-threatening needs such as broken arms, sore throats, and cuts can visit this center. It is a walk-in clinic, and no appointments are needed. Three doctors and several RNs, LPNs, and medical assistants work at the clinic, which is open

seven days a week. The clinic stays open until 9 P.M. on weekdays.

**Gig Harbor Medical Clinic**
**St. Joseph Medical Center Same Day**
**Surgery Gig Harbor**
**6401 Kimball Dr. N.W., Gig Harbor**
**(253) 858-9192, (253) 858-4335**

These two clinics are both housed in the Gig Harbor Medical Pavilion, and both are run by Franciscan Health Services, which also runs St. Joseph Medical Center, one of the major hospitals in Tacoma. The Gig Harbor Medical Clinic is a family healthcare clinic with several doctors and nurse practitioners serving patients. The Same Day Surgery center is an ambulatory surgery center used by area doctors. The center has RNs and ORTs on staff. It also has lab and X-ray facilities and serves as a pre-admission clinic for patients who are undergoing major surgery at one of Tacoma's inpatient hospitals.

### Harrison Hospital Urgent Care Center
**450 South Kitsap Blvd., Port Orchard**
**(360) 895-6250**

In order to better serve the South Kitsap County residents, Bremerton's Harrison Hospital opened this clinic in 1995. Walk-in customers go to the clinic for routine injuries like minor cuts, sore throats, and sports injuries. The clinic also includes offices for primary care, home healthcare, and rehabilitation therapy. Appointments with primary care doctors and specialists are required, but they are not required for the urgent care clinic, which is open every day from 9 A.M. to 9 P.M.

### Virginia Mason Medical Center
**777 N. 5th St., Sequim**
**(360) 683-0900**
**433 E. 8th St., Port Angeles**
**(360) 252-3373**

Virginia Mason Medical Center actually operates five facilities in the Sequim and Port Angeles area. The centers provide comprehensive family healthcare, obstetrics, and diagnosis and treatment for acute and chronic conditions, including cardiac and pulmonary disease. Some centers are also equipped to perform minor outpatient surgery.

### CliniCare
**621 E. Front St., Port Angeles**
**(360) 452-5000**

Nurse practitioners tend to the needs of walk-in patients with routine problems. The clinic is open seven days a week, and no appointments are necessary.

### Clallam Bay Medical Clinic
**74 Bogachiel Wy., Clallam Bay**
**(360) 963-2202**

The Clallam Bay Medical Clinic is a certified rural medical clinic operated by the Forks Community Hospital. The services include general medicine and family healthcare, as well as women's healthcare. The clinic's single, certified Physicians Assistant also serves urgent care walk-in patients here. The clinic is open Monday through Friday from 9 A.M. to 5 P.M., however it is closed for an extended lunch hour from 12 to 1:30 P.M.

### Bogachiel Clinic
**590 Bogachiel Wy., Forks**
**(360) 374-6998**

Two general practitioners provide services, including obstetrics, pediatrics, and urgent care at this hospital-run facility. A third doctor also tends to general surgical patients, and one of the doctors speaks Spanish. The clinic is open Monday through Friday.

### Forks Women's Clinic
**231 Lupine Wy., Forks**
**(360) 374-3143**

To supplement the services offered at the hospital and the Bogachiel Clinic, the Forks Women's Clinic provides general healthcare, obstetrics, and gynecological services for the women and infants of Forks. The clinic is open Monday through Thursday.

### Family Practice Center of Grays Harbor
**815 K St., Hoquiam**
**(360) 533-7104**

Three doctors and a nurse practitioner provide full family care at this clinic. Services include infants and children, general medicine, and geriatric care. Ob/gyn services are referred to the Grays Harbor Women's Clinic, and urgent care needs for non-patients are referred to the hospital's urgent care facility. The clinic is open Monday through Friday, and appointments are necessary.

**Grays Harbor Women's Clinic**
**1020 Anderson Dr., Aberdeen**
**(360) 533-5000**

Grays Harbor–area women in need of obstetric and gynecological care can turn to the Grays Harbor Women's Clinic. Services provided here include prenatal care as well as infertility therapies. Four doctors work at the clinic, which is open Monday through Friday. Appointments are necessary.

**Oakland Bay Pediatrics**
**2300 Kati Ct., Ste. C, Shelton**
**(360) 426-3102**

Two pediatricians provide comprehensive healthcare for infants, children, and adolescents. Services include newborn care, general physicals, and immunizations. The clinic is open Monday through Friday, and appointments are necessary.

**South County Medical Clinic**
**294843 U.S. Hwy. 101, Quilcene**
**(360) 765-3111**

Jefferson General Hospital runs this healthcare clinic in Quilcene. Registered nurse practitioners address basic health matters. Services provided at the clinic include care for acute injuries and illnesses, family healthcare, women's healthcare, and immunizations, wellness, and prevention programs. More serious problems are referred to the main hospital.

# Retirement

The wet and rainy Peninsula may not be a retirement mecca like hot and sunny Arizona, but retirees find the area a pleasant place to rusticate. In fact, some regions are quite popular retirement spots such as Sequim and Ocean Shores. In addition to the ample volunteer options, most communities also offer plenty of recreational opportunities from card playing and bingo nights to walks on the beach and mountain trails and plenty of sight-seeing. While some areas such as the west side near Neah Bay and Forks offer little in the way of retirement living and nursing care facilities, other areas offer quite a few choices. In this section we have listed several skilled nursing and assisted-living facilities. As always, we recommend that you visit and do additional research before making your decision; talk to the staff, talk to the residents, and spend some time looking around to see if the facility will meet your needs.

**Cottesmore of Life Care**
**2909 14th Ave. N.W., Gig Harbor**
**(253) 851-5433**

Cottesmore of Life Care is a Christian-based skilled nursing and rehabilitation center that has been serving area residents for more than 31 years. The center also provides day care for children and incorporates that into an intergenerational program that includes singing and fun activities. Cottesmore also has a public cafe where residents and guests can eat together. Family members often join residents during work lunch breaks. A secure facility serves dementia and Alzheimer's patients, and the center is planning to build an assisted-living facility.

**ManorCare Health Services - Gig Harbor**
**3309 45th St. Ct. N.W, Gig Harbor**
**(253) 858-8688**

Alzheimer's, dementia, and post–acute care services are provided at this skilled nursing facility. The center also features rehabilitation and long- and short-term sub-acute care. The skilled nursing staff is available 24 hours a day, and residents can select from a comprehensive list of activities that are available 11 hours per day. The company's motto of "When your support needs support" is met by respite, vacation care, and senior day-care options. The Arcadia unit is a secure wing specially designed for residents living with memory impairment.

**Merrill Gardens at Gig Harbor**
**3213 45th St. Ct. N.W., Gig Harbor**
**(253) 858-5300**
**www.merrillgardens.com**

Merrill Gardens is a nationally run, 78-apartment retirement community that was built in 1997. Each apartment includes a kitchenette and private bathroom, and residents can select studio or one- or two-bedroom apartments. Services include weekly maid and linen service, emergency call systems, an on-site dining room that serves meals all daylong, and transportation services. The community features a library, large screen TV lounge, salon and barbershop, walking paths, and organized social, physical, spiritual, and intellectual activities. It is situated close to shopping centers, restaurants, and medical services. Residents are also welcome to keep small pets in their apartments.

**Ridgemont Terrace**
**2051 Pottery Ave., Port Orchard**
**(360) 876-4461**

**Stafford Suites of Port Orchard**
**1761 Pottery Ave., Port Orchard**
**(360) 874-1212**

**Belmont Terrace**
**560 Lebo Blvd., Bremerton**
**(360) 479-1515**
**www.ostromcare.com**

Ostrom Management runs these three Kitsap County facilities. Ridgemont Terrace and Belmont Terrace provide 24-hour skilled nursing care and rehabilitation services, including physical, occupational, and speech therapy as well as respite care. Residents live in private suites, and the facilities provide short- and long-term care. Both units feature assisted-living suites with 24-hour emergency alert monitoring, daily medication reminders, and maid service plus weekly housekeeping assistance. Ridgemont also offers apartments for independent seniors as does the new Stafford Suites, which features limited healthcare services, a full-time RN Wellness Director, and a 24-hour staff. Amenities include common spaces, organized activities, weekly shopping trips, and on-site salons and barbershops.

**Bremerton Convalescent & Rehabilitation Center**
**2701 Clare Ave., Bremerton**
**(360) 377-3951**

This 24-hour skilled nursing center features a dementia unit with 24-hour admission. It provides short-term sub-acute care as well as extended care options. Services include rehabilitation, physical and occupational therapy, speech and language pathology, and respite care.

**Alterra Clare Bridge of Silverdale**
**1501 Tower View Circle N.W., Silverdale**
**(360) 697-4488**
**www.seniorhousing.net/ad/alterra_silverdale**

Clare Bridge is designed for people with memory impairments such as dementia and Alzheimer's. The facility is a 24-hour secure skilled nursing center that aims to provide residents with a homelike setting and a family atmosphere. Individual care plans are detailed for each person so the center can work with those who are more independent as well as those who need more intensive care. Residents can visit the beautyshop and barbershop, visit with family and friends, cuddle their pets, and take part in any of the many planned activities. Services provided include incontinent care, diabetic care, housekeeping, hygiene assistance, and medication management, and three meals plus snacks are served every day.

> **Insiders' Tip**
> To search for more retirement housing options, visit www.seniorhousing.net for a nationwide search of nursing and retirement facilities.

**Claremont East**
**2707 Clare Ave., Bremerton**
**(360) 388-1717**

**Clearbrook Inn Living Center**
**12295 Schold Pl. N.W, Silverdale**
**(360) 692-1228**

**Country Meadows**
**12169 Country Meadows Ln., Silverdale**
**(360) 692-4480**

**Northwoods Lodge**
**2321 Schold Pl. N.W., Silverdale**
**(360) 698-3930**

**Alpine Way**
**900 W. Alpine Wy., Shelton**
**(360) 426-2600**

Encore Communities is a locally owned company that provides retirement living and nursing care to the residents of Kitsap and Mason Counties through five facilities. Each facility boasts spacious accommodations that residents can furnish with their own belongings. Common areas include sitting rooms, activity centers, recreation centers, and formal dining rooms with individual tables set for four where residents eat restaurant-style meals.

Residents of the Encore Communities won't grow bored with planned activities such as game playing, church services, coordinated field trips, transportation services, and facilitated support groups. Each center includes an exercise room, and most feature on-site beauty salons and gift shops. Maid and linen service is provided, and residents enjoy free use of the laundry facilities. Individual care plans are coordinated with each resident's private physician.

Independent-living facilities are offered at Country Meadows, part of the 13-acre Silverdale campus, and at Alpine Way in Shelton. Country Meadows features private one- and two-bedroom cottages with attached carports and storage units. Each cottage has a full kitchen with a washer and dryer, gas fireplace, and air-conditioning. Residents can swim or exercise at the community clubhouse and greenhouses and garden spots are also available. Dinner is served daily in the for-mal dining room. Alpine Way features independent-living apartments

Alpine Way, Claremont East, and Clearbrook Inn all feature assisted-living services, including hygiene assistance, managed medication, 24-hour nursing assistance, and three daily meals. Residents live in private and semi-private one-bedroom and studio apartments. Alpine Way and Claremont East also include secure facilities for residents living with Alzheimer's and dementia.

Along with Clearbrook Inn and Country Meadows, the Northwoods Lodge completes the 13-acre wooded campus in Silverdale. Northwoods Lodge is a 24-hour skilled nursing and rehabilitation facility. Residents live in one-bedroom and studio suites that have kitchenettes and private bathrooms. The center is equipped to handle post-operative oncology. The on-site lab allows for blood transfusions and other technical procedures. Northwoods Lodge also includes the state's only on-site pharmacy. Visiting therapists provide rehabilitation services to residents in Encore's other communities.

**Kah Tai Care Center**
**751 Kearney St., Port Townsend**
**(360) 385-3555**

Residents at the Kah Tai Care Center can bring their own furniture and belongings to decorate private and semi-private dormitory-style rooms. The center offers assisted-living options, short-term and long-term care, as well as services for people living with Alzheimer's. The daily activity schedule includes cooking, rhythm and movement classes, bingo, bowling, and discussion groups. Residents go shopping on Thursdays, and pets visit every week to bring some cuddles and cheer to the facility.

**Discovery View Retirement Apartments**
**1051 Hancock St., Port Townsend**
**(360) 385-9500**

One- and two-bedroom apartments serve as home for the independent seniors who live in this retirement community. The apartments include full kitchens, although one meal a day is served in the communal dining room. Weekly maid service, transportation, and organized activities and field trips are among the services provided.

**Suncrest Village Retirement Apartments**
**251 S. 5th Ave., Sequim**
**(360) 681-3800, (877) 421-3863**
**www.seniorhousing.net/ad/suncrest**

One- and two-bedroom, spacious apartments with ample storage space are available as monthly rentals. The apartments are unfurnished so residents can bring their own furniture and decorations. Each apartment includes a full kitchen and access to laundry facilities and manicured grounds. Services for the independent- living apartments, Suncrest Apartments I and II, include a recreation room, emergency call systems, patios, elevators, and a library. The assisted-living facility provides additional services such as a fitness program, recreation room, meals, and housekeeping services, access to a beautician and barber, and a 24-hour, on-call staff. Residents are also allowed to keep pets in their apartments.

**Sherwood Assisted Living and**
**The Fifth Avenue**
**500 Hendrickson Rd., Sequim**
**(360) 683-3348**
**www.sherwoodassistedliving.com**

These two facilities share the same campus. The Fifth Avenue provides independent seniors with the comforts of home, that is if home included crystal chandeliers, oak paneling, and traditional colonial furnishings. Seniors can pick from studios or one- or two-bedroom apartments each with a private bathroom and kitchenette. Weekly maid and linen service and three daily meals are included in the monthly rent. Residents can also visit the exercise and activity rooms as well as the library, beauty shop, and TV room.

Sherwood Assisted Living residents live in dormitory-style furnished rooms, but they may bring some of their own fur-

niture as well. Services include three daily meals in four dining rooms, daily room cleaning, laundry service, and transportation. Daily activities give the residents something to do and range from shopping trips to church services to daily exercise classes. Sherwood also provides a secure unit for residents with dementia and Alzheimer's.

**Park View Villas**
**1430 Park View Ln., Port Angeles**
**(360) 452-7222**

Park View Villas is an assisted-living facility that offers residents studio and one- or two-bedroom apartments. Three meals are served each day in the dining room, and social and recreational programs keep seniors busy.

**Port Angeles Care Center**
**825 E. 5th St., Port Angeles**
**(360) 452-6213**

This 76-bed facility provides 24-hour skilled nursing to residents of the Port Angeles area. Services provided include physical, occupational, and speech therapy. Short-term, long-term, and respite care is offered. Residents take part in activities based on their ability. Activities include sight-seeing field trips, art classes, cards, and games.

**Forks Community Hospital Long Term Care**
**530 Bogachiel Wy., Forks**
**(360) 374-6271**
**www.forkshospital.org**

Up to 36 residents can stay at the Forks Community Hospital's recently remodeled and expanded long-term care center. Some of the semi-private rooms include patios, and residents can bring some of their own furnishings. A professional nursing staff provides personalized care programs. Services include physical therapy, respite care, church services, access to a beautyshop and barbershop, and transportation. Residents can join guided outings and organized activities or take part in the volunteer program.

**Harbour Pointe Shores**
**1020 Catala Ave. S.E., Ocean Shores**
**(360) 289-9663**

Assisted-living makes the senior years easier and more enjoyable at Harbour Pointe Shores, where residents live in private studio apartments. In addition to eating three restaurant-style meals each day with other residents in the dining room, seniors engage in a wide variety of activities, including art classes, game and hobby clubs, and off-site field trips. Additional services include housekeeping, transportation, and hygiene assistance as well as medication reminders, and wound care from the 24-hour staff and trained nurses.

**Fir Lane Health & Rehabilitation Center**
**2430 N. 13th St., Shelton**
**(360) 426-1651**
**www.extendicare.com**

At Fir Lane, residents enjoy the companionship of children who attend the on-site day care and rabbits, dogs, and birds that live on the premises. In addition to guided activities that include arts and crafts and outings, residents can dig around in the wheel-chair accessible gardens. Fir Lane provides sub-acute and transitional care. Services include speech, occupational, and physical therapies, as well as hospice services and a secure unit for those living with dementia and Alzheimer's.

**SunBridge Care & Rehabilitation for Shelton**
**153 Johns Ct., Shelton**
**(360) 427-2575**
**SunBridge Care & Rehabilitation for Montesano**
**800 Medcalf Ln. N., Montesano**
**(360) 249-2273**

Part of the Sun Healthcare Group, these two skilled nursing centers provide specialized wound care, stroke recovery, and 24-hour care in private and semi-private resident suites. The centers also feature physical and occupational therapy, and residents enjoy a wide variety of social activities, including field trips, religious services, three meals a day, and on-site beautyshops and barbershops.

# Worship

No matter how you worship, you'll probably find a place to do it on the Peninsula. Churches of nearly every denomination are scattered over the region. Religion has always played a significant role on the Peninsula from the relationship that the Native Americans had with the land and the animals and the spirit world to the traveling ministers of the 1800s to the modern day religious movements.

Many of the fishing communities around the Peninsula are largely populated by people of Norwegian and Scandinavian heritage, especially in towns like Poulsbo, so Lutheran churches are quite popular. But you're just as likely to find Presbyterian, Methodist, Catholic, Baptist, and Seventh Day Adventist churches as well.

The Peninsula is also no stranger to other traditions. In fact, in the 1800s a utopian community called Home was established near Gig Harbor. Home was a free-thinkers' community that attracted people of different faiths and philosophies from Jews, who were uncommon in the area, to Theosophists to Deists to people who started their own religions. Today, the area still draws people of different faiths. Several towns have metaphysical bookstores and small Pagan and Wiccan populations. You'll also find spiritual healers, psychics, and yoga centers, especially in Port Townsend, which has two metaphysical bookstores and several healers and psychics, and even a place where you can rent sets of votive candles for outdoor rituals.

Fellowship on the Peninsula is important, and community events and concerts are often held in local churches. Religious buildings still play a role in the community as gathering places just as they did more than 100 years ago.

# Senior Centers

Independent seniors who still live on their own may want to use the services provided at area senior centers. Some senior centers provide foot-care clinics and transportation services. Some have food banks and serve low cost or free dinners while others sponsor weekly social events and activities from sight seeing-trips to card games to monthly birthday parties. The senior centers can also help seniors find the resources they need to stay independent and healthy, such as help with nutrition, taxes, and Medicare forms.

**Givens Community & Senior Center,** 1026 Sidney Ave., Port Orchard (360) 337-5743

**Bremerton Senior Citizens Center,** 1140 Nipsic, Bremerton (360) 478-5357

**North Kitsap Senior Citizens Center,** 18972 Front St. N.E., Poulsbo (360) 779-5702

**Port Gamble S'Klallam Senior Center,** Little Boston Rd., Kingston (360) 297-4858

**Port Townsend Senior Association,** 620 Tyler St., Port Townsend (360) 385-9007

**Sequim Senior Center,** 921 E. Hammond St., Sequim (360) 683-6806

**Senior Services and Community Center,** 328 E. 7th St., Port Angeles (360) 457-7004

**Makah Senior Center,** Bayview Ave., Neah Bay (360) 645-2796

**West End Seniors,** Sekiu Community Hall, Rice St., Sekiu (360) 963-2647

**Senior Information and Assistance,** 451 5th Ave., Forks (360) 374-9496

**Senior Center North Beach,** 885 Ocean Shores Blvd. N.W., Ocean Shores (360) 289-2801

**Aberdeen Senior Citizens Center,** 117 E. 3rd, Aberdeen (360) 533-3311

**Brinnon Senior Center,** 306144 U.S. Hwy. 101, Brinnon (360) 796-4350

**Quilcene Community Center,** 294952 U.S. Hwy. 101, Quilcene (360) 765-3842

# Media

News isn't hard to find on the Olympic Peninsula. Almost every town has a weekly community newspaper, and some cities have daily and weekly papers. And when locals need the news faster than the paper can deliver, six radio stations offer a variety of programming over the airwaves, including news.

The history of news on the Peninsula dates from the time before Washington was officially declared a state. *The Daily World* in Aberdeen started publishing in 1889, and the *Port Orchard Independent* started a bit later, in 1890.

Although the Olympic Peninsula doesn't have any television stations to call its own, area cable systems carry state, national, and world programming from TV stations in Seattle. Peninsula residents and travelers can also turn to the Internet for some regional news, since most cities have a Web site with local information.

## Dailies

**The Daily World**
315 S. Michigan St.
Aberdeen, WA
(360) 532-4000
pub@thedailyworld.com
www.thedailyworld.com

Three months before Washington became a state, the *Aberdeen Weekly Bulletin*—which later became *The Daily World*—started business. Now a daily paper with more than 17,000 subscribers, *The Daily World* is known for its local coverage of the Grays Harbor area, including the communities of Aberdeen, Hoquiam, Montesano, Elma, and the coastal areas around Ocean Shores.

Longtime editor John Hughes leads the publication that is owned today by the out-of-state Don Ray Media Group from Arkansas. The newspaper group purchased *The Daily World* in 1968.

*The Daily World* prides itself on being "not so local that they are endangered," but providing continuity in the community with local news and special features such as the annual perspectives series published each year in April.

Subscribing to the *World* costs $9.60 per month for local residents and $14 per month by mail.

**Peninsula Daily News**
305 W. First St.
Port Angeles, WA
(800) 826-7714
john.brewer@peninsuladailynews.com
www.peninsuladailynews.com

Founded in 1916, the *Peninsula Daily News* brings its mix of news, feature stories, and community coverage to 16,000 readers on Mondays through Fridays and to 18,000 readers on Sundays. The paper began as the *Port Angeles Evening News*, then became known as the *Daily News* for a period before becoming the *Peninsula Daily News* in 1984. It is family owned as part of the newspaper holdings of Peter Horvitz.

The *Peninsula Daily News* covers a wide range of communities along the northern edge of the Olympic Peninsula, from Brinnon in the east to Neah Bay in the northwest and La Push in the southwest. According to the publisher, it is very much a local newspaper, more or less like a weekly paper that happens to come out every day. Each morning's newspaper opens with local news on the front page and an inside section with state and world news.

Subscribers to the *Peninsula Daily News* pay $104 per year to get the newspaper delivered.

**The Sun**
545 5th St.
Bremerton, WA
(888) 377-3711
SunNews@thesunlink.com
www.thesunlink.com

An all-local front section combined with national and international news inside the paper is a winning mix for *The Sun* in Bremerton. Known as *The Bremerton Sun* until the late 1980s, the daily paper circulates to 36,000 readers every day and 38,000 readers on Sundays. And its subscribers range from Port Townsend in the north to Grapeview in Mason County in the south.

*The Sun* started publishing in 1935 as one of the Scripps League newspapers. It later became a John P. Scripps paper in 1940 and became part of the E.W. Scripps Company in 1989. But none of these changes have been a major concern for readers, as the paper continues to cover news in all of Kitsap County and the communities of Port Ludlow, Chimacum, Port Townsend, Quilcene, and Brinnon in Jefferson County. *The Sun* also covers northern Mason County with a weekly publication called *The North Mason Sun* in Belfair.

Subscribers pay $11.50 per month to get *The Sun* delivered to their homes.

## Weeklies and Bi-weeklies

**Bremerton Patriot**
520 Burwell St.
Bremerton, WA
(360) 782-1581
editor@bremertonpatriot.com

One of the younger publications near the Olympic Peninsula, the weekly *Bremerton Patriot* started publishing its blend of local feature stories with a heavy emphasis on arts and entertainment, religion, and business in 1999. The paper covers all of Bremerton and circulates to all sections of the city, with more than 12,000 readers of each Saturday edition. The publication also offers hard news coverage.

The *Patriot* is part of the Kitsap Newspaper Group owned by Sound Publishing and it costs $15 per year to be delivered within Bremerton by motor route or $60 per year through the mail.

**Central Kitsap Reporter**
9989 Silverdale Way N.W.
Silverdale, WA
(360) 308-9161
publisher@centralkitsapreporter.com
www.zwire.com/news/newslist.cfm?brd=972

The *Central Kitsap Reporter* dates from 1983, when it was known as the *Kitsap Reporter*. Based in Silverdale, a town with a tradition of having a community newspaper, the *Reporter* circulates to about 18,000 readers with its twice-a-week publications on Wednesdays and Saturdays.

Well known for its school coverage, the *Reporter* touts itself as having all local, community-focused news with all the happenings in Silverdale. It covers news and circulates within the boundaries of the Central Kitsap School District, one of the largest school districts in Washington.

Subscribers pay $26 per year to receive the *Reporter*, or $120 per year for delivery through the mail. The paper is part of the Kitsap Newspaper Group, owned since 1988 by Sound Publishing.

**Forks Forum**
P.O. Box 300
Forks, WA
(360) 374-3311

With roots dating from 1930, the *Forks Forum* is a weekly newspaper offering local news about Forks and the entire Olympic Peninsula coastline from Lake Crescent in the east to Neah Bay in the north. Under the ownership of Olympic View Publishing, the Wednesday paper prides itself in its support of the community as well as in its coverage of natural resource issues and bringing high technology to the area.

The *Forum* has a circulation of 5,300, and although it is distributed for free, area residents can guarantee receiving the paper each week by paying for an annual subscription of $24.

### Northwest Navigator
**9989 Silverdale Way, Suite 109**
**Silverdale, WA**
**(360) 308-9161**
**editor@northwestnavigator.com**
**www.northwestnavigator.com**

Formerly known as the *Puget Sound Navy News*, the *Northwest Navigator* offers weekly news about and for seamen and local residents around Bremerton, the Bangor Submarine Base, and other Naval installations in the area. It goes out to about 12,000 readers per week with feature stories about the Navy and Navy personnel as well as union issues in the Bremerton Naval Shipyard.

The *Navigator* is a free publication and it can be found on base as well as in local business establishments near the Naval bases.

### The Peninsula Gateway
**3555 Erickson St.**
**Gig Harbor, WA**
**(253) 851-9921**
**tom.taylor@mail.tribnet.com**
**www.gateline.com/Gateway/default. htm**

Published since 1917 when it was known as the *Bay Island Reporter*, *The Peninsula Gateway* circulates to more than 11,000 paid subscribers and another 16,000 free copies of a companion shopper publication in Gig Harbor. Under the guidance of Tom Taylor, a one-time owner of the paper, the weekly Wednesday newspaper has been recognized eight times in the last 20 years as the best community paper in Washington for its circulation size.

*The Peninsula Gateway* is now owned by the McClatchy Newspaper group, but it still covers Gig Harbor and the Key Peninsula communities of Key Center and Purdy with solid news coverage and feature stories about people in the community. And since it is actually printed and distributed in Gig Harbor, the paper also has a larger than normal staff for a once-a-week paper, with 52 people making the paper work.

Subscribers of *The Peninsula Gateway* pay $24 per year to get the paper if they live in the county. The price for receiving the paper outside the county varies.

### Port Angeles Messenger
**P.O. Box 207**
**Port Angeles, WA**
**(360) 683-3311**

One of the newest publications on the Peninsula, the *Port Angeles Messenger* bills itself as a shopper newspaper with some community news for the city along with details about events and entertainment in its weekly Friday paper. The *Messenger* is available in businesses and is distributed free through the mail to all city residents to reach its weekly circulation figures of more than 17,000 readers.

### Port Orchard Independent
**2950 Mile Hill Drive S.E.**
**Port Orchard, WA**
**(360) 876-4414**
**publisher@portorchardindependent.com**
**www.zwire.com/news/newslist.cfm?brd=**
**976**

The second-oldest newspaper along the Olympic Peninsula, the *Port Orchard Independent* dates from 1890. It covers all of south Kitsap County, Port Orchard, and the small neighboring communities from Manchester to Olalla and Southworth. Formerly a once-a-week paper, the *Independent* made the move to twice a week in 1996. It now has more than 16,000 subscribers.

According to publisher Rick Peterson, the paper stands out for its community news coverage, sticking to its niche. Locals turn to the *Independent* when they really want to know what is going on in the community.

The *Independent* publishes Wednesdays and Saturdays, and an annual subscription costs $26. It is part of the Kitsap Newspaper Group, owned by Sound Publishing.

**Port Townsend–Jefferson County Leader**
226 Adams St.
Port Townsend, WA
(360) 385-2900
news@ptleader.com
www.ptleader.com/

It is fitting that one of the oldest towns in Washington has one of the oldest newspapers in the state. The independently owned *Port Townsend–Jefferson County Leader*, known to locals as *The Leader*, started publishing in 1898. Today its weekly Wednesday edition is read by about 9,300 people across Jefferson County.

*The Leader* is known for its in-depth coverage of local news, local sports coverage, and an abundant "letter to the editor" section that serves as a public forum for residents. It is also the only newspaper published in Jefferson County, covering communities including Brinnon, Quilcene, Chimacum, and Port Ludlow in addition to Port Townsend.

Subscribing to *The Leader* costs $24 per year for county residents and $36 a year for those outside the county.

**The Sequim Gazette**
147 W. Washington
Sequim, WA
(360) 683-3311
gazette@sequim-gazette.com
www.sequim-gazette.com

*The Sequim Gazette* is the place to turn for weekly local news in the Sequim Valley. Published every Wednesday, the *Gazette* is read by 8,200 paid subscribers and a host of others through newspaper box sales in town. Established in 1974, the paper covers Sequim and its adjacent neighborhoods.

Formerly known as the *Jimmy Come Lately Gazette*, the paper is the last surviving weekly publication in a town that once had three papers. According to publisher Frank Garred, the *Gazette* thrives because it is dedicated solely to the communities and events in the Sequim Valley.

Subscribing to the *Gazette* costs $22 per year for residents in Clallam County and $28 per year outside the county.

## Monthly

**Kitsap Business Journal**
321 Tremont St.
Port Orchard, WA
(360) 876-7900
biznews@wetapple.com
www.KitsapBusinessJournal.com

If it has to do with business in the Kitsap Peninsula or in north Mason County, the *Kitsap Business Journal* is the place to find the news. Since April 1988, Lary Coppola has published local business news that circulates to about 26,000 people monthly. It is available in news racks, at ferry terminals, and through direct mail to area businesses.

In addition to providing news through its paper publication, the *Kitsap Business Journal* offers weekly business updates on its Web site. Readers can also pay $25 per year to receive weekly updates through e-mail, or $25 per year to have the paper sent to them monthly through the mail.

## Radio

**News/Talk**
KXRO 1320 AM, Aberdeen
KONP 1450 AM, Port Angeles

**Alternative**
KRXY 94.5 FM, Shelton

**Classical/Jazz**
KNWP 90.1 FM, Port Angeles

**Mixed Music**
KRWM 106.9 FM, Bremerton
KITZ 1400 AM, Silverdale

# For More Information

## Books

*100 Hikes in Washington's South Cascades and Olympics* by Ira Spring & Harvey Manning. Use this guide to plan day and overnight hikes into the Olympic range. Beginners and advanced hikers will find plenty of trails to suit their needs.

*Backpacking Tips* edited by Bill and Russ Schneider. If you are new to backwoods camping and hiking we strongly suggest you pick up this guide. The Olympic Mountains are beautiful, but their beauty belies danger around every corner. Before embarking on even the simplest of hikes, you need to learn what you need to do to keep the bears away and how to deal with cougar, how to pack for the sudden changes in weather, which foods will keep you energized but won't weigh you down, and how to use the 10 essentials.

*Cascade-Olympic Natural History: A Trailside Reference* by Daniel Mathew. A great reference to keep in the car or take on hikes. It gives detailed information and two sections full of color plates, plus the many line drawings certainly aid in identification of trees, wildflowers, butterflies, bugs, and all the other animals that populate the local woods.

*City of Dreams: A Guide to Port Townsend* edited by Peter Simpson. Organized like a dictionary, this guide will give you a true insider's peak into the history and culture of the city.

*Discover Historic Washington State: A Travel Guide to Hundreds of Historical Places in the Evergreen State* by George and Jan Roberts. Read region eight for a list of historical markers and landmarks on the Peninsula.

*Exploring the Seashore in British Columbia, Washington and Oregon: A Guide to Shorebirds and Intertidal Plants and Animals* by Gloria Snively. Color plates and black-and-white sketches along with detailed descriptions will help you identify all those creatures lurking in the tidepools.

*A Field Guide to the Cascades & Olympics* by Stephen R. Whitney. Take this book with you when you go on day hikes or mountain treks. The guide is stuffed with information and pictures to help you identify plants, birds, butterflies, fish, reptiles, and the mammals of the region.

*Ghost Stories of Washington* by Barbara Smith. So you think that mysterious tap on your back was just a figment of your imagination? Learn about the ghosts in the Manresa Castle as well as those in other spots around the Peninsula.

*Guide to Hurricane Ridge* by Charles Stewart. Pick the guide up for a small fee at the Port Angeles visitor's center or at the Hurricane Ridge observatory. Learn a bit about the flora and fauna, geology, history, and activities available there.

*Hiking Olympic National Park* by Erik Molvar. Easy to moderate to the most advanced of hikes are detailed in this guide. In addition to describing each trail in detail, Molvar has provided the hiker with elevation charts and detailed maps.

*The Land That Slept Late: The Olympic Mountains in Legend and History* by Robert L. Woods. A tidy book that encapsulates some of the myths, legends, and historical mountaineering adventures that took place on the slopes of the Olympic range.

*Mountain Bike Adventures in Washington's North Cascades and Olympics* published by The Mountaineers. If you plan on traveling with your mountain bike, this is a good guide to take along. It offers eight rides on the Peninsula.

*Native Peoples of the Northwest* by Jan Halliday and Gail Chehack. Learn more about the tribes that occupied the Peninsula. In addition to a short history lesson, you will also find out where to go for tribal arts, museums, and celebrations.

*The Northwest Coast: Or, Three Years' Residence in Washington Territory* by James G. Swan. This book was first published in 1857, but it is still a commonly used reference for those who write about and research the Coastal cultures. James G. Swan fled Boston for the less-hurried society of the Pacific Coast where he lived with, studied, and was accepted by the local tribes.

*Northwest Exposures: A Geologic Story of the Northwest* by David Alt and Donald W. Hyndman. Read this book if you really want the inside story on the geologic history of the Northwest. Although all the chapters will help you learn about the forces behind glaciation, volcanic activity, and plate tectonics, chapter 40 will give you a quick history of the Olympic range.

*Olympic National Park: A Natural History* by Tim McNulty. Take our Natural World chapter and expand it by a couple hundred pages. Fascinating reading for naturalists and those who just want to understand what lies beneath their feet and rises over their heads.

*Pacific Northwest Berry Book* by Bob and James Krumm. Know what it is that you are about to bake in a pie or pop in your mouth. Learn which berries are safe to eat as well as how to use them in one of the more than 100 recipes included.

*Roadside Geology of Washington* by David D. Alt and Donald W. Hyndman. Rock hounds and geology buffs will have a lot of fun with this book. You no longer have to drive by that formation without knowing what created it.

*Traveler's History of Washington: A Roadside Historical Guide* by Bill Gulick. Keep this book in the front seat so you don't miss any of the historical attractions that are right on the beaten track.

*Wildflowers of the Olympics and Cascades* by Charles Stewart. This is not a flashy book, but it does have a picture of each plant listed. It will fit nicely in a backpack for those longer hikes.

## Web Sites

### General Information

**North Olympic Peninsula Visitor & Convention Bureau**
**www.olympicpeninsula.org**

This site focuses on the towns in Clallam and Jefferson Counties including Port Townsend, Sequim, Port Angeles, and Forks. Visitors will find lists of attractions, lodging options, and services. You may also order a free travel guide.

**Olympic National Park**
**www.nps.gov/olym**

If you think the Olympic Park is just a place to camp, think again. The National Park Web site gives visitors a comprehensive list of activities available in the park. You will also find information on lodging, camping, facilities, and fees and permits.

**Olympic Park Field Guide**
**www.northolympic.com/onp**

Although this site is technically part of the site mentioned above, we decided to give it its own space since it is such a good resource. You will find information on day hikes, camping, lists of the flora and fauna, including a list of record trees in the park, as well as information on park regulations.

**Olympic Peninsula Bed & Breakfast Association**
**www.opbba.com**

Although the site does not list every inn on the Peninsula, you will find reservation information for those listed.

**Olympic Peninsula Resource Guide**
**www.olympicpeninsula.com**

Visit this site to find resource lists and links to other sites for each area on the Peninsula.

**Olympic Peninsula—The Official Guide**
**www.northolympic.com**

This self-proclaimed official guide to the Peninsula offers information on each city as well as ferry schedules, weather information, and guides to area museums.

**RV Parks of the Olympic Peninsula**
**www.northolympic.com/rvpacc**

If you prefer to take the comforts of home with you, visit this site to find out where to park. You may search for RV parks by city or on a map.

**Tide Tables**
**www.harbortides.com/state_regions.asp?state=42**

If you plan on fishing, harvesting shellfish, or gazing into tidepools, you will want to visit this site.

**Washington State Department of Transportation**
**www.wsdot.wa.gov**
**www.wsdot.wa.gov/ferries**
**(Ferry schedules)**

Check bridge cams, road conditions, and travel advisories with the first site. With the second, find out when your ferry leaves or which runs are running behind schedule.

**Washington State Lodging Association**
**www.travel-in-wa.com**

Here you will find listings for hotels, bed and breakfast inns, hostels, and vacation rentals, as well as tourist guides for the Peninsula and other regions in the state.

**Washington State Parks and Recreation Commission**
**www.parks.wa.gov**

If you want to be sure that you will have a place to camp during your trip, we suggest you visit this site to make a reservation. It can be very difficult, especially during the summer months, to find a place to camp.

**Washington State Tourism: Olympic and Kitsap Peninsulas**
**www.tourism.wa.gov/Region.asp?region=2**

We strongly suggest you visit this Web site before you head to the Peninsula. The Washington State Tourism Department has assembled an excellent on-line guide to the region. In addition to finding driving directions and lodging information for each city on the Peninsula, visitors also can read about the region and order information packets for the rest of the state. This is also one of the easiest ways to find links and phone numbers for each city's chamber of commerce.

## Cities

**Gig Harbor Peninsula Area Chamber of Commerce**
**www.gigharborchamber.com**

Find basic facts about Gig Harbor as well as a calendar of events and list of business resources. Fill out the on-line form if you want an information packet mailed to you.

**Port Orchard–South Kitsap Chamber of Commerce**
**www.portorchard.com/chamber**

Learn more about the Port Orchard area from this Web site: listings for lodging, restaurants, community activities, and relocation information.

### Bremerton Chamber of Commerce
www.bremertonchamber.org

Find out why the Naval base is so important to Bremerton. You can also purchase visitor and relocation guides.

### Kitsap Peninsula Visitor & Convention Bureau
www.visitkitsap.com

Take a virtual tour of the Kitsap Peninsula before you visit. Learn what to do, where to stay, and how to get more information.

### Port Townsend Chamber of Commerce
www.ptchamber.org

For more information on Port Townsend, visit the Chamber of Commerce Web site. We especially like "A Kid's Eye View of Port Townsend and Jefferson County and Its History."

### Port Townsend City Guide
www.ptguide.com

Visit this comprehensive guide to the Victorian city of Port Townsend if only to take the photo tour. While you're there, check out the calendar of events and history section.

### Destination Sequim
www.visitsun.com/index.html

Order a free visitors or relocation guide or look on-line for activities, lodging, and restaurant suggestions. If you wish to spend more time in Sequim, check out the five-day vacation guide on the site.

### Sequim–Dungeness Chamber of Commerce
www.cityofsequim.com

The chamber of commerce Web site offers maps, events calendars, relocation information, and restaurant and lodging listings.

### Port Angeles Chamber of Commerce Visitor Information Center
www.cityofpa.com

Whether you are in Port Angeles for a night before you catch the ferry to Victoria, B.C., or spending a week making day trips around the city, you will want to visit this site to find out where to stay and what to eat. The site also provides a local business directory.

### Clallam Bay–Sekiu Chamber of Commerce
www.clallambay.com

Visit this site for information on the Neah Bay, Clallam Bay, and Sekiu areas. Includes a travel planner, maps, historical information, and lodging options.

### Forks Chamber of Commerce
www.forkswa.com

The guide covers lodging, activities, and weather as well as information on camping and hiking in the area. Don't forget to check the five-day guide to the area.

### Tourism Grays Harbor
www.graysharbor.com

Visit this site for more information on the cities in the Grays Harbor area: Hoquiam, Montesano, Ocean Shores, and Aberdeen.

### Shelton/Mason County Chamber of Commerce
www.sheltonchamber.org

This site is primarily designed for residents, but people who choose to relocate to the area will find this a useful site as well.

# Index

# About the Authors

## Natalie McNair-Huff

Natalie McNair-Huff grew up along the Columbia River in southwestern Washington. One of her favorite vacation memories is of a family trip to the Hoh Rainforest in the Olympic National Park. Even though an ant decided her ear looked like a nice, dry place to hide from one of the frequent rain squalls, that trip led to a lifelong love of the Olympic Peninsula. She currently lives with her husband and writing partner, Rob, in Tacoma where she enjoys frequent views of the Olympic and Cascade Mountains. Day trips and mini-vacations to the Olympic Peninsula keep her sane and give her breaks from the sometimes frantic life of the self-employed.

Since her college days at the University of Puget Sound in Tacoma, Natalie has worked in retail management and as a merchandising analyst, but she still made time to write and pick up a few jobs as a desktop publisher. After a break from the corporate world, she became a freelance contractor in 1995. Since then her days have been filled with writing and cruising the Internet in her work for Web-based companies. She also continues to pick up jobs in desktop publishing and technical writing.

When not working or running out to the Peninsula, Natalie likes to spend time beading, digging around in her organic vegetable and herb garden, playing piano, reading, or writing poetry and short stories. She also likes to take breaks during the day to walk with Rob or pet one of her many animal companions. She loves the Northwest, and can't imagine not living near "big water" and tall mountains. Looking down the street to see Puget Sound or over her shoulder to see that "The Mountain (Mt. Rainier) is out" makes her feel blessed and proud to call Washington home.

## Rob McNair-Huff

Rob McNair-Huff is a lifelong resident of Washington who grew up in the small town of Rochester—just south and east of the Olympic Peninsula. In 1985 he moved to Tacoma to attend the University of Puget Sound where he earned a bachelor's degree in Japanese language and International Affairs. He lives and writes from his home in Tacoma's north end, with a view of the Olympic Mountains to the west and the Cascade Mountains to the east.

Since graduation in 1990, Rob worked four years as a newspaper writer, first as a staff writer for the *Highline Times* in Burien and then as the sports editor of the *Federal Way News*. His writing has been published in such places as the *Puget Sound Business Journal, Today's Careers*, and *Sports Etc*—a multi-sport magazine where he served as editor in 1997. He launched into a freelance career in 1994, editing the 1995 edition of Microsoft's *Complete Baseball* CD-ROM. He then moved into work on the Internet, beginning with a stint creating Web directories and writing site descriptions for Lycos. He continues to work with Lycos as a message boards moderator, and he also works with other on-line clients as part of his business, White Rabbit Publishing.

When he isn't writing, doing research, or living on the Internet, Rob spends his time walking his dog Rhia and exploring outdoors on foot or biking. He is an avid cyclist and sometimes a weekend warrior on a mountain bike.